WHY WE FIGHT

WHY WE FIGHT

The Roots of War and the Paths to Peace

CHRISTOPHER BLATTMAN

VIKING

VIKING
An imprint of Penguin Random House LLC
penguinrandomhouse.com

LIBRARY OF CONGRESS CATALOGING-IN-PUBLICATION DATA
Names: Blattman, Christopher, author.
Title: Why we fight : the roots of war and the paths to peace / Christopher Blattman.
Description: New York : Viking, [2022] | Includes bibliographical references and index. |
Identifiers: LCCN 2021034646 (print) | LCCN 2021034647 (ebook) |
ISBN 9781984881571 (hardcover) | ISBN 9781984881588 (ebook)
Subjects: LCSH: War and society. | Social conflict. |
Ethnic conflict. | Violence. | War. | Peace.
Classification: LCC HM554 .B593 2022 (print) |
LCC HM554 (ebook) | DDC 303.6/6—dc23
LC record available at https://lccn.loc.gov/2021034646
LC ebook record available at https://lccn.loc.gov/2021034647

Printed in the United States of America
1st Printing

Book design and maps by Daniel Lagin

To the internet café, now defunct,
at the corner of Fifth Ngong Avenue
and Bishops Road, Nairobi

CONTENTS

MAPS

WHY WE FIGHT

INTRODUCTION

Napoleon rang the doorbell a third time. "I know this is the place," he said, turning to face us. I stood on the sidewalk beside his partner, Charles, and my colleague Megan. Megan and I, the obvious outsiders, were trailing the duo for the day.

Unlike us, Nap and Charles had grown up on Chicago's West Side. Both had run fearsome local gangs in their youths. Nowadays, however, most folks in North Lawndale knew the gray-haired pair for their relentless prowling of the neighborhood's drug corners and porch stoops—their efforts to coax younger versions of themselves away from a life of dope selling and violence. Guys like Johnny, who was clearly not answering his door.

Johnny led a neighborhood crew. Crews, mobs, cliques—old-timers like Nap kept tossing out terms like these for the young men dealing drugs and trading bullets on the streets of Lawndale. The word he never used was "gang." "These aren't gangs," Nap told me, shaking his head. "We had organization, we had discipline, we had rules. But these kids . . . no way." Today's crews were fragmented, fractious versions of the large, unified criminal structures that once dominated Black neighborhoods like Lawndale. True, Nap was giving us the old ex-gang leader's version of a "kids today" rant, but it was a tirade with truth.

It was a warm autumn day. Along the quiet tree-lined street, the leaves had begun to turn but had not yet fallen, and so the stoops of the three-story family homes were still well shaded. A few young men sat outside talking to friends, keeping an eye on the block. I was still new to Chicago at the time, and the quiet leafy street hardly resembled the image of criminal turf I'd seen on TV. But this, Nap told us, this was the Holy Land. These few blocks were the birthplace of one of the largest and most influential street gangs in American history: the Vice Lords.

Down the street, some of the young men were staring at the spectacle from their porches: our little troop, neon vests over street clothes. Strangers were unusual in the Holy Land. And we were knocking on the chief's door.

Some people would have given up on Johnny at that moment, but there's a reason I call Nap and Charles relentless. Charles hollered, "Hey! Any of you guys know where Johnny's at?" and strode straight toward the closest knot of young men.

All across the city, outreach workers like Nap and Charles were chasing down a thousand Johnnies—the one thousand men we figured were most likely to pull a trigger in the months ahead. The previous year, 2016, murders in Chicago had spiked by an astonishing 58 percent. Nap and Charles represented a new kind of response, to get those numbers down.

Word had gotten around about the goods Nap and Charles were dealing. "You guys from that program?" one of the young men asked. He immediately relaxed and grinned. That program was offering a transition to a new life—eighteen months of a legitimate job and paycheck, with about ten hours of behavioral therapy woven in each week. The job was what interested him most. "What I got to do to get in?" another asked.

Just as Nap was starting his spiel, Johnny's door swung open. A short, confident young man with bright eyes emerged. He was wearing a Superman T-shirt and fitted black sweatpants, lean and well built, like the track athlete he'd once been. A little girl about two years old followed him out. "Sorry," he said, "we were sleeping."

Johnny's brother used to run the mob on the block, but he'd been shot and killed a month before by a rival crew. Now Johnny was "Lil' Chief." He looked us up and down: "What's going on?" As his daughter rode her tricycle up and down the sidewalk, Nap and Charles gave him the pitch on a new life. If they could get Johnny in, with his cred and charisma, other men would follow. And, they hoped, the program would lower the risk that Johnny's crew would retaliate against their rivals. Later on Nap would say, "Did you see how those young men gathered around him like that?" Megan and I nodded. "That's what a chief looks like."

Three weeks later, walking home from a day of manual labor at his new job, a car pulled up. Lil' Chief took sixteen bullets to his right arm, chest, and legs. Fortunately, his old track training kicked in. Johnny managed to sprint to safety in a corner store, bleeding from sixteen places all over the tile floor. Amazingly, he lived. But Johnny couldn't escape his war.

Why? Why were groups of young men like him embroiled in gun-wielding feuds, killing over and over and over again? What could a couple of old guys like Nap and Charles, let alone an outsider like me, do about it?

These weren't questions I'd ever expected to ask or answer. But once you witness the cruel extravagance of violence, it's hard to care about anything else. Even when you see it from a position of safety with the privilege of distance. Everything else fades in importance. Almost two decades ago, that's what happened to me.

WHY VIOLENCE MATTERS

Before the war came, a drive across northern Uganda took you over dry, dusty dirt roads, through miles of swaying grass taller than your head. Green when the rains came, brown when they didn't, the long stalks waved endlessly over flat, arid plains, interrupted only by the occasional trading post or pasture.

Most Acholi families, farmers and herders by profession, lived in clusters of circular huts, with smooth mud walls and conical thatch roofs, in the midst of their fields of maize and cattle. This area of the country, Acholiland, once held more cows than people. It must have been beautiful.

By the time I landed in the north, the grasses were still there, but the cows, the crops, and the picturesque huts were long gone. A civil war had raged for almost two decades. Fear of rebels and the Ugandan army had pushed those families, almost two million people, into dense camps no more than a few miles from their empty and overgrown lands.

The camps were filled with the same round brown homes with the same thatch roofs. But now, instead of idyllic homesteads nestled among greenery and livestock, there were thousands upon thousands of huts laid out on brown bare earth, baking in the sun, cramped together so tightly that you needed to crouch to pass between their eaves. These were places of despair.

The government had cleared the countryside of people and thrust them into these squalid settlements. It made it easier for soldiers to hunt for rebels and harder for insurgents to steal food and supplies—a classic counterinsurgency strategy. It was also a war crime, since it denied millions of people sustenance and freedom.

Forbidden from tilling their nearby lands, these families barely subsisted on the bags of beans and flour trucked in every week by the UN. The doors of their huts were made from gleaming tin cans, hammered flat, all with the identical message "Refined vegetable oil. Not to be sold or exchanged. Brought to you by the American people."

This is not where I expected to be. I was thirty years old, a PhD student in economics at Berkeley. Economists did not hang out in active war zones and displacement camps. My dissertation committee had been unanimous: "Don't go." Yet here I was. What, I asked myself, was I doing?

You see, I was training in a tribe that cared about income and its expansion above all else. That obsession is what had brought me to East Africa in the first place, to study industry and economic growth in Nairobi, a peaceful city a few hundred miles from northern Uganda. The war was small, contained, far away, and hence ignorable. That meant, like the millions of others in that bustling capital, I did my work mostly unaware of the tragedy nearby. That is, until one day a con artist struck up a conversation with me over lunch. As he distracted me, his partner nabbed my backpack, laptop and all. So I spent the rest of my trip in internet cafés, working at Kenya's glacial dial-up speed. If I ever meet that con artist again, I owe him a grateful hug.

Dial-up meant that every email took ten painful minutes to load. There wasn't much to do during those long electronic interludes, so it was natural to talk with others idling at computers nearby. One day I turned to the woman beside me and we began to chat.

Jeannie Annan had just returned from working in northern Uganda's neglected war. A humanitarian worker and a psychology PhD student, she eyed me suspiciously. I was wearing a suit. Good things seldom came from Westerners wearing suits in Africa. But I seemed interested in the war and informed about what was happening, which was more than she could say for most of the people she met. So she gave me a chance.

A few months later, I was traveling the north's dry, dusty roads beside her, marveling at the miles of endless grass, hoping a rebel unit wouldn't pop out. Mostly (I admit) I went because I was interested in Jeannie. But we also had an idea. After decades of conflict, no one knew the true toll of violence on the young men and women displaced, shot at, and conscripted. Jeannie understood the war and the psychological toll of violence, while I knew economics, surveys, and statistics. We joined forces. We hired a local team and spent the next two years surveying people affected by the fighting. Our study was trying to put some hard numbers to the savage toll, discover programs that could help, and test what works. The brutal costs of conflict were everywhere to see. We were the despondent accountants.

I had not yet fallen in love with her, but after a month in northern Uganda, I was well on my way. We started the project together, wrote our dissertations together, graduated, and got our first jobs at Yale together. Today we've been married fifteen years and have a long list of research papers. Our most important collaborations, however, are an eleven-year-old girl and a nine-year-old boy.

That chance encounter over a dial-up connection also changed my career. In northern Uganda, I learned about violence more savage and distressing than I'd ever imagined. The young men and women I met told me stories so horrible I don't even want to try to recount them. I can't do them justice. Those were some of the most emotionally punishing months of my life. In the end, they made me rethink everything.

There and in the years that followed, I learned a society's success isn't just about expanding its wealth. It is about a rebel group not enslaving your eleven-year-old daughter as a wife. It is about sitting in front of your home without the fear of a drive-by shooting and a bullet gone astray. It is about being able to go to a police officer, a court, or a mayor and get some semblance of justice. It is about the government never being allowed to push you off your land and stick you in a concentration camp. Another economist, Amartya Sen, called this "development as freedom." It is hard to imagine something more important to be free of than violence.

As it happens, fighting also makes us poor. Nothing destroys progress like conflict—crushing economies, destroying infrastructure, or killing, maiming, and setting back an entire generation.[1] War undermines economic growth in indirect ways as well. Most people and businesses won't do the basic things that lead to development when they expect bombings, ethnic cleansings, or arbitrary justice; they won't specialize in tasks, trade, invest their wealth, or develop new techniques and ideas.

This is true for cities like Chicago, too, where every year a few hundred shootings probably cost the population a few hundred million dollars. The economist and moral philosopher Adam Smith predicted as much over two and a half centuries ago: "Little else is requisite to carry a state to the highest degree of opulence from the lowest barbarism," he wrote in 1755, "but peace, easy taxes, and a tolerable administration of justice."[2] Clearly, if I cared about prosperity, equal rights, and justice, I had to care about war.

LET ME BE CLEAR WHAT I MEAN, HOWEVER. WHEN I SAY *WAR*, I DON'T JUST MEAN COUN- tries duking it out. I mean any kind of prolonged, violent struggle between groups. That includes villages, clans, gangs, ethnic groups, religious sects, political factions, and nations. Wildly different as these may be, their origins have much in common. We'll see that with Northern Irish zealots, Colombian cartels, European tyrants, Liberian rebels, Greek oligarchs, Chicago gangs, Indian mobs, Rwandan genocidaires, English soccer hooligans, and American invaders.

Some people look at the fighting in North Lawndale or northern Uganda and think, "Oh, those places are at it again," or, "My society is long past that," or simply, "We are different." But that's wrong. True, all these levels of violence and all these societies are distinctive. But even if you're one of the people reading this book from the refuge of a prosperous and peaceful place, we'll see how the logic that explains fighting far away also explains the tumult in your country's past, the ongoing battles between people not so different from you, or why your government (or its allies) still attack other nations. My goal is to give you a framework to understand the common forces that drive these unnatural disasters.[3]

Expansive as that sounds, though, I'm not going to try to explain every kind of contest. When I said that war is a prolonged, violent struggle between groups, I chose my words carefully. One is *prolonged*. Lengthy fights are different from brief skirmishes. Short and deadly quarrels are important, but they're easier to explain through idiosyncrasy, or momentary miscalculations. The real puzzle is why opponents would spend years or even decades destroying themselves and the objects of their desire.

Another key term is *groups*. Individuals fight all the time, but a lot of this interpersonal violence is reactive and short-lived. A book on that would dwell on the traits we inherit from our primate ancestors, our ingrained fight-or-flight instincts, and the ease with which humans identify with members of their in-group. Wars, however, are long struggles where reactions like these recede in importance. Our reflexes are still relevant, as we'll see. But big groups are deliberate and strategic. This means I'll only talk about why individuals discriminate, brawl, lynch, or kill when that tells us something about larger group behavior.[4]

The final crucial word is *violent*. It's normal for groups to compete bitterly.

But one of the most common errors people make is to confuse the reasons a contest is intense and hostile with the reasons that a rivalry turns violent. You see, acrimonious competition is normal, but prolonged violence between groups is not. Wars shouldn't happen, and most of the time they don't.

WAR IS THE EXCEPTION, NOT THE RULE

The fact is, even the bitterest of enemies prefer to loathe one another in peace. That's easy to forget. Our attention gets captured by the wars that do happen, like the ones in northern Uganda or North Lawndale. News reports and history books do the same—they focus on the handful of violent struggles that occur. Few write books about the countless conflicts avoided. But we can't just look at the hostilities that happen any more than a medical student should study only the terminally ill and forget that most people are healthy.

This book tries to pull us away from this unrepresentative view, because it's just not true. Take ethnic and religious violence, for instance. Political scientists have tallied all the ethnic and sectarian groups in places like Eastern Europe, Central Asia, South Asia, and Africa, where riots and purges are supposedly endemic. They counted the number of pairs that are close enough to compete with one another, and then they looked at the number that actually fought. In Africa, they counted about one major case of ethnic violence per year out of two thousand potential ones. In India, they found less than one riot per ten million people per year, and death rates that are at most sixteen per ten million. (To put this in context, sixteen per hundred thousand is a moderate murder rate in a large US city—a level one hundred times higher than deaths from sectarian riots in India). Even if these tabulations are off by a huge amount, it's clear that most groups, even hostile ones, live side by side without fighting. Enemies prefer to loathe one another in peace.[5]

We see this at the international level too. There was the long confrontation between America and the Soviets, who managed to divide Europe (indeed the world) into two parts without nuking one another. There is the perpetual standoff between Pakistan and India, the gloomy impasse between North and South Korea, and the constant deadlock over the South China Sea. There was the hasty but peaceful exit of France and England from their African colonies as soon as it became clear they might fight for independence, plus the nonviolent Soviet retreat from Eastern Europe. And then there are the societies riven by political factions, angry and polarized by class and ideology, who nonetheless compete in parliaments rather than on battlefields. Somehow, however, we tend to forget these events. We write tomes about great wars, and overlook the quiet peaces. We pay attention to the gory spectacles, the most salient events. Meanwhile, the quieter moments of compromise slip from memory.[6]

This focus on the failures is a kind of selection bias, a logical error to which we're all prone. The mistake has two important consequences. One is that we exaggerate how much we fight. You start to hear things like "the world is full of conflict," or "humanity's natural state is war," or "an armed confrontation between [insert great powers here] is inevitable." But none of those statements is true.

Overlooking all the conflicts avoided entails a second and greater harm, however; we get the roots of war and the paths to peace all wrong. When people focus on the times peace failed, and trace back the circumstances and events to find the causes, they often find a familiar set: flawed leaders, historic injustices, dire poverty, angry young men, cheap weapons, and cataclysmic events. War seems to be the inevitable result. But this ignores the times conflict was avoided. If people also looked at the times rivals didn't fight, they'd see a lot of the same preceding conditions. All these so-called causes of war are commonplace. Prolonged violence is not. Things that are present in both the failures and the successes are probably not the roots of war.

To understand why, let me tell you about another famous example of selection bias, from World War II. When American aircraft returned from missions over German positions, they were covered in bullet holes along their main bodies and wings. So the US military told its engineers to add more armor to these parts of the plane. A statistician named Abraham Wald disagreed. He said the engineers should do the opposite: shield the engines and cockpit, where returning planes showed no damage at all. He'd deduced something crucial: the missing bullet holes must be on the missing planes. Shots to the cockpit and engine sent those planes crashing. That's why we didn't see bombers with damage to those parts of the craft. The military was mistakenly focusing on a select sample, and so it got the causes of failure wrong. This is one of those mistakes that are obvious in retrospect, and yet we all make them again and again.

The US military was focused on the successes—a kind of selection problem known as survivor bias. When it comes to war, we're prone to the opposite kind of selection—we pay too much attention to the times peace failed. It's as if the US military engineers looked only at the bombers that went down. Those planes are covered in gunfire from tip to tail. When we do that, it's hard to know which shots were fatal because we aren't comparing them to the planes that survived. The same thing happens when you take a war and trace it back to its so-called roots. Every history of every rivalry is riddled with a barrage of bullet holes, like poverty and grievances and guns. But the aggrieved seldom revolt, most poor young rabble-rousers don't rebel, and the most heavily armed groups prefer a cold war to a hot one.

To find the real roots of fighting, we need to pay attention to the struggles that stay peaceful. By this I don't mean happy and harmonious. Rivalries can be hostile and contentious. The groups may be polarized. They're often heavily armed. They disparage and threaten one another, and they ostentatiously display their weapons. That is all normal. Bloodshed and destruction are not.

My hope is that now you'll start to see this everywhere. When you next pick up a newspaper or a history book, amid all the bombast and belligerence, you'll start to pay attention to the politicians making speeches, pushing for conciliation. You'll notice the rivals who fire rockets at one another for a week or two, then halt hostilities. You'll hear tales of councillors whispering, "Peace, Sire," in their sovereign's ear. You'll note the veteran generals reminding the more inexperienced and enthusiastic officers what misery awaits them. The easiest to spot will be the treasurers and other keepers of the purse who soberly point out that war simply cannot be afforded. All these agonies and costs are what drives most rivals to compromise.

WHY EVEN THE BITTEREST RIVALS PREFER PEACE

The voices counseling peace usually win out for one simple reason: war is ruinous. It massacres soldiers, ravages civilians, starves cities, plunders stores, disrupts trade, demolishes industry, and bankrupts governments. About 2,500 years ago, the Chinese general Sun Tzu put it aptly in *The Art of War*: "There is no instance of a country having benefited from prolonged warfare." Even the bitterest of enemies foresee the consequences of fighting. These costs are terrible. That is why adversaries strive for an arrangement that avoids risk and destruction. One-off killings and skirmishes take place in the heat of the moment. Then cooler heads prevail.

The cooler heads look for ways to compromise. As Winston Churchill once said, "Meeting jaw to jaw is better than war." For every war that ever was, a thousand others have been averted through discussion and conces-sion. Negotiation and fighting are alternative ways of getting what you want. That's what Chinese Communist leader Mao Tse-tung meant in 1938 when he said, "Politics is war without bloodshed, while war is politics with blood-shed." Mao was echoing the Prussian general Carl von Clausewitz, who, a century before, reminded us that "war is the continuation of politics by other means."

What we must not forget, however, is that one of these two strategies is devastating, while the other is not. "Compromise or fight" gives rivals a stark choice: carve up an undamaged prize peacefully, or each pay an enormous cost to gamble over the shrunken, shattered remains. War's destructiveness means that both sides are almost always better off finding a peaceful split than going to war.

That's why, throughout history, most foes opted for the peaceful path. Starting seven thousand years ago, for instance, civilizations regularly bought off so-called barbarians—mobile societies of mounted herders, skilled at fighting—to save their cities from getting sacked. Similarly, most empires on record have offered weaker states the option of submission and tribute instead of invasion. Meanwhile, in small towns and villages, a murderer's clan paid blood money to the victim's family to avoid cycles of retribution and feuding. They realized it's better to compensate than to fight.

Or consider the centuries-long struggles between European commoners and aristocrats. When arms, agriculture, or demography favored the peasantry, and the masses grew richer and demanded more rights, the highborn faced a choice: fight or concede. Historians pay more attention to the great peasant rebellions—the handful of times aristocrats were unwilling to comply. More often, however, the elites relinquished some privileges—enfranchising the more powerful merchants, reducing rents for the most troublesome sharecroppers, or distributing bread to the unruliest urban mobs. Europe's slow democratization was a long-running series of revolutions without revolt.

Nations also prefer to placate rather than battle. Before national borders solidified nearly a century and a half ago, rising nations regularly bought or seized territory without a shot, while the weaker powers quietly acquiesced. The European powers tried to avoid warring over colonies, and so the tiny group of monarchs held congresses to calmly carve up Eastern Europe, Africa, and other frontiers. Likewise, a rising United States purchased Alaska from Russia and a large swath of the Midwest from France, and it even tried buying Cuba from Spain as an alternative to invading.

Today's territorial concessions are typically more subtle: rights over underground oil reserves or who gets to build a hydro plant on the Nile River; or (in ongoing negotiations) who controls the South China Sea. Most of the important elements in the negotiations, however, aren't even land. Hegemons from the United States to Russia to China twist the arms of weaker nations to curtail their weapons programs, support a policy, or change a law. Armed resistance is seldom these governments' best response, however unfair the international system might get. Meanwhile, within countries, political factions find ingenious ways to redistribute political influence when power shifts. And powerful minorities get guarantees of a disproportionate number of parliamentary seats or vetoes. It is peaceful bargains all the way down.

Unfortunately, peace doesn't necessarily mean equality or justice. As so many of these examples show, if one side has most of the bargaining power, it can expect to set its terms. The weaker rival might resent its tiny share of influence and spoils, but it'll acquiesce. The world is full of such terrible but peaceful inequities: minority ethnic groups who control the military and the government, dominating the majority; narrow aristocracies that hold all the land and manufactories in their nation, leaving little for the peasants; or military superpowers that dictate the world order to other countries. For most underdogs, the costs and risks of revolution are too great. However unfair, it doesn't make sense to revolt.

COMPROMISE IS THE RULE BECAUSE, FOR THE MOST PART, GROUPS BEHAVE STRATEGIcally. By this I mean that they, like players of poker or chess, are trying hard to think ahead, to discern their opponents' strengths and plans, and to choose their actions based on what they expect their opponents to do. They're not perfect. They make mistakes or lack information. But they have huge incentives to do their best.

The science of strategy is called game theory. It works out how one side will behave based on what it believes its opponent will do. Starting with the first chapter, we'll walk through the strategic choice: compromise or fight. We won't use this game theory blindly, however. Some people use these models to paint a picture of an unreasonably rational race—*Homo economicus*. We'll be interested in this species because they still manage to commit an awful lot of violence. (As we'll see, in special circumstances, fighting is your best strategy.) But groups and their leaders are not always logical or all-seeing, and collections of people don't hold coherent beliefs that the body politic faithfully represents. So this will also be a book about *Homo unreasonablus* and *Homo righteousus*, plus other breeds of humankind that historians, psychologists, biologists, and sociologists have discovered. Chapter by chapter, we're going to meet each one. But our simple game of strategy will always remain our frame of reference because we can trust that, no matter which of these species they represent, most human groups strive in pursuit of their own interests.

FIVE REASONS FOR WARS

So why do we fight? Now that we're thinking in strategic terms, and now that we aren't committing the sin of selection bias, we have a new way to answer that question. In short, something had to interrupt the normal incentives for compromise, pushing opponents from the usual polarized and contentious politics to bargaining through bloodshed. Fortunately, there are only so many logical ways that this politicking can break down. There are five of them, and part 1 of the book lays them out chapter by chapter. Each of the five logics eliminates the incentives for compromise in a distinct way.

This first is *unchecked interests*. The costs of war are the main incentive for peace, but when the people who decide on war aren't accountable to the others in their group, they can ignore some of the costs and agony of fighting. These leaders will take their group to war too frequently. Sometimes they expect to gain personally from conflict, and so they're enticed to start fights. Unchecked rulers like these are one of the greatest drivers of conflict in history.

The second reason is *intangible incentives*. There are times when committing violence delivers something valued, like vengeance or status or dominance. In other cases, violence is the sole path to righteous ends—God's glory, freedom, or combating injustice. For some groups, these ethereal rewards can offset the pain and loss from fighting. Any preference for them will run against the costs of war and tilt a group away from compromise.

The third way bargains fall apart comes from *uncertainty*. If you've ever called a bluff in poker, you've grasped this logic already. You don't know what cards your opponents hold, but you know they have an incentive to fool you. Obviously, your best response is not to fold every time. Likewise, in war, you don't know your enemies' strength or resolve, and they, too, may bluff. So sometimes you call. The fact that you don't have the same information as your rivals means that attacking is occasionally the best strategy, even if fighting is detrimental.

Fourth is something called a *commitment problem*. Usually, when your rival grows powerful, your best option is to concede something. But what if you're warned of your opponent's rise in advance? You can strike now, while you're still strong, and avert your decline. If the looming shift in power is large enough, your incentive to attack may be irresistible. What could your enemy possibly promise you to do otherwise? That they won't take advantage of their newfound influence once they're strong? They cannot commit to that, and you both know it. It's a commitment problem—you'd both prefer a political deal that avoids the ruin of war, but none of these bargains are credible.

Fifth and finally, our *misperceptions* interfere with compromise. We are overconfident creatures. We also assume others think like us, value the same things we do, and see the world the same way. And we demonize our enemies and attribute to them the worst motives. We hold on to all sorts of mistaken beliefs, even in big groups, and when we do, it hijacks our ability to find a bargain we and our enemies can agree to. Competition and conflict make all these misjudgments worse.

NOW, EVEN IF THESE FIVE LOGICS SOUND REASONABLE TO YOU, YOU MIGHT STILL BE SKEP-tical that they alone explain every war. It can seem like there's a reason for every war and a war for every reason. But most of the time, the arguments people give for a particular war are just these five in disguise. We're going to learn to recognize them as such.

For that reason, don't think of the five as a new theory of war, to be propounded over an old one. I'm not saying "Believe these causes, the other books are wrong." Instead, think of the five kinds of breakdown as a typology—a way to organize the huge number of theories and schools of thought already out there.

I'll also show how we don't need to take intellectual sides behind one discipline or another, or one theory of war. These five encompass the lessons that thousands of economists, political scientists, sociologists, psychologists, and policymakers have learned, boiled down into one frame.[7]

Finally, we'll see how the five logics aren't substitutes; they're complements—tragic ones, because they cumulate to make peace more fragile. That's because, except in rare cases, a war never has one cause. The different reasons cumulate and interact. Unaccountable leaders, intangible incentives, incertitude, commitment problems, and misperceptions combine into a toxic brew that poisons peace bit by bit. This makes it hard to pin a conflict on a single reason.

This is what it means to live in a fragile community, city, or nation. The five forces have eliminated most of the room for two enemies to find a compromise. For a while, peace persists, but it's tenuous. War never seems that far away. In this brittle condition, one misunderstanding, or one calamitous event, can eliminate the incentives for peace altogether. A million little forces can tip them into raging combat—an assassination, a stock market crash, a terrifying rumor, a discovery of oil, or the shortsighted actions of an errant or feebleminded leader.

This is why it's so easy to find a war for every reason, and why we can trace back the events of a war and see a million little things at work. But should we blame war on these idiosyncratic forces? Absolutely not—because we can find the same shocks and surprises and mistakes among the opponents who don't plunge into war. Those rivalries didn't erupt into violence, because the five forces hadn't whittled away the room for politics and compromise. We'll learn not to get too distracted by these chance occurrences.

We'll also learn to recognize false causes. Things like poverty, scarcity, natural resources, climate change, ethnic fragmentation, polarization, injustices, and arms don't necessarily interrupt the incentives for peace—at least not by themselves. They're terrible for other reasons. And they add fuel to a raging fire. But they probably didn't ignite fighting in the first place. Focusing on both successes and failures, plus a little strategic thinking, will help us understand which bullet holes are on the planes that survived, and which are on the crafts that perished. The lesson is clear: focus on the five fundamentals.

Finally, the best reason to peer through this frame and the five logics is to understand why some societies are stable, peaceful, and successful, and to figure out how the most fragile and violent societies can become more like them. That will be the subject of part 2. Its message is simple: stable societies are full of rivalries that compete ferociously without fighting. Villages, gangs, ethnic groups, cities, states, and the globe have found a huge number of ways to make their contests less fragile and to counter incentives to fight. They've built themselves some insulation from all five kinds of failure—armor plating on all the right parts of the plane. The essential ones I call interdependence, checks and balances, rules and enforcement, and interventions. Every one shares a secret: they work if and only if they roll back at least one of the five kinds of breakdown.

Before we get to those, however, let me first demonstrate the gravitational pull of peace.

PART I

THE ROOTS OF WAR

Chapter 1

WHY WE DON'T FIGHT

I first heard about the Billiards War from an inmate in Bellavista prison. I'll call him Carlos. Lean, muscular, in his late twenties, he'd run a plaza de vicio—a retail drug corner—before his arrest. Carlos had started working for his neighborhood gang at the age of fourteen, running packages of marijuana. But he showed a good head for figures and didn't steal, and so the gang leader, the *coordinador*, made him a salaried member. Over the years, Carlos worked his way up through the group, first through armed robbery, then selling drugs. Eventually he made it into middle management, coordinating his own plaza. Unfortunately, Carlos also developed a taste for his own product. He was living in Bellavista's drug rehab wing, head shaven, clad in brown medical scrubs, when we met.

Bellavista sits at the base of a valley crowned by lush green peaks. On either side of the prison, up steep mountain slopes, climbs the city of Medellín. This is Colombia's commercial heartland. Along the lower slopes and valley floor lie quiet middle-class neighborhoods of white stucco and ocher tile roofs. Manufacturers churn out the country's furniture and foodstuffs. Farther up, however, on slopes that seem too steep for human habitation, sit the slums—tightly packed buildings, two or three stories high, of rough, bare clay brick and corrugated metal. Standing in the cramped

Colombia and Medellín

narrow streets, you can stretch your arms from graffiti-strewn wall to graffiti-strewn wall.

In each community also lives a *combo*. Like street gangs everywhere, combos run the local drug corners. But in Medellín they do much more. Head to the main thoroughfare in a neighborhood like La Sierra, its bakeries and tiny general stores stuffed with candy, soft drinks, and beer. On the corner, you may find a teenage combo member providing security. Foot soldiers like this one are a kind of order here, selling protection for a price. He stops by the bakeries and general stores once a week to collect a three-dollar *vacuna*, meaning "vaccine."

Medellín's combos don't stop at drug retailing and protection rackets, however. No one sells staples in La Sierra—eggs, milk, cooking gas, the thick Colombian tortillas known as arepas—without a license from the gang. The combo also sets neighborhood moneylending rates, takes a cut of each loan, and is only too happy to buy and collect the debts that later go unpaid.[1]

All these rents and revenues make each Medellín neighborhood a valuable prize to control. As a result, nearly every low- and middle-income area in the city is occupied by an armed gang, hundreds in all. The city is a patchwork of principalities, each overseen by a thirty-year-old thug. It sounds like a perfect recipe for violence.

Prisons like Bellavista sit at the center of this citywide contest, because that's where most of the *coordinadores* live. The city has done its best to arrest as many combo members as possible, and so the squat, whitewashed, concrete bunker is filled to four times its capacity. But by phone and messenger, the gang leaders still run their little empires from within.

The first time I entered the complex, I expected a regimented, morose atmosphere. The reality is more freewheeling. Inmates dress casually in their own T-shirts, track pants, and shorts. Relations with the guards are casual, even chatty. Technically the men are confined to large cellblocks called patios, but "confined" seems like the wrong word. No one leaves the building, but the men move more or less freely about the maze of cinder-block hallways painted a robin's-egg blue.

In Carlos's patio, a powerful criminal group called Pachelly ran the trade in illicit drugs and phones. They also charged rent for cells and beds. All these business lines made patios profitable and strategic territory, just like the streets Pachelly controlled on the outside. The same gangs that dominate Medellín's neighborhoods also control the prison hallways.

A rival gang named El Mesa lived on the same patio as Pachelly, Carlos told me, and their power was rising. Outside Bellavista, El Mesa's territory, foot soldiers, and profits were all growing and so El Mesa's imprisoned members began to chafe under Pachelly's patio rule. One afternoon in 2012, members of the two groups were in the cellblock's game room, playing billiards. Carlos didn't remember the reason the players started arguing and fighting, or why their friends piled on. Some petty insult or cheating, presumably. What he does recall is that the fight got out of hand fast. Members of El Mesa pulled out their guns and fired on Pachelly. How they kept concealed weapons in jail is a whole other story. The upshot: twenty-three inmates and guards were injured by the time the shooting stopped. Astonishingly, no one was killed.

Anger and recrimination spilled outside the prison. Pachelly and El Mesa began to activate their alliances. Hundreds of city gangs lined up on either side, readying their forces. El Mesa formed an alliance with another powerful gang, Los Chatas, led by one of the city's mightiest kingpins, known by the alias Tom. The city geared for war.

Now, if this were the usual book on wars, here is where I'd describe how, over the next few weeks, Medellín spiraled into bloodshed. What began as isolated reprisals spun into a whirlwind of vendettas. Amid the chaos, combos began capturing neighboring territories and settling scores. The fragile peace collapsed among hundreds of combos citywide. No doubt we could trace that bloody contest for Medellín to a host of so-called causes: disenfranchised young men, a city awash in guns, corrupt politicians, and a crumbling social order.

But the Billiards War never happened. El Mesa did grow in power. They did chafe under Pachelly. The gang did open fire over a game of pool. And El Mesa did form an alliance with Tom and Los Chatas. All of Medellín did gear for battle. Despite all that, the violence ended with that one bloody shootout in Bellavista. Instead of launching a prolonged citywide conflict, Pachelly and El Mesa decided to compromise. There was a tense negotiation, and then Pachelly ceded some of its territory—control of a prison hallway here, a contraband business there. None of these businesses were worth a costly battle with a rising foe.

This has been true for decades. For every gang war that ever was in Medellín, a thousand others have been averted through negotiation and trade. Even though the valley is filled to its green peaks with hotheaded armed gang members, the combos of Medellín seldom go to war. They despise one another. They maneuver for drug plazas and prison hallways. They occasionally skirmish. But the region's homicide rate is lower than that of many big American cities.

It's easy to forget this is how most opponents operate. But Medellín's checkerboard of hostile combos is simply an allegory for our wider world. The globe is a patchwork of rival territories. Possessing them brings wealth, power, and status. Rivals covet their neighbors' territory and resources, prey on the weaker ones, and defend themselves from the strong. Most human groups are simply combos in another guise. And, like combos, they strive not to fight.

PEACE IS STRATEGIC

To show you the calculus of compromise, let's stick with the example of Medellín gangs. I want to give you a tool—a simple strategic logic—that helps explain why most rivals avoid war. A little game theory is worth learning because we'll use it throughout the book, to understand both how this peace breaks down and how to build it back up again.

The powerful factions that we met in Bellavista all came from an area called Bello, on the northern edge of Medellín. For a combo, Bello is full of opportunity: extortion, drug sales, money laundering, hideouts, prestige. Let's imagine Bello as a pie the rivals must split. Suppose, for the sake of simplicity, it's worth $100 to each side, like this:

Also suppose that, militarily speaking, Pachelly and El Mesa are evenly matched. This means, if either one decides to attack, each gang has an equal chance of winning—50 percent, like a coin flip. Let's also simplify war and assume that it's an all-or-nothing affair: the winner gets the whole territory of Bello forever; the loser gets nothing.

The two rivals know, as we do, that war has dire consequences, no matter who wins. Gang war brings police attention to the crime bosses and risks their arrest. It kills their little brothers and friends in the group. It undermines their illegal business lines, since no one pays their vacuna or buys drugs in the middle of a gunfight. Combo leaders couldn't care less about civilian casualties. But war hurts the leadership and their bottom line. These losses are powerful incentives to negotiate. I need to put a number to this destruction to work through the example. I could use any figure, but let's suppose that both gangs expect fighting to destroy a fifth of the pie—$20.

The key strategic insight is simple: war's destruction means that, beforehand, both sides are almost always better off finding a peaceful split than going to war. The $20 is like a peace bonus they get to divide. It creates a whole range of territorial splits they both prefer to fighting, because in expectation war will always make them worse off than one of the divisions inside it. We'll call this the bargaining range.

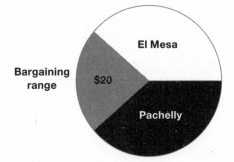

Consider the choice from the point of view of El Mesa's coordinador. He knows his gang has even odds of winning. He thinks to himself, "Should we destroy a fifth of Bello's earning potential, then flip a coin for the shrunken remains? Or can we find a way to carve up the territory as it stands?" In this case, compromise pays. It's simple arithmetic: because war is an even shot at a damaged $80 pie, the expected value of fighting is $40.[2] This means that the leader would happily choose peace so long as the deal gives El Mesa control of at least 40 percent of Bello.

Pachelly faces the same incentives. El Mesa and its coordinador know it too. Thus, neither side fears an attack because each knows the choice the other confronts. Each side can get something in the range of $40 to $60 in peace. How they split it will depend on the details of how the game gets played. But split it they should.

This shows us something important: peace arises not from brotherly love and cooperation, but from the ever-present threat of violence. Each side's bargaining power comes from its ability to threaten the enemy with harm. This power could come from guns, from defensive fortifications, from the money to hire soldiers, from new terror tactics, or from the ability to mobilize millions of people into the streets, munitions factories, or infantry— anything that helps one group triumph over their rival. But you garner concessions only if you can credibly threaten to burn the whole house down. In Immanuel Kant's *Perpetual Peace*, this tense but nonviolent face-off is what the philosopher called the natural state of humankind—not war itself.

This model and these assumptions, simple though they are, give us a few other strategic insights into competition. One is that we should expect peace whether the costs of war are small or calamitous. If fighting demanded only half the sacrifice—less death, fewer interruptions to the drug business, lower risk of arrest—then the bargaining range would be half as wide. Still, every split in that narrower range would be better for both rivals than war. So long as war is costly, there's always a political deal both sides prefer.

This implies something you might find counterintuitive: often, the more ✳ destructive our weapons, the easier it should be to find peace. Vast military investments or new weapons discoveries don't necessarily cause conflict on their own. Mostly they change the balance of power, and hence the splits of the pie. When they make war more ruinous, however, the bargaining range can widen, expanding the dividend from peace. This helps us understand a broad pattern over history: as weapons grow more powerful, wars should grow less frequent. When these heavily armed opponents do fight, however, those wars are doozies. So we expect to see fewer but more calamitous wars over time.[3]

Another insight is that it shouldn't matter how big or small the pie is, or whether it is shrinking or growing. Whatever the size of the pie, so long as war is costly, there will be a bargaining range. That means we shouldn't expect especially poor places to be inherently more conflict prone. And we shouldn't necessarily expect new discoveries of resources, shrinking water supplies, a plunge in commodity prices, or a drought to lead to fighting. Not unless they're accompanied by some other breakdown in bargaining— something that changes incentives and eliminates the bargaining range.

In the case of Pachelly and El Mesa, for instance, we imagined the two sides evenly matched, and so they got roughly equal shares. But what if a cataclysm strikes Pachelly? A federal task force sweeps in, capturing top leaders, freezing bank accounts, and seizing stores of weapons and cash. Suppose this means Pachelly's chance of winning a war against El Mesa falls to 20 percent. All the while, El Mesa has been growing its drug profits, its military power, and its alliances. The bargaining range has shifted, from one that granted Pachelly $40 to $60 of Bello to one that leaves them $16 to $36.[4] From Pachelly's perspective, it looks like this:

The important thing is that the new range doesn't include the old split, so El Mesa is clearly displeased. But this doesn't mean they invade Pachelly's patch of Bello to bring their spoils in line with their power. El Mesa has no need to launch a war. That's because it's in Pachelly's best interests to keep El Mesa from attacking. Pachelly would rather trade rather than fight. They'll cede some plazas to their foe, or keep the corners but pay the rival gang tribute each year.

This shows something important: we should expect peace to be resilient, even when power is unequally held, even when rivals detest one another, and even when they're buffeted by shocks and shifts in power. In general, the side with the least material wealth, mobilizational power, and military strength should expect to get a lesser share of the pie, and to live with it.

A final lesson is this: if a mismatch between spoils and power ever arises, it is better for both sides to deal than fight. In the case of Bello, this doesn't mean the capos have to sit down with an abacus or Excel spreadsheet and figure out their break-even points. But their agents sometimes do meet, each one of them a wily negotiator with a keen sense of value. Or, in some cases, a more powerful gang simply moves into rival territory, capturing a corner or a business, expecting their weakened opponent will concede without a fight. We can see the same informal negotiations and unilateral moves at the level of a country or a village. Their rough-hewn calculus of what they can gain or lose gets rivals pretty far. If they're unsure of just how strong they are, a few skirmishes should clear that up. There's no need for prolonged battles.

OBVIOUSLY, THIS OVERSIMPLIFIES REAL LIFE. THERE ARE JUST TWO RIVALS IN MY EXAMPLE, each group acts in unison, each one observes the other with ease, and war is a one-shot, all-or-nothing affair. Still, we could complicate the game and the conclusion is fairly versatile: if there ever arises a mismatch between spoils and power, it is still better for both sides to deal than fight.

This is an instance of a much more general principle, that rivals have incentives to bargain and transfer resources to avoid wasteful outcomes. The early applications weren't to military conflict, but to commerce. Take negotiations between firms and unions, for instance. Just replace "war" with "labor strike" and the insight is the same. Both groups want the best deal for their group—shareholders on one side, workers on the other. Strikes and stoppages are costly to both sides. So most firms and unions try to avoid them. Under the credible threat of a walkout, employers prefer to grant concessions to workers. Long strikes should be rare, labor economists have argued, because they're costly and inefficient for both sides. For the most part that's true. And when strikes do happen, both parties often regret it.

We see something similar with court battles. Like wars, lawsuits are expensive and inefficient. It's better to settle, and most litigants do. Long, messy court battles happen only when something hijacks the normal incentives for settlement.[5]

About the same time that these ideas were applied to the law and labor, a Harvard economist named Thomas Schelling began applying these strategic insights to wars. Over the next few decades, others refined the logic. My pie-splitting example comes from a Stanford political scientist named Jim Fearon, one of the first to systematically outline how our peaceful incentives break down.[6]

This calculus is embedded in theories of international relations, too. The approach I've laid out resembles the "realist" approach to conflict—a school of thought advanced by some of history's most influential thinkers and politicians, from Niccolò Machiavelli to Henry Kissinger. They see nations as selfishly striving for their own interests, in an anarchic system where there's no overarching authority to keep rivals from attacking one another. Peaceful deals depend on the two sides finding it in their mutual interest not to fight. This is exactly the kind of situation that noncooperative game theory—including our pie-splitting exercise—was designed to capture.[7]

THIS BRINGS US TO WHY WE FIGHT, AND THE FIVE REASONS FOR WARS. EACH ONE OF THE five interrupts the peaceful pie splitting in a different way. They relax some of the simplifying assumptions and realist principles and show which ones are most important to peace. Unchecked interests, for instance, recognize the importance of a group's internal politics, especially that rulers often pursue riches and glory against the interests of their society. Intangible incentives allow for the possibility that societies possess other values and ideals outside the material pie—and that pursuing them can offset the costs of war. Uncertainty removes the assumption that both sides see the same information and understand their rival's bargaining power. Commitment problems introduce changes in power over time, as well as restrictions on how much one side can credibly transfer to the other to preserve peace. Finally, with misperceptions, we recognize that our pie splitters are not coolheaded computers. We misjudge ourselves and our enemies, and this leads us to predictable mistakes.

The next five chapters chart each of these five logics in more detail. But take care. As we walk through failure after failure, it will be easy to forget the core message so far: war is the exception, not the rule. Amid all this misery, however, try not to lose sight of the world's robust constitution, the tools at hand, and the pull of peace.

Chapter 2

UNCHECKED INTERESTS

The dejected warlord stared into his beer. Short, lean, dressed in a grimy white muscle shirt and jeans, the man known as White Flower sat across from me, slouched into a plastic lawn chair. A few months before, the thirtysomething commander had led a thousand mercenaries. Together they ruled a rubber plantation in the West African jungle, worked by ten thousand laborers. Each day legions of these tappers gathered cupfuls of milky resin from the plantation's millions of rubber trees. White Flower and his commanders taxed each one, netting up to $40,000 a month. Tonight, though, he could barely afford his beer.

The night was hot, humid, and pitch-black. Greenville, like most midsize towns in Liberia, hadn't seen electric power for more than a decade. The only light flickered from cook fires scattered along the street's broken pavement. Vendors squatted over makeshift grills, selling oily fish to passersby.

The post-apocalyptic feeling was well earned. It was 2009, six years after the end of Liberia's war. For the fourteen years before that truce, the tiny West African country seldom saw a moment of stability. So total was the conflict, almost one in ten Liberians died. Half were pushed out of their homes. Looting and battles had ravaged and depopulated places like this town.

White Flower's real name was Leon, but he preferred his nom de guerre.

Flanked by two hulking henchmen, the skinny ex-commander had cornered me after dusk, sitting at one of the street grills near my hotel, my fingers greasy with fish.

A few months earlier, White Flower and his coterie had been pushed off the rubber plantation by a mix of Liberian police, UN peacekeepers, and angry tappers tired of paying their "taxes" and getting nothing in return. Worse, foreigners like me were coming through with a promise of jobs and education, trying to coax White Flower's low-level fighters into putting down their weapons. I was studying the demobilization program, not running it. But White Flower wasn't interested in those kinds of distinctions.

Between sips of beer in the dark, White Flower told me a familiar warlord's fable. Liberia is a land with riches for those who were willing and able to harness its wealth, the fairy tale begins. The country, covered in dense tropical forest, funneled its commodities to the West: lumber to France, rubber to Japan and America. Creeks deep in the jungle could be dredged for gold and diamonds, with a lucrative market in Belgium. Those riches could develop the nation, bringing health and education to the neglected

Liberia

masses. Men with vision had to seize these resources for the good of the community, violently if need be.

That kind of rhetoric (and guns) brought the young White Flower to power on the Sinoe Rubber Plantation. Mostly it was the guns. For White Flower knew as well as I that the laborers never saw a single one of the clinics or schools he promised.[1] Also, we both knew he wouldn't hesitate to re-ignite the war if it served his interests. As was true with most Liberian warlords, fighting had made him rich. The conflict brought him land, money, and power, even if the country suffered overall. Given a chance to seize more territory, White Flower would surely do so. His mercenaries and the common folk would shoulder most of the risks and burdens. What did he care?

Fortunately, the Liberian government and the UN peacekeeping force knew White Flower's incentives too. They came prepared. Troops arrived with overwhelming force, a bribe for his troops (including the program I mentioned), and a payoff for White Flower and his henchmen.

Unfortunately for White Flower, though, he was terrible at handling money. After a few months, his windfall was wasted and gone. As the night wore on, his reason for cornering me became clear: he wanted a job on my project team. "I can make sure people here cooperate with you," he explained. I didn't doubt it. But by that point, it was obvious that White Flower was no longer scary; he was defeated and pathetic. I passed on his offer and crossed the street, back to my hotel. It was time for bed.

THE TROUBLE WITH AUTOCRATS AND OLIGARCHS

In many ways, White Flower's fable was the story of Liberia—from its founding as an American colony in 1821, through its history as one of the few independent Black republics in the world, to a long and terrible civil war that broke out in 1989.

Like White Flower, Liberia's story began with natural wealth, resources that a narrow ruling class of businessmen and landowners could capture and use to enrich themselves. In the nineteenth century, freeborn Blacks in the

United States had returned to West Africa and conquered this little strip of coast. Just as the skinny young warlord used his mercenaries to control a plot of rubber trees, the Americo-Liberian elite used their military control to seize most of the country's mines, plantations, guns, business, and Western aid money.

This concentration of guns and economic power left the tiny political class mostly unaccountable to the masses. Gradually, Liberia became one of the more autocratic regimes on the planet. As with White Flower on his plantation, Liberia's president faced few checks or balances. For a long series of leaders and their narrow cabals, the country was their personal fiefdom.[2]

This powerful presidency made an alluring prize, one that warlords, military officers, and opposition politicians would love to capture. If they could seize it in a quick and bloodless coup, so much the better. But if it took an insurgency to nab control, well, many of the sacrifices would be borne by others. This is the key to this chapter: their cost-benefit calculus was skewed. I'll call it a leadership's war bias.

War bias comes about when the people who decide whether or not to launch a conflict have a set of risks and rewards different from the society they supposedly represent. In other words, when the leadership's private incentives differ from the public interest.

This isn't true everywhere. In some societies, wealth, the means of production, and guns are widely distributed rather than concentrated in a few hands. Some peoples have also grown political rules and social norms that check elites, forcing them to seek the consent of the governed. These institutions and distributions of power help align the ruler's interests with the public's. We'll come to these checks and balances in time. The central point is this: societies that possess these restraining elements tend to be more peaceful in part because their leaders are forced to consider the costs of war. Absent these constraints, however, rulers are more likely to launch a fight.

Arguably, this is one reason why countries in sub-Saharan Africa (Liberia included) became some of the most violent places in the world for most of the late twentieth century. Hasty decolonization left the continent with

some of the most unaccountable regimes on the planet. Few rights and responsibilities were spread across different branches of government. Many
presidents weren't just military commander in chief, they were also comp-
troller of the treasury, appointer of every office, and even chancellor of the
university. Authority was concentrated in the capital, and provinces could
seldom tax or spend independently of the center. Power was often personalized as well. The ruling class governed not through stable rules and institutions but rather with their personal whims, their cronies, and their wallets.[3]

This winner-take-all political system carried risks. It gave mid-ranking
military sergeants incentives to grab the presidency in a coup. It gave ambitious warlords enticements to launch an insurgency. It gave stubborn presidents the motivation to resist both, violently if need be. The costs of fighting
would be borne by the disenfranchised masses, but the benefits of winning
would be the leader's to reap.

Don't, however, think of war bias as a problem specific to sub-Saharan
Africa. Most governments for most of human history have been centralized,
personalized, and unequal—and hence severely prone to war bias. The kind
of ruler has varied from place to place—god-kings, emperors, queens, sul-
tans, presidents, shoguns, and military dictators. Their regimes are a familiar cabal of characters: generals, viziers, ministers, high priests, party bosses,
imams, bureaucrats, nobles, and landowners. Some of these oligarchies have
been more inclusive than others. Either way, however, these ruling classes
agreed on one thing: exclude the masses from decision-making. Elites made
any choices that mattered. They determined who received what station in
society. All the taxes and rents accrued to them. They co-opted challengers,
ruling through a mix of bribery and repression.

Centuries before warlords razed Liberia, another despot to the north
put it perfectly. "L'état, c'est moi" (the state, it is I), proclaimed the Sun King,
Louis XIV of France. Unencumbered by elections or a need for popular legitimacy, rulers like him have been more willing to use violence to achieve
their objectives.

In medieval and early modern Europe, warfare was called the sport of kings. For centuries, Europe's monarchies, duchies, and republics waged regular battles. Historian after historian blames incessant war on the greed and private interests of this unchecked elite.[4] An early account of this harsh, selfish calculus comes from Niccolò Machiavelli. The diplomat grew up in Florence in the late 1400s, under the rule of a powerful banking clan turned rulers—the Medicis. For a brief period, the Medici regime fell to a republic. These republican years happened to coincide with Machiavelli's career as a civil servant. When the Medicis seized back power in 1512, however, a dismayed Machiavelli was tossed out of public service. He spent the rest of his years writing, including his famous handbook for dictatorship, *The Prince*.

Machiavelli lived in a tumultuous time—the middle of a centuries-long struggle between Europe's hundreds of tiny polities. Liberian warlords would have found his world familiar and his advice still relevant. The lean, severe diplomat took a ruler's desire for power and dominance for granted. To attain that, he explained, "a prince ought to have no other aim or thought, nor select anything else for his study, than war." People disagree about Machiavelli's intentions. Some say he was seeking favor with Florence's ruling family; others that he despised this form of rule, and merely sought to document its logic and cruelty.[5] Whether it was prescriptive or descriptive, Machiavelli's book explained how rulers can ignore conflict's wider costs. All that mattered to a prince, Machiavelli wrote, was personal aggrandizement. By this logic, war is never to be avoided; it should be exercised to one's personal advantage. In other words, privatize the benefits of fighting and socialize the costs.

These unchecked private interests are easiest to see in their most exaggerated form, which is why I chose late twentieth-century Africa and early modern Europe. It is harder to detect war bias in more open and democratic societies. Even so, its influence, however subtle, is there, and we need to learn to spot it. To see this, let's step away from the extreme cases. Instead, let's shift to Liberia's colonial founders and rulers, the United States—the first modern democracy. When it comes to their founding revolution, Americans are taught a story of liberal ideals. Some scholars, however, also see a Machiavellian tinge.

AMERICA'S IGNOBLE REVOLUTION

Born in 1732, the middle child of an undistinguished tobacco farmer, George Washington found himself on the fringes of Virginia's elite planter society. Luckily, his older brother married into one of the colony's most powerful families. Now the tall, lanky young man found himself with powerful patrons. Those benefactors pulled strings to maneuver Washington into a coveted public office: county surveyor.

Mapping land boundaries promised little profit in well-settled Virginia. Yet to the west, across the Allegheny Mountains, lay millions of acres of unclaimed land—assuming you ignored the native inhabitants, not to mention the French. Within days of his appointment, George Washington headed to the frontier. The young man would help his patrons lay claim to the best lands and scout some choice properties for himself. He was just seventeen.

An acquisitive zeal consumed the young Virginian and his backers. Claiming, hoarding, and flipping cheap land was an obsession across all thirteen colonies. Most great fortunes in the colonies had come from land speculation. Unfortunately for Washington and his patrons, however, France shared their bottomless appetite for territory. French troops began building a string of forts down the fertile Ohio River Valley, right around modern-day Pittsburgh. They ran straight through the claims Washington had staked.

In response, Washington's powerful patrons maneuvered him again, this time to the head of an armed force. Tall and broad-shouldered, Washington looked the part of a military leader. He also showed real talent for command. So his wealthy backers sent him west at the head of an American and Iroquois militia. He was twenty-two.

France's colonial forces far outnumbered Washington's small party. The year was 1754, Britain and France were at peace, and the French hoped to seize the Ohio River Valley without a shot. As the ragtag Virginian militia marched north toward the French Fort Duquesne, the fort's commander sent a diplomatic force to intercept Washington and parley. They wanted to make a deal.

Warned of the French party coming his way, unsure of their intent, Washington made a fateful decision: he would ambush and overpower the approaching men. He marched his forces through the rainy, moonless night and launched a sneak attack.

What happened next is unclear and disputed. Most think the French diplomatic force, taken by surprise, surrendered without a shot. Probably the inexperienced young Washington then lost control of his warriors. We know his militia and their Iroquois guides murdered and scalped most of the French party, including the ambassador. We also know that, as he sat down to write the governor an update, this political catastrophe wasn't even the most important thing on his mind. Before getting to the night's grisly events, Washington spent the first eight paragraphs griping about his low pay.

A British politician summed up the consequences: "The volley fired by

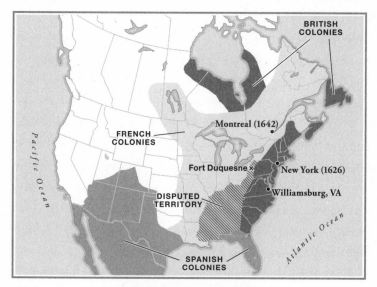

Colonial America, mid-1700s

a young Virginian in the backwoods of America set the world on fire." Washington's ambush sparked a local conflict. Two years later, it escalated into what Europeans call the Seven Years' War. The conflict drew in all Europe's great powers, lasting until 1763. Washington's corrupt and clumsy land claims helped ignite a long, deadly, global conflict.[6]

This is not the typical origin story Americans have long been taught. A more familiar tale portrays Washington as a disciplined, stoic, honorable leader. It describes a man whose love of liberty led him to risk his life and his fortune for independence. It describes a revolution with ideological origins, not selfish ones.

This nobler description is accurate. But what is also true—what biographer after biographer has described, but what schoolbooks sometimes overlook—is that land and his own personal fortune were also at the front of the first president's mind. "No theme appears more frequently in the writings of Washington," writes one biographer, "than his love for the land—more precisely, his own land."[7] Another theme is decadence. George Washington was a profligate consumer. He desired the finest carriages, clothes, and furniture. Land rich and cash poor, he financed his luxurious lifestyle with enormous loans from British merchants.

This relentless quest for wealth dominated Washington's pre-revolutionary years. After the Seven Years' War, he amassed huge western claims. A few he bought legitimately. In some cases, he skirted laws, shadily buying under an assumed name or that of a relative. Other lands he acquired at the expense of his own militiamen—or so some of these angry veterans claimed. As a result of this scheming, Washington died the richest American president of all time. One ranking has him as the fifty-ninth richest man in US history.

How did these private interests shape Washington's decision to revolt against Britain, two decades later? Elsewhere in this book we will see the American Revolution had many causes, including a newfound and noble ideology of self-determination. We can't understand the revolution without that. But we would be foolish to ignore the economic self-interest of the founding fathers, like Washington, as well as the war bias that fostered.

The greatest threat to George Washington's wealth was continued union with Britain. By the 1770s, the British Crown had invalidated some of Washington's more questionable landholdings. Britain also pledged most of the Ohio River Valley to Canada—including some of Washington's most valuable claims. He would have to relinquish all he'd accumulated.

The same was true for many who signed the Declaration of Independence. Like Washington, these elites had an incredible amount to lose from British colonial policy. Most Americans at the time opposed a revolutionary war, but then most Americans couldn't vote in those early years. The founding fathers faced a different set of risks and returns. It is no coincidence that they enjoyed privileges that British colonial policy would undermine—trade interests, vast western landholdings, ownership of enslaved people, and the local legislatures they controlled. If this colonial political and commercial class could not get Britain to revise its trade and commercial rulings, only independence could preserve their privileges.

We need to consider these elite incentives if we're going to ask why the revolution took place. A lot of people see it as inevitable. But Canada and Australia found peaceful paths to independence from Britain. If we're going to take the theory behind this book seriously, then shouldn't the thirteen colonies and Britain have also found a bargain without a fight? The revolution's slogan was "No taxation without representation." Why not strike that deal? We will see several answers in this book. One of them, however, is unchecked private interests. These do not explain the American Revolution on their own, but they certainly made peace more fragile. Let me show you exactly how it works using the pies.[8]

THE LOGIC OF UNCHECKED PRIVATE INTERESTS AT WORK

Imagine that all the thirteen colonies' land, taxes, and other spoils are a pie that the British Crown and the American colonists must share between them. Before the revolution, the Crown held a smaller share than many Americans today realize. It's true that the British profited in various ways, such as selling manufactures and other goods to the colonies. Yet the Crown collected pitifully little in taxes. For every twenty-six shillings an Englishman paid to the Crown, a New Englander paid only one.

Britain was fed up. For years it had lost money on its empire. Then, it racked up massive debts defending the thirteen colonies from France—the war George Washington helped ignite. Enough was enough. It was time for the colonists to pay their share of their continent's defense and administration. And so, the Crown began to levy taxes.

The colonists were outraged. Why should they pay, they asked, especially when they didn't have representation in Parliament? The Americans appealed to an ancient, self-serving, and half-imagined constitutional principle: only a legislature that represented them could levy taxes.

Both sides had arguments on their side. And fighting would be long, brutal, and costly. So why didn't they find a middle ground, where the Americans agreed to pay for their defense and infrastructure, and where Britain granted the colonists more representation? Let's return to the pies. Assume the two sides have equal odds of winning, and that leaders weigh all the $20 in costs, then both sides have more to profit from a peaceful split in the $20 bargaining range:

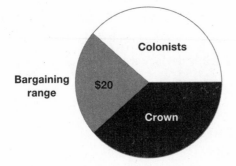

Here's the thing: this claim assumes the group is a unitary whole, and that the rulers are faithfully trying to maximize their group's collective interests, not their own. It means that George Washington weighs the costs and benefits to his citizens as if these were pains and pleasures of his own, that he curbs his bottomless appetite for land, and that he relinquishes precious western territories to Canada, all for the greater good. Likewise, on the Crown side, it implies that King George and the aristocrats that ran England's parliament look beyond their own interests and consider the lowly soldier, or the disruption to Britain's merchants (none of whom had the vote). If both ruling classes behave so, then going to war is a risky, costly wager, akin to each side flipping a deadly coin. Heads they win it all, tails they lose everything. As you might remember, this violent gamble is worth no more than $40 in expectation. Any peaceful split that offers more than 40 percent of the pie is a better deal than war.

What happens when we dispense with this assumption of the benevolent autocrat—the unitary actor, choosing in the best interests of the group? I'll oversimplify the situation to illustrate the logic. Let's make Washington out to be a self-serving land speculator and a leader of a narrow ruling class of founding fathers. Suppose King George and his aristocrats are also equally unchecked and selfish.

In the simplest case, these selfish, unaccountable cabals simply ignore some costs of war. The leaders are looking only at their smaller pie and ignoring everyone else. In effect, the bargaining range narrows, like this:

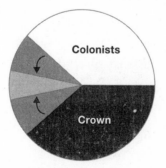

Note, however, that we still don't predict an armed revolution. Fighting continues to cost leaders something. There is still a bargaining range left, at least in this example. Most of the time, there will be. Leaders, even unchecked ones, have a lot to lose from war. It's expensive to wage. They could lose their regime, their life, or their place in history. So they still have incentives to find a deal, even if these incentives are smaller than we'd like.

This is a crucial point. War bias is pervasive in history. Without it, we probably cannot understand incessant warfare in early modern Europe or late twentieth-century Africa. But it rarely acts alone. Rather, it narrows the set of peaceful options and makes the rivalry more vulnerable to one of the other four reasons we fight. This is a theme we will see again and again.

Is war bias ever great enough to spur fighting alone? Yes, it's possible. That's because, for rulers, occasionally war pays. They may get land, plunder, or a greater chance of staying in power. A conflict also opens the national treasury to them, invests authority in the executive, and can offer them a chance to grab more power.[9]

In the example of the American Revolution, for instance, suppose Washington and the founding fathers expected a modest share of the pie if they compromise with the Crown, but could grab a larger share by waging warfare. Not only would the bargaining range shrink to zero, it could also invert, giving the ruling class an explicit incentive for war.[10]

That's not what caused America's revolution. But scour history or the contemporary world, and you can find lots of stories of private incentives leading to war. Take the farewell address of US president (and former general) Dwight Eisenhower. As he left office, he was worried that the powerful business and military elites were narrowing the bargaining range. He devoted his speech to this military-industrial complex, urging Americans to vigilance.[11]

Or consider Shakespeare. In *Henry IV*, the king advises his son to "busy giddy minds with foreign quarrels." We can all imagine an unpopular prime minister who, before a close election, wants to marshal popular support by bombing an enemy. Political scientists call this the rally-around-the-flag effect.[12]

Tragically, another common example is proxy wars. During the Cold War, the Soviets and the Americans supported insurgencies in the other's client states and funded the counterinsurgency effort by their allies. They fought through proxies. The resulting conflicts help explain a great deal of twentieth-century civil war. The superpowers had much to gain in terms of their share of the global pie. But people affected by the fighting had no way of holding the United States and the Soviet Union accountable.[13]

Finally, think of blood diamonds and other lootable natural resources. Political upheaval lets warlords and corrupt ministers sell precious commodities on the black market. Similarly, leaders close to drug cartels might find war, instability, and a covert armed group profitable to the drug trade. These all give unchecked rulers a private incentive to fight.[14]

Here we're not only concerned about the president, queen, or emperor supreme. We also have to worry about the whole ruling cabal. There might be a renegade military general with a stake in the war, or a faction chief getting rich off the black market. If they see the leader pushing for peace, private interests give them an incentive to undermine it. We label these "splinter groups," "extremist factions," and "spoilers." They're often the result of a weak leader, a fragile coalition, or bad luck.[15]

WAR BIAS IS A SPECIFIC EXAMPLE OF A MORE GENERAL PHENOMENON—SOMETHING CALLED an agency problem. It arises whenever one party (called the principal) is trying to get another party (the agent) to act on their behalf. The principal worries that the agent will pursue their own agenda. When you hire a lawyer, a financial adviser, or a real estate agent, for instance, you might worry they'll do things to maximize their fees rather than get you the best deal. If you run a business and hire new employees, you might worry that they'll slack or filch. These are all agency problems.

Politics is full of agency problems, too. Within a country, for example, citizens are the principals while leaders are the agents. These leaders are supposed to behave in the interests of the group. Of course, when unconstrained, they often do not. The citizens don't have the money, the ability to mobilize, the military might, or the institutional rules and norms to hold the leader back. It's an agency problem, because citizens don't have enough power to restrain and discipline the ruler. A lack of checks is easiest to see with god-kings, empresses, or dictators. (They would disagree that they're agents of the people at all.) But it's an issue in representative democracies as well. Elected officials get long terms, can bend the system to help reelection, can use their wealth to mobilize supporters, and can do deals behind closed doors. Citizens may find it hard to pay close attention, evaluate their politicians, or not get distracted by spectacles. All these things insulate and obscure politicians' actions from voters.

Political agency problems and war bias pop up at low levels too. Take urban riots—when people from different races or religions clash. It's tempting to see these sprees as unexpected bursts of mass anger or resentment. US president Richard Nixon once said, "Riots are spontaneous. Wars require advance planning." He was wrong. There's an element of rage and grievance, and certainly some riots are unplanned. But this misses the hidden hand of elites.

The scholars who study riots worldwide emphasize one thing time and again: typically violence happens when political leaders use their wealth, their political organizations, and their influence over the media to build and strategically deploy street disorder for larger political goals. Some of the best evidence comes from India, where several cities have a decades-long tradition of Hindu-Muslim clashes. These aren't spontaneous explosions, however. They are "institutionalized riot machines" in the words of some, deliberately built and deployed to win elections or shape national opinion. Elites develop and use these apparatuses of destruction because they enjoy the benefits while staying insulated from the costs.[16]

A final example comes from court battles. This might seem far afield from warring countries or religious groups, but the theory is similar, and it's a scale that lets us test the theory. Like wars, legal struggles are expensive and risky for both sides. The costs (like fees and long delays) create a bargaining range. That's why most parties in civil disputes find a resolution or settle. Some rivals do end up in front of a judge, in a drawn-out trial, of course. When they do, the reasons often trace back to one of the five reasons bargains fail—including agents biased toward fighting.

One study looked at Mexican labor courts, where employees can sue their employers for back pay. To a layperson reading the law, the rules look like they favor workers. In reality, however, the little guy seldom wins these cases, since the firms find all sorts of technical reasons not to pay. If you go to a government lawyer, who doesn't earn big fees from lawsuits, they'll give you a realistic assessment of your case and help you settle out of court. But go to a private fee-charging attorney and you will hear a different story. Private lawyers emphasize the chance of a big win, and they file satisfyingly large suits, charging high fees. But they don't deliver better results. Their incentives make them war biased, and they dupe workers who don't know the vagaries of the law. It's an agency problem.

We know this because of a simple experiment that gave workers information about their chances of winning a case. If the researchers gave the information to the private lawyer, nothing changed—the attorneys didn't pass it on to their clients, and they still filed their pointless suits. But if the researchers gave the worker the information, they were much more likely to settle, and they were happier and wealthier as a result.[17]

Unfortunately, in war, there isn't an easy fix to the agency problem, like giving people information. Instead, societies must find ways to make the leaders accountable—to counter private self-interest. This is what distinguishes groups—not whether their leaders are self-interested (which is universal) but whether they are checked.

CHECKS AND BALANCES

Politicians respond to incentives. To see a simple example, consider the draft. America voted to conscript its young men into most of its twentieth-century wars. But not everyone voted in favor. Over the course of the century, US legislators with draft-age sons were about a sixth less likely to support war and conscription than those with draft-age daughters (who wouldn't be called up). But as soon as their sons passed the age of conscription, these politicians suddenly renewed their support for the fighting. This is a simple but powerful illustration of the agency problem and private self-interest at work. As soon as politicians were forced to internalize the costs and risks, their calculus changed.[18]

Agency problems disappear only in the imaginary state where politicians treat other people's sons as if they were their own. Some social and political systems do a reasonable job of getting leaders to weigh these costs of conflict. Take George Washington. He was no White Flower or all-powerful despot. However much Washington might have hungered for western lands or the latest in European fashions, he was never so unchecked as to take America to war on his own. This is because there were limits on the general's rule. Washington depended on the Continental Congress to allot him funds. He needed thirteen nascent states, each with a raucous legislature of its own, to send him troops. He faced scrutiny, reproach, and defiance from newspapers and pamphleteers. He led a nation of farmers, craftsmen, shopkeepers, and lawyers, each secure in their property, and each stubbornly convinced of their equality to other men. All the sources of power in colonial America—land, money, guns, decision-making—were widely distributed. In the late eighteenth century, this actually made George Washington one of the more constrained leaders up to that moment in history. He was not fully constrained—even among men of European descent, only a fraction could vote in the early years of the republic. Still, in order to act, Washington needed to build a broad political coalition of planters, merchants, and militias.

In general, this need for the support of many powerful actors makes leaders behave more like unitary actors. It compels them to internalize their coalition's costs of fighting. These cabals have lower potential war bias than a dictator, and, as a consequence, they are usually less likely to wage war.[19]

In my view, there are no good or bad leaders who will act nobly or not in office. There are only constrained and unconstrained ones. Yes, leaders like George Washington will come along who, despite their voracious appetite for land and fine clothes, will still put God and nation before self-interest and refuse the powers offered him. But a stable and successful society must take a dimmer view of humankind, leaders especially, and build our systems for the worst of them.

Chapter 3

INTANGIBLE INCENTIVES

So far, our rivals have had only material objectives: territory, spoils, or control over society's government and institutions. But so many of the things humans value and pursue are intangible. These could be noble: a desire to hold an unjust overclass or colonizer to account; or the righteous pursuit of a principle, such as equality, justice, or freedom. In these cases, even if fighting wreaks destruction, pursuing a higher ideal can supersede that. Violence for the cause might feel virtuous and give satisfaction. Or perhaps certain compromises are abhorrent, and avoiding them is worth any price.

Our nonmaterial motives can also be crude and base. These include rulers who seek glory and a place in history through conquest, a populace that takes pleasure in the eradication of a heretical idea, or a society that is only happy if it dominates supreme.

While none of these motives are alike, they belong together because they share the same logic—they all work against compromise in the same way. Earlier, war was purely costly, and fighting shrank the pie. But as soon as violence is valued for its own sake, or for a reward only fighting can deliver, then the pie-splitting calculus changes. Those intangible incentives negate some of the material costs of war and so make peaceful deals harder to find.

In effect, when parties hold these nonmaterial preferences, they shrink the bargaining range. In extreme cases, they might even eradicate it.

This chapter walks through four examples. Three of them—righteous outrage, ideologies, and the quest for glory and status—have eroded grounds for compromise throughout history. The fourth—an innate human desire for aggression—hasn't. But a lot of people think this exists and causes a great deal of war, so I want to talk about it too.

RIGHTEOUS OUTRAGE

"I'm a campesino," the man explained—an unskilled farm worker. Like his parents before him, he toiled on one of El Salvador's vast coffee plantations. "I worked for the rich, it was heavy labor," he said. "I felt rage, resentment." Salvadoran elites had controlled most of the country's land for generations, in estates called haciendas. The rest lived like serfs, in thrall to the landowners. So, the man finished: "How did I become a militant of the popular movement? It was born out of social resentment, that's how to understand it."[1]

This was an odd conversation for Elisabeth Wood to have. A few years before, she was a physics graduate student at Berkeley. While she was researching nuclear particles, however, current events grabbed her attention. It was the early 1980s. A war had been raging in El Salvador between the elites who owned the plantations and a guerrilla movement of angry campesinos. At stake: who should control the country's land? The military answered to the elites and massacred guerrillas and their sympathizers. It was hard for them to tell sympathizers from serfs, however, and so the merciless soldiers tended to kill them all. Salvadoran refugees flooded into the United States.

Between her classes, Wood volunteered as a translator and paralegal, helping desperate families apply for political asylum. As she listened to their stories of repression and revolt, though, Wood realized she was more interested in these social forces than atomic ones. She began traveling and working in El Salvador. Within a few years, she'd traded physics for a political science degree. And that is how Wood found herself—a slight woman in a small pickup truck—driving up dry riverbeds to isolated peasant homes to talk about the war.

Wood wanted to understand who joined the guerrillas and why. This was a peasant uprising against a narrow class of plantation owners. People must join expecting to get land, Wood anticipated. But that wasn't what she found at all. El Salvador's leftist rebels promised their backers few exclusive reward. The last thing they wanted to do was create a new privileged ruling class. Therefore, any campesino living in a contested area could farm the land regardless of whether they offered the guerrillas any help. They just couldn't snitch to the army. That meant most peasants could be free riders, enjoying the fruits of the armed movement but paying few of the costs.

If that was true, who fought? Why take on the risk and sacrifice? Over hundreds of interviews, Wood saw the same pattern again and again: injustice mattered. Those who supported the guerrillas typically had a terrible experience of violence in their past. Outraged campesinos traced their transformation to government repression against their friends and family.[2]

These participants reveled in the act of resistance itself. For some, even

El Salvador

if their actions were futile, simply standing up against injustice gave them satisfaction and pride. The constant humiliation, the arbitrary authority, and the degradation were too much. "Before the war, we were despised by the rich," one guerrilla supporter explained to Wood. "We were seen as animals, working all day and still without even enough to put the kids in school."

Others took pleasure in the act of punishing wrongdoers or working toward winning actual rights and respect. One person's actions wouldn't affect the outcome of the war. But for the aggrieved, simply doing *something* brought satisfaction and dignity. When Wood asked one man what it had been like before the war, he put his hands together, bent his head and eyes humbly down, and bowed deeply, as if to an imaginary big boss. When asked how life was different now, his pantomime changed. Now he held his head high, his shoulders flung back, and his fist beat the air.[3]

WE SEE THIS IN ALL SOCIETIES. CONSIDER SYRIA, WHERE A SINGLE FAMILY HAS RULED since 1970. The father first took power in a coup, and his son, an ophthal-

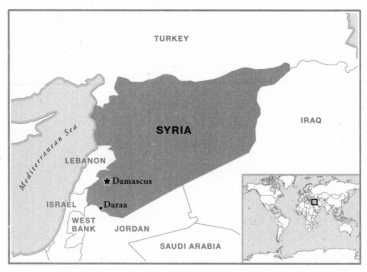

Syria

mologist, rules the nation to this day. But in 2011, his regime looked fragile. That year had begun with a popular revolution in Tunisia, and the toppling of that country's dictator. Then, a few weeks later, a January revolt in Egypt peacefully ousted its autocrat too. By February, the Arab Spring was in full bloom. Like autocrats across the Middle East, the Syrian eye doctor began to worry for his rule.

Soon thereafter, in Daraa, a quiet border city in Syria's far southwest, a group of boys sprayed graffiti on their school wall. They had a not-so-subtle message for their president: "Your turn, Doctor." The next day, the local security police quickly picked up fifteen schoolchildren, some as young as ten years old. They imprisoned, beat, and tortured the children. It was supposed to be a warning to other potential protesters. Their relatives beseeched the authorities: "Please, release our kids." But the police chief dismissed them with a vulgar insult: "Forget your children. If you want children, make more children. If you don't know how, bring us your women and we will make them for you."

Activists organized a march the next day, putting the frightened, indignant parents in the fore. Other families poured into the streets, swelling into a massive protest. The security forces responded with tear gas and firepower, killing two unarmed demonstrators. Their funerals launched larger and angrier demonstrations, more police violence, and larger and angrier funeral processions still. Chaotic videos taken from mobile phones flew across the nation. Within a week, protests against the regime erupted across the nation. The government put them down with sniper fire and tanks. The outrage only grew.[4]

Wendy Pearlman, a political scientist, spent the next years interviewing protesters, rebels, and refugees from the collapsing country. A young woman recalled one of these early marches:

> I was in a demonstration. Others were shouting and I joined them. I started to whisper, *Freedom*. And after that I started to hear myself repeating, *Freedom, freedom, freedom*. And then I started shouting, *Freedom!* My voice mingled with other voices. When I heard my voice

I started shaking and crying. I felt like I was flying. I thought to my-self, "This is the first time I have ever heard my own voice." I thought, "This is the first time I have a soul and I am not afraid of death or being arrested or anything else." I wanted to feel this freedom for-ever. And I told myself that I would never again let anyone steal my voice again. And after that day I started to join all the demonstra-tions.

These are complicated emotions, not so easy to summarize under one label. It seems that here was a desire for free expression, to determine one's own actions, intertwined with moral outrage that someone would deny their rights or insult their dignity. That injustice sparks righteous anger, an emo-tion powerful enough to overcome the risks and fear from speaking out, regardless of whether the aggrieved can succeed.

To Pearlman, the iconic example was the Tunisian street vendor Mo-hamed Bouazizi. After being insulted by a policewoman and failing to get back his confiscated wares, on December 17, 2010, an outraged Bouazizi took his revenge: he set himself on fire in a public square. Police repressed the vigils and protests with violence. Anger sparked nationwide protests. The Arab Spring was born.[5]

THE FIRST TIME I HEARD THESE ACCOUNTS, MY MIND LEAPT BACK TO MY FIRST AND FAVOR-ite game theory professor in graduate school, Matt Rabin. Rabin was known for three things: a wardrobe full of tie-dyed shirts, a deep love of Johnny Depp, and his contributions to modeling quirks of human psychology in economics. Those models won him the MacArthur "genius award."

One day, Rabin began a lecture by asking us to think back to every Holly-wood blockbuster movie we'd seen. At the beginning of each film, the bad guy commits some grievous harm to our hero. Outraged, our hero then spends the next seventy-five minutes going to the most ridiculous, death-defying lengths to see the villain punished, no matter the risk to life and limb. "Of course, that's just a Hollywood script," Rabin admitted. But, he pointed out, people paid real money to watch that movie. Why is that? His answer: "To see justice done."

Fortunately, the science on this question is based on more than box office returns. Rabin was thinking about an experiment that has been run on more people, in more places, than probably any other in history. It's called the ultimatum game. In the usual setup, two college students, strangers, sit down in a university computer lab among a few dozen other undergraduates. Let's call them Maria and Daniel. As the study begins, Maria's screen tells her that she's been given a pot of money—ten dollars—and that she's been part-nered with an anonymous student in the lab. Maria has one decision: How much of her windfall would she like to offer this mysterious other? Nothing, all, or something in between? Maria's screen gives her one last crucial detail: The stranger gets to say yes or no to her offer. If he accepts, he walks away with whatever Maria gave, and Maria keeps the balance. If he says no, how-ever, both of them get zero.

Now, in an emotionless and robotic world, Maria could offer a penny. As you've probably guessed, her anonymous partner is Daniel. A robotic Daniel would judge that a penny is better than nothing, so of course he would accept it. Expecting that, Maria gives the absolute minimum.

That is not what real people do, however. Hundreds of scholars have played this game with tens of thousands of college students across the world. Some of them also headed to secluded corners of the planet, to play with people in completely different societies. They joined forces with anthropolo-gists working on windswept plateaus in Mongolia and with Torgut wander-ers in the semidesert. They played the game with the Achuar, an indigenous people in Ecuador, of whom there are only about six thousand left. The same strange tribe of academics carrying little leather notebooks visited the Orma herders in Kenya's arid grasslands, the Lamalera on a tiny island in Indone-sia, and a dozen other peoples. Each time, this odd clan, with their elaborate titles and coterie of research assistants, asked the locals to join in the curious ritual of exchange.

The results vary a little from society to society, but generally any offer less than two to three dollars and the Daniels of the world say "Screw you" to the Marias. And the Marias of the world know it. That's why, whether it's a jungle or a desert or a drab computer lab, most Marias offer four to five dollars to their Daniels.

What's going on here? Why do Daniels say no to gifts of less than 20 or 30 percent of the total? It's free money! In effect, these Daniels are paying to penalize ungenerous Marias. Punishing unfairness seemed like the right thing to do. Also, it gave the Daniels pleasure. We know this because, while some scholars plunged into jungles and deserts, others teamed up with neuroscientists. They put the players in various scanners and watched their brains during the ultimatum game. When a Daniel punished an unfair offer, the systems in his brain linked to emotional rewards lit up.[6]

Back in El Salvador, Elisabeth Wood saw a parallel tale. "When you keep hearing battles all around, in place of being killed yourself, you pick up arms instead," one campesino recounted. "That is why it grew," he told her, speaking of the lengthy war, "to carry out vengeance for the death of a brother." Others framed their motivations as moral indignation and the desire to make the world a little more just. Either way, the act of fighting back produced satisfaction. It was the right thing to do.

WE CAN FIND A DESIRE FOR FAIRNESS, AND A WILLINGNESS TO PUNISH FOR IT, IN EVERY human society for a simple reason: it helps us cooperate in large groups. To see this, start with small groups, where everyone knows each other and interacts with frequency. Maybe Maria and Daniel live in a village together or are traders in the same market. If Maria cheats Daniel, he doesn't need to get pleasure from punishing her. He'll do it anyway, because punishing Maria for cheating, or refusing to deal with her again and again, makes strategic sense. Otherwise, she'll dupe him again next time. Knowing Daniel's incentives, and knowing she'll interact with Daniel again and again, Maria will think twice about being miserly. The repeated interaction helps to maintain cooperation.

In larger groups, however, this strategic logic erodes. As our groups grow, or nearby groups expand, we're more likely to interact and trade with strangers on a one-off basis. Each time there's a risk of getting cheated. It's like a long series of anonymous ultimatum games. Maria doesn't expect to see Daniel again, and so why should she bother to be generous? Daniel could punish, but what would be the point? It costs him something to shame or sanction her, and he won't see the gains in his future trades. Because no one has a private incentive to enforce, cooperation with strangers becomes harder to sustain. It's a classic collective action problem.

This is where an ingrained emotional reward from injustice becomes useful. It helps solve the collective action problem by giving Daniel an incentive to punish the cheating Marias—pleasure in righteous action. If the Marias of the world know that most people hold such social preferences, they will be less likely to deceive or defraud others. Rabin and others found this fits experimental data pretty well.

This is why many scholars argue that humanity's righteous vengeance is culturally and perhaps even biologically evolved. At the very least, this is a powerful social norm, so useful that we can find it in almost every human society. Even monkeys seem to have an instinct for fairness. One pair of researchers collected twenty-five female capuchins and gave them each a plastic token. If the monkeys returned the tokens, the researcher rewarded them with either a cucumber slice or a grape. Capuchins prefer grapes. So, when one saw her friend get a cucumber slice, she was happy to trade for a cucumber slice too. But if she saw her friend get a grape, and then was offered a mere cucumber for her token . . . well, that was outrageous. She refused to trade. I picture a hopping mad little monkey screeching at the scientist in a rumpled white lab coat.[7]

Anger at an attack, and a desire to punish, helps groups solve another kind of collective action problem: defending themselves and surviving. Fighting is risky, and so individual members have incentives to free ride and let others handle the group's defense. But if enough members have a taste for punishing transgressions, the collective action problem is solved. There will be willing volunteers.

The evidence goes far beyond El Salvador or Syria. Whether they are studying rebels, revolutionaries, sectarian militias, or terrorists, scholars have noted the same motivations among participants in violence: outrage against injustice and unfairness, and a pleasure in exercising agency against a repressive regime or offending out-group. They've found them in peasant uprisings in early modern Europe, in Vietnamese and Iraqi resistance to American invasion, and in the endless cycle of attacks and reprisals by both Israelis and Palestinians. We can find them at lower levels as well, among gangs and tribes, in the long series of attacks and reprisals that constitute so many feuds.[8]

HOW INTANGIBLE INCENTIVES
RAISE THE RISK OF WAR

What happens to the incentives for peace if peasants, sectarians, protesters, and street vendors are willing to punish unfairness? Suppose the pie represents control of El Salvador's vast coffee haciendas. Our two sides are now peasants and elites. The dispossessed campesinos have organized themselves for the first time, increasing their bargaining power. They used to be weak. Now, however, they're a threat to the oligarchic order, with even odds of victory. What happens?

The elites have a choice. They can concede something to the newfound peasant power, breaking up some of the biggest estates into cooperatives, but still holding on to a large share of the land. Or the ruling class can fight and try to keep it all. Victory would cement their system of haciendas and oppression, minus any costs of war. The costs of war create the usual bargaining range, like this:

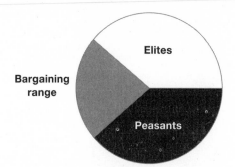

This wedge should give ample room for land reforms and representation to prevent the campesinos from revolt, and keep the elites in charge.

Now introduce a new consciousness, an idea that all humans are equally deserving of respect. Once upon a time, it seemed like serfdom was the natural order of things, or at least inescapable. But no longer. Perhaps the new idea filters in through television and radio, through the example of other nations and peoples. Maybe it comes from the pulpit, as educated priests preach a liberation theology. Or perhaps it arrives in little red books, from union workers, university students, and indigenous leaders who catalog the crimes of colonial settlers, their descendants, and foreign-owned plantations. Why should a tiny fraction of the population possess so much land and wealth? The norm has changed.

Then, a final series of indignities occurs. An overzealous army commander, frustrated by guerrillas who melt into the population, rounds up young men from the nearby village and throws them in jail. The next day, six boys are dead, their bodies brutally beaten and discarded. A priest leads a clutch of mothers to the jail, demanding the other men's release. A scared and callous soldier shoots the cleric dead.

While this is an imaginary scenario, it is sadly not difficult to imagine. Nor it is hard to envisage anger sweeping peasants across the country. People react in different ways—fleeing, giving up, living in quiet fear, or peacefully preaching and mobilizing. But some want to act. The pleasure from resistance offsets the costs of war. The bargaining range has shrunk by a huge amount, and it now looks something like this:

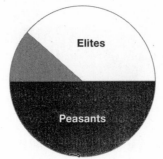

These outrages and a desire for moral action work much like war profits did in the last chapter: they give one side an incentive to fight, one that weighs against the costs. There is a crucial difference, however. The problem is no longer war-biased leaders. Rather, if the group shares this moral outrage, then the leader is merely acting as their faithful agent.

Another crucial detail, however, is that in this example we still predict peace, even with half the bargaining range gone. The army's clumsy cruelty has simply eroded the options advantageous to the elite. It's the same conclusion as with an unchecked leader's war bias: most of the time, the bias or the intangible is not so large that it eliminates the range completely. You would need *a lot* of righteousness to offset the costs and burdens of a long-running civil war. There are examples in history, but they are rare.[9]

Of course, long vengeful cycles of violence do happen, between Israelis and Palestinians, Catholics and Protestants in Northern Ireland, and Hindus and Muslims in some Indian cities. Also, we can find escalating tit-for-tat attacks between villages and ethnic groups, whether it's in the Arabian desert, the Balkans, Southeast Asia, or the African Sahel. One explanation, we will see, is that when one of the other four reasons for war is powerful enough to provoke the first unjust attack, vengeance and righteousness can kick in and sustain that violence.

GLORY AND STATUS

The young fighter pilot was cocky and narcissistic, even by the standards of a flying ace. Dressed in a smart olive uniform, Iron Cross at his throat, Adolf Galland wore his dark hair slicked back and his mustache carefully groomed. His men knew him as the confident, smooth-talking squadron leader, a cigar in his lips and a smile on his face at all times, who never raised a voice in anger. He was hardly the sort of man to follow the rules. If he had, Galland wouldn't be flying, let alone leading the Luftwaffe—Nazi Germany's unequaled air force.[10]

In 1935, seeking glory and recognition, Galland had nearly killed himself in a biplane training exercise. "I had modified the plane beyond normal limits," Galland confessed. His tinkering backfired. He lost control and slammed into the ground. When the pilot woke up after a three-day coma, he found his skull fractured, his nose broken, and his vision partly blinded by windscreen shards. "To this day I still have some of the glass in my eye," he wrote, decades later. It was the kind of accident that grounds a pilot for life. But Galland was ambitious and relentless. Before his physical exam he memorized every letter and number in every possible sequence from every government eye chart. Soon he was flying again.

By then Germany had launched World War II. Hermann Göring was the Luftwaffe's commander in chief and a veteran fighter pilot himself. He was one of the earliest members of the Nazi Party, a morphine addict, and the second most powerful man in Germany after Hitler. He also needed new air force commanders. The elderly officers who'd flown by his side in World War I weren't fit for the demands of modern aviation. Instead, Göring turned to his two best aces to lead Luftwaffe forces in the skies: Adolf Galland and Werner Mölders.

The lean, handsome Mölders was Galland's opposite in almost every way. "When I first met him, I was not very impressed," Galland admitted.

"He did not have the typical fighter pilot's personality, which for the most part is a devil-may-care approach to life, and jovial, with few exceptions." Mölders was Catholic, didn't drink, and didn't smoke. Unlike the gregarious Galland, Mölders was quiet, serious, and analytical. Even so, the two men shared a few traits: a patriotic fervor for their country, a loathing for Göring (they called him "the Fat One"), spectacular flying skills, and, most of all, a thirst for glory—to be recognized as the very best.

In 1940, there was no greater proving ground than the Battle of Britain—Nazi Germany's attempt to bomb London and other cities into submission. The monthslong blitz, Göring hoped, would force Britain to a peace treaty, leaving the Nazis most of Europe. It was the first major military campaign fought entirely by air forces, and an opportunity for Galland to mount the kills he so desperately needed.

You see, success as a fighter pilot had a very simple metric: enemy aircraft shot down, and verified by another pilot. This was the path to medals, public acclaim, and the envy of your peers. Galland wanted it all. "Mölders," he griped, "had received the Oak Leaves three days before me for his fortieth kill." Unfortunately for Galland's pride, Mölders's wing was stationed over the English Channel, and the Battle of Britain meant he'd continue to mount more victories.

At last, Galland got his opportunity to pull ahead. Göring had summoned Mölders to his hunting lodge in East Prussia. Over three days, to Mölders's great frustration, he was forced to hunt stag while Galland gleefully mounted up airborne kills.

Within a couple days, however, Galland, too, received a summons from Göring. As the pilot entered the lodge gates, he ran into Mölders, hurrying to get back to his station. Mölders had arranged a surprise for his rival: "The Fat One promised me he would detain you at least as long as he did me," he called out, "and by the way, good luck with the stag I missed."

At the height of the most important battle of the war, Germany's seniormost military commander had been talked into taking his finest commander deer hunting, all to humor a rivalry for status. "I promised Mölders to keep you here at least three days," Göring told Galland. The consequences of this choice were dire: massive German losses during an important raid on London. When the terrible news reached the hunting lodge, Galland begged Göring again to let him rejoin his squadron. This time, the chastened leader had no objection.

That soldiers strive for recognition is hardly a surprise. Still, the lengths to which these pilots went for fleeting glory should amaze any of us. Four economists crunched the numbers on German pilots, tallying the amazing risks these men undertook.[11]

Simply put, they found that pilots like Galland and Mölders were competing to die an early death. Over the course of the war, an astonishing three-quarters of German fighter pilots were killed or wounded or went missing. What's more, the harder a pilot worked, the more likely he was to perish. In a dogfight between two fighter planes, pilots faced a deadly choice: keep shooting at the enemy or break off. Staying engaged risked gunfire from your enemy's wingman, or loss of control and a crash on the surface. "Flying combat at that time over the English Channel, let alone over Britain, was a very dangerous thing," Galland wrote. "By the time we reached the British coast, we had perhaps thirty minutes of flying time, and less than twenty minutes if flying near London. This time decreased dramatically if you engaged in combat, which forced you to use more fuel."

Keeping these aces motivated was the Nazi key to winning the war. Top pilots downed the majority of Allied planes. But how do you get people to risk their lives for a cause? It's easy to get pilots into the cockpit at the point of a gun. But what you really want is for them to work hard, engaging the enemy, even when that raises the chance they'll die. What could people possibly care about more than their lives? Göring's answer: status. He built an elaborate system of medals and status recognition to keep up pilot effort and kills, even if it spelled their death.

And it worked. We know because the four economists calculated the effects of one kind of public recognition—mentions in the German armed forces daily news. The aces craved this honor and fame. These acknowledgments came at irregular and hard-to-predict intervals—almost randomly. This gave the researchers a natural experiment to help answer the question: To what lengths would pilots go to exceed their recognized peers?

For glory, it turns out they'd pay the ultimate price. In the days after a pilot like Galland was mentioned, rivals in his unit downed more enemies. It drove them to work harder and make more kills. As a result, they died faster too. In normal times, pilots died at a rate of about 2.7 percent per month. In the days after a colleague's mention, that death rate jumped by two-thirds. This wasn't just true of current squadron members, but past ones too. What did Luftwaffe pilots do when they saw their old flying buddies honored in the army press? They set out to even the score, taking ever greater risks, and dying at about 150 percent of the normal rate as well.

Here was a desire that war could fulfill: glory, esteem, admiration, and a degree of immortality. Like most military commanders, Göring understood this. He designed his elaborate system of medals and recognitions with a keen understanding of what people yearned for. It shows just how far humans can go in the pursuit of relative status, even when the cost is mortally high.

THIS STORY OFFERS A FEW LESSONS. ONE IS HOW SKILLFUL LEADERS WITH RUTHLESS aims manipulate people for even the vilest of causes. Generals and propagandists exploit desires like vengeance, glory, and relative status to mobilize populations to fight. Notice, however, I'm describing a story of military recruitment—something that affects a side's ability to win a war, and hence their bargaining power. It doesn't explain why wars begin.

Glory could explain why we fight if groups collectively care about prestige and status—if they are willing to bear the enormous price of fighting, even losing their own lives, for a feeling of greatness or respect. This is possible. Some of the most celebrated philosophers and historians on war— Thucydides in classical Greece, Machiavelli in Renaissance Italy, Thomas Hobbes in early modern England, or Jean-Jacques Rousseau during the Enlightenment—all thought status, prestige, and honor drove peoples to fight. According to the historian Margaret MacMillan, militarized societies and martial cultures continue today. Others have argued that a society can grow furious and willing to fight when its honor is affronted by a rival of equal rank, or when a lower status group climbs above their station—not so different from the way Luftwaffe flying aces reacted to their peers getting recognized.[12]

To put this into our pie splitting, suppose every citizen of every Axis and Allied nation put some weight on their *relative* position. They're not just maximizing how much of the pie they walk away with. Rather, they get pleasure from having more than their rival. In effect, any value placed on relative status will weigh against the costs of war. The bargaining range shrinks, like this:

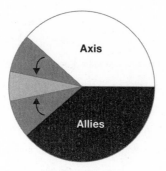

Of course, once again, the incentives for compromise persist. But the peace is more fragile than before.

To me, however, the more common and more dangerous scenario is when unchecked rulers (rather than the populace) desire glory and status. This is a first example of how the reasons for war can cumulate and intertwine. War bias and intangible incentives can be a terrible mix. The Nazis are a good example of this, as we'll see. According to the historian Philip Hoffman, however, a better example would keep us in Europe but go a few centuries back. From 1400 to 1800, the continent was one of almost incessant warfare. And the main reason these kings and queens fought, Hoffman argues, was for glory and to enhance their reputation.[13]

WRITING IN THE EARLY 1500S, THE SCHOLAR AND PHILOSOPHER ERASMUS COULD LOOK around the continent and conclude that citizens build cities, while the madness of princes destroys them. "The people love peace," he wrote. The problem, Erasmus explained, was "their rulers stir up war."[14]

Erasmus, a scholar at Cambridge, had no better example than the local young king, Henry VIII of England. Tall and broad shouldered, with a redgolden beard and flowing hair, Henry was called the handsomest prince in all of Europe. Crowned in 1509, shortly before his eighteenth birthday, the youth longed for war. He loved to joust and hunt. But what he really desired was to reclaim England's ancient rights to rule much of France.

The king's bishops and advisers counseled peace, knowing what havoc war would wreak on the economy and the treasury. The peasants opposed invasion because it raised the price of meat, grain, and drink, and brought home disease. The powerful wool merchants thought war was bad for business too. But to Henry and the carefree young lords surrounding him, France was a glorious prize to be seized. The young monarch was obsessed with the King Arthur of legend and aspired to be like the valiant knights of old. For his foreign policy, he thought of little else but personal grandeur.

Henry first declared war three years into his regime. But he botched the attempt. His Spanish ally duped and betrayed him, leaving English soldiers alone on the battlefield. It was a shambles. But Henry was undeterred. The next year he led another expedition to France. After conquering an inconsequential pair of towns, however, Henry had exhausted most of the treasure his father had left him. Broke, the monarch declared victory, and returned home in jubilation.

Glory is essential to this story because it's not enough to simply say Henry was unchecked. War was incredibly expensive to him, even if he didn't consider all the costs. That's because conflicts bankrupted regimes like Henry's all the time, for it was difficult to raise the funds for these long and massive expeditions. (Around the same time, for instance, Henry's opponent, the

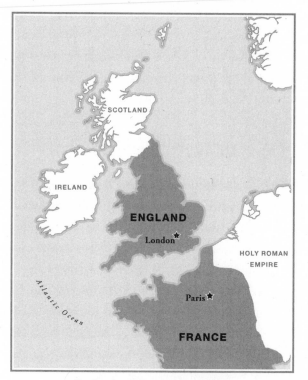

England and France about 1500

French king Louis XII, asked his military chief for the keys to success in war. Three things are necessary, the commander replied: money, more money, and still more money.)[15] To outweigh these costs and good sense, Henry needed some other incentive to wager his regime and reputation. This is where glory comes in—an intangible incentive great enough to overcome the king's personal costs and risks.

Three decades later, these incentives persisted. The middle-aged monarch was now pallid and obese, with leg ulcers left open and weeping. By that time, he'd also run through six wives, executing two, and inventing the Church of England to divorce another. All that time, however, he'd never given up his obsession with glory and with France. In 1544, nearly fifty thousand Englishmen crossed the channel. Henry debased the currency to pay for it. The king managed to take another small French city—albeit at the cost of ten years of normal national spending. Nonetheless, Henry was merry and in as good health as I have seen his grace at any time, remarked one of his courtiers. When power is unequal, unaccountable, and centralized, a society is left vulnerable to the whims and private interests of rulers like him.

IDEOLOGY AND AN AVERSION TO COMPROMISE

A third intangible is a collection of things I'll call ideology. Like glory or status, certain religious principles and political ideals are their own reward. Countless societies have waged war to spread the faith, exterminate a heretical idea, or expand a way of life. Compromising on these principles feels abhorrent. If so, that disutility weighs against the costs of war.

An extreme example is Germany's Adolf Hitler. It's hard to pick just one maniacal ideology among his many. If we want to understand World War II, however, we should start with his glorification of the German race. He wanted it to persist and thrive. But their land was tiny, their enemies were numerous and nearby. Hitler felt certain that if the Germans couldn't expand their territory, they'd eventually be contaminated, assimilated, or dominated by races he loathed. Compromise, Hitler decided, would doom the German people. At all costs, they must obtain the lebensraum—conquest, cleansing, and colonization of the vast lands to Germany's east.[16]

To see a nobler example, consider the point of view of a vanquished and colonized people. The situation is unjust, but the foreign overlords have an overwhelming advantage. By our simple pie-splitting calculus, revolt make no sense. But for some of the oppressed, this compromise is detestable. There is no dignity in subjugation. A bargaining range exists, but over things one side refuses to split.

Think back to colonial America, from the previous chapter. Two and a half centuries ago, the British faced a dilemma. After fighting the Seven Years' War on the colonists' behalf, the Crown's defense debt was huge. Meanwhile, the colonists' taxes were barely paying for their own defense and administration. Britain wanted Americans to pay their fair share. So the Crown passed a tax law. The Stamp Act of 1765 placed a duty on newspapers and legal and commercial documents.

The dilemma was that the colonists refused to pay. At first it was just a few radicals. They said something that, to British ears, was unprecedented and unreasonable: only our own legislatures can tax us. Within a few years, more and more colonists echoed the call: no taxation without representation!

This was a shaky claim at the time. Traditionally, the right to vote and representation weren't considered the same thing. Whether the masses voted or not, the interests of every parish and every colony were still "represented" by Parliament (or so parliamentarians argued). Even most Englishmen could not vote, from merchants in London to the citizens of Manchester. Yet they were expected to pay duties all the same.

It didn't matter. A growing number of colonists were implacable. They refused the principle, denied a compromise, and boycotted British goods until the tax was removed. So Parliament repealed the Stamp Act and tried collecting revenue in other ways. Again and again, Britain sought a compromise where America assumed a share of expenses.[17] Each time they tried to find an acceptable tax, however, the parliamentarians came up against a set of American diehards who could not be satisfied. And more and more over time, those radicals were no longer a minority. Their ideas had spread. Despite my earlier poke at George Washington, historians seldom blame the American Revolution on selfish leaders. Rather, they blame America's ideological intransigence and unwillingness to compromise on this issue. Even if they weren't strong enough to demand it, for the colonists it was liberty and local parliaments or bust.

One historian describes a letter written to Thomas Jefferson in 1815 by founding father (and second US president) John Adams. "What do we mean by the Revolution?" Adams reflected. Not the war, he wrote, for that was no part of the revolution. The true revolution, he explained, "was in the Minds of the People." This transformation came about, Adams later added, through a "radical change in the principles, opinions, sentiments, and affections" of

Americans. The colonists had acquired a new moral reasoning and a conception of political rights.[18]

Likewise, in his *Ideological Origins of the American Revolution*, historian Bernard Bailyn describes the development of the American attachment to ideals of liberty, a belief in higher destiny and purpose, and a sense that they needed to be constantly vigilant against those who would interfere with these rights and providence. Why vigilance? Another historian, Pauline Maier, shows how the radicals came to believe (not without cause) that Parliament and the Crown wanted to exterminate their dangerous ideas and bring the colonies back to servitude. The Intolerable Acts seemed to confirm these suspicions—a series of laws designed to punish the colony of Massachusetts after the Boston Tea Party. "Mistake or passion" could not explain Britain's actions, wrote one founder, John Dickinson. It is "UNDOUBTED," he continued, "that an inveterate resolution is formed" by king and Parliament "to annihilate the liberties of the governed." The idea of compromise with such people became abhorrent. There was a bargaining range, but it was one they were unwilling to accept.[19]

THE COSTS OF WAR CREATE THE INCENTIVES FOR COMPROMISE, BUT WHAT HAPPENS IF every concession in that set is unthinkable to one side or the other? Not because carving up the pie is impossible (for few things in the world are truly indivisible). Rather, some principle, preference, or obsession makes the division detestable.[20]

Take the thirteen colonies. Populous, rich, and growing, they could surely afford to place high demands on Britain. But full rights and representation? This was a price too dear—one that arguably was outside any reasonable bargaining range based on American military prowess. Yet the American radicals would settle for nothing less, and no substitutes.[21]

Some political scientists invoke these "indivisibilities" to explain some of the most die-hard ideological, ethnic, and religious disputes. This explanation can be controversial. For instance, some scholars invoke them to explain the difficulty of a peace deal between Israelis and Palestinians. In these accounts, factions on each side find certain concessions unacceptable—whether it be borders, rights of return, control of Jerusalem, or even who gets to use a specific sacred site. The counterargument is clear: None of these things are physically impossible to carve up! They've been divided countless times in history. What do you mean they're indivisible?[22] To me the answer is clear: Indivisibilities are ideological. In the mind of the true believer, the price of compromise on a religious site, equal rights, or another political ideal is too high. Technically it can be split, but one side or the other is unwilling to accept the split that their actual political power permits.

This is the trouble with rights. Now, I happen to think that an obsessive attachment to human rights is a wonderful thing, one of the great ideological revolutions of our species. If everyone believed in and endorsed the same equal protections and principles, they would be profoundly pacifying, because each group would internalize the suffering war imposes on their enemy. (To some extent, that's exactly what has happened over the past two centuries, as we'll see in part 2.) The problem for peace comes when only one side believes its rights to be inalienable. If I believe in my group's inherent right to a piece of land, to representation, or supremacy, then I am less willing to compromise. There may be no price too expensive to pay to uphold it. It's an ideological indivisibility that obliterates bargains.

I think this is how we should understand the desire for self-determination. The American colonists refused to be subjugated. So did Algerians, Northern Irish Catholics, Chechens, and dozens of other anti-colonial and separatist groups throughout history. Some concessions—to imperialism, to domination—are simply too sickening, or offend a people's dignity too much. Speaking of the colonized, the psychiatrist and philosopher Frantz Fanon wrote that those "who die before the firing squads are not hoping that their sacrifice will bring about the reappearance of a past. It is for the sake of the present and of the future that they are willing to die." Their will for independence, their demand for agency, their conception of rights exceeds what their material bargaining power can win them. Yet the peaceful but unequal compromises on offer are simply unacceptable. "We revolt," Fanon wrote, "simply because, for many reasons, we can no longer breathe."[23]

DO HUMANS EXULT IN VIOLENCE ITSELF?

On a chilly platform in Wales, Bill Buford sipped his tea, awaiting his train to London, when a loudspeaker interrupted the quiet winter evening. An unscheduled train was about to appear, the voice announced, would everyone step back ten feet from the platform, please? As Buford exchanged puzzled looks with his neighbors, the station began to fill with police.

Moments later, it appeared. "I had never seen a train with so many people inside," recalled Buford. Inside, he spied a cross between a party and a riot. Drunken and unruly men chanted slogans and sang in unison. One rider was trying to smash the windows out with a table leg. Buford had just seen his first "football special."

Buford had come to England for university, then stayed on as a journalist. Back home in California, the sport was called soccer, and it was mostly a children's game. In England, Buford realized, things were clearly different. Over the next few hours, he struggled to get home on a succession of trains overtaken by football supporters. The hooligans tore the carriages apart, ripping out the seats and smashing everything in sight.

Buford's friends weren't perturbed by the damage and the violence. Mostly, they were shocked that Buford had never been to a match. Curious, he began attending some games. A stout man in his midthirties, with curly black hair and beard, literary, and American, Buford was an improbable presence in the stands. His plan: befriend a thug or two, confirm his suspicions about who they were and why they rioted, and write it up—a quick story for his magazine. It would be many years, many hundreds of pages, and much bloodshed before Buford found his answers.[24]

Surely (the journalist presumed) hooliganism was merely injustice, status seeking, and class rebellion in a modern guise. He expected to find that the rioters were mostly poor and disenfranchised young men, unemployed, frustrated at their situation in life, lashing out at the ruling classes. And sure enough, there were a few of these. But the first fan he approached, a huge walrus-like slob covered in Manchester United tattoos and drinking unimaginable amounts of lager, was Mick, who turned out to be a successful middle-aged electrician with kids and a huge wad of twenty-pound notes in his pockets. Then there was Mark, the British Telecom engineer, with a pension, a wife, and plans for a future family. Neither one fit Buford's imagined mold.

Any worries he'd met a docile clique of hooligans disappeared on Buford's trip to Turin. Man United was playing the Italian city's club, Juventus. British teams had tried to ban their fans from European games, but Mick, Mark, and their "firm" were undeterred. They flew to Turin with Buford in tow.

The football firms were groups of thirty or forty men, led by people with nicknames like Banana Bob and Sneak Thief. These were unofficial supporter clubs, despised by the large formal associations. The leaders of these little firms "all end up competing with one another," Mick told Buford. Mick's own leader, Sammy, had one of the more loyal followings, with a circle of teenage lieutenants. But what was Sammy leading them into? And what were they competing for?

In Turin, as the match ended, long lines of riot police, with shields and batons, guided the Man United supporters to their buses. The Englishmen had been drinking vast quantities of booze since their early morning flight, starting with duty-free bottles of spirits and progressing to huge liter bottles of beer in Turin's main square, under a hot blazing sun. It was a wonder they could walk at all. Just as the inebriated mass reached the bus doors, however, the man in front veered through a gap in the police. A couple hundred supporters followed, at a light run, Buford among them. It was all—the journalist realized—according to plan.

For—suddenly—there was Sammy. The leader jogged backward. "He appeared to be measuring the group, taking in its size," Buford recalled. Sammy's excitement was palpable. He held out his hands, fingers outstretched, still running backward: "Feel the energy," Sammy yelled to his men. The goal was to evade the Italian authorities. It was time to "go off." This is what they had come for. Sammy had sold them all this holiday package not to spectate a football game, but to rampage.

At one point, recalled Buford, "a cluster of police came rushing toward us, and Sammy, having spotted them, whispered a new command, hissing that we were to disperse." An entourage of supporters spread the message and enforced it. This was no mindless mob, Buford realized. "The members of the group split up—some crossing the street, some carrying on down the center of it, some falling behind—until they had gotten past the policemen, whereupon Sammy turned around, running backward again, and ordered everyone to regroup: and the little ones, like trained dogs, herded the members of the group back together."

Free of the police at last, the Man United supporters spotted a cluster of Juventus fans. The hooligans attacked. Buford watched, paralyzed, as his English companions began kicking a boy in the ribs, repeatedly. They hurled heavy objects through the windshields of parked and moving cars.

The men were joyous. "Somebody near me said that he was happy," Buford recalled. "He said that he was very, very happy, that he could not remember ever being so happy, and I looked hard at him, wanting to memorize his face so that I might find him later and ask him what it was that made for this happiness, what it was like." But the man disappeared in the crowd, and so Buford caught up with Mark, the telecom engineer, instead.

"Every now and then," Mark told him, "even for me, there is something spectacular, something that makes you feel different afterwards. The Juventus match was like that. That was a once-in-a-lifetime experience." Mark went on. "You remember the moment we entered the ground?" he asked. "There were only two hundred of us. It was us against them, and we had no idea what was going to happen. There were so many different feelings. Fear, anger, excitement. I've never felt anything like it. We all felt it and every one of us now knows that we have been through something important—something solid."

In his years among the thugs, Buford heard a similar refrain again and again—about the buzz and the fix, of not wanting to forget it, about being sustained by it, and the joy in the telling and retelling of the tale. In the end, he decided, "violence is one of the most intensely lived experiences and, for those capable of giving themselves over to it, is one of the most intense pleasures."

What makes Buford so persuasive, so chillingly credible on this topic, is that he lost himself in the violence and became part of his own evidence. "There was an intense energy about it," Buford wrote of that night in Turin. "It was impossible not to feel some of the thrill."

At one point, months later, Buford was back with the firm in Fulham. He describes a moment, amid the crashing of glass and the pounding of soft flesh, in that manufactured mob, when he ceased his consciousness as an outsider and an individual:

> There on the streets of Fulham, I felt, as the group passed over its metaphorical cliff, that I had literally become weightless. I had abandoned gravity, was greater than it. I felt myself to be hovering above myself, capable of perceiving everything in slow motion and overwhelming detail. I realize later that I was on a druggy high, in a state of adrenaline euphoria. And for the first time I am able to understand the words they use to describe it. That crowd violence was their drug.

BUFORD'S STORY IS ONE OF HUNDREDS OF FIRSTHAND ACCOUNTS FROM RIOTERS, SOL-diers, and gangsters. Some exult in the social aspect and bonding. Others see meaning in it. War is addictive, they write, violence brings exhilaration, purpose, and identity. "Even with its destruction and carnage it can give us what we long for in life," wrote Chris Hedges, a longtime war correspondent. War, he goes on, "can give us purpose, meaning, a reason for living. Only when we are in the midst of conflict does the shallowness and vapidity of much of our lives become apparent."[25]

There are too many of these accounts to ignore. But what do they mean?

Are we humans innately violent? Do groups fight because they revel in conflict? An innate taste for destruction—what Sigmund Freud called our death instinct—would narrow the bargaining range simply because the average group member got their kicks from hurting the enemy.

There's a long history of this view—that war is ancient and natural. If these thinkers are right, then we would have to try to build societies to contain our worst impulses. Maybe we can channel these instincts into something less damaging, some suggest, like violent sports, grisly public spectacles, or scapegoats. That's the view of René Girard, a famed historian, literary critic, and philosopher. He believed humans have an innate talent for rivalry, jealousy, and quarrel that drives us into wars, feuds, and other bloodshed. Fortunately we have an escape valve, he argued. Girard looked at centuries of history and literature and saw a recurring theme: scapegoats and sacrifices. Why do so many societies find, accuse, and condemn innocents to death? he asked. Because violence against the blameless has a purpose—it channels our worst instincts into less harmless actions and restores harmony to the community. If humans didn't have this release, Girard argued, they would channel their destructive instincts into warfare.[26]

Fortunately for our species, I think this view is mostly wrong. There's no evidence of an ungovernable drive for aggression. Yes, there are moments when men and women lust for blood and revel in the kill. On the whole, however, we're a remarkably cooperative species. If anything, the striking thing about human nature is our capacity to empathize, to work together in large groups, to negotiate, and to make the kinds of trade-offs that preserve peace. In no way are we unthinking war machines.

That doesn't mean humans are pacifists by nature. We know that's not true. Most people enjoy competition and triumph, and certain people in certain circumstances get a buzz from cruelty and dominance. Sometimes, when banded together in small groups, humans also exult in collective acts of aggression—especially, it seems, men. Buford's football hooligans are one example. Street fights among gangs of youth are another.

Some anthropologists also see parallels in ancient forms of warfare between human tribes. They have studied the last remaining hunter-gatherer groups on the planet, and their best guess is that a lot of ancient fighting was stealthy and by surprise. It often happened at night. In small groups, and with overwhelming force, a group of men would invade the settlement next door, kill or kidnap a sleeping victim, then run away. Some of these raids had concrete objectives in terms of territory or material goods, but most accounts point to ethereal rewards as well—vengeance, glory, group bonding, and a thrill in the kill. So, in the right circumstances, we probably do have a little bloodlust after all.[27]

It's not clear any of this is relevant to modern warfare, however. Primitive forms of raiding involve small, close-knit groups, attacking by surprise, with overwhelming force and little personal risk. There's a big difference between that and complex, prolonged combat between large groups. Wars are long, enduring, and exhausting, and carry enormous costs and risks compared to raiding, hooliganism, or brawling. They also require groups to form a coalition, arm, deliberate, and plan, week after week, month after month. We just can't extrapolate from small-scale, low-risk, interpersonal violence to larger group competition.

This doesn't mean we can ignore human drives. If there's an innate tendency that I think we should pay attention to, however, it's that people are *parochial*. Humans are quick to form themselves into identity groups and tribes, and to favor members of their own group over the out-group. Social psychologists call this parochial altruism, and it's a basic tenet of their field. It means we have a regard for others, so long as they're part of our faction.[28]

Parochial altruism is built into the model at the heart of this book. In the pie-splitting exercise, it is why one side cares about the benefits and costs of war to their own group and ignores the costs of war to their competitor. In some ways, this love of fellow group members can be pacifying. Our parochialism is what makes us care about the ruin that war brings to members of our side. To the extent that leaders internalize some of the risks and harms to their in-group, they are less war biased.

A more extreme version of parochialism, however, says that humans don't just favor our own group, we take pleasure in the other group's pain or misfortune. The Germans have a word for this: Schadenfreude. If a taste for enemy suffering is widespread, that would not be pacifying. It would be an intangible incentive for war, canceling out some of the costs of fighting, eroding the incentives to find a deal.

The evidence on antipathy for out-groups is mixed. People exhibit a little out-group envy in the lab, but it's not clear it translates to real-life competition. It's certainly true, however, that some group cleavages are jagged and hostile. Out-group members become demonized. Schadenfreude might manifest itself in these more severe circumstances.[29]

That makes it sound as if societies develop their antipathy naturally. But that's probably rare. Instead, think of human parochialism, antipathy, and aggression as tools of political manipulation. They're cultivated. A leader who wants to go to war for other reasons—material or ideological—can use propaganda and misinformation to demonize and dehumanize the enemy side (just as leaders like Göring used it to manufacture status concerns). This makes unchecked rulers and our parochial nature a toxic mix.

Think of the hooliganism Buford described in Turin and Fulham. Like so many riots, the violence wasn't spontaneous or sudden. It was orchestrated by leaders like Sammy, who sold tickets to join an international rampage. Firms like his competed to give their lads the most ecstatic experience, like some horrific cruise package for sadistic middle-class Englishmen. The best leaders got rich and famous. They profited and gained status from the mayhem. Now imagine Sammy as a charismatic dictator with private incentives for violence. Could he pull off the same feat?

This is one story of World War II and the Holocaust, a classic mix of war bias and intangible autocratic incentives. A tyrant, Adolf Hitler, and a regime with an interest in European expansion, Germanization, and Aryanization. Initially, Hitler didn't have the support he needed. Only a third of Germans voted for his party in the last elections to be held. How to rouse the full nation to his hateful, parochial views? How to get people to support, or at least sit idly by, as he exterminated the "impure" groups? One answer was propaganda.

Before 1933, the Weimar government had denied the Nazi Party airtime on the radio. The government broadcasted pro-Weimar news and propaganda instead. As a result, German towns just inside the radio coverage zone tended to vote more pro-Weimar than towns just outside it. As soon as Hitler took power, however, he seized the airwaves and began a campaign of Nazi indoctrination. "Radio and press are at our disposal. We shall stage a masterpiece of propaganda," wrote Hitler's propaganda minister, Joseph Goebbels, in his diary that month. When Germany held parliamentary elections five weeks later, Hitler's campaign had enough of an effect. The towns with radio signals had shifted toward the Nazis a few percentage points more than those just outside the zone. Over the coming years, places more exposed to Nazi radio propaganda also sent more Jews to concentration camps. The differences weren't huge. Hitler didn't persuade everyone to adopt his maniacal point of view. But this was just one channel of propaganda—a microcosm of the many small efforts and small effects. In the end, his ruling clique persuaded enough.[30]

The same tragic story played out in Rwanda, in 1994, when Hutu extremists hacked to death more than 70 percent of the minority Tutsi population—one of the worst genocides in history. A popular radio station broadcasted and coordinated a campaign of hatred, encouraging Hutus to join in the massacre. Villages with radio signals saw far more Tutsis slaughtered.[31] It is no wonder Goebbels called radio "the most important instrument of mass influence that exists anywhere."[32]

When marshaled by war-biased leaders, our fear and anger can be bent to their aims. Think of our parochialism as the kindling, and the unchecked leader as the match. Alone they are fine, while together they make fire. But take note, this kindling wasn't simply lying around. Aggressive drives aren't stewing in every society, awaiting a light. They need to be gathered and stacked with purpose to be inflamed. And once fighting begins, our proclivity for revenge, status, aggression, and antipathy can be used to marshal people into bigger, bloodier, and longer wars.

TREACHEROUS TERRAIN

What does all this add up to? To understand how to think of intangible incentives, I want you to imagine a flying ace, like Galland, evading enemy fire. In open skies he can dive and swerve at will, avoiding most of the barrage. Should he take bullets to the wings and fuselage, it will be damaging, but probably not fatal. Chance events, like a lightning storm or gusts of wind, are troublesome, but he'll steer through them, for his craft is still solid.

Now suppose the ace navigates treacherous terrain. He is piloting his craft through a narrow canyon. Now it's more difficult to dodge fire. Damage to the craft that, in open skies, would pose little worry now imperils the pilot. A sudden wind could crash the plane into the sheer walls. It's a fragile situation.

This is what it means for the bargaining range to narrow. It changes the landscape a society must navigate. A taste for glory, antipathy for the enemy, or an ideological drive plunges the pilot down toward more hazardous ground, a narrow canyon. Unchecked, able to ignore the perils of fighting, the pilot flies deeper. There's limited room to maneuver, but still a gap to fly through. Now, however, the plane is imperiled by other forces that normally, on their own, might not be enough to cause a crash.

This is why I paid particular attention to the times that glory or parochialism intersected with an elite with private interests in war. The two together are more dangerous than either one apart. The causes for war cumulate and interact. It's a theme we'll see repeated as we encounter more roots of war, including the next one: uncertainty.

Chapter 4

UNCERTAINTY

B ack on Chicago's West Side, I'd been tailing Napoleon English on his daily routine. Some of the younger outreach workers did their patrols on social media. Violence these days often begins with internet gangbanging—an online ricochet of insults and bluster that sometimes culminates in a real-life shooting.[1] Nap, however, preferred to do his outreach the old-fashioned way, wandering Lawndale's blocks on foot, or stopping his car at street corners and front stoops, chatting with the young men who sit there day after day.

At first, those corner dealers and porch fixtures were suspicious of the stocky, gregarious fifty-year-old, with his graying stubble and taqiyah—a woven skullcap signaling his Islamic faith. With time, persistence, and charm, however, Nap usually earned a measure of trust. And, if any of them wondered who the hell this old-timer thought he was, Napoleon told them to ask their father or uncle about Nap Dog.

He talks openly and easily about his younger self. It's a part of outreach. The job means knocking on the most dangerous doors, leaping into fiery disputes, talking each side down, trying to halt cycles of shootings. Having a "background" gives Nap credibility in the dangerous business of making peace.

He grew up in Henry Horner Homes—a public housing project not far from Lawndale. The city built the fifteen-story complex of redbrick apartments in the 1950s to cope with an influx of poor Black families from the American South. They had few frills. The apartments were small and simple, with bare gray cinder-block walls. Even so, before things went bad, many families found the projects a big step up over the slums.

Young Nap was a born entrepreneur. At age eleven, he'd begun hustling for cash outside a nearby grocery shop. There was an old folks' home across the street, he told me, and he carried the residents' bags home for a few coins. Soon Nap was cleaning their apartments, taking them to the store, getting the curtains changed. "I was always the breadwinner in my family," he said, with evident pride.

It was the late 1970s, however, and Horner was already in decline. Broken elevators and burned-out lights went unrepaired. The darkened cinder-block hallways slowly grew a coat of graffiti. And by the middle of the decade, gangs from other parts of the city—Vice Lords, Black P. Stones, and Gangster Disciples—had started colonizing the towers as turf. This meant that, for an ambitious teenager like Nap, Horner offered more lucrative hustles. Nap and his friends could make far more money buying an ounce of weed and rolling hundreds of joints. A faction of the Vice Lords ruled Nap's building and encouraged these enterprising youngsters.

Nap's parents tried to steer him and his siblings clear of trouble, but Nap was fascinated with the older gangsters all around him. Vice Lords used to sit in front of his building and shoot dice. They'd have their guns on them, and eleven-year-old Nap would offer to hold their weapons while they played. Police often frisked the dealers, but no officer ever suspected the little sweet-cheeked youngster of holding all the guns. Nap savored those moments of power and responsibility. He kept hoping something would happen. "I wanted to shoot them guns before they can get a chance to get them back," he told me. "I wanted to defend the community."

Nap's mother tried to get her children out of the projects, moving to a low-rise apartment some blocks away. But for Nap, now fifteen, it was too late. He was already in the life, and he dreamed of one day leading the local Lords. One problem, however, was that he didn't look the part. Nap was a "little bitty guy" (by his own description)—young, short, and chubby. He had to prove his ferociousness. So Nap took to wearing a single black leather glove and a long black trench coat, to give the impression he might be carrying a shotgun. It wasn't an act. Nap spent his evenings gangbanging against enemy groups. I asked what that meant. "Somebody out there," Nap explained, "we shot at them."

With time, that reputation started paying off. The "old man" who ran Horner's Vice Lords faction had noticed. He'd taken a liking to the brash, entrepreneurial young Nap, and started grooming him to take over the Lords' operations at Horner.

Nap's reputation demanded constant vigilance, however. One night, he and a friend (I'll call him Morris) were out gangbanging against the Disciples—longtime enemies of the Lords. This was a normal night out for the two boys. They'd sneak into rival territory and fire at the buildings, just "to pop fear into the other side." Afterward, the boys would head back to Morris's place at Horner, open forty-ounce bottles of malt liquor, and proceed to get drunk.

"One night," however, "we started tussling," Nap told me. Tipsy and wound up from their spree, Nap and Morris were goofing around, like any teenage boys. Except these boys were armed. Morris thought it would be funny to point his gun at Nap's head, thinking he'd taken all the bullets out. Nap wasn't taking chances. As Morris pulled the trigger, Nap swatted the barrel down. A bullet tore through both of Nap's thighs.

Blood everywhere, Morris began freaking out. Nap, however, kept the level head that would one day make him such an effective chief (and decades later a fearless outreach worker). "Take the gun up to my sister's place and hide it there," he told Morris. Then Nap called an ambulance and the police. "My story was believable," he told me, "we was sitting out in front of the building, I told them, and the Disciples rolled past, started shooting, and kept going."

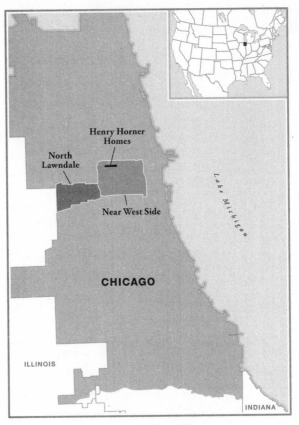

Chicago's West Side

The detectives took down Nap's story as an ambulance crew arrived with a stretcher. But Nap, bleeding and with a bullet still lodged in one thigh, insisted on walking. He didn't want anyone outside to see him being carried, lest he look weak. He managed to make it into the ambulance before his legs buckled beneath him.

One of the detectives must have had a hunch that something wasn't quite right with Nap's story, however, so he had a look around the building. A while later the cops were back, catching Nap at the hospital. "Funny thing," the detective said to Nap, "we found this gun lying in front of the garbage incinerator, covered in fresh blood. Any chance that blood is yours?"

Nap swore silently at Morris's stupidity, then gave the police a ridiculously implausible explanation: he'd forgotten to mention it, but the Disciples came *inside* to shoot him. "They had to write this shit down," Nap told me, shaking his head at the brash absurdity of it all.

Back then, however, convalescing in the hospital, teenage Nap was less amused. He was an up-and-coming Vice Lords leader. "You can run these whole projects," the old guard had promised him. That meant getting shot posed a problem, even if it was accidental. It wasn't just Nap's friends watching, or the older men that ranked above him. There was a much bigger and more deadly audience looking on.

You see, the Vice Lords had long been outnumbered at Horner. Factions of the Gangster Disciples and Black P. Stones held most of the nearby buildings and street blocks. But even if the Vice Lords were the smaller force, it never made sense for the rivals to invade their slice of territory. After all, war is too costly to wage. Instead, the Vice Lords kept a share of the Horner pie roughly equal to their military potential. The difficulty, however, was that the Stones and the Disciples never knew exactly how strong the Lords were. Gangs are clandestine groups. They keep to their own turf, and they have limited interaction with other gangs. It's all highly uncertain. But they gaze across, looking for clues, paying close attention to rumors and news, constantly on the lookout for signs that their enemy's strength and ruthlessness had waxed or waned.

The intensity and stakes only grew as America's drug markets boomed. It was the 1980s, and cocaine and crack markets were surging. Prime territory like Horner Homes became more valuable than ever before. The pie was growing huge, and other gangs' slices looked more appealing than ever. If the Lords were getting soft, the old split would no longer work. Stones and Disciples would expect a larger share of Horner territory. To keep this constant division and redivision peaceful, however, each side needed to know the power of the other, how likely it was that they could win a war, and what it would cost them.

In the middle of this ambiguous, rumor-filled fog, Nap Dog got shot by one of his own guys. Was it an accident or an argument? An internal coup? Rumors flew. The Stones and Disciples perked up their ears. Nap Dog was the up-and-coming young star, the brashest and boldest of the young Lords. What was the new generation of leaders made of? they wondered.

Knowing what was at stake, one of the old guard paid Nap a visit in the hospital. If the teenager was going to take over Horner liked they planned, his name had to mean something, the older man explained. Nap knew how tough he was, his elder implied, but others might not. Nap had to think through this strategically, from the point of view of the other side. The old leader was teaching the young man a deadly but pragmatic version of game theory. "Listen," he explained to Nap, "you going to have to shoot him back. If you don't, it'll be open season over here. Everybody's going to be trying to get you." Nap sighed as he recounted the painful lesson: "There's always someone in your ear telling you to make moves."

Arriving home after two weeks in the hospital, Nap saw Morris sitting outside his building, in the midst of Nap's teen mob, like a boss. They were putting back forties of malt liquor. "I saw that scene and I said, I have got to get this." Nap went up to his apartment, grabbed his .38 revolver ("because that's what he shot me with"), put in some hollow-point bullets ("same shit he got me with"), and came straight down. "Pow," Nap mimed for me. "Pow again." He shot his best friend in both thighs, right where Nap had been shot himself. Finishing his story, Nap sat back. "I had a reputation to defend," he said, looking pensive and sad.

UNCERTAINTY ABOUT RELATIVE STRENGTH

If everyone's strength and resolve were known, there'd be no need for Nap to craft a name for himself. Gangs would look at each other's weapons, soldiers, and leaders and draw similar conclusions about who could win a fight. They wouldn't know the victor for certain. The outcome of a conflict is far too unpredictable for that. But if the two rivals have the same information, they should be able to agree on each other's rough chances of victory.

For instance, they might decide the Lords are strong enough to win three-quarters of the time. But this still means the Stones can edge out a victory a quarter of the time. The first pie splitters we met were perfectly comfortable with these kinds of probabilities and calculations. They compared the expected value of war to that of compromise, and opted for a deal. That kind of uncertainty—the realization of a probabilistic event—isn't a big problem for peace.

The idea that both groups have the same information and agree on the probabilities is a *huge* assumption, however. The world is seldom so stable, transparent, or easy to assess. Most gangs don't know what weapons their rivals possess. They aren't sure of the loyalty of the other's troops, the mettle of their leaders, or the war chest on hand. (They might not even know their own.) In other words, they don't have full information. And even if they did have all the facts, who's to say they'll draw the same conclusions and arrive at the same chances of victory? Even if we ignore all the normal psychological biases and fallibilities, the world is complex and capricious. Over the course of a long-running rivalry, the number of unknowns is impossible to grasp. Judging something as "simple" as the probability of whether your side will win a war is an incredibly challenging task.[2]

Daniel Kahneman, a Nobel Prize–winning psychologist, labels this problem one of "noise." There are so many details, and circumstances change so fast, that smart people with huge incentives to get probabilities right will still get them wrong all the time, even when they have a chance to learn and adjust. For example, here is Kahneman on professional assessors of risk:

> I was working with an insurance company, and we did a very standard experiment. They constructed cases, very routine, standard cases. Expensive cases . . . insuring financial firms for risk of fraud. So you have people who are specialists in this. This is what they do. Cases were constructed completely realistically, the kind of thing that people encounter every day. You have 50 people reading a case and putting a dollar value on it. . . .

Suppose you take two people at random, two underwriters at random. You average the premium they set, you take the difference between them, and you divide the difference by the average. By what percentage do people differ? Well, would you expect people to differ? And there is a common answer that you find when I talk to people and ask them. All the executives had the same answer. It's somewhere around 10 percent. That's what people expect to see in a well-run firm.

Now, what we found was 50 percent, five-zero, which, by the way, means that those underwriters were absolutely wasting their time, in the sense of assessing risk.[3]

These are talented specialists, assessing risk repeatedly, on similar cases, with regular feedback on whether they're correct or not. Getting it wrong could cost them big money. And yet none of these experts can agree on the likelihood something will happen. Other evidence shows this is just as true of stockbrokers, financial auditors, weather forecasters, and even criminal judges. Why should we expect gang chiefs, military generals, or prime ministers to do much better?[4]

Noise is the first way that uncertainty can lead rivals to war. Amid the huge volume of information, the range of unknowns, and the sheer complexity of putting it all together, the two sides disagree on their chance of victory. They arrive at different probabilities. In an influential book, the historian Geoffrey Blainey looked across world wars fought since 1700 and saw exactly this. "Wars usually begin," he concluded, "when fighting nations disagree on their relative strength."[5]

NOISE AND THE RESULTING DIFFERENCES OF OPINION POSE A PROBLEM FOR REASONABLE bargainers. Let me show you how with the pies. Consider two gangs with different starting beliefs about who will win a conflict. Nap and his Vice

Lords, for instance, believed they were well matched against the Stones. The Lords were looking at a pie like the one on the left:

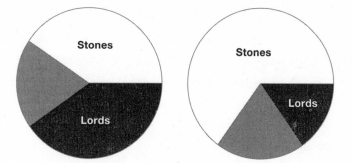

It's a noisy world, however. The Stones saw little bitty Nap Dog, the untested seventeen-year-old chief, and figured that times might have changed. Suppose they thought they could win three-quarters of the time if it comes to a fight. They're seeing the pie on the right.

The first thing you should notice: the difference means the rivals see different bargaining ranges. The overlap will always be less than if they shared the same information and beliefs. So, at a minimum, even if there's a deal both prefer, noise and disagreements about relative strength make peace more fragile than before. The second thing you should see is that in the way I've laid the example out, their beliefs are so different that there's no overlap in the bargaining ranges at all. The incentive for peace has disappeared. This is extreme, but plausible enough that historians like Blainey see it throughout history.

If there's no bargaining range, the enemies learn by fighting. The Stones will go to war until it dawns on them that the Vice Lords are a more equal match. As beliefs converge, a bargaining range appears, and the combatants will find a deal.

Importantly, these wars will only last as long as it takes to reveal true relative strength. In principle, that could happen on the first day of the first clash. But this is the problem with a noisy, changing world. Suppose the

Stones lost the first battle. Was it because they underestimated Nap Dog and the Lords, and they need to revise their chance of victory downward? Or was their expected probability exactly right, and the Lords had a lucky day? After all, a 75 percent chance of victory still means you'll lose one battle in four. Learning to tell the difference between a wrong assessment and an unlucky realization could take weeks, months, possibly even years.[6] It's a murky business. Reality is "wrapped in a fog," the Prussian general Carl von Clausewitz once wrote, thereby giving us the famous phrase "the fog of war."

YOU MIGHT THINK ONE SOLUTION TO THIS HAZE IS PIERCING LIGHTS, AND TO AN EXTENT that's true. War is such a big and horrendous step that both sides want their appraisals to be as accurate as possible. So they try to improve information and communication. Getting assessments right is the main reason rulers build diplomatic and intelligence services, for example. These organizations process the information and pierce through the murk, lowering the risk of war.[7]

Rivals also invest in foghorns. You don't want to be underestimated and invaded by your enemy. Learning through fighting is costly. Who wants to pay for their opponent's ignorance? So rivals spend inordinate amounts of time signaling their true ferocity and crafting reputations. Take Nap—his choice of trench coat, his gangbanging, and the ruthless shooting of his best friend. Partly, he was communicating to other Vice Lords that he was tough, deserving of promotion, and not to be crossed. More importantly, he was sending a loud message to rivals that his gang was not to be trifled with.

Most species prefer to signal rather than fight. Animals have evolved various ways to communicate strength without needing to engage in inefficient conflict—bellowing, hissing, or the display of fearsome-looking horns or teeth. Biologists call this agonistic behavior. Humans have their own manners of doing the same—body language, styles of dress, verbal threats, displays of muscle, parades of weaponry, and rituals to show off potency, from dancing to sports.[8]

Not all signals carry the same weight, however. Wearing a long trench coat, posting Facebook photos of your new guns, or trading insults on Twitter is agonistic. But such talk is cheap. These signals take bravado, but we all know courage is easier on the internet. If you want people to fear you and leave you alone, you need more costly and credible signs.

The best signals are ones that are hard to fake. Maybe that's why the older Lords appreciated Nap's plucky gangbanging against the Disciples, or his cold revenge on Morris. If Nap were weakhearted, he'd never risk those dangers. As more than one gang leader has told me, most kids aren't up to these tasks. A strong group needs to find and foster that mettle.

Let's call these violent episodes "skirmishes." They're not wars—they're too small-scale and short-lived. Often, the whole point of them is to avoid warfare. Sure, some clashes come from youthful bravado and immaturity. But in a shifting and uncertain world, little salvos, gangbanging, and one-off battles are signals of true strength and resolve. They reduce uncertainty and make it easier to find a stable deal.

We see the same raiding and scuffling among rival clans, tribes, and villages, in forests, plains, and deserts. Every society can look back in its past, to an anarchic time before its people had a state. Their ancestors staved off sustained warfare with small clashes and other costly signals, anxiously calibrated to maintain a reputation without spiraling out of control. They weren't fighting a war. Not yet. They were trying to send credible signs of their strength and mettle to avoid all-out conflict.

The same is true of nations, as well. They prefer to broadcast messages nonviolently: testing weapons, firing shots over bows, freezing bank accounts, and holding military parades (the national equivalent of internet gangbanging). When that doesn't work, they turn to skirmishes, preferring ones that are short, small, and revealing. They instigate a limited border raid, seize a lone ship, bomb strategic operations, or launch a targeted cyberattack. Learning by skirmishing is unfortunate, but better than learning by warring.[9]

Sometimes, however, skirmishes and other signals aren't sufficient to resolve the enormous uncertainty. You can imagine the Disciples and Stones wondering whether Nap's attack on Morris proved anything. Maybe the tough-guy image was just an act. The budding leader hadn't been tested for real. Beliefs can update and converge slowly for lots of reasons: because beliefs begin far apart; because new information oozes out gradually; or if signals are themselves noisy or hard to trust. When that happens, battles are one of the only ways to reveal the truth and reach common beliefs. It may start to look less like a collection of skirmishes and more like the prolonged fighting we might call a war. Altogether, uncertainty and disagreements about strength probably explain a lot of conflicts, especially ones of short duration—ethnic clashes, armed standoffs, and brief wars. In a noisy world, we'd expect these to be much more common that prolonged fighting, and they are.

UNCERTAINTY AND THE ABILITY TO BLUFF

Disagreement about relative strength isn't the only way uncertainty affects fighting. Game theorists have pointed out a second way that a lack of information interferes with peace—the opportunity to bluff. Weak parties can send false signals and pretend they're strong to get a better deal. This is one of the more nuanced game theoretic ideas in this book, and so let me walk you through the logic with another episode from Nap.

Shortly after Nap proved his mettle with Morris, the Vice Lords put him in charge of their entire Horner operation. It's hard for me to picture Nap at that age. Instead of his kind face, shaved pate, gray stubble, sweatshirt, and skullcap, I have to imagine a swaggering seventeen-year-old with long black curls, his neck swaddled in gold chains, and an ego so large he named his own pit bull after himself. He wore a size 10 shoe, but he told me he bought his sneakers size 11—just enough room for bullets in the left toe, and a little .25-caliber pistol under his right foot. "The police never looked in our shoes!" Nap explained.

Despite Nap's efforts, the Stones still weren't sure what to make of this short, pudgy teenager. They'd been at peace with Nap's gang for years. But as the drug business boomed, they worried that the Lords controlled more territory than they deserved to. Nap had smarts and resolve far beyond his stature or years, but this wasn't something he could prove. Nap had something called private information—facts the other side couldn't easily verify outside a fight.

Still, there was no need to jump to war. Better to signal and trade territory peacefully than fight. The Stones decided to intimidate Nap Dog and see if he would fold. They issued an ultimatum: he had until the end of the summer to turn his Vice Lords into Black P. Stones. And to indicate their seriousness and test Nap Dog's mettle, Stones began sticking up Nap's dealers—skirmishes to measure each other's strength and resolve. But Nap stood firm. He knew his talents and strength better than the Stones. Unfortunately, his rivals were stubbornly unconvinced. They saw an untested youngster who might be out of his depth, running towers worth a fortune. Maybe the little bitty Nap Dog was bluffing, the Stones worried.

The ability to bluff complicates the strategic calculus. In a world that is simply noisy, you don't want your rival to underrate you and invade. So you have an incentive to signal your strength. But can your rival trust you to tell the truth? You might not want to be underestimated, but you'd love to be overestimated. That would mean getting a larger share of the pie than you deserve. It's a little bit like poker. You'd like to fool your opponent, gambling they won't call.

The weak have powerful incentives to deceive, and everyone knows it. It undermines the credibility of everyone's signals. Was that skirmish a display of true capabilities and resolve, or an elaborate ruse? Nobody wants to be fooled into sharing too much of the pie. This leads to a complex risk-return calculation by both sides. The weak side must weigh the rewards of a successful bluff against the risk it will be called. The strong must weigh the risk of giving too much away against that of attacking an opponent who turns out to be formidable. It's a difficult decision, one where the optimal strategy is never "concede all the time." The crucial insight from strategic reasoning is this: as soon as there's private information, the rational calculation is to call the bluff on occasion, starting a war.

That helps explain why, one afternoon, a member of Nap's crew, out of breath, hammered on his ninth-floor apartment door. "The Stones are here!" he gasped. Nap pulled on a shirt, grabbed his pistol, and sped down the stairs, ready to confront the invaders. Nap got off one or two shots, and then the Stones opened fire. They hit Nap in the hand and arm. Outnumbered, outgunned, and injured, he sprinted back upstairs.

In reality, teenage gang battles are less like a Hollywood shootout and more like a bad high school play—a lethal comedy of errors. Asthmatic and out of shape, Nap Dog heaved himself up the steps. Unnerved and losing blood fast, he managed to miss his floor. He had to backtrack down two flights. That's when he realized he'd locked himself out of his apartment.

Fortunately for him, the Stones were too wary or too disorganized to pursue him closely. So Nap stumbled as quickly as he could to his sister's place. "Help me!" he yelled, hammering on the door. "Call the old man!" His brother-in-law dragged Nap into the apartment, bleeding and losing focus. Nap demanded a phone. "I've been shot in the head!" he told the big boss, "They killed me." "Then how the fuck are you talking to me?" the old man replied. "Give someone else the phone."

This time Nap couldn't walk to the ambulance. He passed out from loss of blood. Paramedics carried him out, unconscious, in plain view of the invaders. The Stones, convinced they'd killed Nap Dog at last, celebrated outside the building. They figured that they'd called his bluff, gambled, and won.

The Stones were mistaken. Nap and the Lords hadn't been faking a thing. Their resolve was firm. "Back in the hospital," Nap told me, "all the old guys were calling me." Once again, Nap had to demonstrate his tenacity. "I had to fight back," he decided. His chiefs were calling to back him up. "They'd already bought artillery," Nap told me, Uzis and other heavy arms. "When they called me, they cocked them guns over the phone: Click, click. Click, click," he mimed.

At stake was more than just Nap's Horner towers. The Lords, Stones, and Disciples were citywide gangs. They had dozens of front lines and potential turf battles. If the Lords looked weak, it threatened every operation. The gang had a reputation to maintain citywide. If they lost that, it would be open season on all of them. So Nap fought back.

Thus began a monthslong battle for Horner Homes. It took time for Nap and his fellow Lords to demonstrate their true potency. Private information isn't always revealed so easily. Once again, it's hard to tell the difference between a lucky realization and a signal of true prowess. Over the following year, the Vice Lords would prove their strength, and all of Horner would flip to their side. They won the whole pie. But that victory happened under the leadership of Nap's younger brother, not Nap himself.

That's because Nap's freedom was one of the war's early casualties. In one of the first retaliatory attacks, Nap killed a Stone and got caught, and the authorities put him away. His resolve and his sacrifice helped give the Lords the reputation they needed to take over all of Horner, but he never got to enjoy it. He was forty-two before he finally got out of prison.

LET ME SHOW HOW PRIVATE INFORMATION AND THE ABILITY TO BLUFF CAN UNDERMINE peace with the same two pies as before. Earlier, with simple noise, the problem was a convoluted world and radically different sources of information. The Stones saw the world on the left, and the Lords saw the world on the right. They had to fight to agree on the truth.

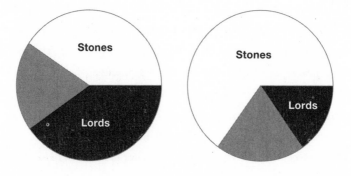

Now, however, uncertainty takes a different form. We'll ignore noise. To keep it simple, we'll simply say that Nap and the Lords have private information, but the Stones do not. The Lords know everyone's true strength. They know they're evenly matched with their opponent—the world on the left. But the Stones aren't so certain. They assign some probability to the case where the Lords are an equal power and some to the case where they are weak and bluffing (the world on the right). The Stones, being the less informed side, need to make a calculated bet.

The Stones know that there's a chance the Lords are weak, and deserve only a quarter share of the projects. The Stones could try grabbing the best buildings in a surprise attack. The weak Lords would give up without a struggle. The problem, of course, is that there's a chance the Lords are strong and would fight back. So grabbing the buildings is a risky move.

Of course, a strong Lords faction knows that the Stones are weighing this option, and the Lords don't want it to come to that. A strong Lords faction prefers to send a clear and credible signal: "Look how powerful we are. Back off." No one wants to be underestimated. The problem, however, is that a weak Lords faction has an incentive to pretend they're strong too. To bluff. If they're successful, then the Stones might leave the Lords with half the towers of Horner.

The Stones know all this too. But because they lack information, they have only bad options: give money away needlessly or risk a costly fight.

What's the Stones' best move? The game theory gets complicated here, but the big takeaway is this: whenever your opponent has private information, your best strategy is never one with zero risk of war. In poker, that would be like folding every time your opponent bluffs. That's a terrible strategy, especially if you get a reputation for backing down all the time. As in poker, you need to be unpredictable—to sometimes call and sometimes fold. This is called a mixed strategy, and it means that the best response to uncertainty can be to attack some of the time.[10]

Add other dimensions of uncertainty, moreover, and the chance of war rises. The situation I laid out is a relatively simple one. There is no noise or disagreement about relative strength. The situation is stable, with relative power shifting just the once. And just one side has private information. As the uncertainty gets more complex, the ways that a bargain breaks down multiply. When both sides have private information, for instance, the risk of fighting usually rises.[11]

REPUTATION IN A WORLD OF MANY RIVALS

Now add other enemies. The simple game above had two groups, interacting one time. The Lords wouldn't gain from a successful bluff in future rounds of play, nor would they lose from a failed one. But, as any poker player will tell you, you bluff with future rounds and other opponents in mind as much as you do with the current one.

This brings us back to Nap Dog and his need for a deadly reputation. Nap and the old men of the Lords weren't thinking of the Stones alone. The stakes were far larger and their time horizon longer. Nap's gang held drug corners across the city. The Disciples, the Latin Kings, and a half dozen other outfits watched the brewing war with interest. If the Lords proved weak, these enemies would be happy to muscle in on Vice Lord corners across the city. Every gang was playing offense and defense on a dozen fronts at once.

This meant an early challenger like the Stones presented a chance for the Lords to set an example—to craft a citywide repute. Amid all the unknowns, the existence of future rounds and other players is a powerful incentive to fight. Reputation exists only because of uncertainty. Without noise and private information, making a name for yourself has no meaning.

Uncertainty and reputation help explain a huge range of costly, risky behavior related to political conflict. One example is lengthy labor strikes. These disputes are full of private information: How long are workers willing to go without pay? How long will the firm forgo production? If this is a one-shot interaction, neither side has incentives for a long strike. But if the union is sending a signal to other employers, or the employer to other units and unions, then both have incentives to craft a reputation. They will man the picket lines longer, or refuse seemingly reasonable deals, paying the price of a disruption today to develop a name for toughness.

Then there's state repression. The need to cultivate a reputation helps explain violence by governments too. Just like a big firm hopes to deter future unionization drives, authoritarian regimes have incentives to crack down on the first protests and make a public example of them. Take how states respond to separatist movements. The governments of Britain, Russia, China, Iran, Spain, Indonesia, France, and Myanmar have all oppressed peoples in their domain, and have all fought bloody conflicts to keep a subjugated province or colony from self-determination. The greater the number of restive ethnic groups in the country, and the more land the nation stands to lose, the more likely that a government fights or represses the first separatists.

Finally, sociologists use private information and reputation to explain blood feuds—low-level warfare between clans, tribes, and villages. From Chicago gangs to Bedouin tribes to Corsican villages to South Sudanese clans, responding violently to a slight is designed to deter future attackers. In Corsica, for instance, groups used to mobilize the entire community to retaliate, even if the slight was small. That solidarity signaled strength, persuading future adversaries to back down, and heading off an endless cycle of skirmishes and retaliations. One anthropologist called this the "peace in the feud"—a war today buys future security.[12]

The fear of future rivals also helps explain why wars, strikes, repression, and feuds can go on for so long. You'd think, after all, that private information and noise should get resolved pretty quickly. That's often true. Once the Stones attacked Nap, for instance, everyone's true prowess should have been clear. A weak Lords faction should have stayed down (now that their bluff was called). Or, the minute Nap and the Lords resumed the fight, the Stones should have said, "Aha—a signal they're strong," and then struck a truce. But if both sides have a wider audience looking on (and if both sides know the other side is thinking along these lines), then everyone knows a weak

Lords faction might still have incentives to keep fighting—to keep bluffing, in the hopes the ruse will pay off. Layer in noise, private information on both sides, and constant shifts in power, and the truth will be hard and slow to discern.[13]

We can tell a story of uncertainty and reputation not just about gangs or firms or unions, but about international conflicts as well. You might think you know why the United States sanctioned, bombed, and eventually invaded Saddam Hussein's Iraq in 2003, for instance. People like to blame a naive, overconfident American administration willing to trade blood for oil. Others, however, point to more strategic and rational roots. You see, Nap's and Saddam's situations were not so dissimilar. Nap remembers seeing Saddam on the prison television all the time, with his dyed black hair and mustache, impeccably dressed in a well-cut suit or army khakis and beret. "Me and the other guys," he told me, "we used to talk about Saddam. You need a leader like him to hold a place like Iraq together." Someone who recognizes the value of a tough reputation. As it happens, Iraq's leader had more in common with gang leaders than Nap ever knew.

AMERICA VERSUS SADDAM HUSSEIN

Saddam was born in a village in the Iraqi badlands, like the landscapes out of an old Western movie. His mother was impoverished, his father absent or dead. Instead of being sent to school, Saddam roamed the alleys. He was expected to bring in money as a farmhand, shepherd, and petty thief, even as a boy.

The young man already showed the ambition and determination that would fuel his rise, however. He fled the village for his uncle's home in the provincial capital and enrolled himself in school. His uncle was a fervent Arab nationalist, political agitator, and Nazi sympathizer, as well as an early member of Iraq's Ba'athist party. Following his uncle's example, Saddam learned to loathe the British-backed government of Iraq. The young man began joining student demonstrations against the regime. Peaceful protests weren't Saddam's style, however. Instead, he began recruiting alley boys, street toughs, and petty criminals. They intimidated shopkeepers into joining strikes and shutdowns. They beat up opponents of the Ba'ath.

Before long, the tall, muscular Saddam became the party's professional agitator and occasional assassin. "He was the tough guy who was brought in to do the dirty business," a fellow member recalled. Saddam's more urbane Ba'athists consistently underestimated the ruffian with the peasant dialect, thinking he'd never amount to more than a party thug and a gangster. Thuggery, however, was Saddam's path to power—slowly building a larger and larger security apparatus of goons, informants, torturers, police, soldiers, and spies, and gradually outmaneuvering his better educated and less ruthless opponents.

Saddam took the same approach to the entire Persian Gulf. In 1980, hoping to annex valuable territory, he invaded Iran, which led to an eight-year war. Next, in 1990, he invaded oil-rich Kuwait. Both conflicts were disasters for Iraq. The dictator was more successful against his enemies at home, however. When the war with Iran ended, for instance, he turned his attention to the Kurds in his country's restive north. He had his air force start with ordinary bombs, to make sure all the windows in the villages shattered. Then came the canisters of poison gas. Over a few bloodstained months, Saddam's forces massacred tens of thousands. Then, a few years later, after the humiliating defeat in Kuwait, he put down an uprising in his country's south. Most Iraqis were Shi'ite Muslims, while Saddam was a Sunni. With Saddam's forces in disarray, the southern Shi'ites rose up. The dictator rallied his forces and crushed the southerners indiscriminately, ignoring details like who had protested and who had not.

Saddam's greatest internal threat, however, came from those closest to him. All tyrants fear an internal coup. To defend against these internal enemies, Saddam imprisoned, tortured, or executed cronies for the mildest of slights. Once, when a cabinet member criticized his rule, the dictator showed no anger. He paused the meeting and asked the minister to join him in another room, to discuss the matter in private. Moments later, the rest of the cabinet heard a single shot. Saddam returned, alone, and calmly continued the meeting.

WHILE THESE SIGNALS MIGHT HAVE DETERRED REVOLUTIONS AND COUPS, THEY MADE Saddam's larger adversaries—Saudi Arabia, Israel, and (most of all) the United States—eager to be rid of him. Here the contest wasn't merely who controlled Iraq, however. America and its allies were competing with Saddam over who would set policy in the Persian Gulf and the broader Middle East. In a sense, the pie was a basket of issues about which the United States and Saddam disagreed: oil prices and production levels; the status and security of Israel; the trend toward democracy versus autocracy; and the safety and rights of minority groups like the Shi'ites and Kurds. The more powerful Saddam Hussein grew, the more he could expect to set this agenda. This was a major reason he'd first set out to get WMD (weapons of mass destruction): they'd help bring about the biggest geostrategic shift in the Middle East in a generation. Every issue in the basket would move in his preferred direction, especially with a nuclear weapon. With a bomb, Iraq would become the first Arab superpower. The threat alone of an atomic weapons program was a valuable bargaining chip with the Americans.[14]

The Americans knew this, of course, and set out to thwart Saddam. In the 1990s the United Nations imposed on Iraq some of the most punishing and far-reaching sanctions in history, partly to halt his various weapons programs. Year after year, UN weapons inspectors tirelessly exposed Saddam's research facilities, factories, and stockpiles. In return, Saddam obstructed and concealed every step of the way.

We now know that, by the time the Americans invaded in March 2003, Saddam's nuclear and chemical weapons programs were exhausted and defunct. Even by the late 1990s, it seems that a decade of sanctions, airstrikes, defections, and inspections had left his regime incapable of developing WMD, especially atomic weapons.

Iraq

But here's the thing: Saddam never made this weakness clear, not until the very final moment—weeks before the 2003 invasion. For years he evaded, blocked, and lied. He and his spokesmen made provocative statements, then contradicted themselves, keeping the Americans (and the UN inspectors) guessing. Even when Saddam did come fully clean, only the nuclear program looked abandoned. Most diplomats and weapons inspectors assumed Saddam still had chemical and biological weapons. One of the few Western envoys in Baghdad on the eve of war, a Norwegian, hostile to the invasion, said he felt certain Saddam had them. That's why the envoy kept stockpiles of protective gear in his embassy. Even Iraq's top generals, interviewed once the war was over, admitted they were never sure what stockpiles the regime might hold.[15]

Why not come clean sooner? Scholars of the war disagree. But one answer is that Saddam knew that weak nations do not set the policy agenda. Bargaining power comes from the ability to threaten harm, and Iraq would get a share of the Middle Eastern pie only equal to its military might. In this grand game of poker, weapons of mass destruction were Saddam's ace in the hole. If he resolved the world's doubts about his scariest and most potent weapons, he'd be giving that up. Not just with America, but with his long list of other enemies inside and outside Iraq. Deterrence by ambiguity. "The better part of war is deceiving," the dictator once said. Ambiguity over WMD was in part a calculated and strategic bluff designed to stay in power and thwart his enemies' agendas in the Middle East. It was a gamble, but Saddam had few options to preserve his position.[16]

THE PRESS, PUNDITS, AND POPULAR MYTH OFTEN TELL A DIFFERENT STORY ABOUT THE United States and Iraq. One is a story of self-interested American leaders. In 1998, when Bill Clinton ordered airstrikes against Saddam in Operation Desert Fox, many worried it was all a diversion from his sex scandal and impeachment trial. Then, in 2000, America elected two people tied up with oil barons as president and vice president. Iraq sat on nearly a tenth of the world's reserves. Protesters accused George W. Bush and Dick Cheney of trading blood for oil. We've seen stories like these before—a leader's private interests marching a country toward war.

A second story you hear is ideological. Some insiders in the Bush administration described a grand vision of democracy in the Middle East. Others saw an aversion to compromising with a despicable tyrant. Outside critics (though almost none of the political scientists and historians) talk about Bush's desire to finish the war his father started, or to avenge Saddam's attempted killing of George Bush Sr. True or false, such accounts are all tales of intangible incentives leading to war.

A final story you hear is one of American self-delusion. Bush, US secretary of defense Donald Rumsfeld, and his undersecretary Douglas Feith famously overestimated the ease of nation building and underestimated the risks of an insurgency and the costs of occupation. That is a story of misperceptions and overconfidence—a chapter we'll come to soon. Arguably, these are errors Saddam made too—failing to appreciate American intentions and resolve, and being impervious to other views.[17]

Personally, I find the "blood for oil" story far-fetched, and the evidence superficial. The ideological accounts are slightly more credible, while the case for overconfidence and misperception is better still. My view, however, is that even if we accept these arguments as true, it's hard to say that any were sufficient to explain the invasion, let alone a decade of escalation and skirmishing. That's because there's a difference between narrowing the bargaining range and eliminating it. Another reason is that none address Saddam's carefully constructed ambiguity about his weapons. A fuller explanation begins with noticing that there was private information on both sides.

The Americans, for their part, had no clue what was happening in Iraq. Unlike in Afghanistan, the United States had few diplomats and sources on the ground. Saddam's regime was also one of the most secretive and paranoiac on the planet, almost impossible for foreign intelligence to penetrate. Even Saddam's own generals were left guessing at his true intentions and capabilities.

The Americans also knew from experience how hard it was to judge Iraq's weapons program, even with a force of international inspectors. After the Gulf War of 1991, intelligence experts were surprised to learn Iraq's covert nuclear program was a mere year or two from a working bomb. When the Republicans returned to power in 2000, some of those same officials were back at the helm—Dick Cheney and Donald Rumsfeld in particular. They knew how noisy the intelligence was, and what a dangerous thing it would be to misjudge Saddam again. It wasn't just the White House and the Defense Department that believed this. Many foreign diplomats, even Saddam's own generals, believed he held on to secret stockpiles of chemical and biological weapons.

As for Saddam, well, no one (least of all him) doubted America's military superiority. Rather, what was ambiguous was the US's willingness to use it. For a decade, the United States had been sending the world ambiguous messages. In 1991, for instance, President George H. W. Bush had held back from invading Iraq, even when Saddam's own people rose against him.

Saddam interpreted this as American weakness. The United States appeared to prove Saddam right in 1993, when it pulled back from regime change in Somalia after the death of eighteen soldiers—a mess famously commemorated in the book and subsequent film *Black Hawk Down*.

Then, the following year, the West dithered during the Rwandan genocide, standing by as a regime organized the mass murder of almost a million men, women, and children—yet more evidence of a lack of American determination, in Saddam's view. Admittedly, in 1995, massacres in Srebrenica finally prompted NATO to intervene in Bosnia with force. But it did so late, reluctantly, and (one could say) only because the conflict was waged in the heart of Europe.

Maybe the new Bush administration that arrived in 2000 was different? It was hard for Saddam to know. But, for two administrations in a row, the United States looked too timid to put troops on the ground. What's more, Saddam had France and Russia on his side. Two permanent UN Security Council members were pledging to block UN approval of an invasion. France also wanted to roll back sanctions and containment measures, figuring Iraq was weak and inspections would prevent Saddam from secret atomic research.

As a result, according to postwar interviews with senior Ba'athist officers, by 2001 Saddam believed the United States would bomb Baghdad but not march on it. He figured the Americans might cut him off from the country's south and north, but he would still be in power. This is more than the dictator believed he would get if he relented to US pressures and settled. While there was a chance the Americans would march all the way to Baghdad, the dictator doubted it. The Americans knew their own mettle, but this was private information.

Each side probed and prodded one another incessantly, testing the other side's strength and resolve. In 1998, Saddam flexed, and tried pushing the bargain in his favor, expelling the weapons inspectors. The United States shoved back. President Bill Clinton ordered strikes on the regime's security

apparatus. These airstrikes—Operation Desert Fox—were designed to signal America's resolve. Like Nap's gangbanging or the Stones' raids, they
would show Saddam (and other enemies) that America was willing to risk
lives, reputation, and money to punish deviations from the status quo.

After 2001, the Bush administration kept threatening invasion, but
Saddam found it hard to distinguish this from a bluff. The dictator's strategy:
to exploit the inherent uncertainty of the situation, and carefully maintain
ambiguity about his military strength and intentions, especially his weapons
of mass destruction. He played France and Russia against the United States
and the United Kingdom. He used every tactic and tool at his disposal—
including the lack of information over what weapons he had and what he
was willing to do with them—to squeeze the best bargain out of the divided
West. As we learned in the pie-splitting exercise earlier, whenever there's
private information, each side's best strategy is seldom one with zero risk of
war. Unsure whether America would invade and topple him, Saddam made
a calculated bluff. It was the greatest gamble of his career.[18]

But this wasn't just a bluff against the Clinton and Bush administrations. This game had more than two players. We know this because, following the invasion, Americans interviewed Saddam's ex-generals and
seized the innumerable tapes Saddam made of every meeting. They learned
something very surprising: America wasn't even close to Saddam Hussein's
chief threat.

Saddam's foremost fear was an internal coup or a popular revolt. The
formative experience for the Iraqi dictator wasn't his defeat by the West in
1991, it was the uprising that followed (and the successive attempts on his
life since then). On the eve of war, Saddam had decided not to defend against
the Americans, but to insulate himself from the risks posed by his own
soldiers and generals. (Gangs, by the way, are similar; Nap had to worry
about the Stones and Disciples, to be sure, but he also had to look out for
Vice Lords gunning for his job.)

Saddam's next concerns were Iran and Israel, his greatest rivals for regional power. Both wanted him dead and gone. But so long as these long-

standing enemies believed Iraq had secret WMD, Saddam thought he could
stave off attacks. What all this meant is that a US invasion of Baghdad wasn't
even a top three threat!

Private information with just two adversaries—Iraq and the US—could
be enough to explain a bluff and a call. Add more players looking on, however, and the incentives to deceive rise. This helps explain why Iraq was so
reluctant to open itself to weapons inspection and come clean. According to
"Chemical Ali"—a senior Iraqi commander, who'd earned his moniker by
using poison gas on Kurds years before—Saddam explicitly rejected the idea
that the regime eliminate doubts about chemical and biological weapons. If
Iraq made such a declaration to the UN, Saddam explained to him, it would
only encourage other enemies to attack.[19]

Saddam wasn't the only ruler in this game with reputation on his mind.
Just as the Iraqi leader was considering his future enemies, the Bush administration was also weighing the message to its other rivals—Iran, and other
nations striving for nuclear power. The American reputation for resolve had
slowly crumbled over the last decade. Invading Iraq would send a clear signal to other challengers.[20]

In other words, Saddam Hussein and George W. Bush lived in a tough
and uncertain neighborhood, just like the Vice Lords and the Stones. There
were many enemies. Saddam had a reputation to keep, or it would be open
season on his rule. Bush had a reputation to mind, too, or there would be
even more nations striving for nuclear weapons. It's hard to understand their
willingness to wage a war unless you consider private information, bluffing,
and their need to craft names for themselves.

NOW, HERE'S THE THING. UNCERTAINTY WAS PROBABLY ENOUGH TO CARRY THE VICE LORDS
and the Stones to war. It can explain other conflicts too. But the political
scientists who study America's invasion of Iraq don't think noise, private
information, and the incentive to bluff were sufficient to get the United
States all the way to war. That's because, on the eve of invasion, Saddam

finally made it clear his nuclear program was no more. At almost the last minute, he allowed weapons inspectors back in. Seeing that his bluff would be called, Saddam made just enough concessions (he hoped) to preserve the peace. Sure, some noise and private information lingered, but not enough (many argue) to explain the invasion in March 2003. So uncertainty can help us explain the long buildup to war, and the narrowness of the range, but not its culmination. To tip the situation over the edge, most experts turn to a commitment problem—our fourth logic of war.

Chapter 5

COMMITMENT PROBLEMS

n 1962, Barbara Tuchman, a little-known journalist and historian, published a history of the weeks leading up to World War I. She had no advanced degree, no academic position or stipend, and up to that point had had trouble being taken seriously. On its release, however, *The Guns of August* sold hundreds of thousands of copies and won her the Pulitzer Prize. More important, that October of 1962, the book sat on the bedside table of John F. Kennedy. Her story would powerfully influence the American president as he confronted the Soviet Union over nuclear launchpads ninety miles off the coast of Florida—the Cuban missile crisis.

Tuchman had a simple explanation for World War I: flawed leadership. The guns of August fired because diplomacy failed in July, she argued. One of the world's deadliest conflicts to date was inadvertent and accidental. The European generals and ministers expected the war to be short and cheap, over by Christmas. They misunderstood their adversaries and multiplied errors with miscommunication, vanity, and overconfidence.

What struck President Kennedy especially hard was a conversation Tuchman described between the German ex-chancellor and his successor. "How did it all happen?" asked the former leader. "Ah, if only one knew," the new one responded. JFK did not want to have the same despondent exchange with the next US president. Tuchman's story prompted Kennedy to restraint, and to find ways to communicate with Soviet leaders. "If anyone is around to write after this," JFK told his brother Bobby, "they are going to understand that we made every effort to find peace and every effort to give our adversary room to move."

Many have looked at the Cuban missile crisis and World War I and come to similar conclusions: a leader's temperament and skill, plus a dash of luck, can save or ruin the peace. Oxford historian Margaret MacMillan attributes World War I to the militarism and mistakes of Europe's leaders, along with intangible incentives at large in the populace: social Darwinist thinking and ethnic nationalism. Others, such as political scientists Stephen Van Evera and Jack Snyder, point to broader problems with the bureaucratic culture that led German military leaders to confidently exaggerate the advantages of a rapid offensive.[1] Popular accounts of America and Iraq in 2003 echo similar themes: leaders with their own private interests, ideologies, and biases, plus an administration that was irrationally exuberant about the ease of regime change.

I buy all these explanations. I think they played a role in each war. I also understand the attractions of a straightforward narrative that focuses on individual flaws and bureaucratic biases, especially because it gives us villains to blame. Any journalist, historian, or academic knows that to have narrative drive, you must leave a lot out. Sometimes that's fine. The problem with analyzing wars, however, is that the same things seem to get omitted again and again, particularly the nuanced and complicated strategic logics. Private information was one of these oft-overlooked forces. Another, the subject of this chapter, is the way that shifting power dynamics make it hard for enemies to commit to a deal.

We need something more than individual mistakes, because errant rulers, overconfidence, and ideological passion can get nations to the first battlefield (and often do). But with something like World War I we must also explain four years in the trenches, millions of people killed, and four empires shattered in a long and unprecedented war of attrition. Iraq too. What kept these opponents at war? Is there nothing deeper at work here than mistakes? Tuchman's insight might have been perfect for the momentary missile crisis in 1962, or for the immediate decisions in July of 1914. But long and devastating wars surely have additional roots.

This brings us to commitment problems. For some, the phrase conjures the dating scene—the people who pull away as soon as things start to get serious, for fear of a long-term relationship. When political economists talk about commitment issues, however, they mean something different—an arrangement that fails because one side can't be counted on to honor it in the future. Both parties want a stable relationship, because breaking up (war) would just be too costly. But one side doesn't trust the other to hold up its end of the covenant. And so things fall apart.

A classic example of a commitment problem is the "preventive war." You're powerful today, but not for long. Your rival will soon dominate you, and you both know it. You could attack now and prevent their rise. War is still ruinous, however, and you might lose, so you'd rather find a deal. Your rival could pledge not to exploit their advantage in the future, and promise you a generous share of the spoils forevermore. But who's going to enforce that? The deal is not credible, because it demands you sacrifice influence now for an empty future promise.

This preventive logic lies behind conflicts as different as World War I, the Peloponnesian War in ancient Greece, and the US invasion of Iraq. Commitment problems are even more versatile that that, however. They're at the heart of civil wars, ethnic cleansings, and genocides too. To see how all these work, let's start in 1914.

THE GREAT WAR

The century before World War I was one of Europe's most peaceful. It wasn't for lack of change, however. From 1815 forward, the Industrial Revolution raced across the continent. Telegraphs, steamships, and railroads collapsed distance and drove unprecedented levels of trade, globalization, and economic growth. The political order transformed too. People formed new ideas of political rights, economic development created new classes, and the merchants and workers driving the industrial economy expected a voice, threatening revolution if they didn't receive one. Meanwhile the old multiethnic empires—Austria-Hungary and the Ottomans—barely clung on. Each year, their emperors' grip slipped in the face of demands for national self-determination. Powerful new nation-states, like Germany and Italy, were assembling around linguistic and ethnic identities.[2]

Still, Europe managed to avoid a general war for almost a hundred years. There were fights between some of the great powers—the Crimean War in 1853, Prussia versus Austria in 1866, or the newborn Germany against France in 1870, to name a few—but these never exploded into continent-wide conflicts.

Rather, ruthlessly but mainly peacefully, European statesmen divided the planet among themselves. The continent's technological edge meant the

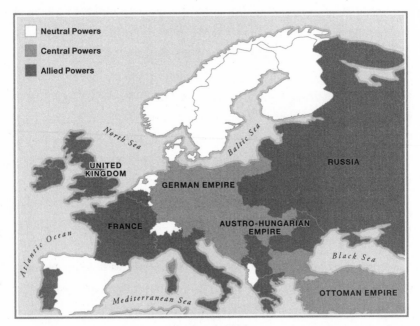

Europe in 1914

world was up for grabs. Armed with a straight-edge ruler, Western powers divvied up sub-Saharan Africa. They wrangled for control of the North African states lining the Mediterranean. Meanwhile, Russia, Austria, and the Balkan states competed for fragments of the dwindling Ottoman Empire, while the British Empire and Russia raced to expand in Persia, China, and central Asia.

Despite the stakes, however, these European powers mostly behaved like the reasonable bargainers in our pie-splitting story. None of them wanted to fight over peripheral territory. Instead, for a century, representatives regularly gathered in congresses, conferences, and committees to divide up distant societies without spending European lives. They loathed in peace, just as we expect.

This long peace ended in 1914 in the Balkans. The region was an unstable buffer between a declining power, Austria-Hungary, and a rising one, Russia. In late June, a young Serb terrorist shot Austrian archduke Franz Ferdinand and his wife in Sarajevo; it was an amateurish assassination of the heir to a fading empire. The murder set off a monthlong diplomatic emergency—what historians call the July Crisis. Over the course of a few weeks, each side activated their alliances and triggered plans to mass mobilize troops. By the end of the summer, all of Europe's great powers were at war: Austria-Hungary and Germany on one side; Russia and France, soon joined by Britain, on the other. The Central versus the Allied powers.

Before asking why they fought, however, we must once again avoid the sin of selection. We can't just look at the failures. For decades, the great powers had managed great crises without fighting. In the fifteen years before 1914 alone, we can see innumerable continental wars that almost but never happened: a British-French standoff in a ruined Egyptian outpost in Sudan in 1898; Russia's muscling in on British and Japanese interests in China to capture Far Eastern ports in 1900; Austria's seizure of Bosnia in 1908; successive clashes over who would control the puppet Moroccan state in 1905 and 1911; two wars between the various Balkan states in 1912 and 1913 in that fragile buffer zone between Austria-Hungary and Russia. A continent-consuming war could have been ignited in any one of these corners of the world. But it wasn't. The incentives for peace were too strong. The great powers usually managed to find a transfer or deal that averted disaster.

What made 1914 different? Yes, Europe's leaders were a mediocre, war-mongering bunch. Their populations were increasingly nationalist. Yet many of the same flawed statesmen leading the same peoples managed the earlier crises without violence. Were they simply less sensible and less lucky in July 1914? Or was there something else at work? Some political scientists and historians look at that moment in history and see the conditions for a preventive war.[3]

ZOOM OUT, HIGH ABOVE GERMANY, TO SEE IT FROM ITS LEADERS' POINT OF VIEW: A NATION encircled by threats. Historically, the Germans focused westward on their longtime enemy, France. More worrisome now was the view east, to Russia, where they saw a behemoth just beginning to realize its full strength. The huge Russian empire was slowly beginning to industrialize, and was better able to exploit its vast resources. In some German opinions, time was running out.

In 1914, the Russian war machine was still recovering from a brutal beating by Japan a decade before. But with French help, the Russians were slowly manufacturing arms, as well as building railroads to their western frontier, to ferry troops and armaments more quickly. As early as 1917, many German generals believed that they would lose any war against Russia.

Foreknowledge gave Germany a window of opportunity to prevent this reversal of power. Moreover, there was little that the country's enemies could do to placate these fears—or so thought many German officials. How could Russia and France possibly promise not to turn Germany into a minor power, or at least not to slowly shave off German territory? This is the commitment problem at the heart of a preventive war—a large, inescapable shift in military power, where the declining power believes the rising one cannot promise to restrain its future self from exploiting its dominance. Act now, top German generals told their political leadership, and the country could forestall Russia's rise. Wait, and the window may close. Some of them had been arguing this for two decades.

Not every commander or head of state was persuaded by the argument. Germany's Kaiser Wilhelm and Austria's archduke Franz Ferdinand, for instance, were skeptical of the case for preventive war. They were inclined to peace. In the July Crisis of 1914, however, with the German window closing and the archduke assassinated, the war party was winning out. "We shall never again strike as well as we do now, with France's and Russia's expansion of their armies incomplete," argued Helmuth von Moltke, Germany's highest-ranking military leader. He believed it was their last chance.

What's more, the July Crisis gave Germany an excuse to attack France and Russia with fewer risks than usual. Looming in German minds was the fear that the other great powers, especially Great Britain, might gang up on them. The assassination in Sarajevo gave the Germans an opportunity. Austria intended to punish Serbia for the slaying of its heir, and in response, it looked as though Russia would mobilize its troops and come to Serbia's aid. If that happened, German diplomats could argue they were simply coming to the aid of their longtime ally, Austria. There was a chance, they thought, that Britain would sit the conflict out (or at least delay long enough for Germany to finish its war with France and permanently weaken Russia). Thus the July Crisis opened up a risky but rewarding opportunity to resolve the commitment problem.

HERE'S WHERE IT'S USEFUL TO LAY OUT THE GENERAL RECIPE FOR A PREVENTIVE WAR. First, there must be a shift in power. Second, the rivals must anticipate that shift (because once it's happened, there's nothing the weakened group can do about it). Together these open the "window of opportunity" for the declining power to counter the rising one. So far, so clear. But now it starts to get tricky, because merely having a window is not enough. The third ingredient is that the power shift must be large. And fourth, the shift in power must be hard to prevent.

We need these last two ingredients to rule out a bargain. After all, both sides still prefer a peaceful deal because war would be costly, and so rivals prefer to trade rather than fight. Germany, for example, would have preferred that Russia avert its rise, or find some way to assure Germany that it would not abuse its future advantage. The third and fourth ingredients make these concessions impossible. The fact that the shift in military might is large means it's harder for the rising power to compensate the weakening one for its imminent loss in influence. Meanwhile, the shift has to be hard to avert, because otherwise the rising power could do something to slow its ascent and make a peaceful deal—transfer some source of its might, or cede something of value to the declining power—just enough to deter it from a preventive attack.[4]

Often power shifts aren't that rapid and large and aren't that hard to avert. That's why commitment problems don't arise with every change in military might. For example, despite massive economic, technological, and political changes, the European powers found compromises again and again in the century before 1914. When the change was sudden, not too large, or divisible, rivals negotiated a transfer of power or territory that preserved the peace. European leaders worked hard to avoid fighting. They reorganized their alliances many times to contain rising powers and blunt their incentives to attack. Some call this the balance of power. A shift in alliances is just power being divided and traded to preserve the peace. There might be no better example of this dealmaking than Otto von Bismarck, chancellor of Germany. He dominated European politics for the two decades before his death in 1890. He was famed for his efforts to find negotiated solutions and avoid war. He even avoided exploiting German military victories, in part to lower the odds of a balancing coalition against him.[5]

At times, however, the shift in power is so large, and hard enough to avoid, that this balancing act and compromise becomes difficult, if not impossible. Many political scientists and historians see this in 1914. Most long wars, some argue, can be blamed on commitment problems like this one. Let me show this with a few other examples, ancient and modern.[6]

ATHENS VERSUS SPARTA

Two and a half millennia ago, there was no such thing as Greece in the sense of a unified nation. Craggy mountains cut the peninsula into valleys and fields of mostly poor soil. Hundreds of islands surrounded the mainland. The towns that developed in these rocky clefts and isles grew to more than a thousand city-states—each one a small urban center called a polis, surrounded by villages and countryside.

At the beginning of the fifth century BC, the dominant polis was Sparta, a three-hundred-year-old military powerhouse. Spartans were the ultimate specialists in violence, shaping their society to produce the best soldiers in the world. At birth, weak infants were killed. Then, at age seven, surviving boys were taken from their homes to the barracks for thirteen years of training. At twenty, they spent another decade training the next generation of children. Only at thirty did they become full citizens. With this came the privilege of thirty more years of military service, before retirement at age sixty.

Every Spartan male could afford to be part of an elite military machine because their society had conquered and yoked nearby settlements to do nearly everything else. These enslaved people, called helots, outnumbered Spartan citizens ten to one. Not surprisingly, their Spartan overlords lived in perpetual fear of an uprising. It created a monstrous feedback loop, where slave oppression enabled and required a fully militarized society.

Led by a narrow oligarchy, the Spartans dominated a huge area of southern Greece, the peninsula known as the Peloponnese. They subdued some of the local cities and built a coalition with others. Allies included powerful oligarchic city-states on the peninsula, like Corinth. Today we call this Spartan-led alliance the Peloponnesian League.

Sparta's chief rival was another powerful city-state, Athens. If this were a film, Hollywood would struggle to come up with a more iconic opponent. Where the Spartans spurned commerce, banning coined money to discourage

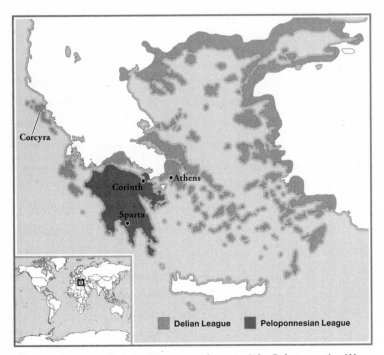

Athens, Sparta, and their alliances on the eve of the Peloponnesian War

material accumulation, the Athenians encouraged markets and built a vast trading system. The Spartans assembled the greatest land army the Mediterranean world had ever seen, while the Athenians based their power on the sea. Finally, rejecting tyranny and oligarchy, Athens slowly established a democracy. This was democracy of a narrow sort—for male citizens only, excluding women, foreign residents, and the enslaved. Still, tens of thousands could assemble and vote, an unprecedented level of political participation.

Athens also sat atop a network of alliances, connecting hundreds of islands and coastal settlements east of the Peloponnese, around the Aegean Sea. Historians call it the Delian League. At first, fear of foreign enemies and pirates coaxed each polis into the coalition. When these external threats failed to persuade islands to join the league, however, the Athenian navy could be convincing. The Athenians were also eager to spread their political system too. Members of Athens's alliance were expected to adopt democratic constitutions, whether they wanted them or not. Gradually, across the Aegean, these seaside cities surrendered their fleets and paid tribute to the center. Athens used this navy to ensure safety, trade, and obedience.[7]

Initially, Athens and Sparta were friendly allies. For a dozen years—from 490 BC to 478 BC—they'd worked together to expel invading Persians from mainland Greece. After that, however, Sparta stepped back and let Athens push the foreign intruder off the archipelago. That was a naval exercise, Athens's specialty. Besides, if the Spartans stayed away too long, they risked a helot revolution.

This decision kicked off a half century of Athenian expansion. As it liberated city-states from Persian occupation, Athens demanded either dues or ships from its new allies. Business, science, and culture flourished. A virtuous cycle of commerce, revenues, and shipbuilding launched Athens and the Delian League toward becoming the new Greek hegemon.

Sparta watched the Athenians' ascent with apprehension. Athens represented a completely different way of life. It wasn't merely a question of values and leadership of the Greek world. The Athenians' semidemocratic system was perilous to a pure slave state with a fragile hold on stability. Their growing power was a threat to Sparta's existence.

At first, the allies managed the shift in power peacefully—it was not so large, indivisible, or inexorable to make peace impossible. For instance, fearful of losing allies to Athens in a chain reaction of desertions, Sparta skirmished with the Delian League on and off. A larger war would have been too costly, however, and eventually the leagues reached a peace accord.[8] In 446 BC, Athens and Sparta signed an agreement they called the Thirty Years' Peace, confidently named for the time it was expected to last. It had two main provisions: a pledge to submit any disagreements to binding, peaceful arbitration; and a vow to never seek the defection of the other league's members. Both sides wanted to build alternatives to a ruinous war.

Unfortunately, the Thirty Years' Peace lasted just fifteen years. Partly, the problem was that Athens continued to rise unabated. The real crisis came, however, when one of Sparta's allies drove Corcyra—a powerful but neutral polis—into the arms of the Delian League. Here was a true commitment problem in the making, a power shift so large that Sparta would be subordinated for good, its way of life threatened. The incentives to prevent that were powerful.

Today we know Corcyra as the island Corfu. Twenty-five hundred years ago, it had the second largest navy in the Mediterranean. It was also nonaligned, one of the few city-states powerful enough to resist the pull of both leagues. Corcyra's naval power was so strong that it would upend the balance of power, no matter whom it allied with.

Corcyra's neutrality ended when a Peloponnesian city-state, Corinth, began quarreling with Corcyra over a minor colony. Sparta tried to rein in Corinth, refusing to support its ally's fight. The risks to the Thirty Years' Peace were too great. Athens, for its part, also tried not to get involved. When Corcyra asked for help, the Athenians tried giving superficial support only. Unfortunately, the Corinthian fleet sank Athenian observer ships. Corcyra and Athens were pulled closer together—a potential alliance that, if it flourished and were cemented, would easily dominate Sparta.

As Corcyra tilted toward Athens, Corinth demanded that Sparta attack them both. If not, what was their Peloponnesian League worth? Otherwise, Corinth threatened to go over to the Athenian side, to join the increasingly stronger party. How many more city-states would rebel and join them? Sparta wasn't just worried about an Athenian alliance with Corcyra; it feared a chain reaction of defections from its league, leaving it weakened and alone with its wrathful helots.[9]

In 431 BC, to prevent this chain reaction from happening, Sparta attacked. Better to get the contest over with quickly, before its position eroded further. A preventive war. The conflict that followed was longer and more destructive than any before. The Peloponnesian War raged for twenty-seven years, engulfing the entire Greek world—the peninsula and archipelago we now call Greece, plus areas we now know as Albania, southern Italy and Sicily, and coastal Turkey.[10]

The historian Thucydides spent much of his lifetime chronicling the war. The fundamental cause, he wrote, was a massive and unavoidable shift in power: "It was the rise of Athens," he wrote, "and the fear that this inspired in Sparta that made war inevitable." Arguably, this is the earliest documented commitment problem.[11]

Two and a half millennia later, Thucydides's claim continues to haunt us. In the late twentieth century, as the Soviet Union rose, the world once again witnessed a great struggle between two visions of civilization. Henry Kissinger, the US secretary of state under Presidents Nixon and Ford, described the Cold War as a new Peloponnesian War between an American Athens and a Soviet Sparta. Did that mean war was inevitable, a journalist asked, and that America (like Athens) would lose? Today, foreign policy experts call this the "Thucydides Trap," implying that rising powers doom the globe to war. Speaking in 2013, for example, Chinese president Xi Jinping told a group of international leaders how "we all need to work together to avoid the Thucydides Trap—destructive tensions between an emerging power and an established power, or between established powers themselves."[12]

Fortunately, commitment problems are much more difficult than that. As we've seen, the recipe requires more ingredients than a rising power. So Thucydides is partly right—the rise of Athens made war more likely, but we need an imminent and hard-to-avert shift (like the Corcyra problem) to really generate a commitment problem. We want world leaders like Kissinger or Xi to realize this—to recognize that war is hard and peace might be easier than they think. Let me show this with our pies.

THE LOGIC OF THE COMMITMENT PROBLEM IN ACTION

Let's simplify the situation, turning the classical Greek world into two players worth a now-familiar $100.[13] Let's suppose that at the outset of the fifth century BC (around the time the Persians were expelled from mainland

Greece) Sparta and its Peloponnesian League could win a war against Athens and its allies three-quarters of the time. The bargaining range looked like this:

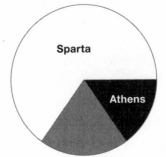

Athens then began its ascent. Athenians discovered a rich vein of silver, then built their famous Long Walls connecting the city to its harbor more than three miles away. These turned the polis into a fortress impregnable to a land invasion and lengthy siege. The Spartans protested, but the Athenians refused to tear down their fortifications. Athens then started expanding its alliances, navy, commerce, and treasury.

At the same time, the Spartans also suffered setbacks. A giant earthquake in 465 BC leveled their city. A helot revolt ensued, killing thousands of Spartan citizens. The population would never return to past levels, and so Sparta could expect a long-term demographic decline.[14] As a result, by the middle of the fifth century BC, suppose that Sparta could foresee a day when the balance of power would be more even, like this:

A crucial detail is that this gradual shift from a 75:25 to a 50:50 match in military power hadn't come about yet. The rebalancing could be averted if Sparta goes to war and wins. The question is whether that war makes sense.

Not necessarily—even with this large shift in power there's no reason to fight. There is still room for a bargain. To see this, we need to add something new to our pie-splitting model: time. Let's imagine there are two periods, today and the future (say, a decade from now). Sparta and Athens are not just bargaining over today's $100 pie, the contest is also for $100 in the future—$200 of pie in total. War would shrink today's pie as well as the future one, by $20 each year. That means war destroys $40 in total. So, today's and the future's war-damaged pies are worth $160 together.

If Sparta attacks Athens today, it knows it has a three-quarters chance of getting the war-damaged pie for both periods—an option worth $120 in all. Meanwhile, Athens expects to win just 25 percent of the time, so its expected value of war is $40. So, anything between $120 and $160 for Sparta and it prefers not to invade. The bargaining range between these two positions runs $40 wide—the same as the total cost of war over the two periods, just as we expect.[15]

Can Athens commit to offering at least $120 to Sparta? Yes, in this case it can. For example, Athens could offer $80 today, and Sparta knows it will get at least $40 in the future. That's fine with Athens. Its tiny slice of the pie today, plus its larger share tomorrow, is far greater than Athens's expected value of war. So Athens lets Sparta enjoy most of today's fruits, knowing that it will be in the Spartans' interest to cede back authority after the rise. There's no commitment problem here, despite a huge shift in relative strength. That's why Athens could refuse to stop recruiting allies, or keep up its long walls. It knew war wasn't in Sparta's interests, and that Sparta could be placated without curbing Athens's rise.

Athens and Sparta sought exactly these kinds of deals. This is why, in the middle of the fifth century BC, to avert a full-scale war, Athens returned a renegade Peloponnesian city-state to Sparta's league and signed the Thirty

Years' Peace, promising it would not permit future defectors. To sweeten the deal, the Athenian leader allegedly bribed the Spartan king and council with a secret transfer of funds. All these efforts bought peace for a time and showed that rivals could accommodate even large rises in power. Clearly, Thucydides wasn't completely right. Rivals can accommodate a large shift in power. War is not inevitable.

But what about larger and more rapid power shifts? In the story above, I emphasized the arrival of a new alliance partner for Athens. Bringing in a third strategic player would make our pie splitting more complicated. To keep things simple, let's take as given that Corcyra will join the Delian League in the future and pool the two largest navies in the world. Now the Spartans think the future is going to look a lot more like this:

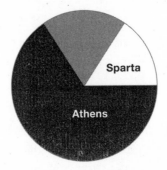

Once this comes about, Athens and its allies will truly dominate Sparta. Sparta is still more powerful today (the first pie), and so it still needs at least $120 not to invade. The main thing that's changed: Athens can no longer commit to giving Sparta $40 in the future. Once the new balance of power comes about, Sparta cannot be fully confident of anything more than $15— the lower end of the future bargaining range. To be certain Sparta will be better off at peace than at war, it needs the balance today—at least $105 worth, if not more. That's bigger than the entirety of today's pie.[16]

Now, there are still a handful of escape hatches here. One would be for Athens to borrow the money from a superpower or a global bank. Sadly, none existed. A second would be to somehow compel Corcyra to stay neutral, or to get it to split its navy between Sparta and Athens. While anything is possible, the practical difficulties are easy to see. Finally, the Athenians could find some way to make a binding pledge to hand over more of the future pie and not exploit their advantage. In the example above, all Athens needs to do is convince Sparta it will get something closer to the top of the future bargaining range rather than the bottom. Such enforced guarantees would be the easiest solution to a commitment problem. Athens could look for an outside power to monitor a deal—an impartial superpower, or maybe an oracle that would curse any violator. Unfortunately, none of these were present.

This is another way of thinking about the commitment problem: it's the child of anarchy. Without a higher power to enforce deals and make pledges binding, big swings in power are hard to manage. Promises are not enforceable. The result can be international wars like the two we've just seen. This is a big general problem. It also helps us explain violence within countries as well.

MASS KILLINGS AND GENOCIDE

"The graves are only half full," blared the announcer, "we must complete the task." Radio Télévision Libre des Mille Collines in Rwanda was exhorting organized gangs of Hutu men to keep up their slaughter of the Tutsi minority. "We made the mistake 30 years ago of letting them flee into exile," the speaker continued, "this time none will escape." It was 1994. Over a blood-soaked hundred days, nearly a million Tutsi men, women, and children died.[17]

Instinctively, most of us think of such acts as the products of hatred and paranoia. Rwanda had both, to be sure. But this emphasis on psychological forces once again underestimates the cold strategic calculus behind mass killings and cleansings.

Genocide is a tactic of the temporarily powerful. The logic should sound familiar by now: today's majority can share a slice of the pie with the minority group for eternity, or they can pay a cost now and avoid having to bargain and share in the future. When the minority is expected to remain small and weak, it doesn't make sense for the majority to pay the price of eliminating them. But if the minority is growing quickly in number, military might, or wealth, then the majority is faced with a diabolical decision akin to that of a Germany facing a rising Russia.[18]

The fear of an encroaching, growing minority consumes many societies. We see it in the native concerned about immigrants with a different language or color of skin (in America or Sweden, for instance); in the exploding population of a minority with a different religion (in China, Israel, or Northern Ireland, for example).

Of course, majority groups seldom leap immediately to extermination; they try to contain the threat in other insidious ways. They disarm the minority, reeducate them in schools, push them to emigrate, bar them from working, jail their leaders, repress their protests, or stick them in ghettos, in camps, and on reservations. They also encourage majority families to have more babies or use the power of the state to grow majority wealth and might. None of these "peaceful deals" are equal or just. The only good thing to be said about them is that they avoid the commitment problem and that they avoid mass killing. (This goes back to a lesson from the introduction: when power is unequally held, the splits of the pie that keep the peace will be inequitable too.)

It's when these strategies fail that leaders turn to violent extermination. Often, the majority feels imminently imperiled—a situation so dire that it overcomes internal opposition and fears of being held to account for this horrific crime. That's one reason most mass killings happen in the middle of an active conflict. This was the case in Rwanda. The Hutu hard-liners in government were losing a war to an invading force of Tutsi soldiers. The civilian massacre was part of the Hutu extremists' final failed gamble for victory. Sadly, these extreme commitment problems are far from exceptional. In the past two centuries, governments have killed many more people in massacres than in battles.

CIVIL WARS

In a remote mountain town in Colombia, nestled amid green rainforest, a local administrator showed a journalist a photograph. It showed a younger version of the official standing next to eight proud men. Each one had been a member of the political wing of the FARC—the Revolutionary Armed Forces of Colombia, a Marxist guerrilla group born in the 1960s. In the 1980s, after two decades of fighting, they'd just formed a political party to negotiate peace and run for office.

Twelve years later, when the journalist first saw the picture, the official was the lone survivor of the group. "All of them were killed," he explained, "none accidentally. It was physical extermination." The Colombian military, their paramilitary partners, and other political allies assassinated the FARC political leaders one by one. By 2002, so many had been disappeared, been murdered, or been pushed into hiding that there was no one left to run in elections, and the state disbanded the party.[19]

Once the uncertainty is resolved, once everyone is exhausted from battle, every insurgent faces a perilous choice: keep fighting or lay down arms and risk the government's taking advantage of their weakness. Many factors kept the FARC fighting in the jungle and mountains for five decades. The systematic extermination of their political leaders was one of them. Even after the rebel group finally signed a peace agreement in 2016 and began demobilizing, the killing began anew. In the years since, dozens of left-wing politicians and demobilized rebel leaders have mysteriously died across the nation, probably by the work of the same murky mix of military and paramilitary actors as before.

This is an example of a tragically common situation: a large government fighting a small but potent rebel force—one that the government would like to find a settlement with, handing over spoils or a share of power. The challenge with settling this civil war is that it often requires that rebels surrender their sources of strength—their troops, their arms, and their secrecy. Contrast this with international wars. Once rival countries stop fighting, they don't need to form a government together. There's no call to merge their militaries, or for one side to disarm. The weaker party in an interstate conflict doesn't necessarily worry about being subsumed by its larger rival in peacetime.

After a civil war, however, unless the two sides split the country, there are pressures to share power and reestablish the monopoly of violence in the state. The challenge is that, once the guns are put down, the stronger side (often the government) has incentives to renege on the agreement, or at least to settle old scores. The risk is highest when the rebels are disproportionately weak, and when the regime is autocratic and unchecked. Once again, the escape hatches are not available. Absent a higher authority to enforce the deal, any arrangement must be self-enforcing. This is tricky to achieve.

The political scientist Barbara Walter has called this commitment problem the single greatest impediment to settling civil war. It helps explain why civil wars last so long; why negotiated settlements are rare; why, when signed, they are seldom implemented; and why sides fight fruitlessly for total victory. As a result, internal conflicts tend to run much longer than wars between nations. The average one runs about a decade. Some, like the FARC, worry their leaders will be killed bit by bit if they surrender their weapons. This is one reason they fought for a half century. There are many more civil wars than there are international ones, and so this adds up to an awful lot of fighting.[20]

BACK TO IRAQ

Now we're equipped to return to Iraq, and to reexamine America's ousting of Saddam Hussein. Iraqis have an old saying that sums up the idea of preventive war perfectly: "It's better to have your enemy for lunch—that way they can't have you for dinner." Some look at the United States and Saddam and see this commitment problem at work. Weapons of mass destruction, especially nuclear material, would change the balance of power between the two countries forever. How could Saddam possibly pledge not to develop them? Uncertainty might help explain the long buildup to war, but it's hard to explain the invasion with private information or misperceptions alone.[21]

From the moment he took office, Saddam Hussein set about seeking a nuclear bomb. The weapon would cement his oppressive and totalitarian regime. It would solidify his position in the Middle East and over global oil markets. He would rise at the expense of every other group, including America, Iran, Israel, and the Saudis. His first big success came in 1980, when France sold the dictator two experimental reactors. The French, cautious and hoping to have it both ways, tried to hand over poorly enriched uranium. Saddam refused, however, and used his leverage to demand weapons-grade material. Iraq was France's second most important oil supplier, and third most valuable trading partner (Saddam bought a *lot* of weapons). So the French relented.[22]

The dictator's true intentions were transparent to all. Israel had used similar research reactors and material to develop its own atomic weapons decades earlier. Now the French deal would be Iraq's path to an "Islamic bomb." The Israelis protested fruitlessly. Meanwhile the United States raised no objections. President Ronald Reagan was more focused on countering Iran, and a stronger Iraq would not hurt. And Saddam Hussein's tyrannical character and power were not yet clear.

Within a decade they would be. Through the 1980s and 1990s, Saddam waged brutal campaigns against Shi'ites, Kurds, Iran, Kuwait, and even his own generals, ministers, and citizens. The West slowly realized what an atomic weapon would mean in his hands.

Still, the first move was not a war. It almost never is. That option is too costly and risky. Instead, the rest of the world first aimed for containment. They had other tools at their disposal that they tried to use first. Iraq had signed the nuclear nonproliferation treaty and had accepted International Atomic Energy Agency safeguards. Those could be enforced through diplomacy, inspections, and penalties. Eventually, these amounted to one of the most extensive sanctions regimes in human history. When sanctions and diplomacy failed, moreover, the United States and Israel still had powerful instruments that stopped short of invasion, such as sabotage and strategic bombings. In short, despite the uncertainty and Saddam's unchecked, reckless rule, the US-led alliance had found a way to contain Saddam—a stable status quo.

By the turn of the millennium, however, a few things had changed. The main one was that containment was failing. Ordinary Iraqis struggled and starved under the brutal sanctions regime. Countries like France were lobbying to end the punishing policy. Meanwhile, Saddam and his family were getting rich selling oil through loopholes. Saddam also managed to use the sanctions to consolidate power. He demonized the United States, and he used his control over scarce imports and foreign currency to reward supporters. All the while, Saddam's military forces were getting weaker. So containment was looking more difficult just as invasion was looking easier.[23]

To the Bush administration, the key worry was this: even if Saddam didn't have atomic weapons in 2003, he couldn't commit to giving up his quest. According to a high-level US intelligence officer, "In the back of our minds, at the fringes of the discussion, was: If we don't do something now, then he would eventually dupe the UN, get the sanctions lifted, and we lose containment. Then he has money and new power, and he opens up his plants, and he is back in business."[24]

These probabilities don't necessarily have to be large. The American vice president Dick Cheney argued something he called the One Percent Doctrine. If there's even a 1 percent chance that a regime like Saddam Hussein's would pursue a bomb, or (worse) would help al-Qaeda obtain a nuclear weapon, he argued, the American government must act as seriously as if it were a certainty. It's a theatrical claim, but so was the image of a centuries-long wasteland where Jerusalem or New York City had once stood.

How real was this risk? It's hard to say. Saddam was secretive, and regime insiders were often unsure of his aims, especially when it came to WMD. As late as January 27, 2003, the chief UN inspector in Iraq, Hans Blix, told the Security Council that "Iraq appears not to have come to a genuine acceptance even today of the disarmament which was demanded of it and which it needs to carry out to win the confidence of the world and to live in peace." Yet after the invasion, based on interviews with former Iraqi officials, a commission decided that the evidence was fragmentary and circumstantial but still consistent with Saddam's planning to restart nuclear research after sanctions were lifted. His incentives to hold on to fissile material and a research program were so great, and were easily enough kept secret, that the Bush administration was convinced he would eventually try.[25]

This is where the logic from the last chapter—uncertainty—becomes important. Saddam, as we saw, had incentives to deceive and to maintain ambiguity. It was hard to remove all doubt through inspections, so noise and concerns about bluffing linger. True, it's possible to imagine blanketing the country with officials from the International Atomic Energy Agency. It would be cheaper than war. But there's a reason that was never an option—the same reason that Saddam severely limited and obstructed inspectors at every turn for the previous decade. Saddam was convinced that the Americans would use what they learned to foster a rebellion, support a coup, or plan a more efficient and effective invasion. How could the United States possibly commit not to do this? Uncertainty and commitment problems comingled.

From the Bush administration's perspective, even the small risk was too great. "Saddam Hussein must understand that if he does not disarm, for the sake of peace," President Bush told CNN in 2003, "we, along with others, will go disarm Saddam Hussein."[26]

REALITY RESISTS A SIMPLE NARRATIVE

This case illustrates my earlier warning about simple stories. It's convenient to blame a war on villains, like Bush or Saddam, and their greedy or overconfident mistakes. But we also have to resist an overly strategic view, one that says war was the rational strategy even if it was a tragic one.

Iraq is just one example. Yes, there were the ingredients for a commitment problem, but the crucial piece—the belief that Saddam would pursue nuclear weapons and that inspections couldn't stop him—was surely exaggerated. The intelligence was flawed and distorted (uncertainty). Top US officials had other biases and motives for war (intangible incentives). And the Bush administration surely underestimated the challenges of regime change (misperceptions). So it's hard to say that the commitment problem alone is to blame. Several logics narrowed the bargaining range until it disappeared.[27]

Or take World War I. Every time someone claims that it followed a preventive logic, a historian points to a clever way out of the bind. Russia's inexorable rise was in the minds of German generals, and was grossly exaggerated, some say. Also, others add, there were deals to be made—a Bismarck would have found a way out of the crisis in July. This brings us back to the arguments by Tuchman and MacMillan—gifted diplomats find peace while the defective ones do not. Who's right?[28]

The answer is both. Think back to the fighter pilot navigating his craft. Historians like Tuchman are focused on the flier's skill. They've shown us that in 1914, Europe's politicians were no aces. They careened their planes into the cliff face. But you'd also be right to ask: Why were they flying in such a narrow gorge in the first place? These same leaders would have been fine cruising in more open skies. Mistakes can make or break a peace, it's true, but only when the bargaining range is perilously thin owing to our five forces. Commitment problems and the four other logics steer the craft from open skies into more the treacherous terrain, one that only a skillful and lucky pilot can navigate. There is seldom one reason for a war.

Chapter 6

MISPERCEPTIONS

Alifelong pacifist, Albert Einstein was so conflict averse that he avoided playing chess. So when World War I broke out, the physicist watched with horror as a militaristic furor spread through every organization in German society, including members of his own academic circle. The scientists who had recruited him to Berlin took on German military positions and research projects. They published nationalistic, warmongering manifestos. The head of the chemistry department, a close friend of Einstein's, began inventing poison gases to waft over trenches and burn through enemy soldiers' lungs.

At first the impish, wild-haired scientist kept his opposition to himself. As the death toll rose, however, Einstein could stay silent no longer. He began attending pacifist rallies and publishing articles decrying the violence. He spent the war and the decades to follow dedicated to a new kind of problem. The mind that revised our entire concept of space and time, the nature of the cosmos, the atom, and light itself turned to one of the most difficult problems yet: understanding and stopping violence.

To Einstein, it was obvious that unaccountable leaders started wars. He thought that a craving for power characterized the governing classes in every nation. What puzzled him was why society followed them with a wild enthusiasm. "How is it possible," he asked, "for this small clique to bend the will of the majority, who stand to lose and suffer by a state of war?" To get an answer, the physicist decided to write to the world's foremost scientist of the mind. Thus, on a summer day in Berlin, in 1932, he sat down at his desk. "Dear Mr. Freud," he wrote, "this is the problem: Is there any way of delivering mankind from the menace of war?"

By 1932, the elderly psychologist was almost as famous and iconic as the younger physicist. But, unlike the kindly, rumpled Einstein, Sigmund Freud was somber and severe. Thin, neatly attired in a dark suit, Freud scowled for his photos, his piercing gaze framed by dark round spectacles, a white beard trimmed short, wisps of hair combed across a balding pate.[1]

The war had shaken Freud as profoundly as it had Einstein. The psychologist was fifty-eight when fighting broke out, far too old to join the war effort. But Freud's sons enlisted, his younger medical colleagues and his patients joined the service, and the psychologist found himself alone and with unusual time to contemplate the unprecedented brutality.

Freud's psychoanalysis focused on the unconscious thoughts, feelings, and urges that shape human behavior. Before the war, he'd fixated on the erotic. But ideas like the Oedipus complex and infant sexuality seemed powerless to explain the forces that drove politicians, officers, and aristocrats to war, or the zeal with which farmers, schoolteachers, and homemakers supported them. There must be other inner drives at work, Freud decided.

By the time Einstein wrote to Freud in 1932, the psychologist had begun to formulate an idea, a twin to the erotic impulse—an instinct for aggression and destruction. As a result of this drive, he told Einstein, "war seems a natural thing enough, biologically sound and practically unavoidable." In his letter, Einstein agreed: "Man has within him a lust for hatred and destruction."

THE TWO THINKERS WERE CORRECT TO LOOK TO PSYCHOLOGY FOR ANSWERS, BUT THE SCI-ence was still in its nascency. Few of Freud's specific ideas about erotic and destructive drives have survived scrutiny. Certainly, the populace can be sometimes roused to hatred, or to lose themselves in a tumultuous rampage, whether it is English soccer hooligans, Indian religious rioters, or Rwandan genocidaires. In chapter 3 we saw how skillful communicators can whip up antipathy for an enemy, especially if they control the airwaves and the information. Despite that, however, I argued that humans don't seem to have an innate taste for violence. Rather, groups manifest this wild hatred with specific rivals (not all of them), in particular circumstances, when relations are especially polarized. Often there is a long history of conflict behind them already. We'll see that misperceptions help turn these animosities into long cycles of violence.

To understand misperceptions, however, we must first understand a much broader feature of human decision-making—our automatic fast thinking—and how it distorts strategic decisions, even when passion and polarization aren't major factors. You see, even if he was wrong about the particulars, Freud's correct and lasting insight was that humans have a deep reservoir of thoughts, emotions, and impulses of which we are only dimly aware. These semiconscious reactions sometimes lead us to hasty judgments or mistakes.

Today people refer to this as fast thinking, a concept famously associated with the psychologist Daniel Kahneman. He and other psychologists have shown how human brains are built to make decisions quickly and efficiently, in ways that bias some choices. Now, not all thinking is fast. A lot of our decision-making is careful and calculated and slow—especially high-stakes and risky decisions, like going to war. But our automatic fast thinking means that even these weighty choices are influenced by things that come to mind quickly and readily. Even when we think our brains are reasoning through problems slowly and rationally, our minds take shortcuts and are influenced by emotion. Most of the time this fast thinking is a boon, helping us navigate a complex world and millions of small decisions. During a crisis or competition, however, our automatic thoughts can lead groups to misperceive a situation in dangerous ways.[2]

This is different from the psychological roots of conflict we discussed in chapter 3, which described the intangible emotional rewards from things like vengeance, status, and parochialism. There was nothing necessarily fast or misconceived about these preferences. We like what we like. If people slowed their decision-making down, it's not clear they'd value these things any less or change their minds. "Regret" is one way to distinguish the logics described in chapter 3 and this one. Intangible incentives are stable and consistent emotional rewards and tastes, and generally people don't second-guess their decisions. Misperceptions are reflexive, erroneous beliefs that lead to hasty actions, and are often cause for remorse.[3] Before we get to the specific mistakes so noxious to bargaining, however, let's first talk about some more basic biases.

THE ELEMENTS OF FAST THINKING

Let's start with some of our most fundamental fast-thinking tendencies.[4] The first is that we're *egocentric*. We're obsessed with ourselves and our group. In earlier chapters we talked about how our selfishness and groupishness are deep-seated preferences, and so they shape our most reasoned decisions. If that were all, then there would be no misperception. But psychologists have also shown that our self-obsession leads us to make errors. For instance, we tend to view the world from our own perspective and forget that others don't see it the same way. Arguably, this is just a special case of something called *availability bias*—we assess probabilities and causes according to their availability and vividness in our memory. Nothing is more vivid in the mind than me, me, me.

Humans are also predisposed to confirm existing and ready beliefs, something known as *confirmation bias*. For instance, we tend to accept our initial hypothesis as true. And once we have a set of beliefs, we tend to evaluate them by seeking evidence that verifies them. Then, having anchored ourselves at a starting point, we selectively search for information, overlooking or failing to look for evidence that is inconsistent.

We're also *motivated*. Humans subconsciously seek out good feelings and avoid unpleasant ones. As a result, we tend to believe and remember evidence that makes us feel good about ourselves and is consistent with our current views. Combined with our confirmation bias and our egocentrism, this motivated reasoning can lead us to favorable conclusions about ourselves. Meanwhile, any stereotypes or misconceptions we have about a disliked group may be slow to change.

Finally, besides our motivation to seek out good feelings and avoid bad ones, our decisions are also shaped by our general emotional state—our *affect*. By this, psychologists mean something more enduring than a snap feeling. They mean something closer to a mood. Our affect shapes how we assess situations in complex ways. For the moment, what's important to know is that there is no such thing as a purely reasoned decision. Emotions infuse our most clinical calculations, even the ones we think are purely rational.

Roughly speaking, you can think of egocentrism, availability, confirmation, motivation, and affect as elemental features of our fast-thinking systems. These elements can combine into more complex and toxic compounds, each one leading to a misperception of the strategic situation. This chapter focuses on the three misperceptions I see as the most relevant to understanding conflict between groups: that groups can be overconfident in their chances of success; that they can mistakenly project their own beliefs and information onto their rivals; and that they can misconstrue motives, attributing the worst intentions to their rivals.[5]

All three misperceptions have something common: they affect how groups and their leaders behave strategically, and so they can disrupt the pie splitting that otherwise gets rivals to peace. You see, any strategic interaction requires each side to form beliefs—to judge their relative chances of success, to predict how their rival will respond, and to understand their enemy's incentives and strategic calculus. When groups or their leadership misperceive these things, it will be harder for them to find a deal.

As we walk through these misperceptions, however, try not to forget this book's mantra. Most of the time war doesn't happen, and so these errors can't be huge and pervasive in every case. Military planners ponder war plans, gaming every scenario and move. Intelligence chiefs send out scouts and spies to get the probabilities right. Parliaments and bureaucracies debate their different views and argue where the money should come from. Even gangs try to think slowly through a decision like going to war, precisely to avoid making a costly mistake. So we will be on the lookout for the circumstances where our organizations and our slow thinking get hijacked by our automatic selves.

MISPERCEIVING OURSELVES: OVERCONFIDENCE

Humans not only tend to overestimate our own abilities; we underestimate the uncertainty around events—we are overprecise. Both are instances of overconfidence, and they arise in part because we're egocentric, motivated to feel good about ourselves and our judgment, prone to confirmation bias, and slow to reevaluate our optimistic guesses. One textbook says that no judgment problem is more prevalent and potentially catastrophic. And when it comes to conflict, Daniel Kahneman has said he thinks there's no bias more significant.[6]

Research has given us plenty of trifling examples. Most people think they're better-than-average drivers, for instance, or that they're funnier than most. Marathoners consistently predict they'll finish the race faster than they actually do. Business school students, entrepreneurs, and seasoned executives all overpredict their chances of success. And, in a survey of a million high school students, almost all of them said they got along with others better than the average person, and a whopping one-quarter put themselves in the top 1 percent.

What we'd like to know, however, is whether we remain so brash when the stakes are high, when we repeat the interaction and have an opportunity to learn, and when the person or group we're making judgments about is close and familiar. To see that, let's start in an unlikely place: a game show.

The Newlywed Game ran on and off American television for almost fifty years. Couples signed up to compete for appliances and furniture. To start, the wives were taken off set. Then the handsome, overtanned host turned to the husbands, asking how they thought their spouses would respond to three questions. Then the wives came back, answered the questions on camera, and reacted with either hilarity or dismay at their husbands' ridiculous predictions. In the second round, the roles reversed, and it was the husbands' turn to be amazed.

A few years ago, Nick Epley decided to stage the show once more, not in a television studio but in a lab. Epley is a tall, gregarious, curly-haired psychologist who studies human judgment. It's not hard to imagine him as a game show host, but he makes a far better behavioral scientist.

Along with a few colleagues, Epley recruited dozens of romantic couples. Some were newlyweds, but most had been together a long while, ten years on average. In the game, partners had to guess whether their other half would agree or disagree with a long list of statements, such as "I would like to spend a year in London or Paris," or, "I would rather spend a quiet evening at home than go out to a party." The researchers added a twist as well; each time a partner made a prediction, they had to rate their confidence in their answer.

Epley and colleagues made three sad discoveries. First, the predicting partner was right only about 25 percent of the time. Second, the partners *thought* they were right about 55 percent of the time. That's a confidence-to-reality ratio greater than two. Third (and maybe saddest of all), this overconfidence ratio was largest for the couples who'd been together a longer time.[7]

Here was a long, intimate relationship—among the closest you can have with another human being. The couples had good reasons to know the likes and dislikes of the other, and then the game added a financial incentive. Not only did the couples get it wrong, they got worse the longer they'd interacted!

This is also something we see in business and finance. Overconfidence doesn't necessarily go away when the stakes are high, when people are experts, and when they're working together in high-performing organizations. Consider Wall Street. Long before he became a bestselling author, Kahneman recalled how a big-shot stock investor asked him to visit his firm. It was

1984. "I knew so little about finance at the time that I had no idea what to ask him," Kahneman said, "but I remember one exchange."

> "When you sell a stock," I asked him, "who buys it?" He answered with a wave in the vague direction of the window, indicating that he expected the buyer to be someone else very much like him. That was odd: because most buyers and sellers know that they have the same information as one another, what made one person buy and the other sell? Buyers think the price is too low and likely to rise; sellers think the price is high and likely to drop. The puzzle is why buyers and sellers alike think that the current price is wrong.

It may seem like a strange thing for economists to say, but people trade too much. Most of the New York Stock Exchange changes hands every year, and foreign currency speculation can reach a quarter of total global trade every day. Even more surprising is that most of these trades lose money. A vast majority of traders underperform the market year after year.[8]

Some of this volume is driven by a huge class of noise traders, especially young men, making overconfident stock predictions over and over again, losing more than half the time. But as decades of research have shown, even the biggest and best-paid mutual fund managers seldom outperform the market. This fact is so well known that cheap, unmanaged index funds have exploded in popularity, and have a better track record of success. Still, the big, overconfident managers and their firms occupy a huge chunk of the market, betting with huge volumes of real money.

Why would Wall Street big shots keep making such high-priced mistakes? Kahneman asked the senior investment manager for his firm's data. As he sifted through the numbers, Kahneman realized that investment managers were doing no better than chance. Sheepishly, he shared the bad news that evening. "This should have been shocking news to them," he recalled, "but it was not." The managers didn't seem to disbelieve him. They simply decided to ignore the inconvenient truth. "We all went on calmly with our dinner," Kahneman recalled, "and I am quite sure that both our findings and their implications were quickly swept under the rug." They preferred information that confirmed their beliefs. They were motivated to accept some data and ignore others. Their overconfidence persisted.

We can see the same pattern with CEOs of huge corporations. Ulrike Malmendier is a UC Berkeley economist. Years ago, she investigated a puzzle in corporate finance: Why do so many companies try to buy and integrate other firms? You'd think it would make them more efficient or more powerful. But most mergers and acquisitions end up lowering the total company's value. Nonetheless, CEOs keep trying them again and again. Malmendier suspected overconfidence.

She looked for ways to spot the kinds of business leaders who made these mistakes. A high level of investment in their own firm was one marker. Other researchers use surveys, language analysis, or persistently excessive earnings announcements. Malmendier found that these overconfident CEOs were more likely to attempt mergers and were more likely to fund these risky ventures by borrowing (which saved them from having to face stockholders). Similarly, other data suggest that football executives overestimate their draft picks; chess grandmasters are overconfident about their memories; firm managers make overly precise forecasts; and physicians cling to a diagnosis for too long.[9]

THAT'S BUSINESS AND SPORTS. WHAT HAPPENS IN POLITICS, WHEN LEADERS ARE DECID- ing on war and peace? Think back to the pies. Suppose the United States faces a group of insurgents overseas. If the American government overestimates its chances of victory, it will make unreasonable demands—that the insurgents can have no place in government, for example, or that their system of laws is unacceptable. If the insurgents are overconfident as well, they, too, will make excessive demands—the complete withdrawal of US forces, or a rejection of democracy. It's as if one side sees the pie on the left and the other sees the pie on the right:

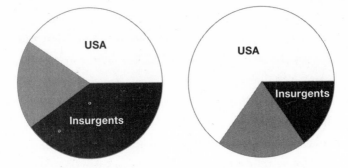

Now, neither mistake dooms the two groups to fight. After all, both sides should recognize that reality is uncertain. And when their opponent's demand is way outside the range they expect, in theory both sides ought to reconsider their beliefs and look for more information. That means it isn't quite as simple as "overconfidence leads to war." Still, the basic insight is this: overconfidence will lead to unusually demanding offers, risking rejection and fighting.[10]

Overconfidence could also help explain why some fights last so long. You'd think, after the first battle, your real strength becomes clear. But we live in a noisy world. If a counterinsurgency campaign goes poorly, is it because the United States overestimated its chances, or because loss was always a possibility? After all, a chance of winning is only that—a chance. We are motivated creatures, processing information friendly to us. We're biased to search for evidence to confirm what we already believe. That could mean we're slow to revise our beliefs, maybe even after fighting for a while. It brings new meaning to historian Geoffrey Blainey's famous quip, "Wars usually begin when fighting nations disagree on their relative strength."

The theory also gives us a strategic insight that's illuminating and frightening at the same time. Say an insurgent group wanted to improve their bargaining position. They could deliberately choose an overconfident leader. They don't want their commander in chief to be *too* optimistic, because they don't want to eliminate the bargaining range entirely. They just want to shut down the less favorable parts of the range, forcing their opponent to accede to aggressive offers, and leaving them the smallest share. Voters in a democracy like the United States could make the same strategic calculation. This is one definition of a hawkish politician—one who is exuberant about military solutions. The same logic has been used to explain why rational people would elect a war-biased leader with a stake in fighting, or even a slightly deranged one. The downside is that electing overconfident leaders will narrow bargaining ranges and make peace more fragile.[11]

It's hard to test for overconfidence with actual world leaders. A lot of the best evidence comes from businesses because there are many firms, straightforward measures of success (like profits), and public data. We don't have the same advantages in politics (and unfortunately no one's yet convinced world leaders to play a version of *The Newlywed Game*). Still, there are several signs that overconfidence shapes war and peace.

Some of the evidence comes from political experts. In a finding that will surprise nobody, several studies show that pundits are too self-assured in their predictions of events. But a lot of the data on overconfidence comes from ordinary people and their political views or choices. For instance, Americans who score highly on surveys of confidence are also more extreme in their political views, more likely to vote, and more likely to identify with a political party. This suggests some people have a higher faith in their political beliefs and are unlikely to admit uncertainty or appreciate varied views. Closer to the topic of conflict, another group of researchers recruited university students and staff and had them play war simulations. They found that many of the players were overconfident about their chances of success, and that they were more likely to attack.[12]

Other studies show how many people think they're immune to bias, a kind of overconfidence in their own judgment. Subjects know that *other* people overestimate their abilities, but they don't think they make that mistake. They realize that others' views are colored by their political ideology or their identity, but when it comes to themselves, people think they see the world more objectively. Even when confronted with evidence of their bias, people tend to think they're immune. (You won't be surprised to hear that some of these studies show that the more someone is convinced of their objectivity, the more biased they seem to be.) Psychologists call this phenomenon naive realism. It's not just overconfidence in our unbiasedness, however; we're also convinced of the correctness of our views and moral rectitude. As the comedian George Carlin said to his audience about driving on the highway, "Ever notice that anyone going slower than you is an idiot and anyone going faster is a maniac?" In politics, I think I'm right, and people who think differently must be biased or wrong.[13]

To actually get at real political leaders, however, scholars mostly look to historical cases for evidence about overconfidence. They find plenty of times that senior diplomats and intelligence agents were bad at assessing risk. A famous example is US president John F. Kennedy's failed Cuban offensive in 1961, a fiasco known as the Bay of Pigs invasion. Some of Kennedy's advisers were certain of success. CIA director Allen Dulles convinced the president that the prospects for landing at the Bay of Pigs were even better than they were for previous successful operations in the region. We also saw similar tales of bombast in the run-up to the US invasion of Iraq, amid uncertainty, when American analysts and politicians grossly overestimated the quality of their sources on WMD and were far too optimistic about governing the country after the battles were won. Likewise, Saddam assured himself and his generals that the Americans would never put boots in Baghdad.[14]

But how prevalent is overconfidence in international affairs, really? If we focus on the failures, of course we'll find stories like the Bay of Pigs and Iraq. Maybe overconfidence is rare. This is why the CEO and Wall Street and football coach examples are so helpful. Those studies looked at all cases, eliminated selection bias, and still found overconfidence to be common. But they also found it was only some firms and leaders. So the question we ought to ask is not if political leaders can be overconfident, but what kinds, and when?

One answer is surely a noisy, uncertain, and shifting environment. When there are lots of shocks and power shifts, many fronts, new technologies, new enemies, and poor communication, it's harder for leaders to evaluate the situation and update their beliefs. Misperception requires this uncertainty to exist.

A few individual traits also seem to matter. One is experience. Evidence from college students playing games in university labs shows that repeated interactions and practice matter. Experienced players make more accurate judgments. (This is consistent with the single largest correlate of which leaders took their countries to war in the last two centuries: those with military training but no actual time on a battlefield.)[15]

The research on stock trading has another tip for you: don't be a young man, for they seem to be responsible for a lot of the trading noise and losses. Some of the lab-based evidence also suggests that men are more susceptible to overconfident assessments than women (at least the Western students tested in psychology labs). And men were more likely to attack in the war simulations I mentioned above. Still, the problem can't be young, inexperienced men alone. Think of all the persistently confident traders and executives with long careers, repeated experiences at the same task, and gray hair. So other factors must be at play.

One is unaccountable power. Some CEOs and traders have a lot of independence. So do some political leaders. It's possible that certain people and personalities are simply more confident, more prone to these mistakes, and that when they're unchecked, the group feels the consequence of their errors. In my view, centralized regimes accentuate that risk.

A lack of checks is not the only kind of group dysfunction, however. Decisions are seldom taken by one person, even in a dictatorship. Just like the most hierarchical companies have boards and layers of management, even autocratic regimes make national security decisions in groups—councils, cliques, and military administrations. So we need to think about what happens when these decisions are deliberated in small groups and in big bureaucracies. We need to focus on organizational dynamics rather than individual traits. We will do that, but before getting there, let's discuss our other two misperceptions.[16]

MISPERCEIVING OTHERS:
MISPROJECTION AND MISCONSTRUAL

On a bright, cold October day in 2018, I wandered West Belfast. Northern Ireland's war had ended two decades before, in 1998, and so I expected the usual historical walk: gray city streets, residents striding briskly by forgotten scenes of struggle, the monuments ignored by everyone except for a few tourists like me. That turned out to be wrong. It is hard to find a city where the past is more present.

I'd heard about the "peace walls" between Protestant and Catholic neighborhoods, covered in brightly painted murals and memorials. I didn't expect them to still stand, let alone to loom so tall. In some places, a two-story concrete barrier was topped with metal netting another two stories high, to keep out rocks and homemade bombs. There hadn't been attacks for a long while, but two decades after the Good Friday Agreement, everyone still felt safer with the fences up.

Then there were the Israeli and Palestinian flags. All across the working-class Protestant Shankill area hung the pale blue Star of David. A short walk away, through a gate in the peace wall they still locked every night at dusk, Palestinian pennants fluttered outside the homes and shops around Falls Road, the heart of Catholic Belfast. How bad must it be, I remember thinking, for people to look at those dismal foes and think, "Yeah, let's celebrate our similarity to them."

It's hard to date the start of the Troubles—one of the deadliest conflicts in Western Europe since World War II. Some would start with the English conquest and colonization of Ireland that began almost a thousand years ago. Others would begin around World War I, when the mainly Catholic Irish demanded independence at last from their mostly British, Protestant rulers. Britain cracked down on this "republican" movement in 1916, prompting a long, Ireland-wide uprising that ended only with the creation, in 1922, of an independent Irish nation covering most of the isle. Only a

Northern Ireland

handful of majority-Protestant counties remained in union with Britain. They formed a new country they called Northern Ireland, with a capital in Belfast.

I'll begin the story of the Troubles, however, in 1969, in a Catholic Belfast neighborhood called the Falls. I'll start on an August afternoon on the normally quiet Bombay Street. Along the long wall of small redbrick row homes marched an indignant Protestant mob, casting petrol bombs into the homes of Catholic workers.

Brendan Hughes stood atop the roof, watching as the rampaging Protestant "loyalists" set fires in the street below him. Young, dusky skinned, with thick black hair and mustache, Hughes was on a short leave from the British merchant marine—a typical job for poor young Catholic men in the Falls, like him. With him on the rooftop was a friend, a young man with an equally common affiliation—namely, with the Irish Republican Army, a Catholic paramilitary and political organization that dated back to World War I.

The IRA had turned to peaceful politics some years before. By August 1969, its local arsenal was thin: a couple of old rifles, two pistols, and a single submachine gun—a relic that looked like a prop out of a 1920s bank robbery. Hughes would one day become one of the group's top leaders. But that afternoon above Bombay Street he wasn't yet an IRA man, so his friend held the automatic weapon. "I was trying to encourage ____ to shoot into the crowd," Hughes later wrote, still concealing the name of his associate. IRA soldiers, however, were under strict orders not to kill that day. "So," Hughes explained, "he emptied a magazine over their heads," breaking the mob up. "They retreated back into the Shankill and we retreated off the roof." That evening, a hundred or so outraged men, Hughes among them, tried marching on Shankill to retaliate. The IRA stopped them from doing that, too, for fighting was too costly.[17]

Hughes had grown up in the Falls, on a block that was mostly Protestant. He was familiar with loyalist venom. "There was one old woman, she was in her nineties, Mrs. McKissick," he remembers, "and every time I walked past her door she would spit on me; every Sunday she would shout: 'Did you bless yourself with the pope's piss this morning?'" Other neighbors celebrated loyalist holidays by putting decorations right outside Hughes's door, the only Catholic house on the street. Then there was the incessant harassment by police. "As a Catholic family in the area, we were constantly singled out for special attention," Hughes recollects. "I was arrested, God knows how many times, taken to court and fined five shillings or ten shillings for not having lights on the bike, for not having brakes on the bike, for playing cards on the street, for playing football on the street."

Even so, violent invasions, like the savage torching of Bombay Street, were new. All through 1969, however, loyalist mobs and paramilitary groups had stepped up their attacks on Catholics. According to one loyalist leader, writing decades later, their reason was simple: "The best means of defence is attack."[18]

Protestants had long been the majority in Northern Ireland. But the Catholics had more babies and were growing in number. What's more, from a loyalist point of view, the Catholics were getting uppity, demanding equal treatment and—worse still—the universal right to vote. This sat poorly if you believed in the old Northern Irish adage "A Protestant country for a Protestant people."[19] Some loyalists also looked at the sometimes riotous civil rights movement sweeping their country and saw a cover for the IRA's true, more devious aim: separation from Britain, and union with the Catholic Republic of Ireland. Many Protestants saw this as an existential threat.[20]

Like so many ruling classes, they failed to see the situation—especially the injustices—from their rival's point of view. Not every Catholic supported the IRA or union with Ireland. Still, loyalists kept up the discrimination, the provocative marches, their supremacist rhetoric, and the occasional, violent attacks. Gradually, the Catholics who weren't republican or rebellious became more sympathetic to those movements. So many empires, colonizers, and ethnic majorities fall into this trap.

As 1969 grew more violent, Britain sent its army in to keep the peace. At first, the troops were there to keep Catholic and Protestant marchers and rioters apart. Soon, however, Catholics found that the burden of curfews, checkpoints, home searches, mass arrests, and internments fell mostly on them. A new, more radical organization splintered off: the Provisional IRA, or "Provos." It rejected the official IRA's peaceful approach and began bombing the police and army.

The state responded with force, hoping to quash the newborn insurrection. That backfired. One Provo described the police and army as his group's best recruiters: "Sometimes the IRA used to come up with some mistake and do something, but then the British Army come out and eclipsed that by doing something even worse," he explained. "We were creating this idea that the British state is not your friend . . . and at every twist in the road they were compounding what we were saying, they were doing what we were saying, fulfilling all the propaganda."[21]

Intimidation and oppression are standard tools for every state. Sometimes

they work. Curfews, arrests, and internment had quelled episodes of republican violence during and after World War II, for instance. But if scholars of
repression have found one thing, it's that such tactics are associated with as
many successes as failures.[22] It's hard to predict whether repression will cow
a population or not, but fail it often does. If the Northern Irish and British
governments had looked back a little further in history, to the years surrounding World War I, they'd remember how their 1916 crackdown had
given rise to the original IRA and an Ireland-wide civil war. Yet here the
state was, fifty years later, trying the same repressive tactics again. As the
first Provisional IRA chief of staff put it in his memoirs: "It has been said
that most revolutions are not caused by revolutionaries in the first place, but
by the stupidity and brutality of governments. Well, you had that to start
with in the north all right."[23]

There was stupidity and brutality on all sides. Starting in 1969, one
historian of the Troubles, Richard English, saw a tragic cycle emerge. It
might begin with an ill-advised loyalist procession through Catholic streets,
the marchers protected by sympathetic Protestant police. It would be followed by an angry counterdemonstration of republicans, throwing stones
and bricks at state forces. In response, army troops would declare a curfew,
search Catholic homes, relieve a local bar of its spirits, and maybe beat or
arrest a few innocent men. So, that night, young Catholic teenagers would
start throwing flaming bottles of petrol instead of stones, and the army
might shoot one dead. In retaliation, the next day a Provo would toss a bomb
into the doorway of a police station for the umpteenth time. The constabu-
lary would then sweep into neighborhoods like the Falls and round up dozens of men, few of them actual Provos (though once in prison some would
be persuaded to join).

Cycles like this drove youth like Brendan Hughes to extremes of cruelty.
On the afternoon of July 21, 1972, he led an operation in Belfast's city center
that set off twenty-two car bombs in seventy-five terror-filled minutes. Nine
people died and dozens were injured in a day remembered as Bloody Friday.

"The war—once ignited—had become a self-fueling conflict," English wrote. "Revenge and politics reinforced one another as motivations for killing."[24]

WE'VE SEEN DEADLY SEQUENCES LIKE THIS BEFORE, IN CHAPTER 3, WHEN WE TALKED about righteousness and vengeance. Unjust acts triggered a strong, lasting, predictable desire to act justly and punish the aggressor. The glow from righteous action would outweigh some of the costs and risks.

Once we started thinking like a game theorist, however, we realized this vengeance story needed a first mover—someone to commit the initial injustice. But who would do that? Barring your enemy from jobs, depriving them of the right to vote, or marching through their streets could make them angry and vengeful. It also makes it easier for your enemies to recruit, gives them pleasure from attacking you, and shrinks the bargaining range in their favor. Acting unjustly might not make strategic sense.

It makes even less sense when you think it could launch a deadly spiral of violence. If you look down the chain of actions and reactions and see that your insult could prompt an arsonist, that arson a riot, that riot a killing, and that killing a mass bombing, and so on, until both sides fight merely for the sake of punishing the other, then you'll take that path with more caution. In a world with vengeful preferences, rivals should launch fewer wars. Violent cycles should be rare. Yet they do happen.

One reason could be uncertainty. It's hard to say what the other side will think is proportionate and just, and whether they will be cowed or aggravated. Many violent cycles surely began with reasonable, imperfectly informed leaders taking a risky gamble on repression, hoping it won't provoke further violence. But historians like Richard English see another reason: a systematic, stubborn failure to see the opponent's point of view, to predict how they will react, and to judge their motives. "Nothing is easier than to denounce the evildoer," the novelist Fyodor Dostoyevsky once wrote, and "nothing is more difficult than to understand him."[25]

In Belfast, for instance, both sides were convinced that their actions were fair and well calibrated, and that the opponents' deeds were malicious. "We all have different narratives of what happened," English told me. "So, I'll start it when you plant the bomb. You'll start it when I invaded your country, which is why you planted the bomb. We each have different starting points for evil. Everyone claims to be reacting appropriately to someone else's violence." They get the probability of a vengeful reprisal and a violent cycle terribly wrong.

A similar story recurs in history after history of conflict: a talent for not seeing the situation from our enemy's perspective, and a stubborn tendency not to revise those views but rather to confirm them in a way that reinforces our bias against the hated out-group—egotism, confirmation bias, and motivated reasoning all rolled together. Together they thwart our attempts to carefully calibrate a response and to find a compromise we both find palatable.

ANY STRATEGIC CHOICE, LIKE FINDING A COMPROMISE WITH AN ENEMY, REQUIRES US TO predict what the other side believes and what they will do. Unfortunately, humans often forget that others hold different beliefs or have alternative versions of events. We unconsciously project our own minds onto theirs. We assume they have the same information as we do. We underrate the events and offenses from the past that matter to the other side. We forget that they interpret history differently. I'll call this *misprojection*.

So rife is this problem that psychologists keep discovering new varieties. They come by different names, but all are variations on a similar theme. They include the curse of knowledge (the tendency, when you know a great deal, to forget what others don't know); hindsight bias (forgetting that others can't easily predict outcomes you already know); false consensus (assuming others would make the same difficult decisions like you); or the lens problem (a tendency to assume others are like you), to name a few. Likewise, some have shown how we exaggerate the probability that others know a piece of information we know, or that others feel the way we feel. We even misproject our future preferences—we let today's weather influence the clothes, car, or house we buy; our current cravings bias our grocery purchases; and so on.[26]

A lot of the supporting evidence comes out of university labs running experiments on Western college students, making decisions remote from war—like whether someone will recognize that I'm tapping out the beat to "Happy Birthday" (they won't, but you think they will). Others use it to explain why some experts are bad at teaching classes or writing books—they lack the ability to see the subject from an amateur's point of view. A few of these studies, however, look at adversarial groups, showing that conservatives tend to think other people are more conservative than they are, voters think that non-voters are more likely to vote like themselves, and so on.

We can see this in our everyday lives too. One day over lunch, my colleague Agnes Callard, a philosopher, compared it to planning an argument with someone in her head. "I think of all the perfect takedowns, all the points they'll make, and how I'll respond. Then I talk to the person, and they have really good things to say back to me!" she said. "It turns out, I was really bad at modeling that person in my head. Even when it's someone I know really well."

We're also bad at modeling other people's reasons and motives—what some call misconstrual, and others call attribution bias. When someone acts against me, do I attribute their action to the person or the situation? Suppose a British soldier shoots a republican protester. Was he inexperienced, in an impossible situation, panicked, and defending himself? That's blaming the situation. Or was he malicious, prejudiced, and working to stamp down the republican cause? That's blaming the person. The sad lesson from social psychology is that we blame the situation for members of our own group, and the person for failings of the other group.

Worse still, misconstruals can interact with the other biases to make them worse. Remember naive realism: I tend to think I see the world objectively, while others do not. Misconstrual means that when I look at my opponent, I attribute the wrongness of their views to their personal failings, such as enmity. I overlook their situation—they were scared, or poorly trained.

For example, one study showed how football fans see the other side as committing gross offenses, while violence by their own side is an understand-able retaliation—even when both sides watched identical videos. The same seems to be true of political partisans. Some researchers showed people tele-vision coverage of a Christian militia storming a Palestinian refugee camp, killing hundreds of civilians, under the cover of Israel's invasion of Lebanon. Pro-Israel and pro-Arab viewers each saw different events in the same foot-age. The only thing both sides agreed on was that the channel covered their side unfairly, because the media was biased against them.[27]

Construals matter because we get less angry at errors, events, or actions beyond someone's control. The situation is forgivable, the person less so. Remember the ultimatum game, where I'll give up free money just to punish you for your unfair allocation? If I learn the small gift was random, or from a computer, or limited by circumstance, my indignation abates, and I let you keep your large share. But if this is uncertain, misconstrual suggests that I will give my in-group the benefit of the doubt, and interpret the out-group's unfair behavior as unjust.

Unfortunately, our projections and construals are also stubborn because we update our beliefs in a motivated way. We tend to believe news friendly to our view and group, and discount facts that aren't. A cute example: people who get good updates about their intelligence test tend to remember it; people who get bad news, less so.[28] But there is nothing charming about holding on to poisonous views about our enemies or ignoring signals that they are seeking reconciliation over war.

Other forces glue our views down as well. We overrate how unpleasant we'll find opposing points of view, for instance, and so we avoid listening to them. To take one example, a group of psychologists showed that US senator Hillary Clinton's supporters overestimated how much they'd dislike Presi-dent Donald Trump's inaugural speech in 2016. If you live in a society where you barely know anyone who votes for the opposite party, you're familiar with these political cocoons. Even when we do realize there's a difference of opinion, we may be bad at judging how big the gap is, and how hard it will be to bridge it.[29]

HOW GROUPS AFFECT OUR BIAS

So far, a lot of the evidence on our three misperceptions comes from individuals. But (with the exception of the most personalized dictatorships) individuals don't decide on war, groups do. What happens when cabinets and legislatures debate and discuss, or when leaders turn to their advisers and agencies for advice? Shouldn't deliberation, expertise, and bureaucratic decision-making reduce our individual biases? The short answer is yes, but not always, and that certain organizational forms and leadership styles are still prone to collective errors.

Let's start with the evidence from psychologists studying small-group performance. They've found that, for many kinds of problem, groups working with good processes make our individual judgments better. For example, when researchers stick people in a lab and ask them to deal with tricky problems, probabilities, and complicated strategic choices, small groups seem to do better than soloists, making fewer logical errors. Groups can also get higher academic test scores, make more accurate forecasts, and recall information better. Groups seem to work especially well for problems that have a clear right or wrong answer.[30]

But when psychologists look at people trying to reach consensus on subjective matters in uncertain environments, like a policy decision or a jury verdict, it's unclear whether groups come to better collective decisions. A lot depends on the people and the process.

Most people have heard the term "groupthink." Psychologists coined it in the 1970s after a series of US foreign policy fiascoes—the failed Bay of Pigs invasion, the Cuban missile crisis, and the invasion of Vietnam. They used it to describe an organizational culture that prizes conformity, discourages deliberation and dissent, and results in persistently wrong beliefs. In the five decades since, a lot of the specific predictions of groupthink theory didn't pan out. Still, researchers think there's something to the general idea. Under some circumstances, people avoid criticizing or disturbing the collective

interest. We get anchored in early beliefs and decisions, and we don't question them enough. Therefore, our optimism and other misperceptions can
get more rather than less extreme over time. When this happens, the group
amplifies rather than eliminates our biases. (This is a good description of my
social media feed, if nothing else.)

One consistent finding is that groups don't necessarily share and aggregate all the information possessed by group members. Some group members
censor themselves. They acquiesce to early ideas and to majority opinions,
either out of deference to the information already given, or to avoid the op-
probrium of others. Also, groups tend to focus on and discuss the information they all share, and they tend to ignore the less widely shared information.
So, if we've all heard the same piece of intelligence saying an enemy has hawkish intentions, and just one of us has heard a different and more dovish piece
of information, we'll tend to spend more time talking about the thing we all
heard, even if the isolated data is potentially more deserving of scrutiny.

The other big finding is that like-minded group members often get
more extreme in their views through deliberation. For example, when people
gather to discuss the appropriate punishment for an enemy or a convicted
criminal, if they all start out lenient, they end up recommending a penalty
that's even lower than anyone's initial proposal. But if most group members
started out inclined to be harsh, discussion makes the consensus punishment
even more severe. It's like a bunch of people from the same political party
working themselves up into a more outrageous opinion after talking to one
another—something most of us can see in our own community or lives.

Broadly speaking, these problems of information aggregation seem to
get better when group discussion is longer, when there are formal processes
for sharing and reviewing all information, when there are norms of accuracy
and problem-solving, when groups are trained to search for more information, or when they formalize critical thinking. The problems tend to get
worse when these processes are not in place.

There's also plenty of evidence that group decision-making gets worse
when members share a social identity. They start to fear that other groups will

take advantage of them, and they're less likely to accommodate rival identities. Most of this research comes from college students in labs. Still, this is
a pretty intuitive result: groups are less inclined to cooperate with foes when
threatened. And in their discussion about whether to go to war, group opinion shifts toward either the pro or anti position, depending on which was
more common among the members beforehand.[31]

Some see the US invasion of Iraq as shaped by these small group dys-
functions at the top. Senior officials in the Bush administration shared an
identity, an ideology, and were like-minded in their hostility to Saddam
Hussein. They failed to create an open culture of discussion and criticism.
Senior analysts and generals had few incentives to challenge the intelligence
on Saddam's intentions or WMD. Unlike with other military exercises, there
were no "devil's advocate" teams set up to question authority. As a result,
some overconfident assumptions persisted, shifting the range of bargains the
administration would find acceptable.[32]

MOST OF THE RESEARCH I JUST MENTIONED DEALT WITH SMALL GROUPS—SIX STUDENTS IN
a lab, or twelve jurors in a court deliberation room. Psychologists, sociologists, and political scientists also study big organizations and bureaucratic
decision-making. A bureaucracy, like a ministry of defense or a presidential
office, brings together many competing interests into slow, deliberative processes to decide important questions of policy. They have systems to acquire
information and bring in multiple bureaus and points of view into the decision. All the little subunits contest the other bureaus. Shouldn't their decisions be more rational and unbiased than an individual's or a small group's?

Again, the answer is often yes. Bureaucracies are ponderous precisely
because they're designed to overcome some of the automatic biases described
here. But not always. For one thing, some huge bureaucracies lack organizational attention and memory. Think of David-and-Goliath-type scenarios—
a superpower dealing with a small client state, a huge central state dealing
with a peripheral minority group, or colonizers dealing with the colonized.

Goliath doesn't have a lot of experience with this David, and he has other problems to deal with. But David's sole focus is Goliath.

Before the Troubles began in 1969, for instance, the British government knew less about Northern Ireland than Anglophone Africa. Parliament spent less than two hours each year discussing the restive province. Once the government realized the Troubles were upon them, they had little sense of history, and were ignorant of republican views and grievances. Now, to make this even worse, suppose every year David stays put, but a new person gets the role of Goliath. "When people in London look at Northern Ireland even now," the historian Richard English told me, "secretaries of state and their colleagues are initially unfamiliar with the place and have to fill a knowledge gap—one which can make mistakes much easier." The rotating British government suffered a kind of collective amnesia. By contrast, English pointed out, "a local politician, such as veteran Sinn Feiner Gerry Adams, has seen waves of British politicians come and go, while his role, knowledge, and engagement have continued year to year." Another historian of the British intelligence services sees this institutional amnesia as a facet of a wider problem, something he's half-jokingly called the "historical attention span deficit disorder" of the state.[33]

Besides this Goliath-ness, however, bureaucracies fail when their organizational form and culture discourages information gathering, debate, and dissent. Consider again the Bush administration and its decision to invade Iraq, but this time let's examine broader bureaucratic failures. The political psychologist Bob Jervis wrote the official postmortem of the US intelligence service. He found that political pressure "created an atmosphere that was not conducive to critical analysis, encouraged excessive certainty, and eroded subtleties and nuances." The national debate was so politicized that staff, even independent intelligence gatherers and analysts, had a hard time getting contradictory views up the chain of command.

Potentially worse still is a culture of conformity and deference to the leader. Personalized systems that elevate and insulate the leader, and centralized bureaucracies full of cronies and sycophants, could magnify a leadership's bias. On the other side of the US-Iraq rivalry, Saddam Hussein is an extreme example. A difference of opinion could mean he'd take you into the next room and shoot you in the head. That's not an environment conducive to dissent. We can imagine the same result even when the penalties aren't so extreme. For example, it's easy to imagine a law-bound and democratic war ministry where the middle ranks defer to the high ranks, hold back information, or don't speak up when they disagree.

In earlier chapters, we talked about the problem of unchecked leaders as one where a lack of constraints meant they could ignore war's costs, or pursue private benefits, against the interests of the group. Now we are adding another dimension to good leadership—building a group of advisers and an organizational culture that minimizes misperceptions. That is probably harder to do in an unchecked system, with fewer bureaus and deliberative bodies.

Constrained or not, however, leaders who want to avoid misperceptions foster norms of openness, debate, and civil opposition, at least in their inner circles and war ministries. They tend to listen first and encourage different views. They task small teams with the job of dissent, questioning assumptions, and harvesting contradictory evidence. In countless ways small and large, effective political organizations and processes don't just restrain a central leadership's ability to ignore the costs of war, they check a leader's fallibility and misperceptions as well.

ANIMOSITIES ON AUTOMATIC

If we're looking for the biggest reason misperceptions matter, however, we need to go back to Freud's and Einstein's original instincts, that "man has within him a lust for hatred and destruction." Einstein had a theory: "In normal times this passion exists in a latent state, it emerges only in unusual circumstances; but it is a comparatively easy task to call it into play and raise it to the power of a collective psychosis." But what circumstances are those? We've covered two at length: when unaccountable leaders with their own interests rile the population up and when organizational cultures fail to make group decisions more rational. Now we add a third: the deadly interactions between misperceptions and passions. Our biases don't simply give us erroneous beliefs about our enemies; they also prompt anger and other emotions. In these charged states of mind, our groupishness and biases grow worse, we react impulsively, and these brash responses can set off the same primal processes in our foes.

A lot of what we know about this comes from studying more mundane individual disputes and emotional reactions. Let's begin there, and then bring it back to competing groups.

IN 1962, AARON BECK NOTICED A PATTERN AMONG HIS PATIENTS. A SLENDER, BOW-TIED psychiatrist, he dealt with ordinary people complaining of phobias, depression, anxiety, or anger. A lot of them came to see Beck because of these extreme emotional reactions. "An anger-prone person," for example, "would blow a minor slight or inconvenience out of proportion and want to punish the offender severely," Beck wrote. Over time, as he treated such patients, he saw a different pattern. When Beck asked his patients to walk through events leading up to the outburst, he noticed that their emotional overreactions were preceded by semiconscious negative thoughts. "These patients showed a regular pattern of thinking errors," he realized. For instance, "they would greatly magnify the significance of a noxious incident. They exaggerated the frequency of such events: 'My assistant always messes up,' or, 'I never get things right.'" Their big emotions and uncontrolled reactions usually followed these automatic thoughts.[34]

Often, this exaggerated and harmful thinking was deep-rooted. Take marriage problems, which Beck saw a lot. His patients often had a lasting, distorted image of their spouses. Chronically feuding couples had developed a rigid negative frame of each other, Beck found. "Each partner saw himself or herself as the victim and the other partner as the villain." A husband estranged from his wife would have an exaggerated perception of the relationship, seeing her as haughty, judging, and critical, with no respect for him. Every moment together had a pervasive, inescapable hostility to it. Starting from that misjudgment, anything she said, no matter how innocuous, would sound mocking or hostile to his ears, making him quick to misinterpretation and anger. "Their minds, in a sense, were usurped by a kind of primal thinking that forced them to feel mistreated and to behave in an antagonistic manner toward the presumed foe," Beck believed.

In this state, his patient grossly misconstrued the other person's intentions. "Each adversary inevitably believed he or she had been wronged and the other persons were contemptible, controlling, and manipulative," Beck noticed. "They would attribute what was clearly an accidental or situational difficulty to the other person's bad intentions or character flaw."

In sum, whether it was between married couples, siblings, parents, or coworkers, their chronic and bitter disputes all shared a few common features: a self-reinforcing cycle of semiconscious negative thoughts driving automatic bad behaviors and outbursts, which in turn entrenched their distorted thinking even further. It was a vicious cycle.

Most of us, including me, can see these patterns in a particular relationship—a parent, child, or friend whose smallest comments or behaviors set us off, often uncontrollably. Negative thoughts like "they always do this" or "they never do that." An impulse to lash out verbally. And a brooding anger whereby we are quick to attribute to them the worst motives.

Some of us fall into the same trap in our dealings with other groups. We don't have this rigidity and reaction toward every out-group, however, any more than we have the same poisonous relationship with all our family members and friends. It's more localized, and some of us may not have this antipathy at all. But when we do get trapped in this rigid frame, tiny provocations can provoke angry and exaggerated overreactions.

That insight alone would rank as a breakthrough. But it was Beck's treatment for the problem that belongs among the greatest medical discoveries of the century. "The formula for treatment may be stated in simple terms," he wrote. "The therapist helps the patient to identify his warped thinking and to learn more realistic ways to formulate his experiences." In other words: know thyself and thus learn control.

What came to be known as cognitive behavioral therapy (CBT) is a series of simple techniques for recognizing your rigid images and automatic thoughts—making the semiconscious conscious—and training yourself to act differently. "Above all," Beck wrote, "they have to become aware that they can be abysmally wrong in their characterizations of other people and their motives, often with tragic results." In other words, become aware of your misperceptions and learn to restrain your automatic reactions. For instance, when an emotion like anger swells, people learn to recognize the distorted thinking that led to it. They also acquire habits that help put their rational brain back in charge—learning to distract themselves, to breathe deeply, to count to ten, or go for a run. Better still, the counselor helps them train themselves to think and react differently: "to become more aware of the rigid thinking that gains control of their minds" and generates the over-reactions, to see the baselessness of their construal, and to slowly unlearn the rigid view they held. "Man is a practical scientist," Beck wrote. We have techniques we can use, with proper instruction, to help become more reasonable.

CBT has been studied thousands of times and for dozens of mental afflictions, including angry and poisoned relationships. It is incredibly effective and persistent. That is important, not just for the suffering it has reduced, but because it provides powerful evidence for Beck's profound insights: that automatic thinking pervades many long-running disputes, that violent and emotional reactions are more counterproductive than strategic, and that our rigid frames and automatic reactions keep us from acting like the reasonable bargainers we need to be.

SADLY, IT GETS WORSE. BECAUSE THERE'S A WHOLE OTHER AREA OF PSYCHOLOGY THAT shows that once we're in an elevated emotional state or mood, the fast-thinking biases we've discussed—overconfidence, misprojection, and miscontrual—can get more severe.

Emotions permeate all our choices. Even the decisions that feel slow and reasoned are influenced by our feelings. A famous example comes from people with damage to the emotional center in the brain (the amygdala) but whose higher reasoning region is unharmed (the prefrontal cortex). These poor souls don't just feel muted and stolid. They can find themselves paralyzed over the most basic decisions. It turns out that all the simple calculations and choices that seem to us to be purely based on reason are intertwined with our feelings and intuitions. Those help make reasoned decision fast. As the philosopher David Hume wrote in 1739, rationality is the slave of passions.[35]

When it comes to competition and conflict, we want to understand how decisions are affected by anger and hostility. I don't just mean momentary flashes of fury; I mean the intense affect that infuses every aspect of the relationship between two long-standing rivals. The answer is depressing. In angry and hostile states of mind, all the misperceptions we've discussed in this chapter get worse. First, anger emboldens. In hostile or heated moods, our minds get brash and self-assured—we're more certain our actions will be successful, and we're more willing to take risks. That means anger amplifies our regular tendencies to overestimate and be overprecise.

Emotions also change how our brains take in news. We see new information about adversaries through that rigid, negative frame. We ignore the old saying "Never attribute to malice what can be adequately explained by stupidity." Instead, we construe accidents as threats. We see neutral acts as mean-spirited. These biases are worst in our paroxysms of rage, but we make similar mistakes in quieter moments when our anger merely simmers. Like the dysfunctional couples Beck counseled, foes create persistent negative views, stereotypes, and overgeneralizations of their opponents. Misprojections and misconstruals are fueled by this smoldering hostility.

Finally, affective states don't just influence our thoughts; they dispose us to take certain actions automatically. The Harvard psychologist Jennifer

Lerner calls this an emotion's action tendency. In hostility mode, we're more likely to lash out in hot, reactive ways.[36] These impulsive reactions can be counterproductive, making the rivalry more bitter than before. In Beck's experience, these exaggerated and reckless responses made the conflict worse, hardening negative views and construals.

Now, just like a lot of automatic thinking, sometimes anger can be helpful. Fury has a productive side—it moves us to want to change the situation and overcome obstacles. Also, genuine rage can credibly signal to the opponent that we're unhappy with the present deal. Visible anger might also provoke concessions and cooperative bargaining strategies. So don't think of emotions being dysfunctional as a rule. They're useful instincts for common stimuli, such as unfair treatment or threats. But this doesn't mean they're always appropriate. My point is that when we're caught in automatic rigid frames, or cycles of conflict, the elevated emotional state we enter can make breaking out of the cycle more difficult.[37]

ALL THIS IS CONSISTENT WITH A LOT OF WHAT WE KNOW ABOUT GROUP CONFLICT. IT FITS events in places like Northern Ireland tragically well. Start, for example, with the intangible incentives we encountered in chapter 3. We're parochial creatures. We think in terms of our group. The more competitive and polarized the relationship, the lower our sympathy, and the greater our parochialism and antipathy. Now we layer on the insights from this chapter: automatic thoughts, biases, and emotional responses. When we're in competition with another group, or have a history of conflict, we're prone to developing negative stereotypes about them—rigid frames—and we cling to false information about them. We're slow to update these beliefs, and we do so in a motivated way, readily absorbing good information about our own group and bad information about our opponent. In the extreme, we demonize and dehumanize our enemies—again, just another kind of rigid negative frame. Here again is David Hume, writing about our talent for demonization, 250 years before most of the research in this book:

When our own nation is at war with any other, we detest them under the character of cruel, perfidious, unjust and violent: But always esteem ourselves and allies equitable, moderate, and merciful. If the general of our enemies be successful, 'tis with difficulty we allow him the figure and character of a man. He is a sorcerer: He has a communication with daemons. . . . He is bloody-minded, and takes a pleasure in death and destruction. But if the success be on our side, our commander has all the opposite good qualities, and is a pattern of virtue, as well as of courage and conduct. His treachery we call policy: His cruelty is an evil inseparable from war.

Misconstruals like these, heightened by passions, echo through modern research on dehumanization.[38]

Our group identity also shapes our emotional responses to events. We feel pride when our group does well, and anger when the group is demeaned or attacked. Members of a group tend to share emotional responses. And the more someone identifies with a group, the more intense their emotional response to victory or a provocation.[39] In surveys and lab studies, there are signs of a vicious feedback loop: misperceptions provoke anger, and then anger elevates these negative stereotypes and support for aggressive or violent actions toward the enemy. For example, American college students who felt angrier following the attack in New York on September 11, 2001, were more supportive of the American invasions of Iraq and Afghanistan. This is a correlation, with self-reported attitudes, so we must be cautious. But some evidence on real-life behaviors and choices comes from Hindu-Muslim conflicts in India. As sectarian tensions and attacks rise, people tend to identify more with their own group, even when it is costly to do so. We know this because some economists collected data on what these people eat. When close to an attack, Hindus avoid beef more and move closer to vegetarianism, while Muslims are more likely to abstain from pork. They start to adhere to their groups' food taboos more strictly—a sign of conflict driving intense group identification.[40]

In addition to examining bureaucratic failures, the political psychologist Bob Jervis spent a career documenting how automatic biases have shaped foreign policy. We misconstrue and misproject on others, even with our allies, and even when differences in cultures and political systems are not involved, he found. But group animosity made them worse. According to Jervis and later generations of scholars, this helps us understand the outbreak of World War I, and the Japanese attack on Pearl Harbor that launched the United States' entry into World War II. Automatic biases contributed to the short-lived American invasion of Cuba in 1961, and to the sadly long-lived invasion of Vietnam. "Enmity and distance on many dimensions make understanding even more difficult," he concluded. Misperceptions don't explain these wars on their own, but they do explain the fragility and how other forces, like commitment problems, could tip nations into fighting.[41]

In the second part of the book, we will see how programs of intergroup contact, group emotion regulation, and attempts to foster empathy can change rigid frames and make enemy groups more amenable to peace (at least a little). Like the evidence from CBT, when these interventions work, it means we diagnosed the correct problem.

IF YOU'RE LIKE ME, THIS NEXUS SOUNDS TRAGICALLY FAMILIAR—POLARIZATION LEADS TO misperception leads to fury, provoking actions that generate more rage, then more misperceptions and further polarization. It conjures Israelis and Palestinians in the Middle East, Serbs and Croats in Europe, Hindus and Muslims in India, Kikuyus and Luos in Kenya, or Catholics and Protestants in Northern Ireland. Long-standing animosities, hostile and simmering always, punctuated every so often with an eruption of extreme violence.[42]

The cycle, to sum it all up, starts from the fact that human groups are prone to rigid negative views of their opponents, and we are only half-conscious of this frame. When this happens, little things provoke automatic outbursts that are often counterproductive. We lash out, often acting against our longer-term strategic interests. This rigid and angry frame of mind also makes all our other misperceptions worse—we're more likely to exaggerate the success of an attack against the enemy group, more likely to misproject our own information onto them, and more likely to attribute evil motives to this opponent. It's a vicious cycle, because violent overreactions and injustices reinforce the negative frames and the angry, hateful feelings, and so they make all our misperceptions worse. That's why this is such a problem among rivals with long histories of injustice and violence. The sequence of events probably didn't cause the rivals to fight the first time. But once the relationship has grown poisonous, it makes any future bargaining range narrower and narrower.

Most of the time these groups aren't actively fighting because it's too costly. Most days Israelis and Palestinians are not lobbing rockets, and Hindus and Muslims aren't rampaging (even in the handful of cities with riots). When they do fight, it's usually short-lived, again because it's so ruinous. But in this trap of misconceptions and hostility, spurts of violence get triggered by the smallest things. A single shock, a sudden shift in power, or a ruthless politician with a close election looming can spark the cycle again: a spate of mutual rocket attacks, a succession of riots and reprisals, or a series of terrorist bombings followed by repressive overreactions. I don't think we can understand the fragility of these rivalries without misperception and passion.

PUTTING THE FIVE LOGICS TOGETHER

The five logics are a diagnostic tool that disciplines our thinking. Every time someone gives you an explanation for a war, you should now think to yourself, "How does that hijack the incentives for peace? How does it fit in the five?" It may not. There are lots of misleading ideas about war, ones that arise from focusing on the failures and tracing back conflicts to false causes.

If you apply them, you'll also make better forecasts of when war will occur. One key lesson of this book so far is that your most reliable prediction will always be peace—a hostile one, maybe, with occasional skirmishes and killings, but not all-out fighting. Another lesson is that the five logics, when present, don't doom us to violence. Rather, when they are present, the five logics make war more *likely*, not a certainty. This means we must think probabilistically—this rivalry seems especially fragile, that one more stable. We must try to judge when our pilots are flying in narrow canyons or open skies, and peer ahead into the dim light to see whether the gorge widens or the weather worsens.

In doing so, we also need to recognize the importance of chance events but not get too distracted by them. Most accounts of war are filled with random human foibles, economic tumult, natural disasters, lucky coups, new and unforeseen technologies, and maybe even butterflies waving their wings. These all play a role. But blaming war on an idiosyncratic event or a person is a little like asking how the world's oldest person died and receiving the answer "the flu." It's true, but the virus wasn't really the issue. Chance events matter only when the fundamentals have left rivals with little room to maneuver. This means that, many times, war will seem to be in the error term. The error term is what's left over after you take account of all the major explanations. It's the little gusts of wind that buffet the pilot, the unexpected engine failure. Without them, we predict smooth flying, and most of the time that's what happens. But a large enough gust could crash the craft. Often, that's how the fighting first breaks out. But it's only because the five reasons pushed the two sides into such a fragile situation.[43]

The path to peace means focusing on these fundamentals. You can still respond to chance events. If a gust blows your craft toward the chasm's side, you steer away. But it's more important to get out of the fragile situation, to pull out of the narrow canyon, giving leaders some room to navigate, free of the risk that one error, one random bullet, or one terrible gust could crash their entire society. Fortunately, we know which direction to point them in. Stable and successful societies have traced a few promising paths.

PART II

THE PATHS TO PEACE

Chapter 7

INTERDEPENDENCE

Eureka used to call itself the pumpkin capital of the world, until the unfortunate day the processing plant moved to another corner of Illinois. But the town still produces students at Eureka College, a small Christian liberal arts school. Its most famous graduate first planted himself there in 1932. Fifty years later, he was back to address a new crop of graduates. Ronald Reagan was a year into his presidency, and the crowd that gathered to hear him speak overflowed the little town.

Reagan chose foreign affairs as his topic for the occasion—what to do about the Soviet Union. The Cold War was midway through its fourth decade. The policy of his predecessors—an uneasy truce called détente—was moribund and failing. It avoided war (that much could be said) but it froze in place an ever-present risk of mutually assured destruction.

Reagan wanted to end the nuclear threat hanging over the globe. The USSR was in decline, and so he also wanted a better deal for America, though he wasn't yet sure how to secure it. Still, Reagan had a guiding principle: "Peace is not the absence of conflict," he explained to his listeners that day, "it is the ability to handle conflict by peaceful means." Few statements better embody the ideas in this book so far.[1]

Here was a struggle where the stakes were nothing less than how to

organize human society—the same quarrel as Athens and Sparta millennia
before, only now on a global scale, with devastating firepower. By the 1980s,
the bombs assembled by either side could wipe out life on earth. The costs
of war were so huge, the bargaining range in the Cold War was literally the
entire pie. How could the West and the East *not* find agreement?

In his speech, Reagan was trying to remind Americans that it's always
better to deal than fight. Most Cold War leaders felt the same way. For
decades, they had managed to avoid direct confrontation. But while the
Cold War never went hot, the rivals came shockingly close to Armageddon
several times. Everyone knows about the Cuban missile crisis of 1962. Another crisis was less public. Early one morning in 1983, in a secret command
center outside Moscow, alarms began blaring. Five intercontinental ballistic
missiles were on their way from America, the readout declared. A few weeks
before, the Soviets had mistakenly shot down a South Korean passenger
aircraft, killing everyone on board. Reagan had also begun calling the Soviet
Union an evil empire. Was this, the Soviet duty officer wondered, a preemptive nuclear attack? Fortunately for us all, the officer wavered. It had to be a
glitch, he guessed, correctly. On a hunch, he called off the retaliatory strike.[2]

The history books overlook these quiet moments when war wasn't
waged. This one, however, was closer and more arbitrary than we'd like.
Near misses like these tell us something important: a fragile peace is a risky,
miserable place to dwell in. Even if all the incentives pointed toward compromise, the United States and the Soviet Union had narrowed the bargaining range to a sliver. Their unchecked leaders, ideological values, ambiguous
intentions, dangerously fluctuating power, and gross misconceptions imperiled the world.

So it's all fine and good for me to point out that war is seldom the best
strategy, or that the bitterest gangs, ethnic groups, and nations find peace
most of the time. But we should aspire to something better than living on
the edge of internecine violence, using the brazen threat of military power
to carve out better deals. It would be nice to have more room for error—to

have our societies' pilots soar in clear and open skies rather than perpetually race through treacherous chasms. This is what Reagan and, eventually, Mikhail Gorbachev wanted to do—to get beyond brinksmanship to a more resilient peace.

Successful societies have done exactly that. These final chapters walk through some of the ways that stable and peaceful societies have managed competition peacefully. I focus on four. The first is *interdependence*. So far, we've treated rivals as independent. They cared nothing for the satisfaction or suffering of their opponent. But successful societies (and the groups within them) aren't so sharply cleaved. They're intertwined economically, socially, and culturally. The other three I tackle in subsequent chapters. Institutional *checks and balances* show us that a stable society is one that compels leaders to listen to the many over the few. Peaceful societies have also created *rules and enforcement* organizations, like the law, the state, and social norms. Finally, successful societies have assembled a toolbox of *interventions* to help stop violence when it breaks out.[3]

These tools for competition management are better than at any time in human history. Recently, the cognitive scientist Steven Pinker brought together reams of findings from sociology, psychology, and other social science to argue that today, within their society, most people are less violent than ever before. By some measures, wars between societies have become less frequent as well.[4] I think we can understand this success through the pieces of part 2—a steady advance in interdependence, checks and balances, the state, and interventions that counter the five kinds of breakdowns and make normal compromise possible. Let's turn to the first of these.

INTERTWINING INTERESTS

The Babri Masjid, or Mosque of Babur, stood for nearly five hundred years in the northern Indian city of Ayodhya. Built of heavy stone, with three imposing gray domes, the building was an enduring source of strife. Hindus considered it holy, the birthplace of a divine hero. The more radical among them believed that Muslim rulers had desecrated the site by building the mosque centuries ago. The building must come down, Hindus insisted. Naturally, the Muslims refused. In the stalemate, the government decided it would be safest if no one used the building, and so for decades it sat vacant. By 1990, its walls were crusted with dirt and overgrown with brush.

The mosque proved to be a perfect issue for the budding Bharatiya Janata Party, however. The BJP represented a Hindu nationalist movement, one that aimed to entrench Hindu values in Indian law and everyday life. But the party had been struggling to build broad support, winning just two measly seats in the 1984 general elections. Then the BJP started campaigning against the Babri Masjid. Destroying it proved incredibly popular—a way to unite the Hindu nationalist vote with anti-Muslim invective. It became one of the BJP's most successful rallying cries.

In 1990, the BJP leader announced he would lead a grand procession across the country. It would start in the city of Somnath, on the far western coast, and wind through thousands of villages and cities across the nation, until it finally arrived at Ayodhya and the despised mosque. Thousands of Hindus joined the procession of vehicles as the party elites gave militant speeches in town after town. It soon become India's largest political movement, the mosque being a powerful symbol of everything they opposed.

Two years later, in 1992, the crowds were back in Ayodhya. A mob of Hindus at least one hundred thousand strong had assembled outside the mosque. They held iron rods, shovels, and sledgehammers. No one was ever able to prove that BJP leaders orchestrated what happened next. But we know the crowd leapt forward, pushing past hapless police, attacking the structure. In an immense cloud of gray dust, the mob tore the Babri Masjid down by hand.

In the days that followed, sectarian riots broke out across several Indian cities. No one knows exactly how many were killed. One estimate says two thousand people, mainly Muslims. For the BJP, it was a political turning point—an incredible vote getter. Today the party is India's most powerful

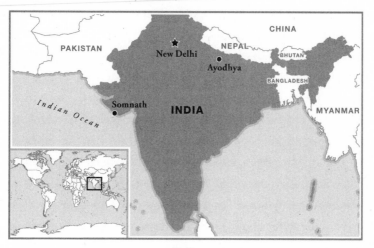

India

political force, and that day in Ayodhya is remembered as one of the most violent, but most important, stops along its journey to dominance.[5]

Of course, amid this spectacle, it's easy to forget that most Indian cities did not break out into violence that year (or any other). Take Somnath, for example, where the BJP leader launched his procession. There was no religious rioting there after the destruction of Babri Masjid. There seldom has been. What makes cities like Somnath different?

Enter Saumitra Jha. The economist had noticed that in ancient coastal cities like Somnath, Muslims and Hindus were socially integrated and economically interdependent. They'd long shared clinics, built interreligious associations, and run disaster and poverty relief organizations for mixed groups. They also started joint business ventures, and they specialized in complementary economic activities—one producing products, the other selling them abroad.

Jha traced these linkages back hundreds of years. In medieval times, Hindu coastal cities had encouraged foreign Muslim traders to settle down, even giving them grants of holy land to do so. That's because the Muslims had connections all over the Indian Ocean, especially the huge textile market that happened every year during the Hajj, the annual Islamic pilgrimage

to Mecca. In a medieval port city like Somnath, the presence of these traders opened new markets and opportunities.

Nowadays, Somnath's harbors have silted up. Today's ships also prefer
deeper, modern docks. But the age-old Hindu-Muslim interlinkages persist
in their social networks, business relationships, and other community institutions. The local communities report higher levels of intergroup trust.
Integration persisted.

As a result, today these medieval port cities have far less sectarian violence. In recent years, Jha found, former medieval ports have five times less
sectarian violence than similar coastal towns. When opportunistic elites
have tried to rile up the population and provoke riots, the integrated populations show little interest. Rather, in places like Somnath, they tend to punish belligerent leaders at the polls.[6]

ECONOMIC INTERDEPENDENCE

To understand what's going on, think back to the pies we split earlier in this
book. We always made the same assumption: groups weighed only the costs
and benefits to their own side. Now think about what happens if the other
group is your business partner, or if you've lent them money. They could also
be your employees or employer, or the main market for your goods. Perhaps
the people from that group make a crucial input into your enterprise. Now
their death, destruction, or disempowerment makes a material difference to
you. It affects your bottom line because you are economically intertwined.

This has a straightforward effect in our model—it raises the costs of
fighting, and the bargaining range is wider than it otherwise would be.
Before, the wedge was $20 wide because one side expected to win a damaged
pie. They didn't care if their rival lost everything. Now, however, the pie is
larger when both groups cooperate, and smaller if they don't. If you launch
a war and win, you not only destroy the usual share of the pie, you also lay
claim to a smaller pie because the complementarities with the other side are

lost. In former medieval ports like Somnath, the bargaining range has expanded to look something like this:

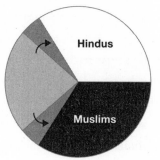

Interdependence doesn't eliminate the risk of war. There could still be a commitment problem, uncertainty, or unchecked leaders that push our two groups to fight. But because of entwined material interests, these forces must now overcome even more powerful incentives for compromise than usual. The gravitational pull of peace has grown stronger.

THIS IDEA ISN'T NEW. IN 1748, ONE OF THE GREAT POLITICAL PHILOSOPHERS OF THE EN-lightenment, Montesquieu, proclaimed that "commerce is a cure for the most destructive prejudices." As a general rule, he went on, "wherever the ways of man are gentle, there is commerce; and wherever there is commerce, there the ways of men are gentle." A generation later, Thomas Paine, a political writer and revolutionary, argued that international trade "would extirpate the system of war." Decades later, in 1848, the philosopher John Stuart Mill described commerce as "rapidly rendering war obsolete, by strengthening and multiplying the personal interests which act in natural opposition to it." Their faith in the pacifying effects of industry fed their belief in a liberal economic order.[7]

Commerce matters for peace for a few reasons. War is almost always rotten for business, even if your economy isn't entwined with the enemy's.

It's hard to make money when rioters burn your shop, submarines destroy your ships, and bombers level your factories. Also, in the modern world, growth often depends on massive investments of skills and financial capital. For this you need to foster the trust and cooperation of investors. You also need your population to devote time and money to education, in the hopes of a future return. All these people want a stable environment, not a society on the brink of civil war. Some political scientists call this the capitalist peace.[8]

Being economically intertwined is an added commercial incentive for peace on top of these normal ones. Like the Hindus and Muslims in Somnath, when the enterprises of one side are wrapped up with that of their rival, these entrepreneurs, financiers, and industrialists have a stake in peace with the rival group. The same logic applies to nations. The fact that China is the second largest holder of US debt as well as a massive trading partner has surely put the brakes on aggressive actions by both sides. What's more, other countries have a stake in the pair getting along. Integrated capital and goods markets mean that damage inflicted on one economy travels through the global economy, giving every trading partner and investor a reason to put pressure on the rivals to avoid tensions and fighting. Integration like this may be why, in the last half century, greater trade flows between two countries are correlated with a lower risk of war.[9]

Unfortunately, we don't have good natural experiments in the international arena, and so it's hard to establish just how capitalist the peace really is. But while you should maintain some skepticism, some of the evidence at lower levels is more persuasive. The medieval ports are one example. Jha also ran a more controlled study, this time in the Middle East. He teamed up with an Israeli economist, Moses Shayo, to see what would happen if Israelis became more aware of how much their economy is wrapped up with Palestinians and peace.

They did this by getting Israelis to trade online before a hotly contested election. Jha and Shayo used a marketing company to get 1,350 people to apply for a study on investor behavior. Half won the lottery to join, getting free shares to trade in an investing app. People started with a portfolio of Israeli and Palestinian stocks, and for the next few weeks they could buy or sell whatever they liked. Typically, regular Israelis like these were insulated from the economic costs of conflict. But watching the market, they gradually grew more aware of the ups and downs, including how markets responded to angry political rhetoric and confrontations. After the election, the marketing firm sent everyone a seemingly unrelated political survey. Those who traded were a fifth more likely to vote for a party proposing peace negotiations. The change was wider than the margin between parties in most elections. If it were nationwide, it might have been big enough to tip the balance of power.[10]

IF ECONOMIC INTERDEPENDENCE WIDENS THE BARGAINING RANGE BETWEEN RIVALS, however, this means the opposite is also true: people are more likely to wage wars when they are economically insulated from one another. For instance, I said that war is rotten for business, but Americans don't always appreciate this fact. One reason, I think, is that their wars have been fought, for the most part, on foreign soils. Many lives were still lost. But US factories stayed open during the nation's greatest battles, and the average American did not experience the full costs of war. Quite the contrary. Defense spending, some argue, has led to American technology and dominance.[11] When superpowers and empires feel neither the personal nor the economic pain of war, then naturally they're more likely to go on foreign military adventures.

Another classic example is oil republics. In general, oil doesn't care if you oppress your people or if you attack your neighbors. It keeps gushing. A ruler doesn't need the consent of the governed to sell petroleum. If anything, it's the reverse: oil feeds authoritarianism. It's the perfect resource for dictators, for it's concentrated in an easily controlled space, and monitoring and capturing the wealth it generates is easy. As a result, oil-rich countries tend to be more elite driven and autocratic, and thus probably more vulnerable to conflict. These resources are the opposite of our interdependent ideal. For peace, you want a diverse economy, with interlinked sectors, and owners who feel pain not gain when the bombs begin to drop.[12]

SOCIALLY INTERLINKED

We've been dwelling on economic linkages, but groups can be socially entwined as well, tied to and caring about people on the other side of a cleavage. Some societies have taken this advice literally, marrying their daughters to the sons of their enemies. For hundreds of years, European monarchs knit their empires and the continent together in a tangle of dynastic marriages. Often, their explicit goal was to end a conflict or head off a looming one. In part they were successful. Polities with related monarchs were somewhat less likely to fight one another.[13]

Intermarriage might work for monarchs, crime families, villages, and tribes, but it's probably not a path to twenty-first-century global peace. Instead, I want to focus on a much more routine, everyday kind of social intertwining, one that comes from having intermingling and interlocking social groups and identities. Political scientists and sociologists see this as one of the essential ingredients for a stable pluralistic society.[14]

A mild but important source of interlinking is simple social interaction. Consider two towns, each with Catholic and Protestant residents. One town grows up with the two groups intermingled, sharing the same blocks, schools, and clubs. The other, for chance reasons, evolves with the groups more separate. If an issue suddenly divides Catholics and Protestants all over the region, which community do we expect to be more resilient? The socially integrated one. Their interactions create affections for one another (the theory goes) and raises the cost of aggression. The bargaining range will widen, because Catholics internalize some of the harm to Protestants, and vice versa, just like the economic case above. When we do not have these social ties, meanwhile, we become polarized from our rivals. It doesn't mean we go to war. We just look like the wholly independent, antagonistic rivals in our original pie-splitting model.

Social interaction should widen the circle of people we care about. The idea goes back at least as far as Adam Smith and his philosophical treatise, *The Theory of Moral Sentiments*. He thought our circle of sympathy would grow to include those sharing the same physical space and those we interact with repeatedly, from business to the ordinary exchange of praise and shame. Smith believed commerce would be pacifying because of this social aspect, not just the direct material stakes.[15]

This cuts both ways, however. As someone grows socially distant from us, our sympathy erodes. We're less altruistic. If we see them experiencing suffering, our brains don't trigger the same pain. When it's a competitor, our sympathy declines further. Their pain might even generate pleasure. From Rwanda to Germany to India we've seen examples of leaders who use propaganda to foster this resentment and blind hatred. Sympathy erosion is a powerful political tool in their hands.[16]

It should be harder to rile up the mob, however, when we are tied to the other side socially. Let's return to India. It isn't just Somnath that avoided sectarian riots. Most cities avoid this violence, especially the ones where Hindus and Muslims are socially entwined. India has a long tradition of intergroup associations, from trade unions to professional associations to sports leagues to the marketplace. The political scientist Ashutosh Varshney spent years studying this civic life. "At moments of crisis," he found, "these organizations policed neighborhoods, killed rumors, provided information to the local administration, and facilitated communication between communities in times of tension." The everyday contact mattered too: "The point is not to get a Hindu fellow to like his Muslim shopkeeper," Varshney likes to say, "it's to get the fellow to recognize his shopkeeper is a good enough guy that he doesn't want to go kill a bunch of Muslims tomorrow." Varshney calls this systematized social interaction an institutionalized peace system and argues that (where it evolved) it countered the institutionalized riot systems that opportunistic political leaders kept stoked and ready.[17]

The idea that a social interaction and an integrated civic life can foster understanding and peace has led to a huge number of "social contact" programs. All over the world, governments and nonprofits try to bring to-gether members of antagonistic groups in sports leagues, schools, and neigh-borhood clubs. A bunch of these have been researched: a Nigerian training school that brought together Christians and Muslims in the riot-prone city of Kaduna; an Indian cricket league that included men of different castes; and an Iraqi soccer league that involved Muslims as well as Christians dis-placed by the Islamic State (to name just a few). These are mostly short in-terventions, with young people, and so they're not the same as generations of civic interaction. Still, contact seems to be pacifying. Across dozens of con-trolled trials, most find more modest social cohesion and less discrimination.[18]

Intuitively, more intensive contact—generations of interaction—should have much larger effects. We don't have much evidence on this, but what we do have suggests that it's far from automatic. The kind of institutionalized peace system Varshney found in some Indian cities needs more than simple contact to develop.

One piece of evidence comes from an ambitious government program in Indonesia. To forge a national identity after independence, the govern-ment took two million volunteers from the large inner islands of Java and Bali and relocated them to almost a thousand new villages in the outer is-lands. There they mixed with one another as well as with local settlers. Some villages were more mixed than others, however, mostly by chance, providing a kind of natural experiment. Among the newly settled places, having lots of ethnic groups led to wider use of the national language, more interethnic marriage, more trust between the groups, and more community engage-ment. But when villages were settled by very few groups, the effects went in the other direction—the ethnic groups became more polarized and antago-nistic. This suggests that there's nothing automatic about contact expanding one's circle of sympathy. Simply putting groups in proximity and closer com-petition may be counterproductive without the civic ties, organizations, and economic linkages that characterize peaceful cities.[19]

Our social interlinking doesn't come from intermingling and contact alone. The antidote to polarization comes from overlapping group memberships and loyalties. This is possible because every one of us has more than one identity. Most of us associate with an ethnicity, but we also think of ourselves in terms of a language, a class, a religion, a political party, a region, and a nationality. In some societies, these identities line up and reinforce one another rather than crosshatch. That's a problem. Take a country like Uganda. In the war-torn Acholi region, where I began this book, most of the people share an ethnicity, a language, a religion, a set of geographic interests, and their livelihoods (in terms of crops and livestock), plus formative political experiences like the war. If you go to another part of the country, like Ankole in the southwest, they, too, have multiple identities, but only a few of them will overlap with the Acholi. That's one reason Uganda is such a polarized place. The Acholi and the Ankole don't have many identities in common. And so they vote for different parties and prefer candidates of their own group. The country also has a long history of ethnic competition and occasional wars.[20]

This isn't true everywhere in Africa, however. To see this, let me tell you about Mali. In its southern core, identities overlap. As a result, politics are less polarized along ethnic lines than in Uganda. One reason goes back to a grand social experiment eight centuries old.

Sundiata Keita founded the Mali Empire along the Niger River, in West Africa, in the thirteenth century. If his realm existed today, its boundaries would stretch from Senegal in the west nearly all the way to Nigeria in the east. Having assembled his domain, however, the young emperor had a problem. Then as now, empires must stitch together polarized peoples, most of whom will never interact. According to oral history and tradition, Keita introduced a legal code, one handed down over the generations. Though unwritten, it was a constitution, one of the oldest in the world—a set of rules under which his peoples would live. Some call it the Manden Charter, others the Kurukan Fuga. It guaranteed an individual right to life and freedom from physical harm. It established the rules by which the heads of clans and age groups would be selected and succeeded. It established certain property rights and outlawed the mistreatment of enslaved peoples. Its whole purpose was to promote peace within the empire's peoples and between them.

With the charter, Keita also created a new overlapping social identity using surnames that would stitch different groups in the empire together. Today it's called a joking kinship or cousinage. Under the rules, for example, someone named Keita (an ethnically Malinke surname) and someone named Coulibaly (a Bambara surname) are "cousins." Typically, their surnames share a common meaning. If they meet one another, despite being strangers, the custom means that their surnames give them a basis for affinity. To signify this, they insult each other with a standard set of jokes. Basically, cousinage is an informal alliance with people from ethnic groups far away, based on related last names, that gives them the right to tease one another. It goes to show how humans have an amazing ability to construct group identities out of the smallest things.

And it works. Cousinage pacifies politics in Mali to this day. Confronted with a politician to vote for, an average Malinke is just as happy to vote for someone with a cousinage name among the Bambara as they are to support someone with a Malinke name. Joking kinship's no panacea. Ethnic violence still happens. Still, the crosscutting linkage has helped to depolarize ethnic politics in Mali relative to others in the region.[21] It's an example of a pattern we see more generally: places where ethnic groups are more geographically dispersed and intermingled seem to be less polarized and conflict prone than the ones where the groups are concentrated together. Places where religion and class cut across ethnic groups also seem to be less violent than the places where the different identities line up.[22]

Another kind of crosscutting identity is nationalism. National prestige, growth, and other success can strengthen large group bonds and weaken the clannish ones that divide us. A Malinke and a Bambara can both identify as a Malian, and potentially find more sympathy for one another as members of a common group. This typically happens slowly and is hard to observe. But one group of economists found a microcosm of this process in soccer. They gathered survey data from thirty-seven thousand Africans in twenty-five countries, and looked at how people responded differently if they were surveyed right after the national football team played. In the days after a national match, people identified more strongly with their national identity and less with their ethnicity. They also said they trusted members of other ethnic groups more. This was all driven by victories, because when the national team lost, there was no change in national identification.

You might think this sounds trivial, but soccer wins and the nationalism it engendered had real effects on violence. The same economists looked at countries where the national team just qualified for the Africa Cup of Nations, and compared them to the countries whose team narrowly missed qualification. In the next six months, the countries that qualified had substantially lower interethnic violence.[23]

Of course, even if national identities reduce conflict between a nation's subgroups, nationalism simply offers another basis for parochialism and competition with other national groups. We never really escape our groupishness and talents for polarization, unless we start to develop sympathy and affinity for everyone. Fortunately, in recent centuries, most societies have widened who they identify with.

MORALLY AND CULTURALLY INTERLINKED

Sundiata Keita realized something fundamental: our social categories are fluid and malleable. They can emerge over time, from trade, through sustained interaction, or from public policy. That means politicians like Keita can try to mobilize and harden identities for good or ill. They can even manufacture brand-new ones. Indeed, even ethnicity is something that got constructed over time. The idea of being French, Acholi, White, or Latino is not a timeless social category. Most of these identities emerged, solidified, and were manipulated in the past century and a half. They continue to evolve.[24]

To a large extent these identities are images in our minds—they are "imagined communities," to use a phrase from the political scientist Benedict Anderson. And one of the most profound changes in the past few hundred years is that these mental communities have gotten bigger and bigger.

Over that time, people began to think less in terms of clans and more in terms of nations, then of broad civilizations, and ultimately of the human race. Each time people extended the bounds of sympathy to a wider group, without direct economic or social interaction.[25]

For example, in the distant past, the average French citizen didn't care if their empire waged war on a small and faraway nation, whose people had different gods, customs, and skin color. These "others" were distant not only in a physical sense but in a moral sense, too—uncivilized, perhaps even subhuman to French eyes. But then a new ideology emerged—the idea of all humans as equal and deserving of dignity and self-determination. Fewer and fewer French subjects were willing to ignore the suffering and humiliation of those faraway peoples. Today, many French people consider themselves part of the same human community as these others, even though they've never met. They are morally and philosophically entwined. Now, any attack by the French state on foreigners will cause a French citizen some degree of distress. That means the French government will find foreign pie grabbing and wars harder to sustain.

The philosopher Michael Ignatieff called this the Rights Revolution. The cognitive scientist Steven Pinker called it the Humanitarian Revolution. They both meant a process by which people began to think of themselves as autonomous individuals, detached from a community identity. Alongside this arose the belief that all humans were equally deserving of dignity and held certain natural rights.

Historians like Lynn Hunt and philosophers like Fonna Forman-Barzilai have traced this individualism and the idea of human rights back to ancient Greece, early Christian faith, and Roman law. Everyone agrees, however, that these ideas flourished most in the period we now call the Enlightenment. "Sometime between 1689 and 1776," Hunt describes, "rights that had been viewed most often as the rights of a particular people—freeborn English men, for example—were transformed into human rights, universal natural rights." Hunt chose the year 1689 for the English Bill of Rights—a document outlining the ancient entitlements and liberties all *Englishmen* shared.

There was not yet a universal circle of sympathy. By 1776, however, the American Declaration of Independence proclaimed something different—that all *men* are created equal and have inalienable rights.

Of course, there was a gulf between these noble words and the slavery, colonialism, and discrimination that both countries engaged in. And the terminology still overlooked women. But still, a large and growing group believed in one equal humanity. That era bred the first large-scale campaigns against slavery, torture, colonialism, and violent punishment. Within two centuries, those noble words would no longer be quite as hypocritical.[26]

Why did these ideas and ideals spread so quickly? Hunt traces them to new ways to read, listen, and gaze. The explosion of novels and painted pictures gave readers and watchers a window into the minds of other people, she argues, cutting across distance and social boundaries, recognizing their shared inner feeling, their common humanity, and thus building empathy. A larger imagined community. If she is right, then today's music, videos, and social media that cross national and ethnic lines may do much of the same work, collapsing borders. Scholars like Pinker and the philosopher Peter Singer also argue for the importance of human reason, and the contagiousness of these new ideas. The age of enlightenment constructed a coherent, persuasive philosophy and worldview, one that bred technological and economic advance. The ideals spread along with this success.

Another possible channel is commerce. Enlightenment thinkers like Montesquieu, Paine, and Mill were enthusiastic about widespread trade not necessarily because of the material integration it fostered. Rather, they thought that exchange enlarged our moral and cultural circle. Commerce had a pacifying effect on humanity's worst passions, they believed, a kind of psychological civilizing process.[27]

These achievements—the Enlightenment and human rights—are part of a pattern that countless philosophers and historians have observed over time: humanity's expanding circle of sympathy. It doesn't move forward automatically or inexorably. Counterexamples are easy to find. But it does seem to be a trend. Why is a huge and unsettled question. Whether novels, contagious ideals, or commerce drove the recognition of human rights is hard to say. I think easier, cheaper communications and travel must be part of the story, however, for they underlie all three. For our purposes, it doesn't much matter. Only the outcome does. This shift extended the bounds of sympathy to include the interests of the other, and thus made fighting even less acceptable than before.

Chapter 8

CHECKS AND BALANCES

Amos Sawyer speaks softly, often letting the young people around him carry the conversation. Portly, with close-cropped white hair and a goatee, the professor has a kind, grandfatherly air. Unfortunately, Sawyer had to flee his home country of Liberia in the mid-1990s, amid a long-running war. He landed at Indiana University in Bloomington. Elinor Ostrom—a longtime friend and a future Nobel Prize winner—had invited him there to teach and to write his books.

At Bloomington, Sawyer met a graduate student studying violence in northern Uganda—Jeannie Annan. When she began her doctorate, Sawyer's homeland was in violent flames. But by the time Jeannie and I were finishing our study of Uganda's war, however, Liberia was experiencing its first peace in more than a decade. One day, Sawyer announced that he was headed home. A new president, Ellen Sirleaf, Africa's first female head of state, had asked for his help. Jeannie asked him what she could do, and he replied, "Come and see." So, the summer of 2008, we moved to Monrovia.

After fourteen years of war and instability, Liberia's capital was shattered. The heat, humidity, swamps, and tropical forest reminded me of Florida at the height of summer, but the resemblance ended there. Monrovia's streets had more potholes than pavement. Half the large hotels and government buildings were empty, gutted, burned-out hulks. The United Nations and the fledgling government had rebuilt and occupied a few structures. The rest were makeshift, multistory villages full of squatters, crouched under ragged, colorful tarps.

Despite the dysfunction, the mood of the capital was hopeful. Fifteen thousand peacekeepers from places like Pakistan, Nepal, and Nigeria patrolled the country. The planes were full of Liberians coming home at last, with bold dreams of starting a business or simply helping out. A skilled and relatively honest government was slowly taking back control. Monrovians began to believe in peace at last.

A council of Liberian cabinet ministers and heads of foreign agencies were trying to entrench the new order. They wanted to address the roots of conflict—a phrase you heard a lot in Liberia those days. Every week the group met around an enormous conference table in a freezing, air-conditioned room at the Ministry of Internal Affairs. Jeannie and I sat in. They debated dozens of projects and ideas, from jobs for disaffected ex-fighters to reconciliation programs for ethnic enemies.

Yet the one root I heard almost no one discuss, on that council or elsewhere, was Liberia's incredible centralization of power. Nor did I ever see a project cross the council table that proposed to disperse decision-making and empower other political actors. National ministers all had a stake in keeping power at the national level, after all. Why give authority away? As for the foreign agencies, they were all tasked with dealing with a central sovereign state. None had the mandate to deal with local counties, civil society, or cities. Nor did they want to deal with layers of squabbling government and regional power brokers. Besides, they liked the current president. Sirleaf had been a capable World Bank and UN official, and seemed to have all the right intentions. And even if Liberia did deconcentrate power a little, why would that promote peace? To many people, it sounded like a recipe for more fractiousness, not less.

Sawyer disagreed. He found the ministers and foreign agencies frustratingly shortsighted. With all the formal power centered in one office, and a

weak civil society, "democracy" in Liberia meant the ability to elect a dictator every six years. That meant there was competition for the number one
office, and not much else in the way of checks on power. For now, the diplomats were happy to see someone like Sirleaf in unfettered command for
six years. Sawyer admired her too. But what if Liberia got unlucky again?
he asked. What if the next election, with the next roll of the dice, the country put another callous warlord in place? A system like Liberia's was like a
huge game of Russian roulette. Most fragile states play the same dangerous sport.

As the head of Liberia's new constitutional commission, Sawyer wanted
to change the game. He wanted town and county governments to be able to
tax and spend, just like provinces and cities can in so many developed countries. He wanted local mayors to be elected by citizens, not appointed by the
president. He wanted the Senate and the House to have real constitutional
authority. He wanted the bureaucracy to be more independent of the current
ruler rather than serve every executive whim. And he wanted supranational
bodies—such as unions of West African states—to have some say over economic policy and human rights monitoring. This, he argued, was the path
to peace and prosperity.

Sawyer could back his argument up with academic studies, and he could
point to the lessons from centuries of constitutional experimentation in the
world's most stable and successful countries. But Sawyer's credibility and
authority also came from his political experience, for he was a former head
of state. After rebels invaded Liberia in 1989, exiled elites gathered in the
Gambia, a sliver of a country in West Africa. Each one represented a different district or political party. As rebel and government forces fought rapa-
ciously for control of Liberia, the exiles selected a humble and principled
scholar to be interim president. Sawyer would last four years in Monrovia
before a cabal of warlords managed to squeeze him out of the executive office.

As a politician, however, Sawyer came from a different mold than these
men of guns and action. He was unfalteringly modest, for one. Jeannie remembers the first time he gave a talk at Bloomington. He introduced himself

as a professor and began his lecture. *"And,"* Elinor Ostrom had to yell out, "you were *president* of Liberia." More importantly, however, a life of activism, scholarship, and finally leadership gave Sawyer an uncommon perspective. He didn't want to promote and empower good leaders like himself or Sirleaf. He wanted to restrain them. In a series of books and articles, he laid out the root cause of failure in so many societies. Unconstrained, overcentralized rule has been the fundamental root of conflict in Liberia, the continent, and much of the world, he argued. Checks and balances were the solutions.[1]

WHY A STABLE SOCIETY HAS MANY CENTERS

One reason for dividing power and holding decision-makers accountable ought to be obvious by now: it gets leaders to internalize the costs of fighting. This addresses our first big reason for wars: unchecked interests. What we haven't discussed, however, is that spreading out power also addresses the other four reasons we fight.

Take intangible incentives for fighting, like glory or vengeance. When power is spread out to many people and arms of government, decisions no longer hinge on a ruler's idiosyncratic tastes. Elected prime ministers and presidents might be just as lustful for glory as tyrants, but they have a harder time taking their nations to war to satisfy that desire. The same is true for misperceptions. Leaders are human. In a personalized system of power, a nation is at the mercy of the bias (or lunacy) of a cabal. When power brokers are restrained and decision-making is institutionalized, however, a ruler's mistakes are modulated by other actors.

More open systems transmit information and reduce uncertainty too. People can signal their support and strength in countless ways: at the polls, on the streets, through a vibrant press, or by garnering likes and retweets. Checked governments are often more transparent as well. Waging politics in the open reduces the noise between nations, and with it the chances one can bluff the other. It also reduces the uncertainty between groups in a nation. (This is why so many authoritarian regimes hold elections they plan to fix, or allow public dissent that they can censor when needed. It's not just for appearances. They reduce uncertainty, giving autocrats a sense of what people or ideas are popular. This helps them adjust their rule and repression accordingly, avoiding revolution.) The institutionalized autocracies that minimize information problems can avoid an awful lot of domestic conflict.[2]

Last, checked leaders are not as prone to commitment problems. That's because power sharing and other institutions help them make credible promises to rivals inside and outside the group. To see why, consider an all-powerful president. A charismatic exile threatens her with invasion. The upstart wants a share of the pie without having to violently fight for it. That's the usual way that political deals get made—from one side threatening to burn the house down. But what can an all-powerful ruler do to placate this challenger? Promise a seat in the legislature? Control of a ministry? Leadership over one of the country's many security forces? What's to keep the president from reneging a few months later and throwing the challenger in jail?

Throughout history, however, *some* ruling cabals found ways to make credible commitments in the form of charters and parliaments and other shackles on power. They did well for themselves. Early English rulers were some of the most successful. There, constraints began with feudal councils in the eleventh century. This was followed by the Magna Carta in the thirteenth century, the first parliaments in the fourteenth century, the Glorious Revolution in the seventeenth century (finally establishing parliamentary supremacy), and then successive waves of extending the vote until every adult in the nation had a share of power. All these institutions helped rulers make credible promises to share power over time, enabling more peaceful bargains between a ruler and their populace. In some cases, a constrained king could also treat with other nations more reliably. After all, a deal with a despot lasts only while the tyrant rules; one with a parliament, in a nation of laws, outlives the current ruler.[3]

In sum, dividing power and holding the deciders accountable can reduce all five risks of war. You might think I mean democracy, but all this time I've avoided that term for a few reasons. For one thing, it means different things to different people. To most, it means holding elections. But "one person, one vote" and majority rule are shallow descriptions of a strong and stable democratic system. Also, electing the president is not enough to solve the problems of centralized power that can lead to war. As the example of Liberia shows, even a clean election can simply give people the power to put in a temporary dictator. It doesn't necessarily stop privileged dealmaking by a winning coalition of power brokers. The preferences and passions of the president can still drive foreign policy. And it's a system still prone to commitment problems—maybe more so because an all-powerful executive can't bind their successors, and because power in a concentrated system can be hard to split with a domestic rival. So, while a temporary tyrant is far better than a permanent one, it's not enough.[4]

Instead, I want us to focus on a narrower idea: distributing power through checks and balances. A system that gives voice and influence to opposite and rival interests makes it hard for a victorious coalition to impose its will on the rest. A system where power is divided is also one that more flexibly adjusts to shifts in the might of one group over the other. Advanced democracies do this, and it's one of their greatest sources of stability. But many non-democracies also check the vagaries of their leaders. This is because not all autocracies are personalized—there is tremendous variation. Some are highly institutionalized. Their central leaders are still formidable, but power is also vested in a party apparatus, regional politicians, an independent military, wealthy tycoons, or vast bureaucracies. They are still tragically unfree, but as we'll see, the checking and balancing makes them stable.

MY FOCUS ON CHECKS AND BALANCES ISN'T A NEW STRATEGY. IT REFLECTS A TRADITION of political thought centuries in the making. Sawyer's fear, that concentrated power would eventually give Liberia a belligerent tyrant, is exactly what worried the designers of the first modern democracy—the United States of America.

With victory over the British, America's founders had to devise a way to preserve the republic from future tyrants. Luckily, George Washington had little desire to become America's emperor. He opposed calls for the presidency to become a lifetime appointment, or for the executive to be addressed as His Majesty. But how could America avoid losing the game of leader roulette in the future? How to prevent a more ambitious and unprincipled leader from taking over? The new nation's founders were obsessed with this risk. They had little faith that voters would deliver a thoughtful and modest ruler all the time. Soon enough, a demagogue and usurper would enter the office.

One answer came from another Virginian politician, James Madison. No one would ever confuse Madison for Washington. Whereas the general was tall, robust, and imposing, the younger Madison was small, less than five feet tall, awkward, weak of voice, and chronically ill. But no one thought, read, stumped, cajoled, wrote, or ranted for the new US Constitution more than he did.

Like the Enlightenment thinkers who influenced them, Madison held a dim view of human nature. One of his maxims was "All men having power ought to be mistrusted." Another was "Any ruler, or body of rulers, will aggrandize himself or itself if given the chance—even elected rulers."

Because of this, the thirteen states first tried operating without a true national executive. For most of the 1780s the president was a largely ceremonial role, intended to serve one year. (They even chose the title "president" to imply someone who would merely preside over the legislature, not an independent authority.) It quickly became clear, however, that to manage foreign conflict and domestic insurrection the republic needed a real executive office. So the framers set out to redesign the country's institutions to balance two main concerns: the need for effective government versus a distrust of concentrated power.[5]

Like Amos Sawyer centuries later, the quiet, unglamorous Madison used his presence in the Constitutional Convention, Congress, and the popular press to agitate for a system of checks and balances. Yes, there would need to be an executive office. But Madison wanted to diffuse power over many layers of government, each having little to do with appointing the members of the others. "Ambition must be made to counteract ambition," he wrote.[6]

Every schoolchild learns the most common check and balance: division into the three branches of government: the executive, the legislature, and the judiciary. But it's a mistake to stop carving up power here. You can also decentralize to other levels of government, giving local and regional authorities the right to tax, spend, and regulate. Another is to foster an independent bureaucracy—the so-called deep state—insulated from elected politicians by procedure and norms of professionalism, and hence a source of continuity and counterbalance to party politics. In addition, to decentralize power you can push some responsibilities up—to authorities bigger than the nation. National politicians can be checked and balanced by commitments between societies—treaties, international organizations, and other agreements and associations. Finally, there are all the organizations, formal and informal, outside the government that lobby, organize, and protest.[7]

Political scientists call this arrangement polycentric governance—a government with many independent hubs of power and decision-making. Polycentrism goes beyond constitutional design, however. Checks and balances don't just come from de jure power—formal rules and institutional design. They also come from the way de facto power is divided. By this I mean the ability to shape the behavior of others without formal authority, law, or even elections. We've been thinking in terms of de facto power throughout this book, every time we talked about bargaining. I see three main sources of de facto power in society. I call them the three Ms: military, mobilizational, and material might.

Military might doesn't need much explanation. The American framers knew how much that kind of power mattered, and how it shouldn't fall into too few hands. So, to check a centralized federal army, Madison proposed that each state should have a militia, and that the constitution preserve their right to carry arms. America, like other nations, has also made its military apparatus polycentric by requiring congressional approval for wars and war budgets, dividing the armed forces into many branches, and fostering a tradition of civilian control over the military.

Then we get to mobilizational might—the ability to raise public consciousness, to shift norms, to get voters to the polls, to shut down the factories with a walkout, to put people on the streets and in the squares, to chastise and embarrass officials. A society with more distributed mobilizational power is one where no one authority controls the newspapers or the airwaves; where an educated public has many civic organizations to coordinate collective actions; where ethnic and religious groups can still incite their followers, but no one leader can marshal the passions of all. Getting people out to vote is only one source of mobilizational power, and in many countries it's not even the most important one.

Last, we come to the material. Are the means of production owned by many or few? A society like the northern states of colonial America, where agriculture and industry favored smallholder farms and workshops, has more distributed wealth, and is inherently more equal and polycentric. Compare that to an economy based on plantations, mines, or oil, where ownership and wealth are concentrated. Places with these resources tend to be more unequal and autocratic—the opposite of polycentric.[8]

Altogether, checked and balanced societies are not just ones where the rules spread influence, but where these everyday sources of power are controlled by the many.

THE POLYCENTRIC PEACE

All this adds up to a compelling theory—that more constrained societies are more peaceful. Testing it is hard. Even the first and simplest step, measuring a society's checks and balances, is challenging, especially because so many constraints are informal and unwritten. Also, we don't have controlled experiments. When rulers become more yoked and accountable, other things tend to change at the same time—there are more elections, more economic development, and more trade. Still, several patterns are consistent with the idea that more checked and balanced groups are less likely to wage war with others or dissolve in rebellion.

Most important, the regimes likeliest to attack their enemies seem to be narrow dictatorships and military juntas, while the ones least likely to launch wars are democracies and the institutionalized autocracies. In other words, it's the places ruled by strongmen with few checks that appear to be the most warlike with neighbors. Correlations like these come from huge databases that pair every country in the world with every other, where for each year they indicate whether a pair fought or not. Researchers test their theories of war by coding up some new variable (like the kind of regime) and seeing whether it correlates with war. They try to control for other variables, like trade and income levels, to increase our confidence that it's not a spurious result.

The political scientist Jessica Weeks coded different autocratic regime types, for instance, to show that not all authoritarians are alike. Personalist dictators and military juntas are the most belligerent kinds of government. Another political scientist, Seung-Whan Choi, tried to measure constraints more directly. He found that de jure divisions of power correlate with less conflict. When presidents must answer to legislative congressional bodies, or share more powers with them, he found they tend to be more peaceful.[9]

This is related to a famous idea called the democratic peace. This dates to at least 1795, to the philosopher Immanuel Kant, who said that if rulers needed the consent of the governed to go to war, they'd weigh the decision more carefully. And it's true: when scholars have done their statistical analyses, they've found that democracies almost never attack one another. When they do go to war, it's against autocracies (and even then, the democracies rarely initiate the fighting). Some democracies do support wars in other nations—proxy wars, funding for a guerrilla movement, or arms for a repressive allied government. In all of these cases, however, the victims of these conflicts are foreign, and have no way to hold the leaders of the democratic country to account.[10]

Yet even though we call it the democratic peace, my hunch is that it's the polycentricity of these places that matters, not just the elections. This goes back to the fact that institutionalized autocracies also don't launch many wars against other countries. Jessica Weeks points to countries like China, where power is widely spread through a large political organization (the Communist Party), powerful bosses, influential firms, and many levels of regional and local government. These societies are, in many respects, polycentric, even if they don't elect their governments. While not as directly accountable to their citizens as in advanced democracies, governments in institutionalized autocracies still face a public that isn't predisposed to attacking enemy nations, and leaders fear the consequences of public ire.

Another reason comes from looking at places that experience civil wars and rebellions. Once again, the studies have real weaknesses. We don't have many natural experiments. But the strongly institutionalized countries, both autocratic and democratic, seem to be the most stable, while the more personalist regimes are more prone to dissolve. Remember chapter 5 and the commitment problem inherent in civil wars: when power is centralized, governments cannot persuade internal challengers to give up their arms. This may be why countries with more constraints on the government are less likely to have long and repeated internal conflicts. This is also why so many ethnically and religiously diverse countries avoid majoritarian rule, and choose more consensus-based forms of government that are more decentralized and allow power sharing. This ethnic and geographic power sharing seems to be a stabilizing force.[11]

Finally, some researchers have tried to peer into specific cases, collecting data on shifts in de jure and de facto power. This research is young but for the most part it tells us that it's possible to improve accountability, checks, and peace in the margin. But how? If you live in a dictatorship, you don't just drop a suggestion in the complaints box outside the presidential palace. How do societies get to strong local government, the separation of powers, and bargaining power more widely held?

THE PATH TO A MORE CHECKED SOCIETY

Among all the volumes written on constraints and democratization, one answer reverberates through them all: checks and balances were achieved gradually and through struggle. Gradually, when technology, economic development, or circumstance gave the mass people a morsel more de facto power—material, mobilizational, or military—they used it to wring concessions from their leaders. This might be an institutional tweak, binding the ruler's hands just a little more. At other times, a slice of the disenfranchised was granted a vote—just enough to ward off rebellion, and no more. The Nigerian political scientist Claude Ake put it nicely: "Democracy cannot be given," he said, "it must be seized."[12]

Some people find it dispiriting to think that checks and balances come slowly and through struggle. Another way to look at it, however, is as countless opportunities for more equality and peace on the margin—little changes to the de jure institutions, little shifts in de facto power, that societies grab bit by bit. This is a scale and ambition that activists, civic organizations, and foreign democracy promoters can work on. I find that heartening, and this piecemeal approach is a theme you will see repeated throughout the rest of this book.

One margin to work on is the de jure rules. The research on this is clear. Little changes matter. One way to see this is to look at the times political parties and activists adjusted the rules to grant the weakest more voice. When Brazil introduced electronic voting machines, for example, it meant that people could see a candidate's photo and party symbol, enabling the illiterate to vote. This had big effects on who got elected, and this pushed policy and spending toward the poor. Or, in Sierra Leone and Benin, some researchers persuaded the political parties to experiment with ways of making voters more informed and candidates more accountable: debates, town halls, and primary elections. These resulted in well-informed voters, better candidates, less vote buying, and more public goods. A grander example comes from China, in the 1980s, when the country began introducing elections for village committees. China rolled the reform out cautiously, over time, first testing to see how the process worked in a few villages before rolling it out to more. The country found that local elections held local leaders accountable, and those villages began seeing real policy changes. Land was more widely shared and income inequality declined, along with corruption. Happy with this success, the Chinese Communist Party eventually made village elections universal.[13]

As usual, the opposite is true: little rule changes can disenfranchise too. We can see this in the United States. After the US Civil War, Southern states used literacy tests and poll taxes to keep Blacks from voting. Counties that introduced these rules saw huge reductions in Black turnout, a rise in the (then anti-Black) Democratic party, and a fall in spending on public goods for Blacks, like schooling. Today, American states are fighting over voting restrictions for similar reasons.[14]

The question for us, of course, is whether these little rule changes affect conflict. Here the evidence is sparse, but I think they do. After a century of voting restrictions on Black Americans, for example, a bipartisan group of Democrats and Republicans pushed through the Voting Rights Act of 1965, which prohibited discriminatory rule changes. This massively increased Black turnout. One researcher compared Southern counties, similar in all respects except that some were subject to regulation by the act and others weren't. Violent political unrest dropped by half in counties protected by the act. Others have looked to England in the nineteenth century and shown similar results—places where reforms enfranchised more people also became more peaceful.[15]

Another margin to work on, however, is de facto power. The idea here is that societies will evolve checks and balances when their material wealth and resources are more equally held, when the populace is widely mobilized, and when the military weapons are widely distributed.

Sadly, hard evidence is scarce, but I think there are a few persuasive ideas. Government programs that promote literacy and access to schools ought to broaden de facto power, for example, raising earning potential and voice. Some kinds of social media expand voice too (while censorship tools hinder it). Economic policies that broaden the industrial base and raise wages should create more open and checked societies over time. So might pro-poor policies that get people out of the worst living conditions and able to focus on goals greater than eating that day. Little by little, policies that distribute the pie more widely should lead to more balanced power in society, and edge a country toward peace.

Outsiders can play a crucial role here. Foreign agencies often have tremendous funds, weapons, and authority, and how they direct those resources has a huge effect on de factor power. When they promote distributed development—building schools and roads, community grants, or jobs programs—they are probably widening de facto power. When they funnel most aid money through the central government, deal only with the sovereign, or train and arm the national military, they are concentrating power rather than spreading it around. Unfortunately, so much of the international aid and diplomatic system is a force for centralization, not polycentrism. That makes the world a little less stable.[16]

Chapter 9

RULES AND ENFORCEMENT

Let's go back to Bellavista prison and the brawl that nearly leveled Medellín. The full story of the Billiards War, however, requires a slightly larger cast, most of all a shadowy group of older, gray-haired, potbellied Mafia leaders. These are the real peacekeepers of Medellín.

During my first months in the city, I didn't know this. We mostly talked to low- and middle-ranking combo members. But this was hard. Young and suspicious, only a few were willing to speak to a clutch of professors. One day, however, as my colleagues and I were leaving the prison after a day of disappointing interviews, the warden paused. "Before you go," she said, "do you want to visit the leaders' wing?"

The warden took us to a cellblock where a group of older men lounged in a meeting room. She introduced us, then took her leave. A curly-haired man with a thick black mustache, dressed in sweatpants and an undershirt, stood up and gave an incoherent and angry speech, his face flushed red. Then he stormed out of the room. He was clearly high. The others were sober, apologetic, almost kindly. Most looked fifty or sixty. One said he was a lawyer for the crime syndicates, another a "businessman," and the last—a cheerful, chatty thirtysomething with a face full of acne scars—we recognized as the notorious young boss of one of Medellín's largest slums.[1]

The older men mostly deferred to the pockmarked young leader. He began asking us questions: Who were we, and what did we want? We must have answered well, because after a while, he sat back, and his whole demeanor changed. He grinned, became friendly, joked around, and invited us to ask our questions. To our surprise, the men responded, often at length.

Unlike the low-level members, the bosses in Medellín's prisons were secure, confident, and powerful. Some topics proved off-limits, like their precise profits. But they were eager to explain how they managed the city's conflicts. Partly it's because they were bored, partly they liked to talk shop, and partly they wanted others to see the role they played in the city's peace.

Over the years we interviewed dozens of different leaders, and we learned that what at first looked like anarchy had a hidden order. The city's hundreds of combos are the lowest level of an elaborate criminal hierarchy. The street gangs eke out a living dealing drugs and shaking down buses and little shops. But the real money in Medellín doesn't come from selling crack to poor slum dwellers. The more sophisticated groups have learned how to shake down the big construction firms and launder money for global drug rings. They're also the wholesale middlemen for the combos' retail drug operations. These powerful Mafia-like organizations call themselves *razones*. As it happens, one of the two gangs that fought the billiards brawl, Pachelly, was a *razón*. So was El Mesa's powerful ally and patron organization, Los Chatas, a razón led by the kingpin Tom.

Years ago, Pachelly, Los Chatas, and the other dozen or so razones came to an agreement: they had to find a way to keep themselves and the roughly four hundred street combos from fighting. The consequences of failure were clear. A few years before the billiards shoot-out in Bellavista prison, two powerful razón leaders had struggled for dominance in Medellín. Every other crime outfit in the city lined up behind one or the other and, for a brief time, the city became one of the most violent places on the planet. To the razones, that war had immeasurable costs. It wasn't just the death toll (massive though it was). The crime bosses also lost the invisibility that had been their shield. Suddenly they saw their pictures in the newspaper, the names of their organizations in print, and elaborate organizational charts as police and journalists began to trace the money. That's how so many of them ended up in Bellavista prison.

To calm things down and protect themselves, the razones slowly transformed themselves into rule makers, mediators, and enforcers. They intuitively grasped the reasons that bargains break down, and one by one they tried to solve them, making compromises possible.

First, each razón organized the combos in its territory. Most of these street gangs already had a business relationship with a razón, for razones were the wholesalers of illicit goods and services. But the razones began playing a political role, too, managing borders and disputes between the combos in their domain, and helping them collude to set drug prices high. So, when a street gang tried to undercut the price of their neighbor, their rival could go to the razón to complain and obtain judgment. Thus, there was no need to launch an attack. This also meant that, for the most part, combos didn't need to worry about an invasion or a rival seizing their drug corners; the razones cracked down on these gang attacks (or at least made sure any fight ended quickly). The combos stayed mostly autonomous and independent from the razones. But each razón established a hierarchy over its nearby street gangs, thus becoming a local hegemon. So, instead of a city of four hundred fractious principalities, Medellín was really a collection of fifteen or so criminal confederations, with a razón at the head of each one.

To settle disputes and manage competition between these confederations, the razones also established a bargaining table and a governing board. They called this criminal council *La Oficina*—the Office. La Oficina made it easier for razones to communicate and negotiate with one another. It also helped them coordinate to enforce their bargains, making commitments more credible. The razones have a name for these arrangements—*El Pacto del Fusil* (the Pact of the Machine Gun)—an unveiled reference to the tool they would use to keep the peace, if necessary. The Billiards War, it turns out, did not simply die out on its own. It was smothered by La Oficina and El Pacto del Fusil. When imprisoned members of Pachelly and El Mesa attacked one another, bosses like Tom sat down, reconciled the rivals, and avoided a city-wide war.

Ironically, by arresting the senior-most combo and razón figures, and holding them in the same cellblocks, Colombia's government helped foster the pact and hold it. Leaders of different factions could interact face-to-face in prison cellblocks, helping them build relationships of cautious trust. They could exchange information, reducing uncertainty. And the fact that they were all locked up together made their commitments more credible. Most criminals in the city expected to pass through prison for a time, and this gave La Oficina powerful tools of contract enforcement and peacekeeping. Ignore their edicts, and they would make life difficult for you and your incarcerated friends. This had the unfortunate effect of making the razones stronger, but for peace this is a price some administrations have been willing to pay.

Thus, in their own territories, each razón of Medellín acted a little bit like a state. They were criminal governors, establishing conventions for competition and interrupting violence when it broke out. A state is just one example of an institution that controls violence. Like all institutions, its effectiveness comes from setting rules and enforcing them. It monitors actors, adjudicates disputes, and punishes violations of the rules within its jurisdiction. As it happens, the world's earliest states closely resemble the razones of Medellín. Local warlords set themselves up as kings, providing security and justice for a price, responding to a population's demand for order amid anarchy. Humanity's first governments were essentially organized criminals with a financial stake in preserving the peace.[2] Like razones, they were unequal, repressive, and only somewhat effective. Their one virtue was that they were better than no order at all. Thankfully, most states today work better than the razones. Modern governments provide more predictable and just rules, and enforce them more reliably. Most are also more legitimate and accountable than a razón. As we'll see, that generally makes them even better at violence control.

If razones resemble nations, then La Oficina and its Pacto del Fusil look like the world's international institutions—regulations and organizations that try to control violence between states. Again, like all institutions, these international ones set rules and enforce them, trying to make cooperation easier. Take the United Nations Security Council. It has a lot in common with La Oficina and El Pacto del Fusil. It is fractious, unequal, weak, full of hard-nosed power brokers pursuing their groups' interests. Also, they're inconsistent and biased in their enforcement of the peace, and only sometimes effective. It's hard for the council to manage cooperation between powerful independent actors, whether they be razones or China and Russia. Still, like La Oficina, the Security Council does some good, and the world is surely a more peaceful place for its existence.

At every level, from villages to gangs to nations and the globe, successful societies have built institutions like these to help groups cooperate. Rules and enforcement are their core function. These institutions take many forms, from written laws to unwritten norms, and organizations large and small. This chapter looks at some of the major ones, why they widen the bargaining range between rivals, and why some institutions are more challenging to build than others.

THE GREAT PACIFIER: THE STATE

Nothing screams Canadian like getting your first job with the Mounties. At sixteen I had illusions of becoming an architect, and so a high school drafting teacher helped me find an internship with the building management department of the Royal Canadian Mounted Police. Two or three afternoons a week, I rode the bus from my suburb to the sprawling headquarters on the eastern edge of Ottawa, where I wandered the halls, tape measure and blueprint in hand. Men and women in uniform would pass by, silently wondering why a gangly child was measuring their rooms and doors. But the plans hadn't been updated in decades. For a year I sketched and redrew, never covering more than a fraction of the hulking structure.

Today, Canada's federal police number about thirty thousand—a long way from the few hundred mounted men who marched west in red jackets from Ottawa in 1874. At that time, Canada had been self-governing for a mere seven years. The new government created the force to patrol and defend the prairies that stretched from Manitoba to the western Rocky Mountains. The region was sparsely settled—a mix of hunters, trappers, and natives. Illegal whiskey traders from the United States were rousing trouble, however. After one drunken dispute over missing horses, a group of traders and wolfers massacred the inhabitants of a native Assiniboine village. Events like these spurred Ottawa to create and march a police force west. Law and order would also ease colonization, they reckoned, and prevent any encroachments from the United States.

Over the next two decades, the Mounties built nearly a dozen forts across the prairies. Canadian, American, and European immigrants followed. As tens of thousands of settlers poured in, the RCMP ranks also swelled, from eight hundred in 1890 to more than four thousand by 1905. In the myth of the Mountie, this early order is what kept Canada's west from growing as wild as the American one, making Canada the pacific nation it is today.

A few years ago, one economist decided to put this claim to the test, comparing violence in prairie communities close to and far from the RCMP

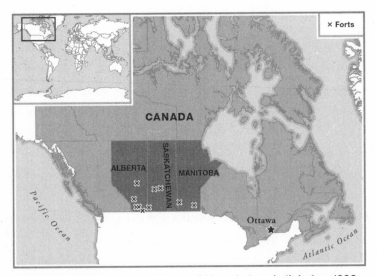

Canada's prairie provinces today, and Mountie forts built before 1890

forts. There are no homicide records from the time, but the 1911 census shows an unusually high number of widows as you get farther and farther from the Mounties. These forts are gone now, but the effects seem to persist. Today, prairie communities farther away from these historical garrisons have about 50 percent more violent crimes and murders. Even their athletes fight more. When the researcher looked at National Hockey League players from the prairies, he saw that the ones born farther from the forts earned 40 percent more penalty time than the ones born close by.[3]

THE STATE AS PACIFIER IS ONE OF THE OLDEST AND MOST WIDELY ACCEPTED IDEAS IN HIS-tory and social science. One of its early and famous exponents was the English philosopher Thomas Hobbes. There's an unwritten rule that every book on violence must print his famous statement—that without a sovereign power, life is "nasty, brutish and short." Anarchy and violence—or as Hobbes called it, Warre—arose whenever "men live without a common Power to keep them all in awe." To end this unpleasant condition, we need a "great LEVIA-THAN," he emphasized, in all caps, or, in other words, "a STATE."[4]

It's no surprise Hobbes felt this way. He was born in the year the Spanish armada attacked England, and he liked to say that his mother gave birth to him prematurely, in terror, over the invasion. Then as an adult, in 1642, Hobbes fled to Paris as supporters of the British monarchy battled those of Parliament, and his home descended into the English Civil War. He described himself and fear as "twins." Like so many of the thinkers in this book, Hobbes was driven by the experience of total mayhem to ask why we fight, and how to keep it from happening again.

The Mounties and Hobbes both show us the value of a professional, neutral third party enforcing a code of laws. This state organ doesn't even need that many personnel on the ground. It just needs the credible threat that it will send whatever officers are required to punish outbreaks of violence and other wrongdoing. Rules and the credible threat of enforcement check the private interests of ringleaders. They counter any intangible incen-

tives for fighting, and they punish violent mistakes. The state can also help
rivals share information, dissuade them from taking risky gambles to fight,
and help parties commit to a deal even when incentives tempt otherwise.
States don't stop all violence within their jurisdiction, but at the very least
they widen the bargaining range between local actors like the whiskey traders, wolfers, and Assiniboine natives.

Over the last few hundred years, organizations of public order have been
responsible for a huge reduction in violence within nations. It's not just security forces like the Mounties. It's also the system of clear rules, predictable
punishments, courts to adjudicate disputes, and public services that make
crime or violence less attractive.

While all these arms of the state matter, however, policing has been the
service most scrutinized. Broadly speaking, the research shows that cities
and neighborhoods with more police are less violent. Dozens of studies—
natural experiments in single cities, analyses of hundreds of cities over decades, and randomized trials of local policing—tend to show that crime,
especially violent crimes, falls with more police officers.[5]

That sounds like a controversial statement at a moment when many
people, especially Americans, have begun to question police forces and their
tactics. In the United States, they point to the killing and abuse of young
Black men by officers of the law. And at the same time, Americans look
around their cities and see carnage. Homicide rates there are extraordinary
for a rich and democratic country.

These views are compatible, not conflicting. We can be critical of counterproductive policing, and promote alternatives, without denying the evidence that enforcing laws creates order. As anyone who studies international
politics will tell you, police states and empires can stop a lot of conflict
within their borders. A peaceful society does not have to be equal or just.
Even repressive security forces can be an effective institution of violence
control. But for good reason, Americans hold their police to a higher standard. Later in this chapter I'll show how a constrained, legitimatized state
is probably the most effective at producing peace. This means America's

police would probably be far more effective at controlling violence in cities like Chicago if they earned the trust of poor and minority communities. Even if they did not, however, the evidence still suggests that US cities would be significantly more violent without large police forces.

As for the alternatives, police are far from the only organizations that set rules and enforce them. There are dozens of other ways that societies can counter violence that don't involve coercion. Policing is just one state instrument, the one with the most attention and evidence. Many other paths to peace exist. As I'll reveal in the next chapter, I've spent the last decade designing and studying some of the alternatives. We will get to these interventions soon.[6] Before that, however, I want to talk about what society looks like in the absence of powerful third-party enforcing rules. This is the condition of anarchy. It's the usual situation for stateless societies, and it's also the nature of the international system. Anarchic situations are not institution-free, however. Absent a state, societies still find ways to craft rules and enforcement mechanisms that minimize violence and war. Without an enforcer, however, these rules must be self-enforcing, and they are hard to create and hold. Let me explain.

ANARCHY AND SELF-ENFORCING INSTITUTIONS

Living in one of the most violent periods in European history, seeing his homeland dissolve, it's no wonder that Hobbes held a dim view of anarchy—what he called a situation of every man against every man, and "a perpetual and restless desire of power after power" among all humankind.

This is not quite right, though, because Hobbes forgot the fundamental incentive for peace. People will compete for riches, honor, command, or other power, just as Hobbes believed, but they'd prefer not to kill, subdue, or supplant the other. It's too dangerous and expensive. That's why stateless societies try to foster norms and create bodies that keep order. Not a state—that's difficult to conjure out of nothing. But some of humanity's other inventions have echoes of the state: tribe and clan structures, for example, with respected headmen and councils of elders, who coordinate with other clans to admonish or punish warlike groups in their network.

Other institutions use norms to shape behavior: religious edicts, rituals, taboos, and other shared beliefs that push people to peace using praise and shame. One example is a culture of honor. It sounds like a moral code, but that's not what people mean by the phrase. Rather, it describes a system that uses the promise of retribution to preserve a degree of peace. You see, in places without police or justice systems, most people don't attack or steal from others for fear of retaliation by the victim's group. Not all these sanctions are violent. The aggrieved could simply refuse to do business with the offender, expel them from the village, or sneer and gossip. Stateless societies have powerful tools of social control. Retribution, however, is often violent— an eye for an eye, a tooth for a tooth, a life for a life.

Why develop a custom of violent reprisal? Because it's a powerful deterrent. A neighboring village will hesitate to raid or assault you if they know you'll retaliate. We saw this with Nap Dog in Chicago's Horner Homes, when I introduced you to uncertainty and his consequent need for a ferocious reputation. When your true strength is ambiguous, your enemies are never sure how strong or resolved you are. Thus, in a lawless society, you have strategic incentives to cultivate a reputation for violence, even if you do not have the taste for it. A culture of honor is what we call it when this strategic response becomes a widely shared social norm. Honor enters in the way this custom is enforced. A victim who didn't respond violently would be shamed by his own community.

Compared with stateless societies without such norms, ones with cultures of honor should be more peaceful. Not as peaceful as societies with a well-functioning state, but better than no institutions at all. When I see street shootings in Chicago, or grisly revenge in the hinterlands of Liberia, I see groups with no Oficina. In the absence of a state, a culture of honor can help to preserve a fragile peace.[7]

Even in places with a strong state, we can still see legacies of past cultures of honor. Some social scientists use this to explain why some parts of the United States and Canada are still more violent than others. To see this, let's go back to the Canadian prairie and the Mounties. All those communities have RCMP officers today. Most have had the police and the state for almost one hundred years. So why do the effects of Mountie forts persist? Why does a hockey player born one hundred kilometers farther from an old garrison throw more punches on the ice? The fort isn't even there anymore.

One answer is that a culture of violence is sticky. Yes, the state is pacifying over time, but not entirely. Norms and cultural institutions are persistent, and so places that fostered a culture of honor see it last. Better if a society never has to institutionalize reprisals in the first place. Steven Pinker—like me a violence-studying Canadian transplanted to the United States—uses the same idea to explain differences in violence over the border, too. "Canadians kill at less than a third of the rate of Americans," he has argued, "partly because in the 19th century the Mounties got to the western frontier before the settlers and spared them from having to cultivate a culture of honor." Obviously, lots of things drive the difference between Canadian and American homicide rates. But the early presence of a pacifying enforcer of rules probably explains some of the US–Canada difference.[8]

This is also one reason the American South is more violent than the North. Many early migrants to the South came from a group called the Scots-Irish, immigrants from herding societies on the fringes of Britain. For generations, the Scots-Irish lived without a strong state to enforce peace, for London was far away. They were like the prairie settlers far from Mountie forts. When their descendants moved to North America, they carried their retributive norms with them. Looking just within the states where they settled, one economist found that US counties that received more Scots-Irish settlers were more violent then, and are more violent today.[9]

As it happens, the Scots-Irish settled in the Canadian prairie as well. When they did, whether their descendants remained violent depended on where the immigrants landed. Those close to the Mountie forts attenuated their violence over time. Slowly, their culture of violence eroded under the rule of state—the Great Pacifier.

I'm a product of this slow pacification. Part of my family descends from Scots-Irish immigrants who settled close to the Canadian capital, Ottawa. So close to the seat of government, they slowly acculturated to authority, until the latest of their line became a meek cartographer for the Mounties and (eventually) a chronicler of peace.

Napoleon English wasn't as fortunate, however. In North Lawndale, like most poor minority neighborhoods in Chicago, cultures of honor persist. The fact that, for so long, the American state oppressed Blacks is surely one reason why. Why trust a justice system stacked against you? Instead, young men turn to retribution to deter their rivals. Relatedly, the journalist Jill Leovy argues that retaliatory violence persists because police forces crack down hard on small infractions rather than solving major crimes. Young men know that they can't count on the police to solve murders. Their gangs provide a degree of self-protection, deterring predation from rivals. It's an imperfect, sometimes violent system, more brutal than one with a legitimate state, but better than a condition of Warre.[10]

ANARCHY AND INSTITUTIONS
IN THE INTERNATIONAL REALM

Our international system resembles these quasi-anarchic, second-best systems of order. Earlier I drew a parallel between razones and states, but actually that's not the best analogy. One or two razones in Medellín resemble states—they've integrated their combos and have created formal systems of finance, security, and social control—but the rest have looser connections with their subordinate street gangs. Most of the time the razón is the hegemon in a hierarchical alliance. This ruling razón protects its combos and resolves their disputes. In turn the combos accept the razón's authority and allow it to capture a large share of the drug profits. Some razones are coercive, compelling a combo to join and stay. But mostly these are relationships of exchange.

As it happens, this is a good description of the international system—a collection of hierarchical alliances. Instead of nearly two hundred nations squabbling in anarchy, the world is composed of a handful of confederations led by the most powerful states. Within these coalitions, the hegemon keeps the peace among members, smooths economic and military cooperation, and negotiates with other hegemons on behalf of the group. Today, an obvious example is the United States and its leadership over North America, Central America, and the Caribbean. France and other European nations have their own hierarchical networks, and the United States leads a larger and looser coalition of all these Western hierarchies. Russia has its own. China is steadily expanding its own, too. The political scientist David Lake has argued that these hierarchical alliances are a powerful force for peace—within the confederations, most of all, but also by reducing the number of groups that have to find a bargain. Rather than dozens of nations bickering, a handful of coalitions negotiate.

Sometimes the hegemon subdues nations through threats and force. We can call this imperialism. It's a fair description of large empires throughout history. Historians speak of the Pax Romana, the Pax Britannica, and even the Pax Mongolica not because these imperialists were gentle in their rule. They were self-enriching and oppressive. But they also tended to outlaw wars. Once conquered, clans and nations within the empire were forbidden from fighting.

Today some imperial coercion persists. The United States built its alliance aggressively when necessary. Still, many of the hierarchies are relationships of mutual exchange—the subordinates defer to the hegemon on certain policies, accept their firms and their exports, ally with them in feuds with other hegemons, and in return these countries can spend far less on their own defense, and enjoy security and trade. Most of these relationships enjoy broad legitimacy and are popular, even when they're biased in favor of the hegemon. Whether or not you think this is a good system of global governance, Lake points out it's the one we have, and so it's incorrect to call the international arena anarchic. Instead, we have pools of regional peace and cooperation.[11]

—————

SOME IDEALISTS ENVISION A WORLD GOVERNMENT. REMEMBER EINSTEIN'S LETTER TO Freud? When it comes to war, "I personally see a simple way of dealing with the problem," the physicist concluded, "the setting up, by international consent, of a legislative and judicial body to settle every conflict arising between nations." Einstein believed this so strongly that he proposed an axiom, a mathematical term for a statement that is either well established or self-evidently true: "The quest of international security involves the unconditional surrender by every nation, in a certain measure, of its liberty of action—its sovereignty that is to say—and it is clear beyond all doubt that no other road can lead to such security."

Fortunately, Einstein's statement isn't quite so axiomatic. A global government is not the sole path to peace, any more than the state is the only way a group can avoid violence. But it's true that we need some form of international institutions to set rules, facilitate bargains, and enforce them.

Not everyone agrees. The political scientist John Mearsheimer is a famous skeptic, and in the 1990s he wrote a famous essay asking the institutional optimists to show more proof. He pointed to something like NATO. Sure, it helped keep the Cold War from turning into World War III, and it's helped to keep the peace in other parts of the world. But what really mattered about the institution? he asked. Was it the organization and the regulations themselves? Or was it the combined power of the states that actually enforced peace in the world? Can we really say the institution itself did something more than the sum of its parts?[12]

I think Mearsheimer is right on a couple of things. The interests and actions of member states matter a whole lot. And the contribution of international institutions themselves is hard to assess. The case for them often gets made on the basis of a mix of data and faith. But since the 1990s the evidence has grown. I think it shows these institutions do matter independently of the member states, and that their impact is at least marginal, and sometimes quite large. International institutions reduce the difficulties of negotiation and coordination, provide routines of cooperation, make enforcement more likely to happen, smooth the flow of information, and improve commitment.

Let me give two examples. I'll start with human rights laws and norms. Earlier, when I talked about intertwining interests, I mentioned the Rights Revolution. As more and more people developed a sense of kinship with rival groups, bargaining ranges widened. But this wasn't a spontaneous shift of culture. It was carefully and painstakingly constructed, and then enshrined in international law. It wasn't easy. For example, the path was long to the Universal Declaration of Human Rights, which was adopted by the UN General Assembly in 1948 and pushed ahead by innumerable activists and diplomats. The declaration didn't bind at the time, and many of the nations that signed on didn't believe in all its provisions. In the decades since, however, that and other efforts have slowly created a vast system of global law, advocacy, observers, and enforcement mechanisms to monitor and protect human rights. Provisions have gotten coded into treaties and new constitutions. And they have shifted norms throughout the world. As a result, publics have changed how they expect their governments to act and what they expect them to do to punish violators. It's checked governments, limited what they can do to repress their opposition, and empowered the weak in these societies to demand more. It's fostered the kind of moral and cultural intertwining that should make peaceful bargains more likely.[13]

Other examples are the League of Nations and the United Nations. These are institutions of collective security, explicitly designed to widen bargaining ranges and reduce the likelihood of war. Like La Oficina, the members have a common interest in compromise rather than fighting. Organizations like the General Assembly and Security Council help to do that. These fix the five problems that lead to war. They provide a forum to meet and exchange information. They include agencies whose role is to monitor compliance with deals and rules, and therefore reduce uncertainty. They provide a coordinating mechanism, expectations, and repeated traditions that help other nations cooperate to punish countries that defect from the rules. And they support agencies that directly intervene to help bargains get made and held, like sanctions, mediation, and peacekeeping.

None of this enforcement works especially well. It doesn't fully constrain nations, especially the most powerful. But I believe this system still produces a more consistent set of rules and more predictable set of consequences than a world without it. As the former UN secretary general Dag Hammarskjöld liked to say, "The UN was not created to take humanity to heaven but to save it from hell."[14]

It's difficult to prove the general effect of something like the entire UN system, but, as we'll see in the next chapter, there is a mass of evidence showing that specific interventions—sanctions, mediation, peacekeeping, and the like—contribute to peace.[15]

Chapter 10

INTERVENTIONS

I wasn't supposed to like John Prendergast. Tall, handsome, with long wavy hair, the charismatic activist ran around Africa with the likes of George Clooney, Don Cheadle, and other stars. A crusader against violence and thuggery, Prendergast had a gift for simplifying and selling solutions. He used his talents to build a hugely successful international advocacy campaign—the Enough Project.

This was exactly the kind of celebrity policy mongering that academics love to hate. By the time I met Prendergast, in 2019, famous African scholars had been beating him up in blogs and books for oversimplified solutions. So I was unprepared to hear him give a more astute take on conflict and unchecked ruling cabals than most of the diplomats and ministers I'd met. He also had a powerful idea about what to do. He'd just reinvented his organization to make it happen.

Prendergast is nearing sixty, and his locks are now gray. As a young man, decades ago, he started his career coordinating aid in a Somali refugee camp. Over the following years, he got into human rights advocacy, and ended up at the nonprofit Human Rights Watch. Then he joined the government. It was 1996. Bill Clinton was president of the United States. The head of his National Security Council pulled Prendergast into the African affairs bureau—a backbench job, about a continent no one in the US government cared about. Except Clinton. "He was obsessed with Africa," Prendergast told me, "he felt so fucking bad about Rwanda."

This was a typical Prendergast remark, or so I would learn: direct, plain-spoken, and completely profane. I can't quite picture him swearing it up with presidents, but somehow the cursing fits his gregarious style and obvious passion. Also, to be fair, topics like impunity for mass killings deserve strong language.

Like a lot of Western leaders and activists, Clinton was inspired to prevent mass murder and conflict by the atrocities of the 1990s, most of all the 1994 Rwandan genocide. "He was asking these questions," Prendergast explained, going back to his first big meeting with the US president, "but nobody knew the answers." This is not surprising—relatively few State Department and other officials made successful careers in Africa at the time. But seated in the back row, Prendergast had opinions. He'd lived in these places. So he broke protocol and started answering Clinton's questions.

Almost overnight, Clinton launched Prendergast to the front lines of US-Africa diplomacy, into peace negotiations and peacekeeping missions across the continent: Ethiopia and Eritrea, Zimbabwe, and Liberia, to name a few. Prendergast felt as if they were helping make real progress. When George W. Bush came to power in 2000, however, political appointees like Prendergast were replaced with new people, as in any transition. So Prendergast decided to return to activism. That's when he created Enough.

It was the mid-2000s, and the killing and conflict that grabbed his attention were in Darfur. I won't try to tackle the crisis here in all its complexity. It's a region in the west of Sudan, a large country in east-central Africa. The simplest description is this: an Arab regime in Khartoum tried to violently pacify the restive, non-Arab population in Darfur, a province in the far west of the country. This morphed into a Khartoum-led campaign of ethnic cleansing and land grabs.[1]

Prendergast and Clooney wanted the killings seen and stopped. They ran publicity campaigns, tried to track and prove the murders were happening,

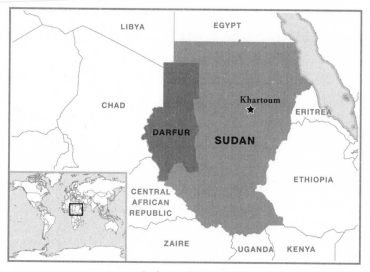

Sudan and Darfur

and attempted to unravel the lies told by Sudan's autocratic regime. They and Enough's legions of young people pushed Western governments to send in the full package—mediators, peacekeepers, truth commissions, and humanitarian aid.

Here's where you'd expect me to tell you Enough's advocacy worked. That mobilizing millions of teenagers and dozens of US politicians made the difference. The killing stopped. The future needs more Clooney campaigns! Maybe that's right. Maybe not. The truth is, I don't know if more advocacy would bring peace. Because that is not the lesson I learned from Prendergast.

For its founder, the Enough movement wasn't working enough. Prendergast wanted thuggish autocrats to stop killing their own people. But the thugs didn't seem to care. "They used to laugh at me," Prendergast told me. Especially in Sudan, he explained. "Oh, it's John," they'd say, "why are you always giving us so much trouble, John? Come on, let's sit down and let's have some tea." By 2015, Prendergast decided that he'd been focusing on the wrong things.

WAR IS A WICKED PROBLEM

Anyone who works on a big social problem knows this feeling. It comes midway through a big project, maybe even a career—a sense that you're wasting energy or it's all for nothing. That's good. Sometimes we're focused on the wrong things, because they don't address the five reasons for war. Other times, we have the right approach, but we could do it better. So it's a good thing to question your diagnosis and worry that you are getting it all wrong, as Prendergast did. Your next step is to tinker with the tools at hand.

Whether it's a neighborhood, city, nation, or the international system, there are a few common paths to peace. This chapter walks through each one:

- Punishing—Using sticks to deter the strong from using violence.
- Enforcing—Ensuring bargains get held until the agreements are self-sustaining.
- Facilitating—Sharing information and making the process of bargaining faster and smoother.
- Incentivizing—Devising carrots to get the powerful to come to the table and stay there.
- Socializing—Cultivating a society that avoids rigid negative frames, misperceptions, and violent reactions.

Each of these contains some good news: community leaders, mayors, national governments, and international do-gooders have all discovered approaches that work, mostly because they make compromises easier to find. The bad news is that all these intercessions have a few other things in common: they're great in theory, wobbly in evidence, hard to get right, and seldom an unabashed success. Also, the impacts are always a little shrimpier than we'd like. That might sound downcast, but there are reasons to be encouraged.

You should be hopeful about peacemaking for the same reasons you value preventive medicine and drugs, even if these measures are less effective for the chronically ill. They keep most of us in good shape and help us recover when sick. If you walked through an intensive care ward, you might not see that. You would be distracted by the incredible effort expended on people who aren't getting very much better. But you'd be silly to decry modern medicine.

Likewise, peace interventions can seem to work poorly because there's a selection problem in who needs the most extreme forms of help, and who keeps showing up for it again and again. But we shouldn't judge a policy solely by how it works in global intensive care—with the Saddam Husseins, the Sinaloa cartels, the Kim Jong Uns, the Somali warlords, the Medellín combos, or the genocidal generals in Darfur. Instead, we need to remember that building a system of predicable, legitimate, effective interventions and incentives deters a great many unseen gangs, ethnic leaders, and governments from violence. This is true at every level—local, national, and global.

If peacebuilding were easy, I wouldn't need to write a book about why we fight. We'd have solved that problem by now. When a social issue as costly as conflict persists, it's precisely because it's hard to address. Peacemaking is a wicked hard problem. It sounds like something a surfer might say, but "wicked" is actually a technical term. A German management and design professor coined it in the 1960s to describe the challenges of social planning and improvement. Some issues are relatively easy to solve—they're isolated, with clear causes; require straightforward technical knowledge to fix; have clear metrics for progress; and don't need that many people to act together. Those problems are not wicked.

Wicked ones are way more complicated. There's no template, there are many possible roots, measuring success is hard, it requires coordinating many actors, and each case is unique.[2] Lots of social problems are wicked: inequality, poverty, drug abuse, and chronic disease.

Preventing and resolving conflict, too—this has all the wickedest features. There aren't just many roots, but five big categories, each class of reasons

difficult to distinguish from one another. These problems often run deep—
down to the organization of power in society—and all of them are difficult
to change. Each rivalry is without likeness or equal. There's no guidebook.
And when you do try something, it's hard to know if it's working. So we
should expect wobbly evidence, shrimpy impacts, and innumerable failures.

For all these reasons, you shouldn't expect any of the five kinds of intervention to be big, bold, and speedy steps to universal goodwill and harmony.
Instead, each one moves society down the path to peace bit by bit, focusing
on what happens when we loosen or tighten a constraint on finding compromise: placing limits on warmongering elites; making war a little more costly;
making information a little more symmetric; making perceptions a little less
biased; making bargaining a tiny bit smoother. When this is the fringe we
are focused on, modest gains are not just okay, they are cause for celebration.
This brings me back to John Prendergast and his dilemma.

PUNISHING

In all the years he tried to call out mass killers, Prendergast realized, the
surest sign he wasn't having an effect was simple: "No one ever denied me a
visa." The presidents and generals took him for tea because none of the advocacy was really threatening them, he figured. Enough wasn't hitting the
core cause of violence and suffering. "That core root cause is the kleptocracies
that are at the center of these countries," Prendergast decided.

The issue was the way that power was distributed in Sudan—it was
concentrated in a clique of self-serving elites. "These governments in Congo
and Sudan and South Sudan and Somalia and other places have been hijacked," he told me. "They've been captured by a small group of people, like
military officials, commercial leaders, and their international collaborators—
bankers, lawyers, and others that set up their shell companies and move the
money out." Their incentive wasn't to find peace. It was to use whatever
means necessary—purges, land grabs, civil war, genocide—to seize more of
the pie.[3]

Prendergast knew that an outsider like him couldn't fix Sudan's institutional structure, creating checks and balances. Even if he could, it wouldn't change fast enough to avert the violence happening right then. But maybe, the activist thought, he could tweak the incentives on the margin. Foreigners were complicit in the crimes of the Sudanese elite, laundering their money and selling the weapons. Perhaps it was up to more upright foreigners to help fix that part of the problem.

A few years ago, Prendergast changed tactics and retooled his organization, calling it The Sentry. Out went the teenage campaigners. Instead, Prendergast recruited a new breed of activist: straitlaced accountants, rumpled economists, and ex-government anti-terror investigators with serious demeanors and conservative hair. The Sentry's sober new crew started following the money. They investigated the shady lawyers, banks, and shell companies who helped Sudan's plutocrats hide their money. They traced the network of illegal arms and diamond dealers, and documented the corrupt generals and politicians squirreling money outside the country.

Some of these enablers were sketchy businesspeople in the Middle East, the Caymans, or other tax havens and pariah states. A lot of the money, however, passed through big American and European banks. Prendergast and Clooney put these Western institutions in their sights. "George and I were like, when do we have to start fucking going out and protesting, impugning these banks for working with these warlords?" he told me. But it turned out the bankers didn't need protests. The business executives were happy to see them. So was the US Treasury Department.

Having George Clooney didn't hurt. "Without him we wouldn't have access to all these CEOs," Prendergast explained. Celebrities open important doors. Mostly, however, Prendergast got cooperation because Western banks were out to get the kleptocrats and their enablers too. The thugs and thieves undermined the credibility of the whole financial system. Plus, the US government had been pressuring big financial institutions for years to shut down the villains funding terror. "Just give me the fucking evidence," one official told Prendergast, "and we'll go get them."

Prendergast had just a couple dozen investigators, while the banks had throngs of compliance officers and legions of forensic investigators. The Sentry's team knew the terrain and could start the cases. The banks and the US Treasury Department could finish them. (And to keep the banks motivated, a little pressure from Clooney and a looming threat of protests probably didn't hurt.)

Today, Prendergast can point to some unsavory people who have now been sanctioned: politicians who pumped oil money into hidden accounts, corrupt diamond tycoons, or their unscrupulous lawyers and financiers. They've been frozen out of their liquid assets, shut out of the entire global finance system. They are weaker, and they are mad. Sudan's military leaders don't invite Prendergast to tea anymore. And they sure don't give him visas.

PUNISHING THE POWERFUL FOR ROGUE AND SELFISH BEHAVIOR IS NOTHING NEW, OF course. It's a common approach. When it's our own institutions checking our own leaders, we call those penalties public shaming, censure, and impeachment. When it's our government deterring private actors, we call it regulation, injunction, and prosecution. Most societies try to set up predictable systems of rules and a schedule of penalties to keep bad people from doing harmful things. We do this not just for the joy of disciplining offenders, but to change their incentives and keep them from offending in the first place. International laws, courts, sanctions, and organizations like The Sentry do the same. It's just that they're usually performed by outsiders to the society. We talked about institutions like the law and courts in the last chapter. Now let's talk about these foreign investigators and sanctions.

Foreign sanctions have been tools of statecraft for a long time. Most, however, have been broad-based. They were indiscriminate, banning all trade with an offending country, punishing entire societies for their leaders' misdeeds. We saw this in the 1990s, in Iraq. The United States and its allies have imposed other long-running sanctions on Cuba and Iran as well.

The trouble is that this strategy takes a big toll on innocent people, and it's hard to tell whether the wrongdoers at the top feel the pain. In the 1990s, for example, the trade sanctions against Iraq shrank the economy by half. All the while, Saddam Hussein and his family grew wealthy. The tyrant's hold over the populace even strengthened because sanctions gave him the power to hand out scarce food, currency, and supplies for money or loyalty. By the end of the twentieth century, failures like this had made diplomats and scholars skeptical of broad-based sanctions regimes. The deterrence effect wasn't apparent, but the human costs sure were.[4]

Policymakers began searching for more discriminating tools. One they called targeted sanctions. These punishments would single out leaders and the corrupt cabals around them. Instead of banning all trade, the policies identified specific individuals, froze their bank accounts, banned their travel, and forbade legitimate companies from working with them. Prendergast was one of many tinkerers around the world, trying to get the approach right. That's because the big challenge with targeted sanctions is finding the right people, marshaling the evidence, and penalties. That's what The Sentry was able to do.

Sanctions aren't just a tool of statecraft. Governments fighting gang violence have been taking a similar approach. In the United States, cities call it focused deterrence rather than targeted sanctions, but the logic is similar. When there are powerful gangs, enforcing every little law is crazily ambitious and all-consuming. Worse, it distracts authorities from stopping the most terrible crimes. Under focused deterrence, police and prosecutors narrow their attention to feuds and wars. They draw bright red lines that they say gangs cannot cross. Usually, that line is shooting people. The next time a body drops, they tell the gang leaders, we will come down hard on the suspected group. So get your people in line.

Some Latin American governments, like Colombia's, have told drug cartels the same thing. It's a predictable, targeted incentive to stop doing the most harmful things. Ben Lessing, one of my coauthors on the Medellín gangs projects, calls all these forms of deterrence "conditional repression"—

cross the line and we will crack down. Whether it's a genocidal political or criminal boss, it's one way to get leaders to internalize some of the costs of violence they ignore.[5]

Conditional repression sounds like a sensible idea, but does it actually work? The short answer is "probably yes." I would also add, "modestly." How we know, and why I'm optimistic, is worth explaining. The lessons will apply much more broadly, to almost every kind of intervention.

LIKE MOST INTERVENTIONS IN THIS CHAPTER, JUDGING WHETHER A POLICY LIKE SANC- tions does its job is hard for a simple reason: it's difficult to count the bodies of people never killed. If rulers expect to be punished for a genocide, or for invading a neighbor, a lot of them will be deterred. If gang leaders believe that bodies dropping will bring in prosecutors, they'll keep the peace with rival outfits. We don't observe these quiet successes. Instead, we see only the few defiant regimes or mobs whose desire to flout the rules is so strong that they still crack down on their people or attack their neighbors in spite of predictable penalties.

That's easy to forget. We look at the Saddam Husseins of the world and we're tempted to say, "See, sanctions don't work!" When researchers look at the sanctions actually levied, only a minority change the behavior of the target. At best a third succeed (depending on how you define success). But judging sanctions on this record alone is making a mistake that I hope read- ers of this book now recognize: a selection problem. We cannot appraise interventions only by the times they were tried. We also want to account for the moments when, anticipating a punishment, a dictator decided not to purge his enemies, a drug lord opted against a hostile takeover, or a tyran- nical majority chose to tolerate instead of cleanse an irksome minority. When it comes to conditional repression policy, most of the value is in the actions we never see—the regimes deterred.

This is hard to quantify. To know what works, normally we try to find a reasonable comparison group and look at how targets perform with and without the intervention. We've taken this counterfactual approach many times in the book. Think back to the Mounties and the culture of honor. Towns farther away from the forts were compared with the closer ones. It's not a perfect experiment, but the two kinds of towns looked similar otherwise, so it was useful. We've also seen real randomized experiments, like the Israelis who were assigned by lottery to stock portfolios during a tumultuous time, to see if they became more conscious of the economic costs of conflict.

When weighing something like sanctions, finding the right counterfactual is challenging. For starters, there's seldom an obvious comparison group. Suppose we want to know if The Sentry made the Sudanese government less repressive. We'd need to find countries similar to Sudan, with incentives for violence, where the Prendergasts of the world didn't agitate or investigate. We might be able to find some examples, but they would be few in number and never quite the same as Sudan. Also, we'd worry that the ones who get the sanctions are different. Most of all, however, even if we found these comparisons, they wouldn't tell us anything about the deterrent effect—the degree to which rulers in Ethiopia, Congo, or elsewhere moderate their corruption because they fear investigation and targeted sanctions. Some of the most promising policies are nearly impossible to evaluate and quantify.

This makes the job of tinkerers especially hard. You don't know for sure whether your approach is working. You're forced to rely on your own judgment, or unusual indicators (like whether plutocrats invite you to tea). But people who really want to change a nasty situation don't just give up. Instead, they do a few things. First, they stop selecting on successes and failures, and they start thinking about the counterfactual. Second, they get careful and creative. They look for nature's experiments where, by circumstance, some groups got the program and others did not. Or they compare historical cases, looking at ones with and without the intervention, and with and without evident success. Finally, they stay humble, resist hasty judgments, and don't overclaim.

PEOPLE HAVE APPLIED THIS APPROACH TO TARGETED SANCTIONS, AND THE evidence—slim as it is—makes me cautiously optimistic. First, when it comes to broad-based sanctions (not the targeted kind) the scholars who counted all the cases concluded that the policy often works, at least when the objectives are reasonable. Overly ambitious goals, like regime change, or stopping an ongoing war, are seldom achieved. But sanctions have had far more success at other behavior changes—keeping regimes from supporting terrorists, from military buildups, or from obtaining more dangerous weapons.[6]

Second, there are signs that targeted penalties cause plutocrats pain. Most of the evidence is anecdotal, because we don't have data on their financial holdings. Occasionally, however, these elites have companies that trade on the stock market, and the share prices of these organizations reflect their strength. In these cases, researchers have looked at the stocks of these companies before and after sanctions, and compared them with similar but less politically connected ones. In Iran, for example, after a breakthrough in negotiations that could end the heavy international sanctions, stocks boomed in companies controlled by Iran's supreme leader and the Islamic Revolutionary Guard Corps. This was a sign that the sanctions had real bite.[7]

That's just the regimes that actually had sanctions applied. It doesn't get at the deterrence effect of conditional repression. I haven't seen any data on this at the country level. There are lots of stories of success, but it's hard to quantify them. We do have data on another breed of thug, however: organized criminals and cartels. The evidence is still emerging, but conditional repression seems to make gangsters and mafias less violent. One example comes from focused deterrence programs in American cities, where police and prosecutors commit to crack down on the most murderous groups. There have been twelve studies, and on average they found the strategy brought gang killings down. Granted, the data are small and a little shaky. And most of these studies compare homicide rates in cities that tried the policy to a selection of those that did not—a good comparison group, but no randomized trial. Still, the consistency of results is promising.[8]

Another example comes from the way that different countries deal with international drug rings. "Backed into a corner, cartels fight," Ben Lessing argues, but "given an attractive alternative to conduct their business in less violent ways, most do." The Colombian government did this well, he argues. They gave drug lords a warning: cut down on the violence or we will come down hard on you—including extradition to the United States. Lessing believes the policy helped to bring peace to Colombia. The Mexican government took another approach. It went after drug lords naively and unconditionally. This strategic misstep did nothing to broker peace, Lessing argues. In fact, it prolonged and expanded the violence.

In the end, targeting penalties at the thugs and autocrats who cross red lines is not so much a proven strategy as a persuasive idea, closely in line with our theory of why we fight, with reasonable but imperfect support. That's fine. Modest improvements on the margin are going to be a theme, and I want us to learn to love them.

ENFORCING

Let's turn to another modest success: armed peacekeepers, unarmed mediators, and other third-party facilitators and enforcers. Prendergast was growing disillusioned with some of these actors, with good reason. Take UN peacekeeping missions. Their fans idealize them as impartial heroes in powder blue. Skeptics label them the "peacekeeping-humanitarian complex" giving every country the same "Failed State Package."[9] They're both correct. Peacekeepers could work much better. Still, by addressing the reasons bargains break down, they nonetheless make strides toward peace.

The first time I met a blue-helmeted foot battalion, I admit I wasn't impressed. They were from Pakistan, stationed in Liberia's north. The foot soldiers were poor and not very educated. Almost none of them spoke English, and so the patrols couldn't manage the simplest interactions with Liberian civilians. They drove around in pickup trucks with guns, and seemed to do their best never to get out of their vehicles. None of this is unusual—you can hear similar stories of peacekeepers anywhere in the world. The Pakistanis, of course, were mainly Muslim as well, and so some locals saw them as partisans in an area of the country long known for Christian-Muslim violence.

I knew them partly because I ate at their canteen. Whenever research took me to Liberia's north, my colleagues and I would drive to the outskirts of the county capital to dine in the shabby trailer that served as the officers' mess hall. Aid workers were allowed to buy food there. The kitchen can't have been clean, as there was always a good chance I'd be sick to my stomach the next day. But I was tired of the Liberian diet of spicy, oily potato greens, mystery bush meat, and a vegetable aptly name bitter balls. I couldn't resist a delicious plate of biryani and dal. The officers often spoke English, were well educated and polite, but (as far as I could tell) were disdainful of the locals and keen to go home.[10]

Peacekeeping is a business, one of America's ambassadors to the United Nations once explained to me. She had the unenviable job of making peace missions less dysfunctional. Poor and middle-income countries get big pay-offs from rich nations to send their troops to restless places like Liberia. These troop-sending countries spend a tiny fraction of that payoff on the soldiers and officers, of course, and they pocket the rest of the money. It's no secret—the payments are a massive subsidy to their militaries at home, all because the rich nations don't want to put their own people in harm's way. So the wealthy countries outsource peace. Once there, these developing country battalions are notoriously inefficient and plagued by management issues. And they rarely have the skills or even the language to solve big problems.[11] However, I soon learned to appreciate these missions despite their flaws.

THEY FOUND THE GIRL'S BODY NEAR THE NEW MOSQUE. FOURTEEN YEARS OLD, KAMARA had disappeared the day before, walking home over rolling hills of dense tropical foliage. She'd been picking cassava on her family's forest plot.

Kamara was a Lorma, a group that practiced a mix of Christianity and local traditions. The town of Konia, like most places in Liberia's northern reaches, was cleaved by faith. "The Mandingo are foreigners," the Lorma would complain about their mainly Muslim rivals, "and they control all the businesses." "We've been here for generations!" the Mandingo would bite back. "The Lorma persecute us; they make us stay inside when the devil comes out." They were referring to a common traditional ceremony, a kind of costumed parade through the village, meant for the eyes of the Lorma alone. "We lose money, and their devils abuse us," the Mandingo would complain to visitors like me.[12]

It sounds petty and superstitious, but there were deeper issues in the town—which sect would control the best market property, who has rights to farmland, who would become the town chief or magistrate, and what laws would they enforce? Most so-called religious quarrels in Liberia have such secular roots. Occasionally these disputes turned violent, and sectarian mobs turned on one another with fists and machetes. During Liberia's long war, the region around Konia was one of the most contested places, and the brutal fighting fell along this religious divide.

Kamara's murder tore this cleavage back open. Her angry, grieving parents confronted the mosque's imam. Someone had told them that Muslims consecrate new mosques with the blood of children. But that was outrageous. The imam had no idea what happened, he explained. And why would they put the body there if they were guilty of the crime? Unfortunately, there was no one to investigate and determine the facts. There was no impartial or trusted authority to judge the evidence and make a decision. There was zero promise of punishment for offenders—no Leviathan.

It was just a few years after the end of its civil war, and Liberia's police barely functioned. They were few, they were untrained, and they lacked the most basic equipment. They didn't even have uniforms. The courts were far away, backlogged and corrupt. The jails were almost nonexistent—small wooden shacks. If you wanted an arrested relative fed, you brought them their food. At the time, few of these officers were impartial. Sometimes they were worse than that—the one time my team and I investigated a murder, in a town not far from Konia, we quickly learned the culprit was the local chief of police.

Clearly, there wasn't going to be state justice for Kamara. So her clan did what most societies do when they don't have a formal system: they organized a mob. A large group of Lorma marched on the imam's house, roughed him up, and damaged his property. Then they threatened to burn down the mosque.

News of the violence spread. Every town in the region had a similar sectarian divide. Suddenly, these rivals all went on alert. In each town, Muslims and Christians were outraged by the injustices committed by the other group. They failed to see the other's point of view. This was the same mix of rigid frames, anger, misperceptions, and righteous anger that we talked about in past chapters. Enterprising politicians on either side could leverage this opportunity for short-term political gain. All the ingredients for a breakdown were there.

Over the next few days, mob attacks and riots swelled. Churches and mosques began burning across the county. Liberia's vice president came to give a speech in the local capital, and we heard reports that a mob surrounded and stoned the building, trapping him inside.

Events like these would be dangerous at any time, but the years right after a peace agreement are especially perilous. Kamara was murdered in 2010. The country had been quiet for about eight years, after fourteen years of some of the worst fighting and political instability imaginable. This postwar period is a fragile moment in any country. The fear is that local troubles will undermine the bigger peace.[13]

This is because the decade after a conflict is a time when de jure and de facto power are in flux. If you play the game well, and get lucky, you and your group can end up with a peaceful deal where you have a huge share of the national pie—the natural resources, the aid dollars, the ability to set policy, the creation of the nation you desire. This was true in villages, too: who would control the markets, the best land, the political posts—everything was up for grabs. The stakes are seldom higher.

At the same time, the bargaining range has shrunk. In addition to all the parochialism and passions, all the conditions are there for a commitment problem. It's subtle but important. Think about this in terms of the pie-splitting game, one where, at the end of the civil war, your group had even odds of winning if you kept fighting. That means you can expect roughly half of the nation's spoils in the bargained peace. In the months and years following a peace agreement, however, all the rules are being rewritten (the de jure power in society) and control of the wealth and guns and popular support are in flux (the de facto power). If you act quickly or cleverly, you could grab most of this power, raising your chances of victory far higher. It's like a handgun lying between two enemies at the climax of a Hollywood film— neither one can credibly commit not to reach for it. This is one reason why civil wars so often start and stop, start and stop.

Worst of all, at this crucial moment, local institutions and channels of communication are frail. In Liberia's case, there were few police, the courts were too few and corrupt, the government bureaucracy was barely up and running, and groups were polarized and mistrustful. So not only is there no one to hold either side to commitments, each side is shrouded in a fog—a haze of noise and private information. Altogether, it's a terrible mix. The bargaining range is so small that one destabilizing event, like a murder and an isolated ethnic riot, can be enough to ignite a wider war. Keeping it under control, getting a nation through that perilous moment, is the fundamental function of a foreign peacekeeping mission.

BACK IN NORTHERN LIBERIA, AS THE RIOTS UNFOLDED, THERE WAS ONE GROUP WITH THE ability to act: those underwhelming Pakistani peacekeeping troops. They were the local arm of a broader UN mission, roughly fifteen thousand soldiers strong in all, from dozens of countries.

As the mob violence ballooned, the UN battalion was slow to get involved. At first, I thought this was idleness and cowardice. Only later did I learn about the tricky line they have to walk. Liberia's police and civilian authorities need to stand up on their own, eventually. After eight years, it was time to give them the first opportunity to respond. If the peacekeepers stepped in right away, local institutions would have the wrong incentives, and the peacekeepers would never be able to go home.

When the pickups full of blue helmets finally did roll in, they were able to clear the rioters from the county capital without much trouble. The mob was unarmed and disorganized, and it folded at the first sign of authority and discipline. Simply being able to send officers into these hot spots was hugely valuable, extinguishing sparks that could light a nationwide fire. Still, these monolingual foot soldiers were incapable of settling the Konia dispute, let alone the deeper tensions between Muslims and Christians. Fortunately, the mission was bigger than just a few troops. The United Nations had been preparing for this moment for years.

Ever since the peace agreement, UN agencies had been placing radio towers all around the country. They blasted popular music, had the best news service, aired entertaining shows, and played some clumsy peace propaganda, too. In remote villages, they were often the only broadcast around. The real purpose was for moments like the one in Konia. Whoever controlled the airwaves controlled the message. Also, the mission had built a good relationship with the most senior imams and ministers all over the country. The UN force put representatives from both faiths on the radio to calm fears, dispel rumors, and talk all sides down. Along with the patrols in pickups, that helped things calm down in a few days.

What I saw in that brief episode is a microcosm of what peacekeepers do every day. The day-to-day work of a mission is to help deals get made and stick. It's not done in grand gestures but in small, ordinary actions—like a well-timed radio broadcast, or quelling a mob. They also do a bunch of slow institution building, helping rivals share power, fostering new systems of accountability, and building up the state's ability to control violence.

For starters, these missions try to shape the incentives of unchecked elites. Splinter groups hesitate to launch a sneak attack with a well-armed UN mission in place. Warlords are pushed out of their strongholds and surrender their weapons. Peacekeeping forces also give unchecked leaders reasons to stand down. We've already seen an example: the short-lived buyout package for White Flower, to get him and his thugs off the rubber plantation.

The missions also reduce uncertainty and misperceptions. Besides setting up radio stations, they monitor whether both sides stick to the terms of the deal. They supervise arms decommissions and troop drawdowns. They create forums where both sides can meet, talk, and build trust. They eliminate speculation and reduce fear and anger, diminishing everyone's need to hold on to their guns. When accidents happen, like the flare-up in Konia, peacekeepers can arbitrate and mediate on the spot. They counter the worst misconstruals. They get cooler heads to reign.

Finally, the ground troops also enforce deals. In that imaginary Hollywood film, it's the third actor stepping into the scene and kicking the handgun away. Now the rivals can credibly commit to walking away. Likewise, with a mission, each side worries less about preventive and preemptive strikes, should their rival gain a momentary advantage. Sometimes, by the time the peacekeepers draw down, the local norms and institutions have gotten strong enough that bigger deals can hold.

It's important to be clear about the kind of conflict we're talking about, however: internal wars, where at least two armed groups (one of which is usually the government) wage a conventional military conflict. Something has kept these rivals from finding a bargain. There are other forms of international armed intervention: to stop mass slaughter, to reverse coups, or to topple an authoritarian regime. But many of these are attempts to stop repression, not war. The roots of tyranny and oppression are different, and the five logics don't necessarily apply. Since the diagnosis is distinct, so are the solutions. People sometimes forget this. They look at peacekeeping in civil wars and extend the lessons to regime change. We won't do that. Humanitarian military intervention is a different question for another time. Our focus here is not on every ill in the world. It is on prolonged organized fighting between groups.[14]

When it comes to calming internal wars, however, we have learned this:

peacekeepers help entrench peace. Not always or as well as they could, but they generally make terrible situations a little better. A small, passionate army of political scientists have tried to calculate what happens when these missions intervene. Page Fortna, a political scientist at Columbia, made one of the earlier and best-evidenced cases for what peacekeepers do. She compared the internal wars that did and didn't receive troops and found that these missions were associated with more lasting calm. The obvious worry is that peacekeepers went to the easy places, manufacturing a correlation with peace. But Fortna and others found signs that peacekeepers get sent to the more difficult conflicts on average. If true, the correlations *understate* what peacekeepers can do. Political scientists have also compared long versus short missions, large versus small ones, and those mandated to use force or not. In general, larger and longer and more empowered missions seem to reduce the killing and diminish contagion to neighbors.[15]

Liberia is a good example. Its long war ended in 2003 when the United States sent a multinational force led by two hundred marines, supported by warships off the coast. That (plus international pressure and West African mediation) pushed the warlord Charles Taylor out of the presidency. It also changed the incentives of other warlords big and small, established a truce between the fractured parties, and paved the way for the larger UN-led force to enter.

In some ways, a war like Liberia's offered peacekeepers ideal conditions. For one, Liberia is a small country, in terms of area and the number of people, and so fifteen thousand troops proved an effective presence. What a contrast to places where the conflict is spread over a vast terrain, like South Sudan or the eastern Congo, where UN forces have struggled. Another advantage in Liberia is that its people identified with the West and its ideals, and there was no world power backing one side. If an insurgent group sees the West or the United Nations as ideological enemies, a mission will struggle more. And conflicts backed by superpowers are unlikely to end without the cooperation of all the patron states. So there are limits to what blue helmets can do.

The one disadvantage peacekeepers faced in Liberia was that they walked into an ongoing fight. For obvious reasons, it's easier for outsiders to guarantee a peace agreement already in place, and so UN missions tend to work best after warring rivals have found a truce. In the case of Liberia, however, war was waged by opportunistic warlords, where all sides were relatively weak. Arguably, unchecked commanders and a commitment problem were all that stood in the way of a deal. So it was feasible for peacekeepers to march into an ongoing fight and impose a truce in some cases. But there are never any certainties in war. Intervening is risky, and the mission could have gone disastrously.[16]

Altogether, even if peacekeepers aren't a magic solution, their record of modest success implies there probably would have been fewer war deaths in the last thirty years if the world had more and bigger missions. For all their weaknesses, I don't think we should do away with these forces, any more than I would eliminate a police force owing to their deep and systemic problems. Instead, I think the evidence says that fixing these enforcement organizations makes sense. More accountable and representative forces are the path to peace.[17]

We need to be careful labeling these enforcement missions alone, however. A lot of the credit I have given to peacekeeping forces doesn't belong to the troops. There's usually a small army of civilians working alongside the troops on disputes, reconciliation, and the incentives for peace. The evidence these missions work includes the efforts of these lower-profile people. A lot of what they do, what makes these missions effective, doesn't fall into "enforcing." They're expediting bargains with information and procedure. This noncoercive facilitation is a crucial intervention too.

FACILITATING

When Tony Blair assumed leadership of the UK Labour Party in 1994, he turned to Jonathan Powell to be his chief of staff. Tall and lean, his dark curly hair beginning to gray at the temples, Powell had been a British diplomat for sixteen years. He wasn't the obvious choice for the job. Nor, when

Blair became prime minister three years later, was Powell the natural pick to lead peace talks with the IRA. "I had no training in negotiation," he explained. More ominously, a half century before, the IRA had shot his father through the ear. Years later, they stuck his brother on a death list. "I didn't feel warm and cuddly about these people," Powell recalled. Indeed, the first time he met IRA leaders Gerry Adams and Martin McGuinness, he refused to shake their hands.

Negotiations changed his mind. By the end of the year, he and Blair held their first public meeting with the IRA leaders at the prime minister's home in London. Right away, Powell's point of view changed:

> Adams and McGuinness came into Downing Street. They came down the long corridor that takes you to the cabinet room at the end of the building. And I brought them into the room and took them round to the far side of the table with the windows behind them. And in an attempt to break the ice, Martin McGuinness put his hands on the back of the chair and said, "So this is where the damage was done, then?"
>
> I was horrified. I said, "Yes. The IRA mortars landed in the garden behind you. The windows blew in. My brother, who was with John Major at the time, dragged him under the table to get him away from the falling glass." And he looked horrified and said, "No, no, no. I was talking about the treaty with Michael Collins in 1921." It was a completely different sense of history on the two sides. You had to break through this to have any chance of getting an understanding.[18]

Powell never forgot the lesson. Rivals have amazingly different mindsets, beliefs, and memories. As we saw in earlier chapters, they misperceive and selectively remember. They live in "intellectual ghettos," Powell realized, "only talking to each other and very rarely getting to understand how they're seen elsewhere."

This misperception is true of any two rivals, but it's worse when one of them is hunted or clandestine. Insurgents and terrorists "are completely ignorant of the outside world," Powell realized. "They have never left the country, they have been confined to rural areas for years, they live in hiding or underground, they are surrounded by trusted people only like them, and it is very risky for them to mingle with foreigners." Meanwhile, officials like Powell often have their own muzzles and barriers, banned by convention or even law from so much as talking to their rebellious enemies.

Powell learned that he had to engage with people he hated. That was really, really hard. After concluding the Good Friday Agreement, however, he decided that he could use his insight and experiences to help other enemies find resolutions. He'd seen firsthand the difficulties of negotiating on your own with the other side. Foreign mediators had made a real difference in his own negotiations with the IRA. Maybe he could do the same. Over the next two decades, Powell helped mediate peace in the Basque region of Spain, in Colombia, and he presided over occasional failures like Libya.

Partly, Powell learned the importance of little things: gestures of respect, long amounts of time spent together, and being able to meet in secret. Mediators can help make this happen. Most of all, however, Powell realized the importance of process. He now likes to quote former Israeli prime minister Shimon Peres, who used to say that both Israelis and Palestinians knew what the terms of a peaceful deal looked like: "The good news is that there is a light at the end of the tunnel," Peres remarked. "The bad news is that there is no tunnel." The job of a mediator, Powell decided, was to help build this passageway and usher both sides down it.

If there's a problem with these mediator accounts of peace, however—and there are many such accounts, new books by more diplomats every year—it is that they always sound a little bit like magic ("build a tunnel") and a little trivial (gestures of respect, or agonizing over the size and shape of the negotiating table). It's possible that mediation is a delusion. Maybe these diplomats don't do much more than murmur incantations and arrange rituals in the hopes that peace will magically emerge. Or perhaps the real peace comes from great powers guaranteeing the settlement, and the mediator is incidental.

Fortunately, that's probably not the case. There's no mystical force at work. Rather, mediators help end violence because they tackle the reasons that bargains break down. Like other good remedies, the tactics map to the five reasons for war. Most of all, mediators try to reduce uncertainty and private information. If states disagree about their relative power, or if they worry that the other side is bluffing about its intentions or strength, trusted intermediaries can gather accurate information and relay it. They also try to reduce the emotional and perceptual errors that frustrate so much bargaining—helping each side see the conflict from the other's point of view, building a shared understanding of the history, salving anger, and basically trying to make real people behave more like the rational bargainers in our models.

Mediators also foster trust. When I say "trust," I don't mean some intangible feeling we can't put our fingers on. In my view, trust is straightforward and concrete: It comes from understanding your opponent's constraints and costs—the things they do or don't have an incentive to do. I trust you because I know it's not in your interests to betray me, not because I've judged your character. Some of these incentives are hidden, however. Rivals need credible signals. Having a reputable mediator vouch for them is sometimes good enough.

In the mid-1970s, for instance, Egyptian president Anwar Sadat told Israeli prime minister Golda Meir, "You must take my word seriously. When I made my initiative in 1971 I meant it. When I threatened war, I meant it. When I talk of peace now, I mean it." Could she believe him? US secretary of state Henry Kissinger had spent time with the Egyptians and he vouched for Sadat. "I have to tell you honestly," he told her, "my judgment is that Egypt is genuinely willing to make peace with Israel." Talks continued, and the two sides reached a peace agreement in 1979.[19]

—————

THAT'S THE THEORY. WHAT ABOUT THE EVIDENCE? MEDIATION IS A TRICKY THING TO EVAL-uate, but a clue comes from an unlikely place: summer vacations. You see, a lot of mediators are legislators and bureaucrats back home—like Jonathan Powell, for example. And many come from Europe, North America, and other northerly climes. This gives them something in common: every June or July these politicians' legislatures go into recess, or their governments wind down for a little while, freeing them to go other places.

The political scientist Bernd Beber noticed this quirk when he was a graduate student at Columbia. He also saw that truces and peace talks break out all the time, more or less evenly through the year. If your negotiations began during the northern summer months, however, he found they were more likely to receive a foreign mediator.

This is important, because the Jonathan Powells of the world are never randomly assigned. They have to be invited and they also must want to go. This is going to mess up any comparisons. Because the conflicts that get mediators will be systematically different from those without them. If mediators go to the easier cases, or the ones where great powers are willing to enforce the settlement, then mediation will be spuriously correlated with peaceful outcomes. What we'd like to do is find a natural experiment, one with randomness in where the Powells of the world go, but nothing else changes. That's what was so useful about the summer vacations. Beber showed that the probability of your getting a mediator is higher if your truce begins in the summer, and that these agreements were more durable. It helps to disentangle the tricky cause and effect.[20]

It's not just civil and international wars that benefit from mediators either. Remember La Oficina and El Pacto del Fusil, back in Medellín? Recently the pact began unraveling. Homicides tripled within a few weeks as a handful of combos began skirmishing, and the city's criminal organizations geared for war. So, secretly, the government decided on a transfer of every major criminal boss in Medellín to a different prison, all at the same time. Instead of being scattered over a dozen different institutions around the country, the bosses all found themselves in the same holding area for a few days, waiting for a transfer. Then, by "coincidence," a criminal trusted by all sides was arrested for some minor offense and placed in the same patio—a natural mediator. We don't know exactly what happened behind those metal bars. By the following week, however, murders had fallen back to their previous levels. Similarly, you can see examples of secret facilitation of criminal peace across the Americas. Such mediation has brought homicides down in some of the most violent cities on the planet. (The only tragedy is that some governments criminalize this important service, and prosecute the bureaucrats, politicians, community leaders, and priests who help gangs negotiate.)[21]

Besides large wars and gangs, mediation and negotiation skills can help preserve the peace at a much more local, interpersonal level too. That happens to be why I was in Konia, in Liberia's north. A local visionary named James Ballah had an educational program he wanted to push out to the most violence-prone towns in Liberia. I was trying to figure out if, like Prendergast or Powell, he had found a better path to peace.

Ballah's idea was this: train local chiefs, ministers, imams, and concerned citizens on how to negotiate and mediate better—a crash course in the skills of alternative dispute resolution for a big chunk of each village. It sounded a little wacky, but that was my day job: finding the inspired, too-good-to-be-true James Ballahs of the world, helping them scale up their ideas, and testing to see if they worked. Local officials in three counties flagged 250 fractious towns and villages. Then specialists in dispute resolution techniques visited nearly one hundred of them, running workshops every few weeks for months on end.

To imagine these places, start by picturing endless miles of rainforest. Then picture a huge clearing with ramshackle homes of plaster and corrugated metal. A handful of the villages were next to a highway. Most villages were a long walk over remote trails. If there was a road, it had washed out years before. People were isolated and dirt poor. They eked out a living growing a little dryland rice or vegetables on untilled land. There were no oxen or tractors. You almost never saw livestock. People farmed what they could manage with a hoe in the wet tropical forest.

A lot of their disputes were over land. They didn't own much else to fight about. Each year, a fifth of the villagers told us they'd had a disagreement over farm boundaries, property inheritance, or who could use the best market spot. Half of these quarrels were hostile and aggressive, and a quarter resulted in destroyed property or a brawl. Occasionally, one led to a village-wide uprising, like the mob riled up by Kamara's death.

Ballah's trainers did a few things. They taught some basic negotiation techniques: framing problems in positive and cooperative terms; speaking one's mind plainly and addressing disputes directly; avoiding accusatory statements; and "active listening"—repeating back the other person's concerns after they express them. They also educated villagers about their automatic biases, especially misperceptions and misconstruals, and they practiced techniques for dealing with them. This included ways to manage anger—such as counting to ten, or walking away to cool down. Through village meetings, they also tried to create consensus around certain procedures. Violence was decried, of course. But they also got villagers to agree on some standards of appropriate behavior—a collective expectation that people would follow the techniques they learned, and treat anger or accusatory statements with scorn. The trainers also legitimized dozens of different groups—ethnic leaders, town mayors, and even average citizens—to mediate and judge conflict. But once you chose a forum or informal court to hear your case, everyone agreed that you couldn't leave if you didn't like where it was going. This forum shopping had been a kind of commitment problem before the training came along.

Their efforts had real effects. We visited the villages a year after Ballah's program, and then two years after that, comparing the places that got the program to those that didn't. Ballah was right: a third more disputes got resolved, and violence fell by a third. It didn't stop all the fights, but Ballah and the trainers made a huge difference.

There was no sorcery here. The trainers were helping local leaders and villagers acquire the same skills and techniques that professional negotiators and mediators use. They designed their program to reduce uncertainty and misperceptions, and to foster commitment. They did so by helping create some coherent norms—widely shared informal rules of behavior—one of the most basic institutions in successful societies. It was a microcosm of what good negotiation and mediation can accomplish, at any level. This, I came to believe, is what Shimon Peres meant by building a tunnel.[22]

SOCIALIZING

I want to zero in on a crucial piece of Ballah's program, however. The techniques and norms were designed to reduce uncertainty and increase commitment. That was huge. But it wasn't just facilitation; it was also a program of socialization. The community had to sit down and decide on appropriate behavior. They practiced these new conventions inside and outside the training sessions as they tackled their backlog of land disputes. Learning to recognize your biases, listening to your enemy and trying to understand and sympathize with their point of view, and controlling your anger and impulses—these are all habits. They can be learned and acquired. They were reinforced by social norms and convention. Societies can engineer these norms for themselves.

The sociologist Norbert Elias called this the civilizing process, and he wrote a famous book by that name. Elias examined Europe over the last one thousand years; there he documented a gradual decline in violence—knife fights, honor duels, and brawls. Alongside that decline he observed the slow invention of manners, niceties, and standards of refinement. Common to all these was the accumulation of habits of self-control, more sympathy and consideration for others, and a more rational and forward-looking mindset. Elites often led this norm change, by altering their own behavior and acting as examples. Recently, Steven Pinker expanded on Elias's argument, arguing that the civilizing process is why violence in most societies has declined.

According to Elias and Pinker, some of the credit goes to a gradual cultural enlightenment, some to checks and balances, some to the state—all the subjects of the last three chapters.

As Ballah's experiment suggests, however, this civilizing process can also be engineered. Of course, "civilizing" is a troublesome term. So is "social engineering," though if we are being honest, that's precisely what it is (even when people are doing it to themselves). In past chapters, we've talked about how elites use this for selfish purposes—propaganda and misinformation that fires up outrage and antipathy. Now let's talk about the ways people like James Ballah have tried to socialize their societies for the good.

IT WAS A CLOUDLESS AFTERNOON IN MONROVIA'S RED LIGHT MARKET, AND THE SUN seared down on our heads. The luckier market vendors hid from its glare under tattered beach umbrellas, their wares piled into rusting wheelbarrows or arranged on tarps laid out over the packed brown dirt.

I was trying to meet the city's underclass. Not the ones selling used shoes on dusty tarps, or hawking shampoo in their arms—they were poor but, like most Monrovians, they were upright and peaceful citizens. It was the figures along the fringe who interested me: the ones who clustered in the small thatch huts that served as drug dens, or who stood with empty wheelbarrows, ready to carry your goods for hire, but who made most of their money from pickpocketing and armed robbery. Most were ex-fighters from the civil war. Men like these, the government worried, would be tomorrow's rioters, mercenaries, and rebels.

I was wandering through Red Light with Johnson Borh, a tall, smiling, meaty man in his midthirties. He ran a community organization for ex-fighters and street youth, and so here we were, tired, our shirts damp with sweat, looking for the least law-abiding men we could find. We rested in the shade of derelict buildings, or to the side of massive refuse piles, or inside little thatch drug dens, listening to the youth describe their daily hustle.

One day, as we stepped away from one of these meetings into the bright light, a young man across the street spotted Borh and waved. He was young and skinny, tidily dressed in threadbare clothes, selling used shoes from his pushcart. After he and Borh caught up, I asked how they knew one another. "Well," the man replied, "I used to be like them," as he pointed to the dealers we'd just met, "but then I went through Johnson's program." The next afternoon the same thing happened, with a different man, and again the day after that. They were all proud graduates of Borh's organization. "Tell me again what you do?" I said to Johnson. His summary, full of buzzwords and hyperbole, was little help at first. So we spent the next two days at my computer, in a cavernous bar, writing up what he did day by day, activity by activity. Afterward, I went to Jeannie, a psychologist. "What does this look like to you?" She paged through my notes. "This looks like cognitive behavioral therapy," she replied, "unusual, but it could work."

IN LIBERIA, FIFTY YEARS AFTER AARON BECK INVENTED CBT, BORH HAD NEVER HEARD OF the famous professor or his method. But Borh knew what had impact. For fifteen years, he'd absorbed trainings from visiting social workers, downloaded handbooks for dealing with delinquent youth, and borrowed Western ideas and techniques. Beck's discoveries were embedded in all these materials. For Borh, each day was an informal experiment. If something worked, he kept it. If it didn't, he threw it away.

I sat in on a few sessions. Twenty men sat on scarred plastic chairs, on the third floor of an abandoned six-story building. Borh met the outcasts three times a week, in the mornings, for just two months. They covered a lot. Most of all, they learned and practiced techniques to cope with angry emotions and hostile confrontations. They practiced trying to see their adversaries' points of view. All of these are standard CBT techniques for managing problematic thoughts and emotions. The men also tried a new identity on for size. They practiced dressing and acting like normal members of society, going to banks and supermarkets between sessions. They learned through experience and practice that other people would be understanding and welcoming rather than spurn them. With Borh's help, the young men resocialized themselves.

Borh had run this program in small groups for years, but there had never been a large-scale test. We revamped it a little, and rechristened the program STYL—Sustainable Transformation of Youth in Liberia. He and I recruited colleagues and raised money, and a year later we launched a randomized control trial with one thousand of the most violent and unstable men in the city.

The results amazed me. They still do. A year after the program, assaults and criminality had fallen by half among the men who underwent the program. This transformation was greatest and most sustained among the group that got therapy plus some cash to start a small business on the side, like shining shoes or selling used clothes. They did best not because they had more income, since those businesses often failed after a few months. Rather, the temporary enterprise let the men keep practicing the new behaviors, solidifying their new upright identity, and reinforcing their attempts to change. Ten years later, we went back. Those men were still half as likely as the others to commit crimes or violence.[23]

AT THE SAME TIME BORH WAS DEVELOPING STYL, A YOUNG MAN IN CHICAGO KNOWN AS Tony D found a similar calling. He'd grown up poor. But Tony made it to a community college down the block from home, where he discovered psychology. "It called to me," he explained, "this idea of emotions and behaviors." After going to graduate school, he started tinkering, too, letting a program develop organically. "I started forming these circles, doing clinical counseling, engagement and men's work," he recalled. "I started talking to boys about manhood and challenging them to look at themselves." Like Borh, he wasn't just shooting for self-awareness and emotional control. He wanted the boys to develop a new, bigger, more peaceful identity. He called his program Becoming A Man, or BAM.

As my coauthors and I were helping scale and study STYL, a group of economists and psychologists at the University of Chicago's Crime Lab did the same with Tony D's organization. Our results came out at almost the same time. None of us had ever met or compared notes, but we found the same thing: Borh and Tony D had created some of the most effective anti-violence programs ever measured.[24]

The two studies help launch a conversation in America and beyond. Cities in Latin America began experimenting with similar programs. Aid donors began to subsidize local attempts. Today, there are copycat programs happening all over the world. That includes Chicago. When gun violence spiked in 2016, the city looked to STYL and BAM as models. Instead of targeting street youth and high school kids, however, a group of nonprofits in Chicago decided to work with the city's most likely shooters. Whereas STYL and BAM worked with delinquent young people who had never killed, Chicago tried finding and working with one of the most trigger-prone populations in the world. The Rapid Employment and Development Initiative was born. READI offered a combination of CBT and jobs. You've already met one of its top outreach workers—Napoleon English. READI was the program that had us pounding the streets of North Lawndale at the outset of this book. The program's early results are promising, including signs of a fall in homicides.[25]

I RELATE BORH'S AND TONY D'S STORIES NOT BECAUSE THE SOLUTION TO WORLD PEACE IS universal CBT. Nor do I think wars are triggered by spurts of anger (though those outbursts don't help). Rather, in these studies and in Ballah's negotiation program, I see a microcosm of the civilizing process Norbert Elias described. Self-control is a habit. So is looking ahead to the future, controlling your anger, recognizing your biases, or trying to see the world from another person's point of view. All of us can change. Even adults. Even the most far gone.

Some of our patience, restraint, empathy, and consideration is imbued in our genes, but mostly it is learned and reinforced. Successful societies have interventions and institutions that saturate our lives with these lessons, and they construct laws and norms to fortify them. They socialize their young to nonviolence. In Western countries, for instance, the average preschool curriculum is socio-emotional, working through a lot of the same skills and norms that Ballah and Borh tried to impart: talk out your differences, learn to breathe, violence is not acceptable. In a village or a grandmother's lap anywhere from France to Kenya to China, the teachings are similar: respect others, listen, control your anger, focus on the future. These are also the same things Aaron Beck taught his adult patients in the United States. Some people and communities just need a little remedial help to acquire these skills or norms. Especially after a war. Sometimes this socialization comes from outsiders, but most of the time people remake their own societies: governments, communities, elders, and brilliant local social entrepreneurs like Ballah, Borh, or Tony D. It's peer to peer more than top down.

The same skill development is crucial in business and law. If you're a lawyer or a mediator or a manager, not only do you hone these abilities, you try to instill them in your clients and staff. Professional mediators and negotiators counsel people on how to avoid anger as well as the most extreme forms of bias—demonization, misprojection, and self-righteousness. Nothing is more harmful to everyday negotiations. As these experts will tell you, these habits don't always come naturally. We could all use a little remedial help.[26]

And just as communities try to foster these habits and norms informally, governments use media and propaganda. Our airwaves are flooded with subtle and not-so-subtle socialization into social harmony. They acculturate us to avoid violence, or they encourage us to adopt the perspective of others. In America we start early, with *Mister Rogers' Neighborhood* and *Sesame Street*. In cleaved nations like Rwanda, the authorities broadcast soap operas and talk shows to promote peace. All of their methods are deliberate, and often cognitive behavioral. The scholars who study these media programs and other perspective-taking exercises proved them to be effective and durable.[27]

Earlier in the book I asked where our integrated, peaceful social identities come from. Why do people have wider and wider identities, or a more sympathetic, humanitarian view of the world? I think the answer is "bit by bit," sometimes accidentally, but often deliberately. In part, peace is the product of socialization.

INCENTIVIZING

So far, we've talked mostly about sticks, like sanctions and security forces. Or we've talked about socialization, which is often quite subtle. What about carrots—big explicit ones, dangled right in front of our faces? Can't the world promise aid, jobs, renown, or other rewards to leaders who keep the peace? The short answer is yes, but know this: these carrots can taste bitter.

In the unequal, unchecked societies most prone to conflict, peace usually means dealmaking between powerful people. Order comes when elites have a stake in stability. This means, in the short term, that they often enjoy unequal power and unequal spoils. Sadly, often the key to preventing another armed uprising is co-opting the people who have the de facto power and making it worth their while not to fight. Allowing them to form parties and run in elections; buying them off; embedding them in a patron-client network with the ruling coalition. This is the darker side of peace.

Imagine a country with two well-armed factions, each one headed by a powerful cabal, each one with its own private incentives for war. Something must counteract their war bias. Giving unsavory people a huge share of aid, resource rents, or seats in an assembly is one way to do this. The West and Russia did this in the 1990s among the former Soviet republics. That's a major reason so few of these newly independent nations collapsed into conflict in those tenuous years. America did the same thing after invading Afghanistan, embracing warlords and feigning blindness to their thuggery and theft to maximize the parts of the country at peace. And rich countries pledge foreign aid to conflicted African countries knowing full well that this pipeline of cash will fill the pockets of rulers.[28] These policies spring from an unsentimental realpolitik, rationalizing that inequality is worth it to stop the death and destruction. It's a kind of competition management—a subsidy for peace.

But rewarding kleptocrats and thugs for not fighting has two problems. One is that this inequality and corruption is at odds with many people's ideals. Domestic reformers and international activists are caught in a trap: policies that eliminate elite privileges and corruption are noble and well-intentioned, but in the short term they could increase political violence. Patronage is the glue that holds many fragile societies together. Ignoring this fact—pursuing anti-corruption or full democratization blind to the incentives of powerful armed actors—can risk a return to war. We forget this at great risk.[29]

The second problem is that romancing oligarchs and warlords seems to run directly against one of the secrets to a successful society: making power more accountable and spreading it out in society, through checks and balances. Centralized authority amplifies every one of the five reasons for war, so why would anyone bolster it?

This might be the toughest trade-off in peacebuilding, one the world is still struggling to get right. Should superpowers buy off dictators and warlords to avert a civil war? Should a principled president bring a powerful and corrupt sectarian leader into government? Should a city come to an implicit bargain with its Mafias and gangs: keep the peace and you can keep your drug profits? You can buy an end to fighting in the short run, and it's possible the bandits in charge will see their own self-interest served by keeping the peace. But this is a delicate balance, and violence is never far away. It's not clear how stable and long term these arrangements will be.

THERE IS NO EASY ANSWER. TO RESOLVE THIS TENSION, THE IDEALISTIC ACTORS I KNOW try to balance realpolitik in the short run with broadening de facto and de jure power in the long run. One example comes from the experience of ending civil wars. At the same time that they're buying thugs off, international nonprofits and UN agencies are hastily organizing elections, often just one or two years after the fighting has stopped. Meanwhile, domestic politicians are trying to reconstitute the bureaucracy, creating a class of independent professionals, and helping it deliver health and education to the poorest. They also subsidize industry and make trade deals to reignite the economy and bring back big business. Indeed, since the end of the Cold War, almost every post-conflict effort has been designed to usher in a transition to democracy, respect for civil liberties, a market-oriented economy, and the rule of law. After World War II, the Marshall Plan aimed to do the same.[30]

There's much to be cynical about. Take the hastily organized elections. Who are outsiders to rewrite the rules for another people? Critics also worry these polls are empty rituals of democracy rather than the real thing, "giving aid donors an election barely clean enough to receive a low passing grade, but dirty enough to make it difficult for the opposition to win," according to one skeptic. Also, elections with a cabal of warlords in charge is an invitation to vote buying, intimidation, and election fixing.[31]

Or what about the bureaucracy building, and the influx of health and education aid? You might think that sounds like a great idea. But expecting weak states to do so many things just sets them up to fail. Countries like Liberia or Afghanistan barely had a civil service when the fighting waned. Whether it's outside agencies, idealistic politicians, or local voters, no one can reasonably expect the Liberian or Afghan state to run a welfare system. Most of all, it distracts them from urgent tasks only the state can do—like rebuilding security forces and justice systems. This premature load bearing risks collapsing the whole structure, these critics point out.

Others admire the aims—democracy, social services, and open economies—but decry the execution as naive and hurried. Remember, these postwar periods are delicate moments. Everything is up for grabs. Elections and market economies create intense competition at the precise moment when these societies are least equipped to handle them.[32]

I share these concerns, but I'm more hopeful. My view balances the realpolitik with idealism. Talking with terrorists and making deals with warlords is the darker but necessary side of peace. Rivals shouldn't shy from it. At the same time, every bargaining range is just that—a range. Of the available deals, concerned insiders and outsiders can work to get the most equal deal available. They can also try to influence that bargaining range, putting in place rules and policies that will slowly tilt de facto and de jure powers in the direction of justice.

Personally, whether you're a citizen of the society or an outsider, I think this means playing the long game, trying to shift power to a broader and broader group: investing in mass education and poverty reduction; university training abroad, in liberal democracies, for the next generation of elites; and training and building the bureaucratic professional class. I think it also means little rule changes, like the ones we saw in our examination of checks and balances: making voting a little easier, making elections a little cleaner, enfranchising a few more people on the margin, pushing elections out to lower levels, sharing a little tax and spending power out to provinces and towns. All the randomized and the natural experiments showed these little changes made elections more competitive, pushed policy toward the well-being of the masses, and made these places a little more peaceful.[33]

Chapter 11

WAYWARD PATHS
TO WAR AND PEACE

People have plenty of intuitions about war: that men are more likely to wage it, that the poor are more likely to rise up, or that sometimes war can be good for society—helping to settle an unstable arrangement or spurring us to advance. If true, these would point us to additional secrets to successful societies and other important interventions. Some would bolster policies that already seem like a good thing, like ending poverty, or getting more women in power. Or they could imply something more controversial, like allowing some wars to run their course.

Each claim has some truth to it, but each claim is only a partial truth. Some claims start us down a misleading path, especially when they skirt the strategic nature of competition. This is a problem—wrong diagnoses generate wrong solutions. So before we finish up, I want to show you how you can use what we've learned in the book to evaluate these kinds of claims.

People talk about why we fight all the time. Pick up an op-ed or a history book and you'll read a compelling case that climate change is going to bring political disorder, and so the most fragile places need help managing water wars and other turmoil. Or you'll hear a political speech blaming unrest on the vast number of unemployed youths, and so we need a jobs program for peace. By now, however, you've learned not to focus on the failures. You see the common logic behind the five reasons for wars, and you have a little game theory to help you ask in every case: Shouldn't there be a deal that avoids fighting, and if not, why? Which of the five logics does this explanation fit into? We can use these lessons to spot wayward paths to peace. I'll walk through a few examples, showing how things like creating jobs and increasing women's representation are important for their own sake, but they won't speed rivals to compromise. We'll see why fears that the world faces a future of water wars are probably overblown. And other ideas—like war has big benefits for society—I'll argue are dangerous myths that we should challenge rather than accept.

PUT THE WOMEN IN CHARGE?

Twenty years into the Peloponnesian War, the poet and playwright Aristophanes staged what would become one of the most famous plays of all time, *Lysistrata*; it is still performed today. Women in Athens couldn't vote, but the conflict was killing their sons, brothers, and husbands. So Lysistrata, the lead character, calls on her fellow women of Greece to deny their husbands sex until Athens and Sparta find peace.

Soon, a Spartan emissary approaches the city. In most productions, an exaggerated prop makes his condition obvious: he has a massive erection. Women in his home have heeded Lysistrata's call, he grumbles. No sex for Spartans. He pleads for a treaty. By the end of the play, representatives from each polis have gathered to reconcile. In most productions, this is a large, distressed crowd of men adorned with enormous fake phalluses. Lysistrata lectures them on the need for peace as the men carve up land rights. A celebration ensues.

This is not, sadly, the story of how the Peloponnesian War ended. (Following the play's premiere, the fighting raged on for several more years.) The play isn't an enlightened treatise on gender either. It's a bawdy comedy, written by a man, acted entirely by men, in a society dominated by men, playing up stereotypes for hilarity. Still, it captures a common view: if the women were in charge, we wouldn't have so much fighting in the first place.[1]

It's undeniable: most warriors in history have been men. Most of the leaders who've declared war—men. Raids on the neighboring village, gang, or tribe—also men. Fistfights, brawls, duels—again, overwhelmingly males. It's true on almost every continent, in almost every society. It's even true in related species.[2]

In surveys, women favor peace somewhat more than men. Most of the evidence comes from a few advanced democracies (largely the United States). Still, the results are pretty clear. If, for example, you tell people a hypothetical story of a dispute between nations, and ask whether they should fight or negotiate, women are about a quarter less likely to support violence than men.[3]

Does this mean putting more women in charge would lead to a more peaceful world? Yes and no. Yes, in the sense that excluding anyone from politics is going to make peace less likely. Bringing women into decision-making ought to make societies more representative, more checked, and therefore more pacific. This is mechanical. If only half of a society gets a say in the big decisions, then we create the agency problems we encountered in the very first reason for war. So, whether it's women, an ethnic group, or a religious minority left without a say, leaders in those societies are going ignore some costs, narrow the bargaining range, escalate the risk of war, and make peace agreements harder to hold. This is a difficult claim to test with data, but the enfranchisement of women probably spurs more peace because it reduces political distortions.[4]

Still, that's not usually what people mean when they say that women make for less belligerent politics. Rather, the claim is that, from Lysistrata to today, women have peaceful predispositions, and they will temper the excesses of men. Here's where the evidence is shakier.

At the individual level, it's obvious that men are more aggressive one-on-one or in small groups. Some of this might be a systematic and strategic bias toward using force, or strong social norms, as the US survey data above suggests. But most of this aggression is reactive, situational violence. It's not clear this hot thinking translates into more wars. Groups deliberate. Passions and urges are filtered through layers of decision-making and bureaucracy. There's an "aggregation problem" with any story of psychological drives and values—group actions aren't simply the sum of its members' feelings. Male aggression is no exception.[5]

We don't know whether reactive male aggression gets filtered out by groups. But one thing seems clear: male leaders don't take their societies to war more than female ones. When a group of political scientists pulled together over 120 years of data on leaders around the world, they found that countries led by women were about as likely to start a fight as the rest.[6] Amid the many other bargaining failures, perhaps men's excessive belligerence just doesn't matter than much.

There are some problems with this evidence, though. First, a lot of these women leaders come from democracies, and they're checked and balanced by parliaments and bureaucracies full of men. If the women were unencumbered, or if they were well represented at every level of decision-making, maybe politics would be more serene. We'd need to compare male-dominated governments with ones where women have a more equal say. Unfortunately, that evidence doesn't exist yet (partly because equal representation is still rare).

Second, there's a selection problem. What if the women who run for office and get past a prejudiced electorate are as macho as the men? Then of course they're just as likely to wield violence. This is the kind of charge people levy against former British prime minister Margaret Thatcher, once branded the Iron Lady. Some Indians gave Prime Minister Indira Gandhi the same label. If it's true, then history isn't a reliable guide to how female politicians would act in the future. Research certainly shows that women face more hurdles gaining office. We don't know whether this makes them more warlike. But the women seem to be more able leaders than the men, on average, because they had to leap over a higher bar. This differential selection means a century-long leader analysis can't tell us what we need to know.[7]

A grand experiment could help answer the question, one where we randomly assign an unchecked woman to lead some countries, while the rest get an unchecked man. As it happens, nature did just that in Europe in the five centuries before World War I. Because of the vagaries of royal succession and accidents of birth order, some states were idiosyncratically more likely to get queens than others. These female monarchs were more, not less, likely to find themselves in conflict. The reasons why show how perilous it is to make simple generalizations about gender and warfare.

HENRY VIII WAS MERELY DISAPPOINTED WHEN HIS FIRST SURVIVING CHILD, MARY, turned out to be a girl. Over the next two decades, however, disquietude slowly turned to distress as the royal couple failed to produce a male heir. Clever, charismatic, and corpulent, Henry had gathered an immense amount of power as ruler. But he was only the second in his family to be king of England, and he had no wish to see the Tudor line go extinct. A queen had never ruled England before. Therefore, Henry sought a son.[8]

After countless miscarriages and stillbirths, the king grew desperate. When his mistress became pregnant, Henry defied the pope and had his union with the queen annulled. They had been married twenty-four years. He promptly wedded his young and beautiful lover. To his dismay, however, she bore him another daughter, Elizabeth.

More miscarriages followed, and still no male heir. But Henry hesitated to divorce a second time. Instead, he accused his second wife of adultery, then had her head cut off. A few days later, Henry married her beautiful lady-in-waiting. She, at last, bore him a boy, Edward.

The next decade held more weddings, more divorces, and more untimely deaths for the king's unlucky lovers. But no more sons. Thus, when Henry died—obese, ulcer ridden, and purulent—the Tudor line seemed to rest on nine-year-old Edward alone. The boy never assumed full power. At fifteen, he fell ill, slowly wasted away, and died. He had fathered no children, and his father Henry had no living brothers. As a result, the next three rulers of

England were women. First, Jane Grey, Henry's niece, ruled for a few days. Then Henry's firstborn, whom history remembers as Bloody Mary, deposed her. After Mary's death, Henry's second-born, Elizabeth I, ruled for forty-five years.

Oeindrila Dube wondered whether she could use episodes like this one to figure out if women leaders were more warlike. A political economist, she spends much of her time looking for ways to curb violence, mostly in the contemporary world. But if you want a big sample of female heads of state, the modern era offers too few. You have to go back in time. And in early modern Europe, an unusual number of monarchs were women. Even more importantly, biology and the rules of succession injected some randomness into which countries got them and which did not.

Many factors led some countries to have queenly rule; others led to an unbroken series of men. Among these forces, however, were accidents of birth order. Some rulers, like Henry, drew a girl first. Perhaps their fathers did the same, meaning the king had sisters in the line of succession too. Together with her colleague S. P. Harish, Dube noticed that kings were more likely to be succeeded by a woman if they had older sisters or a firstborn daughter—things that were more or less random. After all, every royal pregnancy was a flip of a biological coin. Statistically, this helped the researchers parse out whether women were more likely to find themselves embroiled in war than men.[9]

The answer surprised them. Queens, it turned out, were almost 40 percent more likely to find themselves at war than kings. These reigns weren't more peaceful at all. What was going on?

Henry's daughters give us some clues. One is that men perceived queens to be weak. "Nature," said one English politician, criticizing the idea of a woman like Mary on the throne, "doth paint them forth to be weak, frail, impatient, feeble, and foolish." Perhaps King Philip II of Spain shared this low opinion, for after Elizabeth took the throne, he assembled an armada to unseat her.

Even when rallying her own troops against the invasion, the young queen had to address such prejudices. "I know I have the bodie, but of a weak and feeble woman," Elizabeth exclaimed, "but I have the heart and Stomach of a King." To signal her fortitude, "I my self will take up arms," she said. "I my self will be your General, Judge, and Rewarder of everie one of your virtues in the field." She succeeded. After Philip's defeat, Elizabeth's allies sold medals stamped with sunken Spanish ships and the inscription "Done by a female leader."[10]

This is a pattern Dube and Harish saw across the centuries: overconfident kings who persistently underestimated queens (especially the unmarried ones) and decided to attack. Partly this is a story of uncertainty. If everyone's strength were clear, then there would be no reason to underestimate women. This noise is intermingled with stubborn misperception. Part of the reason that queens had to show the "heart and Stomach of a King" was the systematic biases of the male monarchs around them.[11]

But don't take this to mean that queens were peaceful but for those nasty predatory kings. Dube also found that queens, once married, were more aggressive toward nearby states. With their sudden strength and expertise, these royal couples attacked their weakened neighbors. This is a little puzzling, since they should have squeezed their opponents for a better deal without waging war. One possibility is the inherent war bias of a powerful king and queen. Merge two royal families, and they may indulge their private needs for glory and treasure all the more.

All told, it might be true that women are inclined to compromise on an individual level, but this is only a partial truth. To the extent gender shapes conflict, it is far more intricate than "women prefer peace." Strategic interactions, plus the forces we've discussed—uncertainty, agency problems, commitment, misogyny—make predictions about war more nuanced than the sum of aggressive impulses.

TO AVERT CONFLICT, END POVERTY?

Before the laptop-lifting con man in Kenya, I wanted to be an economic historian. I'd get up each morning and trudge to the university library at

Harvard, then later at Berkeley, take the elevator down to a level deep underground, and make my way to neglected corners full of government tomes. I'd like to say they were dusty and antiquated, but mostly the stacks were just dimly lit and lonely. There I'd find digests of Latin American trade data going back 150 years, or French statistical yearbooks from a former African colony. I was searching for data—price movements in diamonds, production levels of palm oil, and discoveries of silver.

I wanted these data because I was thinking about war and the role of poverty. For most countries, commodity prices were a huge source of economic fluctuation. That's because most places for most of their history exported just one or two crops or resources. A plunge in world prices could be calamitous. For people who worked in these industries, those plummeting returns meant less income. The government also lost out on resource and trade taxes. Soon, public finances (seldom in a comfortable position to start with) would be in crisis. Civil servants, pensioners, and even (at last resort) the army would go unpaid. These cycles of boom and bust took a toll on long-run development. All told, countries with more volatile commodities have been far less likely to prosper over time.[12]

I had a hunch these swings caused conflicts too. "Economic anarchy produces political anarchy," one historian wrote, "which in turn makes economic anarchy worse." It makes a certain sense. When people are poor, soldiering looks more attractive. So if wages fell, or as mining or plantation jobs disappeared, it should have been easier to recruit fighters.[13]

Meanwhile, other evidence was percolating with a similar refrain. Ted Miguel, my adviser at Berkeley, found that times of drought in Africa were followed by years of war. Together with Juan Vargas, Oeindrila Dube also looked at Colombia during its decades-long guerrilla war and saw that plunging coffee prices led to rising attacks in the places that produced coffee. Dives in income seemed to cause fighting. This made sense. Wars are more common in poorer countries, after all. And the logic I just gave—hungry men revolt—is intuitive.[14]

So I was surprised when my commodity price study yielded nothing.

Falling prices didn't seem to cause wars—not even the huge plunges, or the ones in the most fragile places. "I must have made a mistake," I thought to myself. I put the paper aside, planning to work on it later. Like most null results, however, it languished in a file drawer. Then I met Jeannie and got wrapped up in studying African civil wars on the ground rather than from a library. Over the years, however, the belief that poverty and falling incomes cause conflict became an established view in economics. Maybe my result was wrong.

Then I started thinking strategically, through the lens I've described in this book. Why should poverty or plunges in commodity prices matter? Think back to the two groups fighting over a pie. Suppose it shrinks in half. Why fight? War is still ruinous. The two sides continue to be better off splitting a shrunken pie. They might even be *less* likely to fight after a plunge in income, especially if the costs from war don't shrink as fast as the pie. Something about the "hungry men revolt" story was amiss. Every time someone tells us "___ causes wars," we need to instinctively leap to the strategic frame: How does this shape the incentives for compromise?

When it comes to poverty and war, there's been a mix-up. Poor people don't start wars. They'll join one, however, if it's already raging. The "hungry men revolt" story was a good explanation for why some wars got more *intense*, not why they began. Falling commodity prices made people hungry and desperate, and they were easier to recruit into crime and rebellion. So, when a war was already underway, anything that made people poor swelled armies and casualties. In a time of peace, however, each side would gladly pull the hungry into their military, enlarging their armed forces, but these soldiers drilled rather than fought. The two sides still had the usual incentives for peace.[15]

This fit the data pretty well. In Colombia, for instance, plummeting coffee prices produced more battles because the war was already underway. And, globally, a colleague and I found that times of falling prices made wars longer and more intense, but not more likely to break out. Droughts in Africa showed the same pattern.

For me, it was a lesson in always thinking about conflict more strategi-cally. Economic anarchy might produce political anarchy, but only when the five fundamental logics of war had eliminated the bargaining range.[16]

This means that ending poverty and smoothing shocks probably won't prevent war. There are plenty of good reasons for countries to diversify the products they trade, help farmers become less reliant on rainfall, and build safety nets for people and businesses beset by bad luck. But conflict mitiga-tion isn't one of them. We could take these actions in active wars, to help them end, but my guess is that this would be a colossally inefficient way to spend scarce peacebuilding funds and attention. To me it's armoring the wrong parts of the plane. If the goal is avoiding violence, I think the tools described in the last chapter are going to be more effective.

OTHER WAYWARD ROOTS OF WAR

These stories—that "women wage peace" and "hungry men revolt"—echo something I've been saying throughout the book: when you hear someone say that such and such inflames conflict, my hope is that you stop and ques-tion it in light of what we've learned. In which of the five logics does it be-long? Perhaps none at all. Perhaps it's merely a driver of competition, not fighting. Or maybe it's neither—a wayward path.

There are dozens of things that make wars hard to win and that allow conflict to drag on. Poverty and falling wages are one. Others include rug-ged terrain, outside powers who fund insurgents, or opportunities to sell and traffic drugs, to name a few. But we shouldn't confuse these with forces that make conflict more likely to break out. Let me walk through three more wayward paths.

One is an exploding population of youths—the dreaded demographic "youth bulge." Young men carry out most acts of political violence, goes one line of thinking, and so countries swelling with youths are going to be inher-ently less stable. On reflection, though, it's not clear why a large number of young people affects the war bias of the country's leaders, uncertainty, or commitment problems. Perhaps there's more general testosterone or aggression? Maybe. But take two countries with the same wealth per person. The one with more young men is going to have a larger supply of fighters, implying (if anything) a more intense and destructive war. This should enlarge the bargaining range and insulate the rivalry from breaking down. The truth is, there just isn't much of a link from demographics to the incentives for peace. That's probably why age and population measures are poor predictors of war, especially once you start to get the tricky problems of causality correct.[17]

Another fear that's mongered is hardened ethnic identities and the inevitable conflict this supposedly creates. Enough riots and civil wars get fought along racial and tribal lines that some worry these cleaved societies are fundamentally unstable—prone to animosity and misperceptions. But too many of these stories forget that every society is cleaved, and that most ethnic groups don't fight. Perhaps that's why most studies fail to find a link between conflict and the number of ethnic groups or the inequality between them. If anything matters, it is the degree to which two rivals are polarized, and whether misperceptions and passions pervert their relations, not ethnicity itself.[18]

Last, we get to climate change. There are dozens of ways the climate crisis is stressing the planet and will upend our lives. "More fighting" might or might not be one of them. Take water wars. It's easy to find news headlines predicting a bleak future of conflict over dwindling water. But water scarcity is common; fighting over it is not. This makes sense. If the pie is the water supply, whether it's big or small, war is still costly. The size of this squelchy pie shouldn't affect the bargaining range. (The drought studies told us the same thing: sudden drops in water might make existing conflicts run on, but not more likely to break out.)[19]

Of course, climate change is broader than water, and here the evidence is a little more concerning. Across a range of studies, it seems that increases in temperature are followed by more interpersonal violence and more fighting between groups—both new fights breaking out and existing fights getting longer and more intense. What's going on here?

When it comes to homicides and small-group violence, hot days can make aggression worse. But that isn't likely to drive prolonged fighting between larger groups, so we probably need some other explanation. These temperature shocks worsen the economy, but (as with commodity shocks) we don't think hot or hungry men rebel unless there's already a fight to join. Social scientists have yet to work out what's going on. To me, the most likely explanation is that the roots of the war lie elsewhere—in one of the five reasons we've discussed—and that extreme climate events are shocks that send the most fragile countries over the edge into violence.[20]

If that's right, then if it wasn't a drought or temperature spike, some other shock would have set off fighting—an errant leader, a botched assassination, a girl's murder and the ethnic riot that ensues. Climate change joins the legion of idiosyncratic forces that make it hard to navigate a narrow canyon. I'm not suggesting we ignore it. When chronically ill patients get the flu, we treat it with urgency, even though it's not the root problem. Likewise, fragile places need buffers against these shocks. But we should never forget the fundamentals.

LET THEM FIGHT IT OUT

Finally, let me address a troubling claim—that war isn't just death and destruction, that on balance it might be good for society in the long run.

One version worries that the problem with peace interventions is that they freeze an unstable balance of power in place. When one side wins definitively, the chances a conflict breaks out again in the future seem to be much lower. If correct, maybe the outside world shouldn't step into messy civil wars, or push for negotiated settlements. It's painful to imagine, but the country will be more stable if the world stands by and waits, some argue. Let's call this the Decisive Victory view.[21]

Another version goes further, arguing that conflict cleanses and reinvigorates society. The Stanford classicist Walter Scheidel calls war the Great Leveler. Human societies tend to become decadent and unequal over time, he explains. Conflict has made societies more equal throughout history. Some of this comes from making everyone equally miserable, pounding society back to subsistence. But war can also be a positive force for reform, he says. Without the threat of violence, the Great Leveler view goes, it's hard to find examples of the great egalitarian reforms: the enslaved emancipated, or land distributed from elites to the landless.[22]

Maybe most influential of all, however, is a claim made by the sociologist Charles Tilly that war made the state. This is the idea that the modern world has powerful institutions of violence control—states—because of long periods of incessant conflict. That's because making war is expensive, and so rivals need to raise vast sums of money to arm and pay soldiers. To collect these taxes and field large armies, these societies need a capable bureaucracy. The key dynamic in this War Made States view is this: If you fail to build a powerful Leviathan, your society will be swallowed by societies that succeeded in doing so. As a result of this brutal survival of the fittest, strong states emerged over time.[23]

If any one of these views is right, maybe war's not entirely bad, and we shouldn't work so hard to avoid it. "Look," you can imagine a representative to the UN Security Council arguing, "we could send an aggressive peace-keeping mission into Syria and halt the fighting. But that's going to produce an unstable division of power, prop up a weak opposition, and it's not going to solve the fundamental schism between the two sides. Any settlement will create a weak and divided state. Better to let them resolve their own differences, see who the victor is, *then* support them in building a strong state and a transition to democracy. It'll be more stable in the long run. Otherwise, we'll be there for thirty years."

"Better to fight it out" is an extraordinary claim, however, and so I think we need extraordinary evidence. To me it's a half-truth. It omits some important points.

One is that it ignores the people who suffer, die, and don't enjoy the fruits of the decisive victory, the great leveling, or strong states. It's an example of survivor bias, the same kind of selection problem that led the US military to armor the wrong parts of their planes. If we ignore the suffering and the lives lost, and only catalog the benefits for those who endure, then of course the Decisive Victory or War Makes States views look attractive. But we can't weigh the well-being of the survivors alone. Our sample has to include the people who would live in the absence of fighting. This makes the decision thornier. If war has some future benefit for society in terms of equality, stability, or strength—and this is still a big if—then these views require us to make some difficult trade-offs. How many lives today are worth an uncertain advantage a generation hence? Also, who gets to make that decision on their behalf? I can imagine circumstances where the considered answer is "fight it out," but let's not pretend this trade is easy, let alone the best default.[24]

A second problem should make us question whether war has future benefits at all in terms of stability, leveling, or stronger states. It's yet another example of selecting on success. It comes from focusing on the times when fighting produced more equal societies, stronger states, or new technological advances, and overlooking the failures—the wars that failed to revive economies, boost technology, or foster efficient administrations. We can't cherry-pick the cases. But this is sometimes what happens.

As an example, consider the evidence behind the War Makes States view. Outside of the stretch in Western European history that Tilly studied, incessant war has rarely bred large and sophisticated states. Tilly focused on Europe from the end of the Middle Ages to the Napoleonic Wars—the mid-1400s through 1814. Historians call this period the Gunpowder Revolution, because the invention of firearms set off a spiral of technological advances—guns, cannons, defensive fortifications, mass armies, and so on. Wars that were once won with hundreds or at most thousands of troops now demanded tens of thousands and sometimes hundreds of thousands. Big states managed this better than small or disorganized ones.[25]

But history has many more long periods of fighting, and most of these didn't generate spirals of state building: China before its consolidation more than two millennia ago, or the centuries it spent defending itself against invading nomads; eighteenth-century India after the decline of the Mughal Empire; sixteenth-century Japan before the long rule of the Tokugawa shoguns; Russia and the Ottoman Empire from the sixteenth to the eighteenth centuries; or Latin America in the nineteenth century. Sometimes these episodes produced fitter governments or more egalitarian societies. But mostly, these long periods of conflict were simply destructive, leaving whole societies more vulnerable to failure and conquest. They fractured coalitions, set economic development back decades, and bled governments dry. In short, the Gunpowder Revolution was exceptional at best.[26] We can see other, far less productive arms races throughout history; most of the time they are a massive waste. Instead of being spent on health or education or infrastructure, arming dumps public monies into equipment and employment that (ideally) never gets used and (at worst) gets blown up.[27]

A third issue is confusing competition with war. A rivalry can push us to innovate, reform, build, and expand. It's not clear there's enough of an extra advantage from actually getting violent. We might get most of the benefits—a great leveling, technological advance, or a stronger state—from *rivalry*, not warfare. Historians call this process defensive modernization. Facing a powerful enemy, societies reshape themselves to be more competitive. For example, many of the technological advances attributed to war actually happened in peacetime. The moon landing, supersonic aircraft advances, and the internet all grew from an intense Cold War rivalry, for example, not the actual process of fighting. Changes made in anticipation of a possible fight are different from those made in the midst of fighting.

Some counter that it's only in the hot crucible of warfare that societies make the most painful sacrifices—such as the changes needed to build a tax system or to equalize the political structure. Let's call this the Urgency view. As far as I know, however, no one has shown it's generally true, let alone that the marginal benefits from fighting outweigh the terrible costs. Several scholars have found that cities and countries are more developed if they have had more wars with other nations. The problem with this correlation, however, is something called omitted variable bias. We don't have good measures of "intense but nonviolent rivalry." Competition for people, territory, and influence drove a huge amount of reform and technological change. It only sometimes broke out into violence. But without a measure of this more peaceful competition, and defensive modernization, any conflict-development correlation grossly overstates the role of actual fighting.[28]

Finally, the last mistake is to overlook the tremendous amount of stability, equality, and state building that's happened without war. The last eighty years have been some of the best for stability, democracy, and state development in history, and they've also been relatively peaceful so far as international conflicts are concerned. Since 1945, the United Nations has gone from 51 member states to 193. Over seventy-five years, these fledgling nations went from former colonies with sparse administrations to large and sophisticated states with a growing array of public services. Democracy has gone from the fragile system used by a handful of peculiar states to the global norm. Standards of living have also surged. Some of the most successful societies, such as Ghana, have hardly seen a day of warfare. When we look at the growth miracles of the twentieth century, from South Korea to Botswana, warfare doesn't play an obvious role in their success. Clearly there are alternative paths to success.[29]

POSSIBLY THE BEST EXAMPLE OF PROGRESS WITHOUT WARFARE IS THE SLOW EXTENSION OF political rights and power that has unrolled over the past three centuries. At the outset of this period, most states were protection rackets run by elites. Occasionally, however, something increased the de facto power of the masses. Maybe it was a new way to communicate and collectively organize (like the printing press or Facebook), a prosperous new place to escape to (like the New World), a weapon that worked best with mass armies (like the musket), or a new way to hide your production and wealth (like the potato, less easily counted by hungry taxmen). This raised the bargaining power of non-elites. With this new influence, the masses demanded a bigger slice of society's pie. They called for public goods and a voice in proportion to their power. The alternative was armed revolt.

But we now know that violent insurrection, like war, is an inefficient way to bargain. The elites knew that too. So they made concessions. They offered the most powerful outsiders a place in the treasury, the privy council, and other influential bodies. (Basically, they bought off the most powerful segment of the disenfranchised, widening the elite.) The other thing the elites did was carve off and give these challengers real power, creating things like parliaments, provincial governments, or independent agencies and bureaucracies. Last, the elites handed over more of the pie as public goods, from roads to public health to justice and schools. To deliver the goods, they had to build a stronger state.

Altogether, stability, states, and equality emerged as a process of internal struggle, between the elites inside the halls of power and the merchants and masses outside it.[30] You may recognize some of these changes—they echo the interventions and secrets of success we saw before: checks and balances, stronger states, and co-option of the influential. An internal rivalry, sometimes violent but often peaceful, has been a motor driving some societies to stability and prosperity.

Of course, to the people living in fragile societies, this is not especially encouraging information. They do not want to hear "Wait centuries and hope for a confluence of historical factors that may or may not help your society emulate Western Europe, China, and Japan." They want a more direct path to peace. There are innumerable outsiders interested in helping them. What exactly are they all supposed to do? My answer, in brief: be a peacemeal engineer.

Conclusion

THE PEACEMEAL ENGINEER

W hen it comes to war and peace, people have three kinds of reactions. One is to be intellectually engaged but emotionally detached. War is such an eternal human struggle; how can anyone not be captured with curiosity? The suffering . . . well, sometimes that seems distant and abstract. A second response is helplessness: "How could anyone ever solve such a massive problem, especially me?" It seems overly ambitious and hard—not just understanding something as immense as conflict, but fixing it, too. The last reaction I see is an urgent desire to do something. Not necessarily a savior complex, but a sincere longing to contribute to something larger than yourself.

Many people—and I am one of them—feel all three at the same time. But I think the challenge only feels massive, impersonal, and impossible if we think about trying to solve it all at once—to strive for world peace, rather than a slightly more peaceful world. There's a difference. The right response is not a huge leap. Bold steps would lead us astray. The true path to peace is different. It's winding, often hard to find, full of obstacles. Charging ahead at full speed would only take us to the wrong destination. The correct approach starts by saying, "Careful, diligent steps will move us in the right direction."

That sounds like a platitude, but it's not. It's science. Dozens of economists, political scientists, anthropologists, sociologists, and practitioners have tried to understand why some policies work and why some fail. Few studied war and peace. Rather, they looked at social change of every sort, from crime to city planning to healthcare. Across all these areas, the same lessons appear again and again.

Let's begin with Karl Popper. The title of this chapter is a twist on his plea:

> The piecemeal engineer knows, like Socrates, how little he knows. He knows that we can learn only from our mistakes. Accordingly, he will make his way, step by step, carefully comparing the results expected with the results achieved, and always on the look-out for the unavoidable unwanted consequences of any reform; and he will avoid undertaking reforms of a complexity and scope which make it impossible for him to disentangle causes and effects, and to know what he is really doing.[1]

Popper was a philosopher of science. He asked how we come to know things as true. That work led him to a famous idea: we can never prove a theory; the best we can do is to try to falsify one through careful experiments. To Popper, science was an instrument for solving practical problems, with small adjustments and readjustments, continually improved on bit by bit.

Popper didn't limit his focus to science, however. Eventually he applied the same principles to building a better society. How could he not? Born in 1902, in Austria, to Jewish parents, he lived through the chaos of World War I, the hunger and disorder that followed it, and the rise of terrible new ideologies, Communism and Nazism (at least one of which wished to see him exterminated). It wasn't just the ideologies themselves Popper disagreed with, however. He took issue with their method. These were grand schemes, pursued by concentrated state power. Their leaders were utopian engineers, not piecemeal ones. Evil or not, Popper believed this utopian approach would "easily lead to an intolerable increase in human suffering." The real path to human progress, he thought, looked a lot like the path to scientific advance. We can never find the perfect route or reach the ideal destination, but we can get better approximations over time through slow, careful, and pragmatic tinkering.

So much peacemaking—so much policy in general—ignores Popper's advice. A powerful central government or foreign agency oversimplifies the problem and articulates a grand vision. Their ambitious goals, central plans, sweeping changes, and undeserved faith in best practices lead to mediocrity at best, and disaster at worst. To change the world instead of wrecking it, we need another doctrine.

THE PEACEMEAL COMMANDMENTS

I want to boil down decades of research and practical insights into ten general principles—rules we can follow in any sphere. It's not going to be a specific set of directions, however. The path to peace isn't that simple. The reason goes back to something one of my mentors, Lant Pritchett, liked to say: "I can give you the Ten Commandments, but not the Torah, and certainly not the Talmud, even though that's what you'll need." What was he talking about? Well, Pritchett is one of the rare people who tries to be a piecemeal engineer as well as to write and teach about it. He spent a lot of his career at the World Bank, then the Harvard Kennedy School. I think of him as the Mark Twain of international development, full of folksy humor, clever quips, and simple stories with a deep meaning. Now, Pritchett is Mormon, and I was raised Catholic, so we shouldn't expect an analogy about Jewish scripture to work very well. But if you're forgiving about the details, it's a nice metaphor.

The real Ten Commandments, you see, are simple. A set of elementary rules for how to live well. Don't kill people. Be good to your parents. These are reasonable guidelines. But they don't tell you everything, and to live a fully pious life you need a bit more detail. Another five hundred words isn't so useful; what you need is a huge manual of rules and lessons. You need the

Torah. It's the same with policymaking. The general principles are powerful, but if you want to apply them to a specific area, you need volumes.

Even then, you will still have more questions. How does this apply to my circumstances? To this peculiar situation and society? To answer that, well, you need the Talmud—a vast body of case law and ruminations, produced by generations of thinkers, trying to apply the commandments and the Torah to complex, shifting circumstances. Each society will have to write their own. So I will stick to the big commandments.

A set of general principles should speak to everyone. Maybe you're like me: an international do-gooder and meddler. Perhaps you're a politician, a civil servant, or a community worker in a fragile place, trying to figure out how to make your home more stable. Or maybe you just need to decide where to give your donation or your vote. These principles are for all of us. Like the actual Ten Commandments, they're an ethos, a way of acting responsibly in a difficult world.

Be warned: some of them will sound pretty basic. Then again, so does "Thou shalt not commit adultery." A lot of common sense is awfully uncommon. The reality is, if you work on any kind of social problem, you're bound to make a lot of these mistakes. We all do. They're hardwired into our minds and our organizations. Take none of them for granted.

I. Thou Shalt Judge the Easy from the Wicked

Not every problem is difficult to solve. There are times the path is straight and clear. Consider the challenge facing New York City's health commissioner on Good Friday, in 1947, when he heard the test results from three unusual deaths: smallpox. Tens of thousands could die. The government's response was swift and uncomplicated. Within a month, New York vaccinated roughly six million residents. The ambition didn't stop there, however. Outbreaks like this one helped spur a global campaign against the virus. By 1980, smallpox had been eradicated from the face of the earth.[2]

Sometimes standard templates work just fine. Smallpox was a problem with a clear cause, scientifically well understood. The solution—a vaccine—had been around for several hundred years. A specialist in the city's central apparatus knew precisely what to recommend. The actual task, while immense, was routine and logistical: roll up your sleeve, stick a needle in, next please. The treatment (jabbing) and success (not dying of purulent boils) were straightforward to measure and track. Lots of things can go wrong in a health campaign like this one, but as social problems go, mass vaccination proved to be one of the easiest to manage. With a few adjustments, the same tool kit can be pulled off the shelf, shipped to a faraway place, and made to work reasonably well.

At the other end of the policy spectrum lies what we called wicked problems. Instead of a straightforward cause, they have multiple mysterious roots, all intertwined. Instead of clear metrics, success is hard to observe. Instead of a handful of actors, many must coordinate to respond. Instead of a standard technical fix, the solution is unique to the case.

There's nothing more wicked than peacemaking. The source of trouble involves five broad reasons for war, all interacting. Fixes like "build a more interdependent economy" and "check the power of political oligarchs" involve many actors, no one body of expertise, and a custom solution for each case. And if somebody figures out how to do it in their own society, it will be a source of ideas and inspiration for others, but certainly no blueprint. In West Africa, the Yoruba have a saying for these kinds of issues: *Ona kan o woja* (there are many paths to the market). Likewise, with something like conflict, everyone must find their own route.

Too many people forget that social dilemmas are not all the same. They skip the step where they ask, "What kind of problem am I trying to solve?" They approach every issue like it's a mass vaccination campaign—a straightforward crisis with a known solution that just needs a little money and political will. Then they wonder why they failed. Your first commandment is to avoid this blunder, to develop a filter for distinguishing the rare and simple logistical problems from the ones that are wicked hard.

If you're a voter, this means you don't reward politicians for promising quick fixes or demand your government find hasty solutions. If you're donating to a charity, you have a harder choice. You might say, "Let's solve the simple problems and avoid the complex ones." Many do, and there's a whole movement that says we should give to the causes that have the highest proven impact. That's fine. I give to them as well. But the proven ones are, almost by definition, solutions to the easiest problems. I hope you spare some change for the organizations tackling wicked problems, too, like violence. Because the answer to the hardest and most harmful challenges facing humanity is not to avoid them.

What if you're actively working on the problem? There's no simple logistical fix, but this doesn't mean there are no maps or guides. Just as no one finds the route to the market by wandering aimlessly, no peacemaker finds their path with a blank map. We have a framework, for starters. We think strategically now. We know that rivals have strong natural incentives for peace. And we know there are five ways these incentives erode. Whatever contraption we design to carry us down the path to peace, we know it needs to get enemies to loathe in peace.

We also have a sense of wayward paths to avoid. There are huge challenges like poverty and injustice that we could spend a lot of energy trying to fix, but we now know that tackling them won't take us down the straightest path to peace. There are many poor and divided societies. Most of them aren't going to dissolve into violence. The peacemeal engineer needs to focus attention on the ones where the ability to find a compromise is most frayed or has fallen apart, for the most urgent task is to end the most extreme suffering and disasters.

Finally, we have examples and experiences to learn from. There are many successful societies to model after. But here we must be careful. It is one thing to scour the world for good ideas, adapting and refining them, seeing if they work. It is another thing to blindly imitate and replicate on a grand scale. But that's what an amazing number of policymakers do. Avoiding that is the next commandment.

II. Thou Shalt Not Worship Grand Plans and Best Practices

My first year working in northern Uganda, a delegation from a funder came through. They asked me and Jeannie to act as guides. A couple of days into his trip, his first to the country, the delegation's head said something I've found hard to forget: "What this place needs," he explained over dinner, "is a TRC." I nodded knowingly, then leaned over to Jeannie and whispered: "What's a TRC?" As it happens, I'd heard of South Africa's Truth and Reconciliation Commission—a court-like process where victims could record the crimes against them, and perpetrators received amnesty for confessing. I just didn't know it by this casual acronym.

Now, the delegation lead was an intelligent man. I'm sure he wouldn't take a process tailored for one situation—an industrialized country recovering from repression and apartheid—and blindly copy it in an impoverished nation with a long-running civil war. But his comments reflected his conviction—a common one—that there are some general-purpose solutions for peace.

The allure of the formula, the best practice, the scalable innovation, or the paradigm is hard to resist. These ideas sweep through business management, international development, public health, policing, and a hundred other fields. Now, it's true: like mass vaccination, there are some formulas that work. But, somehow, the existence of a few best practices tricks us into thinking there are blueprints for all.

Humans have an amazing ability to oversimplify a situation, especially when we are making decisions for other people. It's our inner utopian social engineer at work. Put any one of us in charge, and I guarantee that most of us will slip into this mindset: we instinctively avoid complication, and we tend to latch on to a localized success and see a template to be easily exported or copied.

We can see this blind blueprint following in one of the wickedest

challenges imaginable: building better institutions for more stable societies. Just compare the lists of "good governance" reforms that international
agencies recommend for any two fragile countries. The places are wildly
different, but the recommendations are suspiciously similar.

This isn't just a mistake made by foreign advisers. Local politicians oversimplify the path to integration or democracy, thinking a national election
is enough. Another example comes from post-conflict countries writing new
constitutions. These are the fundamental rules for their society, the basis of
any bargain between powerful groups, and historically the object of debate
and hard negotiation. Amazingly, though, most new nations have simply
copied their documents from generic constitutions without any national
discussion. And when countries design their own governments after a long-
running conflict, they typically mimic a handful of highly developed societies. Rather than customize rules and institutions for a weak and underfunded
state, they set up a lengthy and familiar list of ministries—of planning,
justice, health, gender, sports, and youth. Most of these bureaucracies are
aspirational. The forms are there but not the function—a best practice
blindly followed.

Some call this isomorphic mimicry—the same phrase biologists use to
describe how a frog or a butterfly imitates the patterns of a more poisonous
or powerful species. It's useful to look like a functioning government, even
if you're not. Others call it institutional monocropping. As a result, govern-
mental form in fragile countries has become as diverse as the developed
world's bananas.[3] In a normal society, mimicry would simply be a path to
mediocrity. In a fragile one, copycatting is perilous. Instead of spreading
power widely, elections for a powerful president provide a ritual of democracy. A generic constitution lays out some rights and regular elections, but
it doesn't resolve the fundamental problem of sharing power in society.
And with all their ministries, weak states get distracted from their core and
unique functions—defense, policing, justice—and instead busy themselves
trying to imitate a more stable and advanced welfare state.

Countless thinkers have pointed out the peril of simple, centralized, one-size-fits-all solutions, in every walk of policy (not just peacemaking). An early intellectual hero of mine, the activist and writer Jane Jacobs, wanted dense, lively, diverse cities. She loathed the powerful urban planners who aimed for visual order and zoned districts. They held uniform ideas of how humans should live. "There is no logic that can be superimposed on the city," she protested. "People make it, and it is to them, not buildings, that we must fit our plans." The urban planner's grand visions and blueprints were responsible for destroying great American cities, Jacobs argued.[4]

Another is the political scientist and anthropologist James Scott. His book, *Seeing Like a State*, carries a Popper-like subtitle: *How Certain Schemes to Improve the Human Condition Have Failed*. In it, Scott tells us, "The despot is not a man, it is the Plan." He looked at hundreds of years of idealists trying to make society better—from housing projects, to scientific agriculture, collectivization, and other confident, state-organized schemes—and found the same syndrome again and again. The natural inclination of these planners was to simplify and order the world to make it easier to improve, and then to implement ambitious and utopian schemes. The beneficiaries of these blueprints often suffered.[5]

III. Thou Shalt Not Forget All Policymaking Is Political

Another mistake utopian engineers make is to think their job is to solve a technical problem, to plan and implement in a nonpartisan way and to strive for the best solution. This is a noble goal. Bureaucracies are admired and legitimate when they're neutral and technocratic, following rules instead of granting personal favors. Still, no program is apolitical. Every new rule and every intervention changes the balance of power. Every policy has winners and losers. And the losers will try to undermine the change every step of the way.[6]

A lot of planners forget that. They focus on the technical aspect of the problem and try to find the "optimal" solution. They forget they're political actors, navigating a complex social problem. They convince themselves they're outside the fray even when they're embroiled in it.

This tendency gets worse when people work outside their native political habitat. After immigrating to the United States from Canada, I remember asking an American classmate, "This is the richest country in the world. Why isn't there healthcare for all?" What followed was a long answer that touched on party politics, the history of American insurance, and the peculiar way in which states elect presidents and Congress. If I'd asked her how to fix it, she'd probably have said, "I have no idea." Like me, my friend was a master's student studying international development. Imagine an aid agency hired her after graduation to work in Malawi's health system. After a couple of years, suppose I asked her the same question: Why is healthcare so broken in Malawi, and how can it be repaired? I bet she could give me a thoughtful answer. But I'd also bet that it would be less complex than her US response. Likely there would be fewer arcane political details and history. The political incentives and personalities would be scarce. The reforms she'd recommend would be straightforward and confidently given.

Take any one of us out of our normal environment, and we have a tendency to oversimplify the world—even if it's our own city or country. In short, we become "anti-politics machines." This isn't my term. It comes from a book of the same name, by a Stanford anthropologist named James Ferguson. In the early 1980s, when he started the book, he was working in Lesotho, a tiny kingdom surrounded by South Africa. Instead of studying the people of Lesotho, like most anthropologists might do, Ferguson was fascinated by the development advisers hanging around. He decided to take the tools and techniques his field used to understand small-scale societies and apply them to this serious, suited, advice-giving tribe.[7]

One of the projects he observed helped the people of Lesotho—called Basotho—sell their cows. This doesn't sound important, but cows are the main form of Basotho wealth. During droughts these livestock can die, erasing the nation's savings. Unfortunately, without transport and other infrastructure, there was no way for everyone to sell their cows at the same time, so cattle died in the fields. What the Basotho needed, it seemed, was access to long-distance markets so they could use the cows as a kind of savings account, to draw down in bad times. A bonus: it might even turn into a productive export business.

It turns out the planners in Lesotho—a mix of central government and foreign agencies—overlooked some important details. Not being able to sell cows was the whole point of buying them. Most Basotho men worked far away in South African mines. When they sent their money home, they didn't want their wives to spend it, so they bought assets that were hard to liquidate. If you create a market for cows, you threaten their whole system of social control. The people with power (in this case, the migrant men) actively worked against the project. It failed spectacularly.

The foreign aid industry is famously utopian and politically blind. Bill Easterly, one of the industry's chief critics, sees agencies full of utopian planners. A planner "thinks of poverty as a technical engineering problem that his answers will solve," he wrote. The alternative is to be a searcher—someone who "admits he doesn't know the answers in advance; he believes that poverty is a complicated tangle of political, social, historical, institutional, and technological factors." The searcher (just another name for the piecemeal engineer) remembers that development involves growing and splitting a pie. This is a huge, messy contest—full of social and political competition.[8]

This makes Easterly wary of foreign peacebuilders too. He's not alone. The political scientist Séverine Autesserre is another critic of centralized, top-down peacemaking. Starting in Kosovo, then Afghanistan, eastern Congo, South Sudan, Palestine, and Timor-Leste, Autesserre went from being a conflict and humanitarian worker to studying the crises. Wherever she went, she saw the same insular community. Recalling her first days on the job, she says, "I had naively expected my colleagues' attitudes and behaviors to be as varied as the countries they came from and the organizations they represented." Instead, she realized that "they shared a common collection of practices, habits, and narratives that shaped their every attitude and action." Once she learned to fit in in one locale, Autesserre could work in Southeast Asia, central Africa, or central Asia and never feel out of place. It was all one country: Peaceland.

Some aspects of Peaceland were helpful. Its denizens brought funds, good ideas from elsewhere, and some rare forms of know-how. Also, as we've seen, their presence and their programs made bargains easier to make and hold. But there were also some dysfunctional habits and unintended consequences. They valued the skills they had (technical knowledge) over the ones they didn't (an understanding of the local context and politics). Like all planners, they also preferred simplified narratives for the conflict over complex ones. They were anti-politics machines.

What Autesserre realized is that the planner culture was perpetuated and reinforced by a range of small, everyday failures: their security procedures kept them from living, shopping, and even walking among locals; their organizations put outsiders at the top and locals at the bottom, enforcing power disparities; they designed their projects with limited local input, external funding, and international implementation. "They worked hard, endured many deprivations, occasionally risked their lives," Autesserre realized, "and became frustrated when—to their surprise—the situation worsened." Their myopia came from a hundred small blinds and obstructions.[9]

These examples involve foreigners meddling in other countries. But they aren't the only outsiders prone to being anti-politics machines. In some places, who are the only people who seem more out of their native political habitat than the expatriates? The local elites. Especially in the most unequal societies. When a city official in Chicago is making plans for the South Side, when a state bureaucrat in New Delhi is thinking how to improve life in the villages, or when a police chief in Medellín is wondering how to control gangs—these planners are separated from their subjects by class, education, and maybe race and religion as well.

Some people react by deciding that outsiders and elites shouldn't meddle at all. It's an understandable reaction. But I don't agree. Bureaucrats are not doomed to be anti-politics machines or denizens of Peaceland. Many approach each problem with humility. They pause and think hard about whose interests will be served. They focus on and spend time in fewer places, for longer. They work harder to have insiders at the top of their organizations.

And, instinctively, many follow the other peacemeal commandments to come. Peacemeal engineers like these are a major reason we have greater peace and more successful societies today than at any other time in history.

IV. Honor Thy Margins

Popper was not the first to suggest an incremental approach to governing. Two millennia ago, in the *Tao Te Ching*, the philosopher Lao Tzu wrote that one should govern a society like one cooks small fish. The colleague who told me about this explained the advice this way: Little fish are small and will easily fall apart if you turn them again and again. And if you put on too much seasoning, the flavor will be too strong. So, when you cook small fish, be careful and put only a little spice in each time.

Lao Tzu wasn't just advising us to be gradual, however. He was telling us to be marginalists. There's a difference. One moves slowly; the other focuses on results. You can make a gradual change that delivers nothing in terms of impact. What matters is that you are paying close attention to whether your actions have the desired result and at what cost. As Popper explained, piecemeal engineers make their way "step by step, carefully comparing the results expected with the results achieved," strenuously avoiding reforms of a complexity and scope that make it impossible for them to disentangle cause and effect. Marginalism requires the mindset of a tinkerer: an open mind to many alternatives; trying to squeeze out the greatest gains at the least cost; being self-critical; trying to see what works; and being attuned to consequences both intended and unintended.[10]

To see how incremental interventions don't always improve things on the margin, consider how many American cities deal with gun violence. Open a newspaper, listen to a mayor, or consult an activist, and you might hear any one of these sensible-sounding priorities: reduce school dropout; lower unemployment; treat drug addiction; increase social workers; fund or defund police on the streets. There are lots of reasons these might be sensible policies, but "cost-effective ways to reduce homicide" is not one of them.

These are all incremental changes, but not one of them is thinking on the correct margin. That's because we have little reason to think that dialing them up will decrease violence by much. Only a trivial number of dropouts, jobless, and addicts shoot guns. So even the most effective school, jobs, drug, or social programs aren't going to reach the small number of people who kill. Someone thinking on the margin would have noticed, after decades of these programs, that they weren't squeezing out great gains from their immense efforts and expenses.[11]

Similarly, not all marginal interventions are incremental. Take peacekeeping missions. Sending an armed force of fifteen thousand blue-helmeted troops into the country doesn't sound so piecemeal. Nor, really, does any element of the Failed State Package. In some ways, that's a reflection of the size and nature of the problem, plus what's needed to get results. When it came to civil wars, we saw how a commitment problem is often the greatest barrier to a settlement—what rebel group would put down its arms without a guarantee the state won't eradicate them? Add to this all the uncertainty, the passions, and other barriers to a bargain. A hundred peacekeepers here or there—it's not clear that this increment is enough to solve the commitment problem. Maybe some problems require either larger steps or no steps at all.[12]

Now, the fact that a peacekeeping mission isn't incremental might help explain some of its middling record. There's an element of what Popper warned us about—an act of such scale and complexity that it's hard to know whether it works and how to improve it. That's why some say the world should do less policing of weak states, even if that's a hard truth to accept.

I struggle with this (we all should) but I come down on the side of peacemaking interventions. One reason is that marginalism means paying attention to whether peace responds to the intervention. If a larger increment is needed to be effective (as in a commitment problem), then the marginalist might depart from a small and gradual increase. Another reason is that even an unexceptional improvement in great suffering is better than none at all. I also happen to think the commandments can make intervening less mediocre. We've talked about seeking your own path, being averse to blueprints, and attuning to the politics. Now let's discuss how interventions can be experimental, iterative, patient, realistic, checked, and accountable (the six commandments to come). The bigger and bolder the intervention, the greater the need to work harder at these peacemeal principles. Therefore, if I have to guess why UN missions and so many other foreign interventions fail, it's not that they're too big; it's because they violate the other commandments.

V. Thou Shalt Find the Path by Exploring Many

If we cannot follow blueprints, then what? Part of the answer is to explore and experiment. But "experiment" means different things to different people. To a scientist it means to run controlled studies. To an American college student, it means new drugs and romantic partners. Those are all fine goals, but what I mean is structured trial and error. "A grocer who opens a new shop is conducting a social experiment," Popper wrote, and "we should not forget that only practical experiments have taught buyers and sellers on the markets the lesson that prices are liable to be lowered by every increase of supply, and raised by every increase of demand." Likewise, finding the right policy—including the path to peace—is often a process of tinkering with different things, a process of revelation and discovery.

To see what I mean, suppose I asked you what you need to get from St. Louis, Missouri, to Portland, Oregon. You'd answer, "A driver's license, a phone, a car, gas money, someone else to take shifts, and some music." Plug the location into your map app, and you'd likely arrive in a couple of days. This is not a wicked problem. It's a simple logistical one, even easier than mass vaccination. Now, however, suppose I tell you it's 1804. There are no cars, phones, or maps. This was the task that US president Thomas Jefferson gave the explorers Meriwether Lewis and William Clark. It took them on a two-year, four-thousand-mile journey to the western coast of the United States. In 1804, what do you need?

This is another parable from Lant Pritchett, one he developed along with Matt Andrews and Michael Woolcock. Any good answer involves a miscellany of equipment, a team with a wide range of skills, and plans for a very long journey. You probably want several teams trying it in different ways, maybe even competing. But the greatest difference in 1804 is the philosophy and approach you require. You're going to have to choose paths tentatively, backtracking often and trying new things. Bold, irreversible ventures might get you and your party killed. You need to experiment bit by bit. That's how you approach wicked problems. Some of the great policy successes of the last century, like the explosion of wealth and industrialization in East Asia, get attributed to a systematic process of trial and error—of self-discovery and progress through experimentation.[13]

What does this look like in practice? Shortly after Liberia's war ended, the country's cabinet ministers, UN agencies, and major development organizations created a commission. With a large pot of money to disburse, they invited all comers to propose new ideas. The only requirement: they had to identify conflict drivers and tackle them. Dozens of clever program proposals crossed the table, competed with one another, and got funded. Every program had to have a diagnosis and justify its cure—saying precisely what margin it was improving. Every funded organization had to have a plan to monitor results and adjust to failure. Several got rigorous and did formal research on their impact, leading to some of the studies in this book. Even when the commission's innovation subsidy ran out, however, what lived on in Liberia is a tendency to informal experimentation and trial and error. Nonprofits kept trying new things. More researchers began to study conflict mitigation and recovery. A few years ago, when a big international research group assembled all the rigorous peacebuilding lessons in the world, a shocking proportion came from that tiny little coastal nation in Africa.

Cities can take the same approach. A decade ago, my colleague Jens Ludwig founded the University of Chicago Crime Lab, building a partnership with the mayor's office, the police, foundations, and the city's nonprofits. They share data, look at the evidence together, come up with new programs to try, field-test them, and study them. We've already talked about one of those big successes, the Becoming A Man program. It emerged when the Crime Lab staged an open competition among the city's social entrepreneurs for ideas.

This is not the typical city or peacekeeping mission's style. Open calls for new ideas, transparent competition for scarce funds, local officials and nonprofits with equal seats at the table, a focus on data and measurement, and careful attention to what's working and what's not—this is the opposite of the way the United Nations or most mayors' offices operate. It needn't be.

VI. *Thou Shalt Embrace Failure*

Most public policy is atrocious. If you stare at all the failed projects littering the landscape like dead bodies, you risk getting depressed. But the average policy is not what's important. Because none of the great ideas—the world-changing ones—would be possible without the endless number of failed attempts. To be a piecemeal engineer, Popper reminded us, what is needed most is "the realization that not only trial but also error is necessary." We must learn "not only to expect mistakes, but consciously to search for them." Imagine trying to get from St. Louis to the West Coast in 1804 without accepting that you're going to have to backtrack and stumble. To charge forward, to stick with mediocre decisions, to refuse to acknowledge you took a wrong turn.[14]

It sounds commonsensical, but once again it's awfully uncommon. Almost every big project I've seen started the same way: a mayor, a government ministry, or an aid agency comes up with an idea; they write up a program manual outlining who will get what; they get funding from the central government or an outside donor; their approach gets laid out ahead of time in the grant proposal; they immediately implement at scale, to thousands or tens of thousands of people. A hundred things go wrong. They tweak the rollout to fix the worst problems. But the core design never changes, no matter how flawed. Three years into their five-year grant, the implementers have little idea if the program is working, and they are beset by nagging worries that it is middling at best. Everyone involved knows about the mediocrity, but they're fearful to admit it. Their organizations insulate them and the project from accountability.

Every time I see this happening, I suggest the same thing: "Hold on. Why don't we figure out what we want to achieve and come up with five or six different ways we could do this. Roll them all out rough. Pilot for three or four months. Tinker. Watch. Collect some data. Interview people. *Then* we write the program manual with the one or two best ideas, finalize the design with the donor, and roll it out to a larger group." It doesn't have to take more time. In a five-year plan, what better way can you think of to spend years one and two? And it doesn't mean spending more money. In fact, it costs less when you don't toss funds at mediocre solutions for years. I have made this argument dozens of times—that the path to peace and prosperity needs to be discovered through piecemeal tinkering. Few take me up on it, from Colombia to Uganda to Liberia to Chicago. It's like watching a car crash in slow motion every time.

Organizations need to institutionalize this iteration and failure, running through it as rapidly as possible, discarding bad ideas. Biologists call this evolution. The problem: Unlike organisms, organizations are really bad at the process of creating variation and selecting out the losers. They don't run enough little social experiments, and they don't discard the bad ones quickly enough.

Maybe what we need is a buzzword and a *Harvard Business Review* article to legitimize the idea. In the last few years, we've gotten one: "Design Thinking." The idea has been around for decades. It grew popular in organizational behavior and engineering circles in the 1960s and then caught on in the tech industry more recently. Now it's spreading. It's more of an art than a science, and there isn't much hard research on the process. But the idea is straightforward: generate creative ideas, rapidly prototype them, test them out, and reiterate.[15]

I learned about design thinking from Jeannie, now a senior executive at the International Rescue Committee, one of the world's largest humanitarian and refugee agencies. She created and runs its internal research and development lab, Airbel. Jeannie got tired of watching humanitarian agencies get multimillion-dollar grants to run a program at scale, only to see them end in mediocrity. So, a few years ago, alongside her usual group of humanitarian workers and researchers, she hired a bunch of people who style themselves as "designers"—professionals who specialize in the process of testing and iterating. They started applying design thinking to alleviate violence and suffering.

One area they worked on is violence within families. Domestic abuse is endemic in a lot of places, and brutal beatings are something many women silently endure. Unfortunately, the existing interventions don't work that well. The world needs new approaches. Her team began trying out new techniques—text messages and WhatsApp groups for men to try to change norms around violence; or educating faith leaders to become better couples counselors, using scripture to fight oppression. These weren't in the normal playbook of big secular nonprofits like IRC. These were lessons the team learned by drawing on what worked elsewhere, then interviewing, prototyping, and testing different ways of helping women. Only when they thought they had a promising model did they ratchet it up and study it more formally. A team of dozens at IRC does this kind of thing daily, in as many countries. Unfortunately, rapid experimentation like this is rare.[16]

VII. Thou Shalt Be Patient

How long will all this take? You can experiment and iterate and fail quickly in certain realms, especially where the program is quick and the result immediate—like disaster relief or election monitoring, for example. But you can't reduce corruption, improve democracy, foster new social identities, build state capacity, or reduce gang killings in an instant.

Unfortunately, however, even when ambitions are as enormous as "good government" and "open societies," some of the wisest policymakers have unrealistic time frames—another failing of the utopian engineer. Take Afghanistan and Iraq in the twenty-first century. After almost twenty years, some of the most measured experts look on these as failed experiments in building capable states and open societies. Liberia seems like a disappointment, too, where great expectations went unmet.[17]

Maybe the problem is with the expectations. Afghanistan and Liberia were never going to develop high-functioning states in a couple of decades. Either country would count itself among the best performers in human history if it got there in a hundred years. The problem is the collective delusion that we should expect better. To show this, three of the scholars we've already met—Andrews, Pritchett, and Woolcock—ran a simple thought experiment. They gathered all the data available on the capability of a country's state. Not whether it's democratic or autocratic, but whether it delivers effective public services, provides rule of law, has a capable bureaucracy, and is relatively uncorrupt. They turned these data into a summary measure of capability. At the top you find Singapore. Near the bottom you find countries like Afghanistan and Liberia. The middle features Turkey, Mexico, and Egypt.

Let's consider a country like Guatemala, not at the bottom of the scale, not at the midpoint, but in between. Here's the question: In the best case, how long before Guatemala can raise its capability and pass the midpoint of the scale, to the level of a Mexico or Turkey? The result: longer than you think. At current rates, the sad answer is never. But let's be more optimistic. The world has learned a few things, and the incentives to govern better have never been higher. Let's imagine the nation turned into a top performer, growing its capability at some of the fastest rates of any country in history. If Guatemala performs in the top 10 percent, it will pass today's midpoint in about . . . fifty years. Over the same time frame, if Afghanistan or Liberia excels at the same rate, it will reach the level of today's Guatemala.

This can feel dispiriting. A student in one of my classes, a Nigerian, put it well: it's hard to come to peace with the idea that your society won't overcome its struggles in your lifetime. But, as she also wrote, collective delusion won't speed anyone along the path to peace.

VIII. Thou Shalt Set Sensible Goals

"Have you been to see the Ministry of Finance?" Melissa Thomas remembers someone asking her. She was a development worker and a political scientist. It was 2008, and he was referring to the government of South Sudan, the world's newest nation and one of its weakest states. "It's a guy. In a trailer," he said in exasperation, "yet somehow everyone expects him to do everything that a ministry of finance does."[18]

I see this everywhere. Voters in the poorest and most fragile states want their governments to run primary schools, build a clinic in every village, and rebuild the roads. Local politicians think they also ought to run the power agency, reconstruct the port, and regulate a dozen sectors. International donors ask them for more: cut poverty, malnutrition, and corruption in half in five years' time.

There are two big problems with this. First, it risks taking a success and labeling it a failure. Think back to Guatemala, and the decades it will take to reach the corruption of Mexico or Turkey. If Guatemala (or Afghanistan, or Liberia . . .) reduced corruption by 3 percent in a five-year span, that pace would put it among the most successful societies in history. If local taxpayers or foreign donors deride them for the 97 percent remaining, what's the incentive to improve? Setting unrealistic goals for poverty, governance, or infrastructure undermines our collective confidence in the state.[19]

Worse, it makes the classic mistake that "when everything is a priority, nothing is a priority." This warning has special bite in a fragile society. Anyone can run a school or a clinic. But only the government can police, run a system of courts, enforce property rights, and control violence. Getting kids educated and keeping them alive past the age of five is incredibly important.

But a society with a weak state must make difficult trade-offs—what they do versus what they let the nonprofit sector handle.

This means we need to add another margin to the ones we discussed above: What's the bandwidth of the state (versus other actors) to tackle the problem, and which should it focus on first? This is a question seldom asked. But the marginalist should always remember a government's organizational capacity is its scarcest constraint. Impose on it with caution.

To me, it helps explain an earlier commandment: embrace failure. If you want to understand why ministers, bureaucrats, and others in the development and peacebuilding community are so averse to failure even when they set themselves up for it, surely part of the answer is that the rest of us have delusional expectations. Taxpayers, donors, and voting publics want their politicians to meet unrealistic objectives error-free. Changing this political culture is beyond the reach of one book, but individually we could start with striving to be tolerant of trial and error, praising rather than punishing the people who adjust their views when the evidence changes.

IX. Thou Shalt Be Accountable

If we really want to know, however, why bureaucracies get mired in bad best practices, why there's too little experimentation and iteration, and why so many organizations seem satisfied with mediocrity, I think the answer comes down to this: too little accountability.

All these thinkers we've been talking about have looked at successes and failures and come to the same conclusion: organizations are successful when they get feedback on what's working, when they have powerful incentives to improve, and when the winners from a particular policy can't lock in their advantage. When James Scott said, "The despot is not a man, it is the Plan," he traced the failure of grand utopian schemes back to a lack of such accountability. How else could great leaders impose their irresponsible visions on a society? And when Séverine Autesserre and James Ferguson diagnosed anti-politics machines of peacebuilding and development, they blamed it on imbalances of power. Only a strong and unchecked political class, foreign or local, could afford to ignore the interests of the people they were supposedly trying to help.

Most people think accountability comes from above or below and forget it can come from *beside*. It arises from being flanked by many piecemeal engineers, spreading out the ability to experiment and iterate. Elinor Ostrom called this system polycentric—decision-making with many centers. She is the rare woman and the rarer political scientist to have won a Nobel in economics. She spent her career at Indiana University, where she worked on these ideas along with her husband, Vincent, and a crew of graduate students—including my wife, Jeannie. Amos Sawyer was a colleague as well, an influence on her (and deeply influenced by her too). The ideas I traced in part 2 on the secrets to success—on how too much centralization makes a place conflict prone—are the product of their intertwined views.

Earlier, however, I celebrated polycentricity because of its peacebuilding properties. Sawyer wanted to fragment central authority and bring in more intergovernmental competition to reduce the agency problems, the commitment issues, and the idiosyncratic values and mistakes that cause so much fighting when elite cabals run a country. That's not why Ostrom pursued polycentricity, however. For her it was about effective government. Both are right: the same checks and balances that promote peace can also make governance more adaptive and functional.

When there's only one governing authority making decisions, Ostrom argued, there's only so much experimentation it can do. It will do just a few things at a time, and once the new ideas are in place, it will probably be a while before they change again. Also, one false assumption or one mistake can be a disaster for the whole region. A design process with many designers is bound to be speedier and more successful. I don't mean working by committee. I mean lots of piecemeal engineers working in tandem or in competition. Some hold up federalism as an example—that is, where provinces and states experiment with minimum wages, tax breaks, and environmental regulations. Piecemeal engineers also spur healthy competition within a locale by setting up many agencies, or by giving funding to lots of foundations, nonprofits, and community organizations.[20]

Distributing power isn't the instinct of many peacebuilders and other do-gooders, however. I'm used to hearing the refrain "more coordination" not "more competition." From Chicago to northern Uganda, many of the governments and nonprofits I've worked with often grumble when another organization copies "their" idea, enters "their" village or territory, or competes for "their" donor. Only a handful of central governments or donors deliberately fund competition.

But decentralization probably matters most for wicked problems like peace. The more complex and changing the situation, the more important it is for the testers closest to the problem to navigate by judgment. One study of aid organizations, for instance, found that the agencies that succeed tend to push the decision-making out as far as possible. Tragically, some of the largest organizations—the United Nations and American agencies—tend to be the most inflexible, controlling, and failing.[21]

But while a government of many centers can have different levels and branches checking and holding each other to account, to me the most important direction of accountability is down. Good peacemeal engineers give away power to those below them.

Influence can be spread out in countless subtle and indirect ways, each one raising the incomes or voices of many. Schooling and literacy programs, small business development, basic incomes, community development grants, and other kinds of decentralized programs all move the needle in the direction of empowerment. So, most likely, do transparent systems that put information in the hands of the public: how much the local schools received in public funding, who got public sector jobs and at what salaries, or politicians who must declare their assets and criminal record. Get this right, and I think the evidence is overwhelming: better policies emerge, and bad ones die.[22]

Too many peacebuilders do the opposite—they empower the center unthinkingly, reducing its culpability. International agencies funnel tremendous resources through a country's central state, for example. This is partly a function of a global legal system that invests authority in the central sovereign. One longtime US State Department official told Séverine Autesserre, "But, Séverine, we are State. We get states. We're not set up to work at the local level."[23] Typically, an embassy, a United Nations mission, the World Bank, or an international nonprofit isn't allowed to deal with regional governments, fund cities, or disburse help to villages unless the center agrees.

Presidents, mayors, ministers, and agency heads, even the enlightened ones, also tend to hoard power and build up the center. It's an easy trap to fall into. Even if your heart knows that a less concentrated system would be better in the long run, in the short run handing away power usually means giving it to your enemies, to people you despise or whose policies you disagree with. Few politicians are capable of it. All these incentives to centralize power are often greatest after a war. Everyone's focused on reconstituting the center (or grabbing it). The worry—a legitimate one—is that empowering other levels of government and civil society makes the state weaker, not stronger. Thus, "polycentric" is not a word you will hear in almost any circle—from foreign governments, to international organizations, to the local politicians in power.

I think of it differently. People will grant the state, governments, nonprofits, foreign agencies, and experts more power when they trust these authorities. And trust comes from knowing they are limited and controlled. There is a fundamental congruence between making the center strong and making it more accountable. What all this means is that holding power and desiring peace and stability involves a paradox: you have to wield your influence responsibly while also trying to give it away.[24]

X. Find Your Margin

A little more than twenty years ago, after finishing university, I'd decided to work in business. I was months from becoming a chartered accountant, and I was miserable. It wasn't because solving the world's problems seemed too big. I was ignorant and unconscious of all that. I didn't read much about the world. My only real trip outside Canada had been a childhood visit to Disney World. I had a vague sense that I didn't like what I was doing and that I could do something more engaging and meaningful, but I didn't know much more than that.

The change began with books. I don't remember where I started. Maybe it was Jane Jacobs on why some cities thrived or collapsed, or Ernst Schumacher on how to start small and make your community a little better. They were grappling with wicked problems bigger than themselves. They explained how our normal everyday choices could make a difference.

The next books that called to me dealt with other places, like David Landes or Jared Diamond on why some nations were rich and some were poor. The inequities and issues in my hometown were real, but these global ones seemed more urgent. I subscribed to some international news magazines too, and one day I noticed an advertisement for a program in international development. A few months later, I quit my job, gave up on accounting, loaded up a moving truck with a friend, and moved to the United States.

One reason I wrote this book was for people like my younger self. Someone with a vague sense they'd like to know more or do more. I wanted to give them a mix of ideas and inspiration. Years later, I discovered a quotation from the philosopher David Hume that put it better: indulge your passion for science, he said, but let your science be human, and have a direct reference to action and society. In other words, let your quest for understanding be accompanied by a desire to act.

I could leave the message at that—be inspired to learn and do something. But a desire to act isn't quite enough. We're marginalists now. We need to pay attention to the effects of our actions, which means acting well. But how to do that? I remember graduating from my master's program, having matched my desire to do something with several degrees, but I still didn't know what to do or how to do it. I was caught in the problem that began this chapter—intellectual engagement and a desire to act, but a sense that the problem was too big to make headway. So I also wrote this book for people like my slightly less young self: for those already inspired, about how to act smart and responsibly.

Over time, you see, I realized there were thinkers and doers who had found some answers. They changed the way I looked at the world. Only nobody seemed to be talking about them, and no one brought all the ideas together. Instead, people held lots of mistaken ideas about warfare, and policymakers seemed either nihilistic or utopian in their approach to engineering peace. That didn't seem right. Maybe that was an increment I could work on, I thought. After all, one way to change the world is to spread a set of powerful and contagious ideas on others. I found my margin.

I think this is all any of us can do: find the area where we think we can make an impact and work there, bit by bit. It could be what you read next, how you vote, how you give, where you volunteer, or (if you work in a government or an organization) whether you take up the commandments and try to do better.

But I can't tell you what to do next. There's no Talmud or Torah. Like the path from St. Louis to the American West Coast in 1804, or the path to peace today, there is no template. I can give you some concepts, tools, and maybe a little extra enthusiasm. But it is a journey of self-discovery, full of trial and error. You will have to find your margin. Good luck. And remember to go peacemeal.

ACKNOWLEDGMENTS

I dedicated this book to a slow and now defunct internet café in Nairobi because it set me on the path to meet, work with, and (most importantly) marry Jeannie Annan. This book would have been impossible without her and that chance encounter. But it wasn't enough to merely meet. Others had to propel us along.

I was in Nairobi only because a World Bank manager named Vijaya Ramachandran hired me to run a survey of factories after I emailed her out of the blue. When I expressed horror that the bank flew its staff and consultants business class, putting them up in five-star hotels, Vij found me charming. She said that I could fly however I liked, but that my hotel must have four stars, if only for security and insurance. That's how I ended up at the Fairview, perfectly pleasant lodgings but for the lack of wi-fi. So I trudged down the road to the cybercafé where I met Jeannie. Thanks, Vij.

Six months after we met, however, Jeannie and I had fallen out of contact. I was back in Berkeley, she in Bloomington, Indiana, and the idea of working together hadn't occurred to either of us. I planned to be an economic historian of sorts, studying how commodity volatility led to coups and conflicts. For advice I called on Macartan Humphreys, a brand-new Columbia professor, who had looked at the problem of natural resources and wars.

I knew he was interested in child soldiers and rebel recruitment as well, so as I left his office, I offered a parting thought: "Let me tell you about this woman I met," and I described Jeannie's interviews with Ugandan rebel conscripts. I still remember Macartan's response: "What a fascinating research project." As I walked out of the building, I thought to myself, "That *is* a fascinating research project." Standing on the New York sidewalk, I dialed Jeannie's number. "Tell me more about northern Uganda," I said. Within an hour, as I strolled the streets of Morningside Heights on my phone, we cooked up an idea for expanding her qualitative study into a large-scale survey. Two years later, the project (to my enduring surprise) worked out almost exactly as we envisioned it that wintry afternoon. Thank you, Macartan.

We weren't in northern Uganda yet, however. My PhD proposal defense was still six weeks away. When I got back to Berkeley from New York, I slipped a new proposal under my committee members' doors. "Ignore that economic history idea," I implied, "I'm going to go to an active war and run a survey of child soldiers." When I arrived at the defense, the committee had a surprise for me. "We met last week," they told me, "we decided this child soldiers project is a bad idea." The professors had coordinated to read my original proposal instead. "Do the historical commodities study instead," they counseled. What I didn't tell them: my flight to Uganda departed in two weeks.

I was heartbroken. I lay in bed for a day, demoralized. Recognizing the depression setting in, I decided to take up running, and went on my first ever jog. That helped. I also went to see my dissertation chair, Ted Miguel. That helped more. Owing to a quirk of the Berkeley system, your main adviser doesn't sit on your proposal defense. Four other faculty do. I asked Ted what to do. Fortunately, he shared my enthusiasm for unusual questions, and had an appetite for risk. "Listen," he said, "go." But instead of staying for nine months, Ted suggested that I come back after three. Work on the commodities paper too. See what happens. It was the best possible advice. So thanks to Ted too.

Of course, when we landed, Jeannie and I were still complete novices. She had years of experience in the region, and I had many months of running complex surveys, but we were still out of our depth. A few generous people saved us. Filippo "Pippo" Ciantia ran an organization called AVSI, which housed and drove and supported us for a year. A human rights researcher, Dyan Mazurana, and an anthropologist, Tim Allen, adopted us, and taught us how to find money and work responsibly. Godfrey Okot and Filder Aryemo were our first staff and guides, and they became lifetime friends and colleagues. And two UNICEF directors, Cornelius Williams and Andrew Mawson, believed in our work and bailed us out of the $80,000 that Jeannie and I had unwisely borrowed from my student loan to run the study. (Pro tip for PhD students: Don't do that.) Fortunately, UNICEF eventually paid for all of our research. Thank you, Pippo, the AVSI family, Dyan, Tim, Filder, Godfrey, Andrew, and Cornelius.

My committee, by the way, was right in so many ways. The financial, professional, and personal risks Jeannie and I took were enormous and unwise. It was a lot of hard work, but I'll be the first to say we got lucky. One of my dissertation committee members, Gérard Roland, who had counseled me not to go to northern Uganda, said as much when I graduated: "Congratulations," he said with genuine enthusiasm, "you really pulled it off." Then he put his arm around my shoulders. "But for the record, Chris, if I'd known this was about love, I would have told you to go!"

There are a few other important people to thank. Most of all, my parents, Jim and Rita, whom I resemble in thought and deed more and more every day—proudly so. I'm grateful they forgave me for not telling them I worked in a war zone until it was over.

Also, my children, Amara and Callum, who managed to be their best selves in the pandemic year I finished this book. The deadlines would never have been met without their hardiness (not to mention the help of our tireless babysitters and friends, Laura and Diana).

My agent, Margo Fleming at Brockman Inc., believed in this book before I even met her, fought for it, and shaped it more than she knows. Then there is Wendy Wolf, my editor, whose voice never left my head ("Write your book!"). She helped me write like a person, not a professor. Chapter by chapter, freelance editor Andrew Wright found all the loose ends and pushed every paragraph to be more compelling and persuasive. Before him, Bronwyn Fryer helped me find my storytelling voice, while Yale editor Seth Ditchik prodded me for years to write a book, helping me reject more than one mediocre idea.

Once I started writing, a horde of friends, colleagues, and students fixed my mistakes and offered ideas. Thanks to Thomas Abt, Anjali Adukia, Matt Andrews, Kent Annan, Nelson Annan, Scott Ashworth, Sandeep Baliga, Maria Angélica Bautista, Bernd Beber, Chris Berry, Eli Berman, Tim Besley, Monica Bhatt, Bear Braumoeller, Ethan Bueno de Mesquita, Leo Bursztyn, Agnes Callard, Adam Chilton, Ali Cirone, Michael Clemens, Paul Collier, Tyler Cowen, Emine Deniz, Ciaran Donnelly, Oeindrila Dube, Bill Easterly, Kim Elliott, Richard English, Nick Epley, Jim Fearon, Bridget Flannery-McCoy, Andres Fortunato, Sonnet Frisbie, Scott Gehlbach, Don Green, Eric Green, Tim Harford, Sara Heller, Soeren Henn, Anke Hoeffler, Sarah Holewinski, Dan Honig, Chang Tai Hsieh, Cindy Huang, Chinasa Imo, Macartan Humphreys, Adebanke Ilori, Stathis Kalyvas, Megan Kang, David Laitin, David Lake, Ben Lessing, Betsy Levy-Paluck, Anup Malani, Yotam Margalit, Edward Miguel, Nuno Monteiro, Roger Myerson, Suresh Naidu, Monika Nalepa, Emily Osborne, Gerard Padró-i-Miquel, Bob Pape, Wendy Pearlman, Paul Poast, Roni Porat, Bob Powell, Lant Pritchett, Russ Roberts, James Robinson, Domenic Rohner, Danny Sanchez, Raúl Sánchez de la Sierra, Shelly Satran, Alexandra Scacco, Mehdi Shadmehr, Jake Shapiro, Jesse Shapiro, Konstantin Sonin, Paul Staniland, Santiago Tobón, Ashu Varshney, Joachim Voth, Jeremy Weinstein, Rebecca Wolfe, Elisabeth Wood, Yuwen Xiong, and Noam Yuchtman. Daniel Lagin made the beautiful maps you see. Gabriel Bartlett rid the final manuscript of errors. Finally, in addition to providing comments, Joel Wallman and Dan Wilhelm hosted a book conference at the Harry Frank Guggenheim Foundation, which was a great gift to me and the book. Jim Fearon, David Lake, and Joel Wallman gave nearly page-by-page feedback—another great gift.

All my coauthors on all my projects share a little part of this book. So do the massive research teams. For research assistance on this manuscript, including stories, models, references, and maps, thanks to Peter Deffebach, M. Samiul Haque, Sebastián Hernández, José Miguel Pascual, Camila Perez, and Estefano Rubio. Also, my Colombia research team helped gather the material for the Medellín story, including David Cerero, Peter Deffebach, Sofía Jaramillo, Juan "Pipe" F. Martínez, Juan Pablo Mesa-Mejía, Arantxa Rodríguez-Uribe, and Nelson Matta-Colorado. In Uganda, Liberia, and Colombia, I couldn't have managed any of these teams or projects without the international research nonprofit Innovations for Poverty Action.

Last, let me thank Russ Roberts. One June day in 2017, he interviewed me for his *EconTalk* podcast. I'd like to write a book, I told him, but I probably won't do it for another decade. "Why are you going to wait ten years?" Russ pushed back. "Even if you finish it, it's going to be eleven; and then it's got to get published—that's twelve—and I will be seventy-four years old!" I laughed, signed off, and stood there for a moment. "Why wait ten years?" I thought. I opened a blank page and began. If you've read this far, you may be the kind of person with a book in you too. Russ was right: Why not start now?

NOTES

INTRODUCTION

1. A large literature has shown how wars collapse economies. Take civil wars, for example, like Uganda's. The second half of the twentieth century saw more internal conflicts than ever recorded. They were devastating, causing incomes to collapse by a fifth. For more on how wars affect health, schooling, and other outcomes, see Blattman and Miguel (2010) and Blattman (2011). The impact of civil war on national incomes comes from calculations by Mueller (2012), based on what happens to national output after a five-year civil war. Looking across all countries and wars, he and other economists have also shown that each year of war is probably associated with 2 or 3 percent lower national income (Mueller, Piemontese, and Tapsoba 2017). These comparisons, however, probably underestimate the effects of conflict on growth (Rohner and Thoenig, 2021). It's hard to get similar estimates of the effect of gun violence on the American economy, but simply based on what people seem to be willing to pay in home prices to avoid violence, Cook and Ludwig (2000) show that this amounts to nearly $100 billion in the United States. On development as freedom, see Sen (1999).
2. The statement comes from a 1755 paper of Smith's, quoted in 1793 by Dugald Stewart (Kennedy 2005).
3. A couple of things I don't do in this definition are also important. First, I don't use the word *political*. Some definitions emphasize that war only happens between political organizations or interests. My definition does not. I want to leave room to include organizations and motives built around money, religion, and other interests. Thus, gangs and sects can go to war. Also, although I emphasize violent fighting between groups, I don't have a level of violence in mind. When scholars code databases of wars, they sometimes use thresholds such as the number of battle deaths per year. That approach is fine for large-scale civil wars and international wars but it starts to get arbitrary for smaller groups. (What's the threshold for a gang war, for instance?) It's also not clear we need a threshold in this book, since I am not trying to tally statistics but to impart some concepts. Not using a death tally also allows for a war to arise from the destruction of

property, even if there are no deaths. Ultimately, the definition I use is closest to that of Levy and Thompson (2011) and Wolford (2019). Both have long and useful discussions of the trickiness of defining war, as does Sambanis (2004).

4. For more on these biological, evolutionary, and cultural roots of interpersonal violence and aggression, see Berkowitz (1993), Wrangham and Peterson (1996), Collins (2008), Pinker (2011), and Sapolsky (2017). A nice summary of my point comes from the anthropologist and primatologist Richard Wrangham (2019), who contrasts the reactive aggression that governs most interpersonal human behavior (including the behavior of small groups of humans) and the more proactive, planful, coalitionary aggression that humans feature in war.

5. For Hindu-Muslim violence in India, see Wilkinson (2004) and Varshney (2003a). Practitioners of the two religions live together peacefully in most cities in India; even where there are riots, these conflagrations are relatively rare and not particularly lethal. For Africa and Eastern Europe/central Asia, see Fearon and Laitin (1996). They look at ethnic conflict in post-Soviet republics, as well as late-twentieth-century Africa. Of forty-five non-Russian nationality groups in the post-Soviet world, Fearon and Laitin count only two cases of sustained communal violence between a minority and a majority group. Looking at Africa, they count about one case of ethnic violence per year. But in any given year there are nearly two thousand potential ethnic conflicts, in terms of pairs of ethnic groups that regularly interact with one another in their country. A final example is mass cleansings, killings, and genocides. We will see the connection between these events and wars later in the book. Research shows these terrible events are relatively uncommon, despite the huge number of majority groups who could benefit from getting rid of the minority group. See, for instance, Valentino (2004).

6. See Weisiger (2013) on the rarity of long international wars. Note: The Soviets and Americans inflicted pain and violence on the rest of the world through proxy wars, it is true. Why they fought indirectly but not directly is something we explore in chapters 2, 7, and 8.

7. Instead of a grand unifying theory of conflict, think of this as a grand unifying typology. Though my classification differs in some ways, it's deeply influenced by Fearon (1995), Powell (2002), Humphreys (2003), Kalyvas (2007), Collier and Hoeffler (2007), Walter (2009a), Jackson and Morelli (2012), Levy and Thompson (2011), and Ted Miguel's half of our collaboration (Blattman and Miguel 2010).

In the lingo of political science, the two core "rationalist" explanations are asymmetric information and commitment problems. Technically, the logic of unchecked private interests is also rationalist, though a surprising number of people overlook it. I say surprising, because in my opinion this is the most pervasive cause of war in history. Together, this duo and trio have been labeled the "bargaining theory of war." I avoid all these labels, because I find them unhelpful. So I bury them here in the endnotes for the curious and the pedantic. There's nothing "irrational" about values—our preferences are our preferences. Also, we can have a bargaining theory that encompasses values as well as irrationality in the form of persistent misperceptions and systematic mistakes. In fact, we could hardly understand real-life negotiation and compromise without them.

CHAPTER 1: WHY WE DON'T FIGHT

1. For details of the organization of crime and criminal rule in the city, see my collaborations with Gustavo Duncan, Ben Lessing, and Santiago Tobón (Blattman et al. 2021a, 2021b).

2. The expected value of an action is a measure of its predicted worth. To calculate it, we take the value of all the possible outcomes, multiply each one by its probability, and sum them up. War offers a 50 percent shot at $80 plus a 50 percent shot at nothing—an expected value of $40. We'll use this approach throughout the book. We'll ignore something called risk aversion, a common human preference that implies you prefer a $40 sure thing to a coin toss for $80 or nothing. It's a way of discounting riskier options, and if it exists, it will tend to push rivals further toward peace.

3. To be clear, though, it's not quite as straightforward as "more arms, more peace." In the simple, one-off decision I lay out here, more armaments widen the bargaining range and make peace more likely. That will be true in the real world too. But in the real world (or in a more complex model) there's a second factor to consider: the huge cost of arming, especially when we expect the rivalry to last for years. Troops and weapons are expensive. If launching and winning a war now means you can save money in the years to come, you'll weigh that against the cost of fighting today. That means there are circumstances where it might make sense to attack your enemy now, to avoid having to spend so much money on arming in the future. Now, both of you would prefer to sign an arms treaty, and reduce the spending on troops and weapons. But if neither side can credibly commit to arms reduction, then there are times war will be the best option. (This dilemma is an example of a commitment problem, the subject of chapter 5.) We can see an example in the 1950s. The United States considered an attack on the Soviet Union to avoid the economic and political costs of a nuclear arms race (Powell 2006). Fortunately, the costs of a war outweighed these fears, and so (like many rivals) they settled on peace.

4. If the two sides go to war, El Mesa has an 80 percent shot at the damaged $80 pie, for an expected value of $64. So they won't want to ever give Pachelly more than the balance, $36. Meanwhile Pachelly has a 20 percent shot at the $80, an option worth $16. Hence the new bargaining range runs from $16 to $36 for Pachelly. The old split was somewhere between $40 and $60, which is outside the new bargaining range. To preserve peace, Pachelly has to cede more to El Mesa.

5. The idea that rivals have incentives to bargain and transfer resources to avoid inefficient outcomes comes from Ronald Coase (1960) and is so famous that it received an august name: the Coase theorem. On labor strikes, see Kennan and Wilson (1993). On legal battles, see Landes (1971), Posner (1973), and Gould (1973), and a review by Cooter and Rubinfeld (1989). Systems of predictable and calculable law (along with a host of societal institutions) exist to minimize these impediments to bargaining and to avoid prolonged legal fights.

6. See Schelling (1960) and Fearon (1995). Other early contributions on applying game theory to wars include Wittman (1979), Brito and Intriligator (1985), Azam (1995), and Walter (1997).

7. The realist, pie-splitting model is very much a "neoclassical" view of conflict. In it, competition is normal, but doing so peacefully is efficient, while fighting is not. A prolonged violent conflict is akin to a market failure—we shouldn't observe them in an efficient world. Of course, we do observe them, because just like the market, the world isn't always so well behaved. The five reasons are the main ways that the efficient peaceful equilibrium breaks down. This is no coincidence. Modern realist theory, sometimes called neorealism, emerged partly from models of neoclassical economics—nations behave like unitary actors, maximizing their self-interest above all else (Waltz 2010).

Several of the five reasons depart from standard realist principles, however. For instance, if you believe that groups are a collection of interests, and that they don't behave like a unitary whole, then you must consider their internal politics. The first of the five reasons for war considers one important aspect: principal-agent problems be-tween leaders and the populace. The second reason allows groups to have a wider range of values, ideals, and preferences beyond maximizing wealth or power (something that is associated with a school of thought called constructivism rather than realism).

Maybe the most important departure from realism comes in part 2 of the book, when I walk through the ways that humanity has tried to build cultures, rules, orga-nizations, and norms that shape people's incentives, reduce political market failures, and push groups to bargain peacefully. The view that it is possible to build these insti-tutions of cooperation is associated with the school of thought called liberalism. Of course, believing these efficient institutions are possible doesn't imply they will auto-matically come about. There are many factors that interfere with groups developing efficient institutions, our five reasons among them (Acemoglu 2003).

I personally don't find these labels—realism, liberalism, constructivism, and so on—so helpful. Partly they're just bundles of different assumptions—what groups do and do not try to obtain, how unitary they are, what kinds of cooperation are feasible, etc. Better to just consider the assumptions one by one, without labels, and treat each one as an empirical question: is it true or not? Maybe more important, to me these schools of thought mix up people's views of how groups *do* behave with how they think groups *ought* to behave. This book is mostly concerned with how groups do behave, and how they respond to efforts to change their incentives. For reviews of these schools of thought, however, see Doyle (1997); Frieden, Lake, and Schultz (2013); and Drezner (2015).

CHAPTER 2. UNCHECKED INTERESTS

1. For a history of Liberian plantations and other resource invasions, including White Flow-er's rise and fall, see Cheng (2018). For the results of our study of the program to de-mobilize and reintegrate these ex-fighters, see Blattman and Annan (2016). We found what you might expect: helping the fighters on the plantation become farmers led them away from illegal work, like illicit mining, and even seems to have lessened their inter-est in mercenary work when a war broke out in neighboring Côte d'Ivoire.
2. See Sawyer (1992, 2004), Ellis (2006), and Liebenow (1987).
3. See, for example, Mamdani (2018), Ayittey (1998), Jackson and Rosberg (1982), Ake (2000), or Sawyer (1992).
4. For example, Gennaioli and Voth (2015) and Hoffman (2017).
5. For quotations, see Machiavelli ([1532] 2006). For the argument that Machiavelli was not in fact seeking favor or sincerely recommending such self-interested behavior, but that he was a republican being ironic and biting, see Benner (2017).
6. I base my description of George Washington on some standard biographies (Chernow 2010; Middlekauff 2016; Taylor 2016). For a summary of self-serving motives in US presidents, including Washington, see Bueno de Mesquita and Smith (2016). Wash-ington's worth, below, comes from Klepper and Gunther (1996), and the tax revenues statistic below comes from Galiani and Torrens (2016). For a fuller and nobler account of the ideological origins of the revolution, see Bailyn (2017). I'll return to these ac-counts in the next chapter.
7. This quotation comes from Dorothy Twohig, quoted in Chernow (2010).
8. I owe this presentation to Jackson and Morelli (2007). For a discussion of how these incentives shaped major wars in the last century, see Weisiger (2013) on the interaction between these elite incentives and commitment problems.

9. Kleinfeld (2019) has also shown how unaccountable and predatory elites can drive a wider range of disorder and violence than simply warfare alone can. Unchecked leaders are problematic for many reasons.

10. Suppose, for example, the founding fathers get 30 percent of the pie if they choose peace. The colonists as a whole will never get more than $60 out of a peaceful deal. Even in that optimistic case, $18 goes to Washington and the founding fathers, and $42 to the rest. Suppose going to war and winning, however, offers the founding fathers outsize benefits—50 percent of the shrunken pie instead of 30 percent of the undamaged one. The expected value of war for the group is $40 still. The leaders' half share is $20—more than their $18 payoff from peace.

11. In his farewell address to the nation, US president Dwight Eisenhower warned Americans of the risks of having a huge military establishment: "In the councils of government," he said, "we must guard against the acquisition of unwarranted influence, whether sought or unsought, by the military-industrial complex." Military generals benefit from more troops under their command, for example, and a chance to prove themselves at warfare. Any one of these motives tilts incentives away from a peaceful bargain. A longer discussion of the evidence is in Frieden, Lake, and Schultz (2013, 143–44).

12. For a discussion of the rally effect literature, see Levy and Thompson (2011). In 1997, Hollywood had just made a film about this exact premise, *Wag the Dog*, a thinly veiled allusion to US president Bill Clinton's bombing campaigns amid his sex scandals.

13. Most civil wars during the Cold War were actually "proxy wars" between the great powers (Westad 2005; Kalyvas and Balcells 2010). For a more general take on proxy wars throughout history, see Berman and Lake (2019). In the case of Liberia, it's surely no coincidence that the warlord Charles Taylor invaded at precisely the moment the United States withdrew military and foreign aid from Liberia's government, limiting the Liberian government's ability to buy off warlords and opposition figures like Taylor.

14. See Reno (1999) and Keen (2005) on West Africa, and Snyder (2006) on the phenomenon of lootable resources and warlord incentives more generally. Ross (2001) looks at the case of Indonesia. Lootable resources often contribute to the length and intensity of conflict more than its outbreak, as we will see in chapter 11.

15. See Stedman (1997) on spoilers in peace processes, and Bueno de Mesquita (2008) on extremist factions. Many non-state armed groups have trouble holding their coalitions together and are plagued by splinter factions. Pearlman (2011) blames episodes of Palestinian violence on the difficulties of managing renegade groups. Splinter factions, incidentally, may also have ideological motives—the subject of chapter 2. Finally, in addition to the agency problems that lead to spoilers, weak coalitions can create commitment problems as well. I come back to this in chapter 5.

16. On Indian riots, see Brass (1997), Varshney (2003a), Wilkinson (2004), or Mitra and Ray (2014). On riots in general, including the pervasive role of elites, see Varshney (2003b), Horowitz (2000, 2001), Esteban and Ray (2008), and Wilkinson (2009).

17. See Sadka, Seira, and Woodruff (2020).

18. See McGuirk, Hilger, and Miller (2021).

19. Bueno de Mesquita, Smith, Morrow, and Siverson (2003) develop a model of politics where conflict depends on the size of the political coalition that is needed to support a leader in a given set of political institutions. They call this coalition the "selectorate." Under democratic institutions, leaders need a larger coalition or selectorate to support them, relative to nondemocratic situations. Keeping a larger coalition satisfied is more costly, and risks a leader being thrown out of office. Therefore, losing a war is relatively

more costly for democratic leaders than for nondemocratic ones, and generally makes them less prone to war. But democracies that are politically biased enough can indeed go to war.

CHAPTER 3. INTANGIBLE INCENTIVES

1. All quotations come from Wood (2003).
2. Of course, for these injustices to lead to insurgent support, you had to be in areas where insurgents were present. People outside these areas might have had plenty of terrible experiences in their past, but there wasn't a local movement to join.
3. In the jargon of the literature, Wood couldn't find an instrumental motive for fighting. That is, fighting didn't bring the campesinos any gains (such as land from the insurgents) or help them achieve some goal. Rather, fighting was an act of resistance. Wood called it a pleasure in agency, by which she meant satisfaction gained from acting as a free and moral person. This wasn't the only driver of participation that Wood found. One was relatively simple: there had to be a local movement to support, and so a history of local mobilization (often by Catholic priests, catechists, or activists preaching a theology of liberation) was important too. There also needed to be a guerrilla cell nearby. And the military could not be too powerful. After all, no one was suicidal.
4. For the story, see Tarabay (2018), Pearlman (2017), and Asher-Schapiro (2016).
5. See Pearlman (2013).
6. On the ultimatum game and other games of fairness, see Fehr and Gächter (2000). A longer review comes from Bowles and Gintis (2013). It fits experimental data fairly well (Charness and Rabin 2002; Chen and Li 2009). For the academics who traipsed around the world, see Henrich et al. (2004). For Matthew Rabin's take on vengeance beyond Hollywood heroes, see Rabin (1993, 2002). For how this works in the brain, see Sapolsky (2017) or Fehr and Krajbich (2014). Two of the most famous experiments are de Quervain et al. (2004) and Sanfey et al. (2003). Scientists have also found that disrupting the part of the brain that operates during the ultimatum game leads the Daniels of the world to accept unfair offers, as in Knoch et al. (2006).

   One interesting tidbit: It seems to matter that on the other side there's a thinking and feeling Maria who acted intentionally. If the game tells Daniel that a machine chooses for Maria, or it's random, most Daniels will be happy with much less than two or three dollars. Context matters too. When games like these are framed as competition, the Daniels of the world are less concerned about unequal outcomes. For example, see Blount (1995) and Falk and Fischbacher (2006). Finally, for a broader exploration of virtuous violence and the enforcement of social norms, see Fiske and Rai (2014).
7. For arguments on the evolutionary advantage of cooperation, see Boyd et al. (2003), Bowles and Gintis (2004), or Fehr and Gächter (2002). For the monkey study, see Brosnan and De Waal (2003). For a broader exploration of such virtuous violence, and the enforcement of social norms, see Fiske and Rai (2014).
8. For a range of scenarios, see Moore Jr. (2016). On wars, see Gurr (2015); Dell and Querubin (2018); and Haushofer, Biletzki, and Kanwisher (2010). For smaller groupings, see Bastaki (2020). We also see it in more mundane locales, like the workplace. When factory workers don't get the contracts they expect, they slack or sabotage. When New Jersey police didn't get the raise they expected, they stopped risking their lives to arrest people. On fairness in the workplace and labor markets, see Fehr, Goette, and Zehnder (2009); Kube, Maréchal, and Puppe (2012); and Mas (2006, 2008). For an argument that all violence is moral, see Fiske and Rai (2014).

9. There's one more reason to predict peace most of the time. Knowing that their oppression, attack, or atrocity will provoke outrage and a willingness to fight, why would a rival act unjustly in the first place? Just as Maria avoided cheating a stranger, knowing it could provoke rage and punishment, the elites of El Salvador (or Syria) should be just as strategic, avoiding the worst provocations. That first transgression makes even less sense if elites think it could launch a deadly spiral of violence, where they're never assured victory. I return to this point in chapter 6.

10. I base my account on a few sources. Some of the general history is covered in the article by Ager et al. (2018). Many quotations and descriptions come from firsthand accounts of the pilots themselves: Galland (2014), Heaton and Lewis (2011), and Pierce (2014).

11. See Ager et al. (2018).

12. On glory and prestige, see Slomp (2000) and MacMillan (2020). For a political science view on wars fought over affronts to honor and status, see Markey (1999) and O'Neill (2001). For furious reactions to groups rising above their station, and how these emotions fuel a desire for conflict, see Petersen (2001, 2002, 2011) on ethnic conflict in Eastern Europe. He also emphasizes a role for righteous anger and a desire for vengeance.

13. See Hoffman (2017). In Machiavelli's instruction manual for statecraft, *The Prince*, a chapter is even titled "How a Prince Should Conduct Himself so as to Gain Renown." Today, most leaders are more constrained than these early modern monarchs. Still, glory and status exert a pull on our presidents and prime ministers, and foreign affairs scholars still see world politics and wars as fights for standing, honor, and personal vengeance (Dafoe, Renshon, and Huth 2014). Is it worth it? One example comes from US presidents. Over the years, historians have ranked presidents in terms of their importance and standing. Bueno de Mesquita and Smith (2016) averaged more than twenty different rankings for presidents and compared them to the number of war deaths per capita during their term. Sure enough, the more soldiers died under him, the more highly historians rate the president in hindsight.

14. For the Erasmus quotation and the details of Henry VIII, see Ackroyd (2013).

15. The quotation comes from Slantchev (2012).

16. See Weisiger (2013) for an analysis of World War II and Hitler's ideology. Weisiger emphasizes how this ideology led Hitler to believe that he must launch World War II to prevent German cultural demise. As we will see, this preventive war logic is a classic example of a commitment problem. But let's be clear: the source of the commitment problem was Hitler's refusal to compromise on German purity or integration, or to be subservient to a larger power. So while I agree with the preventive war interpretation, it's also tightly bound with ideology. This is true of many commitment problems, especially the ones that have to do with "indivisibilities." We'll come to these in a moment.

17. British parliamentary debates from this time also show many signs of bargaining failure, from overconfidence to uncertainty and private self-interests. What is interesting, however, are the many parliamentarians who seem to be aware of war's costs, and who push for peace and conciliation as a result. See, for instance, the debates discussed in chapter 1 of McCullough (2005). For a description of the sometimes clumsy attempts to bargain, and the many failures on the British side as well, see Wood (2002). As an alternative explanation, Galiani and Torrens (2019) have argued that American representation would have shifted the balance of power within Britain in favor of radical political reform. Fearful of this path, the British incumbent coalition chose to go to war.

18. Thompson (2019). Likewise, when he wrote his *Rights of Man* in 1791, political activist and philosopher Thomas Paine wrote how American independence was "accompa-

nied by a revolution in the principles and practice of governments." See also Hunt (2007) on the invention and spread of human rights in this era.

19. See Bailyn (2017) and Maier (1991).

20. Game theorist and political scientist Bob Powell (2006) has pointed out that indivisibilities are, technically speaking, a variant of a commitment problem (the subject of chapter 5). In terms of modeling the problem, I agree. But my view is that this seeming commitment problem is actually born of preferences. In most cases, the indivisibility is a cherished belief, not a practical impossibility. It is because of values that there is no set of transfers that satisfies both parties, and no means to split the issue that both sides can commit to. If there were an issue or territory that was truly impossible to divide (such as a highly strategic territory), then this would be a commitment problem and nothing more.

21. Think of this as a hypothesis for the revolution, and not the established account. One could also make an argument that uncertainty and errors of judgment played an important role. In such a view, an overconfident Britain underestimated the colonists, and misjudged the furor their laws and acts would create. Moreover, the colonists' intransigence, far from being an ideological preference and indivisible principle, was an unreasonable paranoiac fantasy about the evil intentions of the empire.

22. For more on sacred sites and indivisibilities, including this case, see Hassner (2003).

23. The first quotation is from Fanon ([1952] 2008), the second from Fanon ([1963] 2004).

24. See Buford (2001).

25. Hedges (2003). Another recent example is Ehrenreich (2011). She describes war and violence as a rite of sacred ecstasy, biological and cultural in its roots.

26. For a discussion of the long line of thinkers who argue humans are inherently nice or inherently violent and evil, see Wrangham (2019). On scapegoating, see Girard (1977). Even though Girard sees scapegoating as a release to avoid more serious forms of conflict, scapegoat theory has also become one of the most common theories of mass killing and genocide. It is the idea, commonly applied to 1930s Germany or the United States in the 2010s, that economic and other malaises lead otherwise good people to find and persecute an out-group. See, for example, Staub (1989). For a skeptical account, see Valentino (2004). For sport as safety valve, see an example from Russia by Volkov (2016).

27. This is a huge literature, with endless debates and disagreements, and I oversimplify it here. That's partly because I am not writing a book about individual and small-group aggression, and these drives probably don't explain most war. There are several rich and thoughtful summaries of this literature, from what millions of years of evolution and cultural development and civilization can tell us about individual and small-group aggression. Examples from anthropology, history, and evolutionary science include Wrangham and Peterson (1996), Beck and Deffenbacher (2000), Gat (2008), Ferguson (2011), Martin (2018), and Wrangham (2019). For the brain science of aggression, see Sapolsky (2017).

28. See Tajfel (2010), Akerlof and Kranton (2000), Cikara, Bruneau, and Saxe (2011), and Cikara and Van Bavel (2014). Experiences of violence also strengthen in-group bonds (Blattman 2009; Bellows and Miguel 2009; Bauer et al. 2016).

29. On parochial altruism and antipathy, see Smith et al. (2009), Cikara et al. (2014), and Chen and Li (2009). On evidence against clear antipathy toward other groups, especially outside the lab, see Habyarimana et al. (2007) and Berge et al. (2020). Others trace these parochial instincts to millennia of biological selection. See Glowacki, Wilson, and Wrangham (2020), Wrangham and Peterson (1996), Bowles and Gintis (2013), and Pinker (2011).

30. See Adena et al. (2015).

31. See Yanagizawa-Drott (2014).

32. More hopefully, however, media can also play a peaceful role. Just as pro-Weimar messages reduced Nazi support before 1933, radio and other media favoring ethnic harmony and reconciliation have fostered trust and forgiveness in Rwanda in the decades since the genocide. See Blouin and Mukand (2018); Paluck (2009a); Paluck and Green (2009).

CHAPTER 4. UNCERTAINTY

1. On internet gangbanging, see Patton, Eschmann, and Butler (2013).

2. For a similar argument, see Jervis (2017a).

3. See Tyler (2018).

4. For a review of these and related arguments, see Kahneman et al. (2016); Gartzke (1999); and Friedman (2019). Asked what "beyond a reasonable doubt" means, one survey of US federal judges "produced answers with a minimum of fifty percent, a maximum of one hundred percent, an average of ninety percent, and a standard deviation of eight percentage points" (Friedman 2019).

5. See Blainey (1973).

6. For formal models, see Smith and Stam (2004) and Powell (1996). Note that we should be a little careful to predict fighting: knowing that your enemy has come to a different conclusion should force you to ask whether the other side knows something you don't. You should reconsider your beliefs, at least somewhat. This is known as Aumann's agreement theorem, and it says that two groups acting rationally and with knowledge of the other's beliefs cannot agree to disagree (Aumann 1976). But how do you know what they know? How do they clearly and credibly communicate their beliefs? Noise will interact with incentives to deceive—a second dire consequence of uncertainty. We will turn to this in a moment.

7. Even these bureaucracies have their shortcomings. Thousands of diplomats, spies, and analysts generating vast amounts of information, pushing it up long chains of command, over vast distances, is a slow and imperfect solution. After a surprise attack or a failed invasion, it's usually easy to find the analyst or intelligence memo that told you so. Elevating that information in advance is a great deal harder. On the difficulties intelligence and diplomatic services have in practice, see Jervis (2010) or Betts (1978). The problem gets even worse when diplomatic and intelligence services are hijacked. Perhaps military generals see a path to glory or promotion through war. Or a faction of ideologues in the defense ministry want to spoil the peace process by sowing fake news or mounting a sensational attack or assassination. Unchecked bureaucrats and generals with tangible and intangible incentives for war make it harder to share the same information and draw similar conclusions. On unchecked private interests trying to extend the war, there is a huge literature on such "spoilers," led by Stedman (1997). That is just one example of other causes of war interacting with uncertainty. Uncertainty interacts with human irrationality as well. Our brains are bad at thinking probabilistically, and we have trouble making complex assessments of many factors. For example, you cannot be overconfident in your expectations of victory unless reality is uncertain. In a world of noise, the bounds on human rationality drive two rivals' beliefs further apart and slow convergence. A famous example of this argument comes from Jervis (2017b). We'll return to this in chapter 6.

8. See Young (2019).

9. Most interstate wars are relatively short, and an even larger number end with skirmishing and don't even get counted as wars (Weisiger 2013). On crafting a reputation to

avoid feuds, see Thrasher and Handfield (2018). For formal discussions of signaling in war, see Fearon (1997) and Wolton (2019). This gets harder in a world with many rivals. For example, who really launched that cyberattack? In a world with many hostile rivals, attribution can be difficult. See, for instance, Baliga, Bueno de Mesquita, and Wolitzky (2020). Besides that kind of uncertainty, in this crowded environment, every signal you send affects your deals with your current rivals as well as your future ones as you craft a reputation. We'll get to some of these dynamics shortly. On crafting a reputation to avoid feuds, see Thrasher and Handfield (2018).

10. If the Stones think the Lords are almost certainly weak, then their optimal strategy is to attack all the time. The Lords know this, however, and if they're sufficiently weak, then they won't even risk a bluff. They'll admit their weakness and hand over territory. This is called a separating equilibrium. A pooling equilibrium happens when the Stones can't distinguish the strong from the weak, but figure the Lords are likely so strong that it's not worth the risk. The foggy middle range is called a semiseparating equilibrium. This is where the Stones optimally play a mixed strategy—they don't choose one definite action; rather, they choose a probability to invade and then roll the dice. It's as if, in poker, you decided that 20 percent of the time you'll call against the opponent with the good poker face, and 80 percent of the time you'll call against the one you have more reason to suspect is faking it. Another analogy that might help you think about a mixed strategy is a soccer goalkeeper defending against a penalty kick. The player doing the kicking is essentially picking a random corner to kick to, and the goalkeeper is choosing a random corner to defend. This is their optimal move under uncertainty.

These incomplete-information scenarios appeared first in literatures on labor and legal disputes. They were carried into the literature on warfare by game theorists such as Brito and Intriligator (1985). For reviews of the logic and the earlier game theoretic and economic literatures, see Fearon (1995), Powell (2002), and Ramsay (2017). For a more recent technical review of formal models, a terrific synthesis is Baliga and Sjöström (2013).

11. For example, Roger Myerson won his Nobel Prize in part for showing that, when both sides have private information, there are circumstances in which it may be impossible to reach the efficient outcome, in this case peace (Myerson and Satterthwaite 1983). Two-sided incomplete information is a good description of the situation at Horner Homes, for the Stones had their troubles sending credible signals too. When they tried to shake Nap down for their corners, he worried they were bluffing as well.

12. On price wars and big businesses crafting a reputation, see Kreps and Wilson (1982). On labor strikes, see Kennan and Wilson (1993) for a review. On state repression, see Walter (2009b). On blood feuds, see Thrasher and Handfield (2018), Gould (1999), or Bastaki (2020).

The issue of feuds brings us to the ambiguous meaning of honor. In the last chapter, we identified tastes for status and respect. That is one conception of honor—a desire for recognition. That is distinct from the strategic pursuit of honor in the sense of maintaining a reputation. As we will discuss later in the book, in environments without formal institutions of law and justice, having a name for violence and retribution is a powerful deterrent of crime and victimization (Nisbett and Cohen 1996). It's rational to cultivate that reputation, because in some cases it's the best strategic response to uncertainty—a way of signaling strength and resolve. Thus, to keep terms clear, when I speak of "glory" and "honor" in this book, I mean a taste for status for its own sake, achieved violently. And when I say "reputation," I mean the strategic value of violence that arises in situations of uncertainty.

13. New models show how uncertainty about how tough one side is can lead to prolonged fighting as one side tries to bluff by putting up a strong defense. See Baliga and Sjöström (2013) and Fearon (2013). When it comes to multiple players, however, the game theory hasn't been fully worked out. For an analysis of this kind of behavior in firms, see Kreps and Wilson (1982).

In addition, consider that uncertainty could ignite a war, after which other forces sustain it. Once fighting starts, there are always self-serving politicians, warlords, businesses, and generals who have an interest in keeping the battles going. Moreover, the violence can provoke anger, vengeance, and a taste for waging on fruitlessly. In short, uncertainty can kick us off, but war bias and tastes for violence interfere with talks for peace.

14. See Lake (2010) on the stakes of the bargain. See Coe (2018) for a game theoretic model of how weak regimes combat superpowers through unconventional means, like weapons of mass destruction and support for terrorists, and how the superpower uses diplomacy, containment, and even war to thwart its weaker rival.

15. See Anderson (2004).

16. This logic is one half of the explanation for the invasion put forth by Debs and Monteiro (2014). The other half is a commitment problem, and we continue with that in the next chapter. This logic is also an integral part of the explanation offered by Baliga and Sjöström (2008). The "better part of war" quotation comes from Woods (2006). Not everyone buys this deterrence through ambiguity argument, however. For instance, Braut-Hegghammer (2020) argues that the ambiguity wasn't a calculated strategic gamble, but rather the actions of a confused bureaucracy that sometimes failed to comply with Saddam's orders to reveal information about weapons programs, plus a worry that admitting to cheating in the past wouldn't get sanctions lifted.

17. This story of the Bush administration's overconfidence is told by several journalists and academics, including Ricks (2006), Jervis (2010), Saunders (2017), Lake (2010), and Chilcot (2016). For Saddam's mistakes and failure to update on new information, see Hafner-Burton et al. (2017). For bureaucratic errors, see Braut-Hegghammer (2020).

18. For an elaborate and careful argument, including a more sophisticated formal model than what I provide in this book, see Baliga and Sjöström (2008).

19. See Woods (2006). Uncertainty also helps us explain things the other explanations do not, such as the breadth of the coalition for invasion—not only American neoconservatives, but also some of the most liberal human rights crusaders (some of whom later ran foreign policy in the Obama administration) and a Democratic-controlled senate, where the war resolution passed with more than a three-quarters majority. Even European diplomats hostile to the war—even Saddam's own generals—saw that the tyrant was a threat to the West. They mainly differed on the means to contain and depose him; see, for instance, Woods (2006) and Gordon and Trainor (2006).

20. See, for example, Butt (2019). This is also, arguably, the rationale given by Bush in his post-presidential memoir; see Bush (2010).

CHAPTER 5. COMMITMENT PROBLEMS

1. See Tuchman (1994), Abrams (2017), and Pace (1989) for details of Tuchman's life and the book's impact. See MacMillan (2013) for an account of World War I that emphasizes unchecked leaders, intangible incentives, and misperceptions. Her account of Europe over the centuries also echoes similar themes (MacMillan 2020).

On the "cult of the offensive," see Snyder (1989) and Van Evera (2013). They explain how the great powers erroneously believed offense was the best defense. Cautionary voices told their leaders no, the technology of war had changed. Attacking infantry could be mowed down in heaps by machine gun posts; field artillery would pin down and pommel men in lines of trenches; railroads could dump fresh recruits off at the front as quickly as the old ones died; and war would be a slow, bloodstained process of attrition. These voices were right (this story goes), but they were ignored. While MacMillan emphasizes many foibles and mistakes, she also endorses Snyder's and Van Evera's claims that military leaders held an ideology of the offensive. Rather than learn the horrors of offensive war from the 1904 war between Japan and Russia, "the lessons were not that the attack no longer worked," she explains, "but that it had to be pressed harder, with more men."

We can draw parallels to these views and the concept of overconfidence discussed in chapter 6, ahead. An alternative view, however, is that each side (the Germans in particular) knew that an offensive strategy would be a gamble: a quick invasion of France gave Germans their best shot at knocking France out, before turning to Russia. It's a gamble they lost. Distinguishing a systematic error from a gamble lost is tricky business.

2. For the events leading up to and during World War I, I rely on the sources mentioned above (MacMillan 2013; Snyder 1989; and Van Evera 2013) as well as Clark (2013), Levy and Vasquez (2014), Wolford (2019), Levy (1990), and Lebow (2014).

3. Proponents of the preventive war view that follows include Levy (1991), Van Evera (1999), and Copeland (2001, 2014). For textbook treatments, see Wolford (2019) and Frieden, Lake, and Schultz (2013). Several others—Snyder (1989), Fearon (1995), Powell (2006), and Levy's contribution to the Levy and Vasquez (2014) volume—are also supportive of the preventive logic but take a less singular view, seeing irrationality or uncertainty as contributing to the war.

Note that there's a second potential commitment problem in some of these accounts of World War I: the first strike advantage, also known as the preemptive war. Suppose, by striking first, that Germany would be far more likely to win the war. If so, this, too, could create an irresistible incentive to invade—a power shift so large that no transfer from France or Russia could offset Germany's interests in fighting. Some German generals believed that a rapid invasion would win a war in months. Their strategy began with a surprise attack on France while the slow Russian war machine rolled into gear. A few weeks later, if Paris fell, Germany could use its own railways to rush men and armaments to its eastern front to block Russia's belated invasion. There was no guarantee such a preemptive strike on France would go as planned. And there was a risk Britain would join the Allied cause. Nonetheless, to many war planners, this was Germany's last best shot. The war would never be winnable again. As is the case with all commitment problems, at its heart is a large shift in power, an inability to commit not to use it, and anarchy—the absence of some third party who can hold an opponent to account for striking first. Some political scientists and historians think the first strike advantage was in the minds of a few generals only—a mistake. There was a myth of an offensive advantage (Snyder 1989; Van Evera 2013). If so, this is less a commitment problem than a misperception. The preemptive war story carries more weight in nuclear strategy and explains why countries strive to improve their second-strike capability, creating the dreadful doctrine of "mutually assured destruction." This is a vast literature. For an example, see Schelling (2020) or Kaplan (2015).

4. These points may make sense in retrospect, but they were hard-earned insights from years of game theory and empirical debates. Besides the power transition theory contributions mentioned above, the seminal game theoretic contributions include Fearon (1995) and Powell (2006, 2004). A nice synthesis is Baliga and Sjöström (2013).

5. See Taylor (2011) and Clark (2006).

6. For the argument that long wars can mainly be blamed on commitment problems, see Weisiger (2013).

7. As Ober (2015) lays out, for cities across the Aegean, this alliance building was preferable to waging war against Athens for their independence. Members of the Delian League got benefits from cooperation—peaceful seas, more trade. More importantly, however, resistance would be too costly. The bargain gave the most powerful polis, Athens, more of the Aegean pie than anyone else. It's an example of (mostly) peaceful bargaining in action—unequal but less damaging.

8. This series of minor wars is sometimes called the First Peloponnesian War. Even though the skirmishing lasted fifteen years, it paled in comparison with the subsequent and larger war. The two conflicts began in similar fashion, however, with the fear of a chain reaction of defections. One decade after Sparta and Athens fought the Persian wars together, a disgruntled polis from the Peloponnesian League (Megara) switched its allegiance to the Delian League. Sparta feared a cascade of followers. This arguably created a commitment problem in the same way that, a few decades later, Corcyra's tilt toward the Delian League led to a massive and destabilizing shift in power. To the best of my knowledge, however, there is no game theoretic analysis where an expert in these Greek wars looks at them through the lens of bargaining (or modern psychology). So my diagnosis here should be taken with caution.

9. Whether a powerful third party will stay neutral or join one alliance (or whether a loose alliance member will peel off and join the other side) is a profound source of instability, a major source of commitment problems for the two main rivals. I think of this issue as the problem of weak coalitions. A more technical book would dwell on the formation of groups and alliances, and the problem of multiple players in a game. Instead, let me make a few points here.

First, if we introduce a third player to the pie splitting—one who can opportunistically switch sides, or attack and spoil a deal between the others—then peace is no longer the only equilibrium. There will be circumstances where peace is optimal, and others where it is impossible to design a set of transfers that satisfies all parties at the same time. In technical terms, there are multiple subgame perfect equilibria, including both peace and war. For a general overview of multiplayer bargaining, see Muthoo (1999). For applications to conflict, see Gallop (2017) and Ray (2009). In brief, having more than two players allows for the inefficient outcome (war) even when there is no uncertainty and any two sides can commit to a deal. This remains a research frontier in the game theoretic analysis of conflict.

Second, more actors can introduce more noise, more players with private information, and multiple incentives to bluff. Not only that, but the information can shift when alliances form or dissolve (Walter 2009a). One piece of evidence consistent with this hypothesis is that civil wars tend to be longer if there are more players (Cunningham 2006). To the best of my knowledge, no one has worked out the claims game theoretically.

Finally, weak coalitions have a great deal in common with selfish, war-biased leaders. Even if the Austro-Hungarian emperor general internalized all the costs and benefits of war for his fellow citizens, surely he overlooked the consequences for most Germans. Likewise, it is hard to believe that Corinth considered the interests of all the Peloponnesian states when the city insisted that Sparta lead them in an attack against Athens. To the extent that one member can carry an alliance to war, for the sake of reputation, groups must sometimes follow errant and war-biased allies to war.

What this implies is that a multipolar world of loose alliances (or, within a country, a loose political coalition) may be inherently less stable than a small number of cohesive and long-standing factions. You should view this as a hypothesis rather than the truth, for this is one area of research where the formal theory and the rigorous evidence have yet to catch up to the claims. If only because we are becoming a more multipolar planet, this seems like an important topic for political scientists and economists to dwell on further.

For case studies of alliance formation in civil wars, see Christia (2012). For the problem of weak coalitions among Palestinians, and its connection to violence, see Pearlman (2011). There is also a much longer tradition of studying alliance formation in international relations, early work including Walt (1985).

10. My illustration zeroes in on the Corcyra problem. A fuller and longer history would highlight other possible causes of the war. Historians point to the outrage with which Athenian and Spartan elites reacted to each other's provocations, and the shortsighted, stubborn refusal to avoid a dangerous entanglement like an Athenian alliance with Corcyra (a mix of intangible incentives and misperceptions). They point to a narrow Spartan elite, who could foist so many costs of war on the enslaved helots who served the warriors, and they accuse Pericles, the Athenian leader, of fanning the flames of war in the pursuit of glory and a personal interest in war (a case of a selfish, unchecked leader). And finally, they point to innumerable other crisis points that preceded full-scale war. My own reading is that the slow accumulation of power by Athens was not large or sudden enough to create a commitment problem. If Thucydides is right, the power shift had to have been more sudden and larger. The Corcyra problem and the way it endangered the system of alliances strikes me as underexplored and underappreciated in the literature. But that will be for the specialists to sort out in the future.

11. For Thucydides's *History of the Peloponnesian War*, I typically use the Landmark Thucydides (1998), edited by Robert Strassler and translated by Richard Crawley. When citing passages, I refer to this volume. A common translation of Thucydides 1.22.6 reads more elegantly: "The growth of the power of Athens, and the alarm which this inspired in Sparta, made war inevitable." For background to the war and the period, I draw on several additional sources: Kagan (1996, 2004), Doyle (1997), Hanson (1998), Plutarch (2009), Martin (2013), and Ober (2015).

12. Power shifts are the focus of a long research tradition in international relations, sometimes coming under the heading of power transition theory. Major contributions include Organski and Kugler (1980), Gilpin (1981), and Van Evera (2013). These ideas are encompassed and formalized by some of the game theoretic work of Fearon (1995) and Powell (2006). The journalist questioning Kissinger comes from Doyle (1997, 50). The Xi Jinping quotation comes from Graham Allison in his contribution to Rosecrance and Miller (2014).

13. Here again I draw on the simple formal model in Fearon (1995), who was among the first to work out the commitment problem in interstate conflict. Another game theoretic contribution from the same time, focusing on the commitment problem in civil wars, is Azam (1995). Earlier contributions include Schelling's (1960) on credible commitments in avoiding conflict, as well as a vast body of work on commitment problems in institutional economics, labor economics, and other subfields.

14. Martin (2013) notes that "eventually, Spartans failed to bear enough children to keep their once supremely powerful state from shrinking to such a small population that by the later fourth century B.C. their city-state had become inconsequential in international affairs. This change—Sparta falling from its position as the most powerful state in Archaic Age Greece to a bit player in international affairs by the time of Alexander the Great—is perhaps the clearest evidence from antiquity of the crucial importance of demography to history."

15. What this means is that in any deal that leaves Sparta with $120 to $160 overall, both sides prefer peace. Sparta's expected value of war is 0.75($80 + $80) = $120. Athens's is 0.25($80 + $80) = $40. Athens's 50 percent future chance of victory isn't relevant in today's decision, because the war is being fought now, when the balance of power is 75:25.

     Note that to keep the arithmetic simple, I don't discount the future, and a dollar today is equal to a dollar tomorrow. This doesn't affect the basic conclusions. In fact, as long as both sides value the future similarly, discounting will generally reduce the chances of conflict (by making today's costs larger relative to future payoffs).

16. Technically there are still bargains that will give Sparta a reasonable expectation of $40 in the future. But they are not assured. If we introduced a third period (or more), then the range of possible bargains that could appease Sparta quickly disappears.

17. The quotation comes from Dowden (1994). For an accounting of the death and displacement, see Verwimp (2003). For a fuller account of the Rwandan genocide, see Des Forges (1999) or Straus (2006).

18. For a review of the literature on mass atrocities, including the strategic logic, see Straus (2015); Esteban, Morelli, and Rohner (2015); and Anderton and Brauer (forthcoming). Insurgents, terrorists, and minority groups use mass atrocities strategically as well. But here the logic is often different. Violence serves a communicative function, to signal strength, or to provoke fear, and thus push the hegemonic majority closer to the smaller group's wishes. See, for example, Kalyvas (1999, 2006).

19. The quotations come from Schemo (1997). Members of the political wing, called the Patriotic Union (*Unión Patriótica*), were murdered by a mix of military operatives, paramilitary fighters (many of them linked to the government or elites), and major drug organizations in the country.

20. On commitment problems in civil war, see Walter (1997, 2002, 2009a), Elbadawi and Sambanis (2002), and Fearon (2004). This discussion glides over the issue of why governments require rebels to disarm if it causes prolonged fighting. One account comes from Powell (2013), who shows that when there are big returns from a monopoly of violence, it will create incentives to keep fighting. These incentives could come from the international community, which vests so much authority and legitimacy in a single sovereign, and generally only treats with and gives funds to a sole head of state.

     Commitment problems can also help us understand why civil wars break out. Picture a country with a declining majority: a president and a ruling party whose popularity is falling. The ruler fears that, should the opposition take over, it will use its control over government to sideline the old elites, prosecute ex-officials, and persecute or kill their followers. The opposition party would like to promise it will do none of these terrible things. But the way that institutions are structured, nothing can stop the opposition leader from actually taking these repressive actions once in power. And so, the ruling party, which understands exactly how a transition would play out, decides to arrest and intimidate the opposition, stifling its ability to run. It purges the opposition's sympathizers from the military to minimize the risk of a coup. In short, it pulls the country in a more autocratic and unchecked direction. Control of the government is a prize more valuable than before, and both parties want to possess it. Its peaceful path to power cut off, the opposition launches a rebellion. Scholars have used this logic to explain why African dictatorships are so prone to coups and conflict, why secular governments in the Middle East and North Africa prefer to fight Islamist parties, and why ethnic minorities violently sought their own state after the collapse of the Soviet Union. See Roessler (2016), Fearon (1998), and Kalyvas (2000).

21. The saying comes from Coughlin (2005). The account that follows is closest to Debs and Monteiro (2014). Another account, laid out by Baliga and Sjöström (2008, 2020), devel-

ops a formal model of strategic moves and ambiguity generally and in the case of Iraq. Both see a commitment problem plus private information as the main ingredients for war. I also discuss the view from Coe (2018) and Coe and Vaynman (2020), who see private information as less important and regard the matter mainly as a commitment problem.

22. See Dowell (1980) and Benjamin (1980).

23. Another thing that had changed was the events of September 11, 2001. The 9/11 attacks made the administration of George W. Bush realize that it had worse things to fear than a new balance of power in the Middle East. Enemies like al-Qaeda were seeking material for a dirty bomb—conventional explosives wrapped with radioactive material, enough to make an area the size of Manhattan or Washington, DC, uninhabitable for generations. Saddam, some in the Bush administration worried, was one of bin Laden's most likely suppliers. Iraq didn't need to finish developing a bomb; it simply needed to hide and hand over a little of the French uranium. "We cannot come all the way to you in the United States," Saddam had threatened the US ambassador in 1990, "but individual Arabs may reach you" (Coughlin 2005). A decade later, the Americans noticed something concerning. On the morning of September 11, Saddam placed his troops on the highest state of military readiness since the 1991 Gulf War— before the first plane crashed into the Twin Towers. We now know that these links to bin Laden were largely illusory. It's easy to overplay the fear that Saddam would transfer WMD to terrorists. Arguably the Bush administration did just that (maybe sincerely, or maybe disingenuously out of a desire to sell the war to the American public). It doesn't matter. If Saddam got WMD and kept them for himself alone, the power shift would still occur. Containment was still failing.

24. The quotation comes from an unnamed senior military intelligence official in Ricks (2006).

25. Blix is quoted in Gordon and Trainor (2006). For the postmortem on WMD, see the "Duelfer Report," especially the "Preserving and Restoring WMD Infrastructure and Expertise" section of the Key Findings (Duelfer 2005).

26. Debs and Monteiro (2014) make the most persuasive case for this mix of uncertainty and commitment problems. Coe and Vaynman (2020) make the counterargument that you don't need private information—the weapons program was always verifiable, and the problem is that Iraq couldn't allow the United States or the United Nations full inspections because that would give them information that would help them overthrow him in other ways. In this view, the issue is commitment problems all the way down. For the quotation, see CNN (2003), reproduced in Debs and Monteiro (2014).

27. For the psychological elements of this case, see Jervis (2010) and Lake (2010).

28. Hundreds of articles and books have been written on the causes of World War I. It must be the most overstudied, overexplained conflict in human history. Historians are fond of pointing out that there are so many sources of primary material, and so many thousands of books and articles, that it's possible to find any hypothesis for the war and evidence to support it. For the added role of asymmetric information, see Fearon (1995). For the argument that there was an irrational overconfidence in offensive strategies, see Van Evera (1999) and Snyder (1989). For more on the flawed and unchecked leaders simply not up to the daunting task, see MacMillan (2013) and Lebow (2014).

CHAPTER 6. MISPERCEPTIONS

1. For the letters, see Einstein (1932) and Freud (1932), or the reprints in Einstein (2017). Unless otherwise indicated, direct quotations come from this correspondence. My portrait of Einstein and the circumstances leading up to and around the letters draw

mainly from the biography by Isaacson (2008), as well as from collections of the phys-icist's essays (Einstein [1933] 2011, 2017). My portrait of Freud, his life, and his broader ideas come mainly from the biography by Gay (1998), as well as from some of Freud's own work (Freud [1930] 2021).

2. The idea is that human decisions are shaped both by our semiconscious fast thinking (also called System 1) and our more conscious, deliberate, and slow thinking (also known as System 2). This two-system model is a simplification, but has been widely adopted for its usefulness and intuitive nature. See Kahneman and Tversky (2013), Thaler and Sunstein (2008), Simon (1956), Epley and Gilovich (2016), and Jervis (2017a, 2017b).

3. The split between chapters 3 and 6 parallels the way many behavioral economists distinguish between what we know about psychology and models of decision-making. For instance, Rabin (2004) divides what we know into three kinds of assumptions: (1) preferences—the things we gain utility from, and what I have been calling intangible incentives; (2) erroneous beliefs—how we assess the states of the world and probabili-ties of those states; and (3) miscalculation—cognitive limits and other constraints on expected utility maximization. These three have a direct correspondence to expected utility maximization: what we are maximizing, how we assign probabilities to different states of the world, and how we may fail to maximize expected utility. I meld erroneous beliefs and miscalculation in one chapter because it's not clear to me they are distinct. So many of our beliefs are automatic and tied up with our brain's heuristics and shortcuts.

4. I'm especially indebted to Nick Epley, Betsy Paluck, and Richard Thaler, who performed damage control on this summarization of the elements and compounds of mispercep-tion. My elements roughly correspond to research and categorizations by Epley (2015), Epley and Gilovich (2016), Thaler (2016), Kahneman (2011), and Tversky and Kahne-man (1974).

5. In his speech accepting the Nobel Prize for his contributions to behavioral economics, Richard Thaler summed up the trouble with psychological explanations like this: "The fact that there is a long list of biases is both a blessing and a curse," he said. "The bless-ing is that there are a multitude of interesting ways in which human judgment diverges from rational expectations, each of which offers the possibility of providing useful insights into economic behavior. The curse is that the length of the list seems to offer theorists a dangerously large number of degrees of freedom" (Thaler 2016).

6. On overestimation versus overprecision, see Moore and Healy (2008). Overestimation gets the mean wrong, overprecision the variance. On the importance of overconfidence, see Bazerman and Moore (2012). When it comes to war, Kahneman and Renshon (2007) argue that "excessive optimism is one of the most significant biases that psy-chologists have identified."

7. For details of the new *Newlywed Game*, see Epley (2015) and Eyal, Steffel, and Epley (2018).

8. For the original story, see Kahneman (2011). For related research, see Odean (1999) and Barberis (2018).

9. For reviews of the CEO evidence, see Malmendier (2018); Bertrand (2009); and Moore, Tenney, and Haran (2015). For the other experts, see also discussions by Hafner-Burton et al. (2013), Massey and Thaler (2013), and Tetlock (2017).

10. For a selection of models on overoptimism, see the debate between Fey and Ramsay (2007), Slantchev and Tarar (2011), and Fey and Ramsay (2019). Fey and Ramsay stress that overconfidence might not be sufficient for war. In general, however, mutual op-timism will increase the risk that hard offers are made and rejected, compared with a scenario where both sides are certain but not optimistic. It narrows the bargaining range at the least.

As an alternative, note that it would also be overconfident for the US government to underestimate the cost of counterinsurgency. In that case, it would shrink the bargaining range the United States perceives and finds acceptable compared with war, increasing the fragility of the situation.

11. See Jackson and Morelli (2007) and Smith (1998) for examples.

12. See Ortoleva and Snowberg (2015), Johnson et al. (2006), Hafner-Burton et al. (2013), and Tetlock (2017).

13. See Pronin, Lin, and Ross (2002); Pronin (2007); and Ross (2013).

14. On the Bay of Pigs, see Schub (2015) and Jervis (1976). For US intelligence failures, see Jervis (2010). For experiments with national security professionals, see Friedman, Lerner, and Zeckhauser (2017).

15. See Horowitz, Stam, and Ellis (2015).

16. Some political scientists sometimes call this the aggregation problem (Hafner-Burton et al. 2017). This has led international relations scholars to approach the causes of war at different levels of analysis, from the individual to the small group to the country and the international system (Levy and Thompson 2011). One of the earlier and most influential accounts is Jervis (1976), with updates in Jervis (2017a). For a wider view of political psychology in international relations, see McDermott (2004).

17. Hughes recounts his career in Bean (2010).

18. The quotation comes from David Ervine, a onetime bomber for a loyalist paramilitary group, who later founded the Progressive Unionist Party, and in the 1990s helped negotiate a cease-fire and peace. Ervine recounts his career in Bean (2010).

19. Some Catholics did have the vote, but a property-owning requirement benefited the Protestant community, as did the plural business vote for parliamentary elections. The adage was derived from a 1934 parliamentary statement by James Craig, who said the following: "We are a Protestant Parliament and a Protestant state," thereby drawing a parallel with what was claimed in the Irish state to the south about being a Catholic state.

20. In some ways, this was a commitment problem in the making. The Catholic population was growing. Many wanted union with the Catholic Republic of Ireland to the south. If they ever gained a majority, it threatened the loyalist way of life. How could Catholics commit not to do this once they outnumbered the establishment Protestants? Now, this probably wasn't a true commitment problem. The demographic shift was slow. And there are a huge number of ways to make credible commitments in a constitutional democracy. So we need something more to explain the violence.

21. The quotation comes from Tommy Gorman, in English (2008).

22. See, for example, Davenport (2007); Chenoweth, Perkoski, and Yang (2017); and Aytaç, Schiumerini, and Stokes (2018).

23. Quoted in English (2008).

24. This is an example of how the IRA had its share of miscalculations too. The most blatant ones began with a series of murders and restaurant bombs in 1972. That's also the year that the IRA began disappearing people. These indiscriminate and brutal attacks outraged their opponents and cost them popular Catholic support. You could argue it culminated with Bloody Friday. The IRA had called in a warning (as usual) but the number and spread of bombs was more than the state could manage. The operation was planned and commanded by Brendan Hughes. You could argue that some of these were simple miscalculations and errors. But the IRA kept making the same mistakes, including a horrific series of pub bombings in later years. Some date the decline of the IRA from these early 1970s misperceptions and mistakes.

25. See Dostoyevsky ([1873] 2013).

26. For some of these examples, see Pinker (2015). For the lens problem and some supporting research, see Epley (2015) and Epley et al. (2004). For the curse of knowledge, see Heath and Heath (2006). For exaggerating the probability others know what we know, see Madarász (2015); Fehrler, Renerte, and Wolff (2020); and Eyster (2019). For mispredicting our future selves, see Loewenstein, O'Donoghue, and Rabin (2003); Conlin, O'Donoghue, and Vogelsang (2007); Acland and Levy (2015); and Busse et al. (2012).

27. The social psychologists Ross and Nisbett (2011) wrote, "We do not recognize the inherent variability in our own construal of events; hence we predict our own behavior with too great confidence. We similarly fail to recognize both the random (or at least unpredictable) differences between our own and others' construals of events and systematic, stable differences. Consequently, we predict other people's behavior too confidently and, when confronted with surprising behavior on the part of another person, attribute it to extreme personality traits or to motivational differences between ourselves and the other person, rather than recognizing that the other person may simply have been construing the situation differently." For some of the examples listed, see Hastorf and Cantril (1954); Vallone, Ross, and Lepper (1985); and Ross (1990).

28. For the IQ example, see Zimmermann (2020). An early summary of motivated reasoning is Kunda (1990).

29. See, for example, Dorison, Minson, and Rogers (2019).

30. For a review of this evidence, see McDermott (2004), Charness and Sutter (2012), and Tindale and Winget (2019).

31. For the original formulation of groupthink, see Janis (1972). For a formal behavioral model of groupthink, see Bénabou (2013). For a recent history, see Sunstein and Hastie (2015). For summaries of this information processing and aggregation research, and the phenomenon of getting more extreme through deliberation, see reviews of the field by Kerr and Tindale (2004), Sunstein and Hastie (2008, 2015), and Tindale and Winget (2019).

  On whether collective decision-making moderates or amplifies overconfidence, we do not have a lot of research. But groups show these biases in lab conditions (Cacault and Grieder 2019). For a theoretical case, see Backus and Little (2020). Ashworth and Sasso (2019) also examine how policymakers can structure incentives to minimize expert overconfidence.

32. See Jervis (2010). On top of that, he notes that "analysts may also have been influenced by the desire to please policymakers, not so much by telling them what they wanted to hear but by being able to reach a firm conclusion rather than writing in the typical and disliked style of 'on the one hand, on the other hand.'" For related views, see Lebow (2020), Levy and Thompson (2011), and Lake (2010).

33. See Andrew (2004, 2009). "The state is human too," English reminded me. "It's some normal bloke or woman doing a job, being worried, trying to get promoted, et cetera—with imperfect information and imperfect judgment."

34. The quotations come from Beck's late-career reflection on anger and violence (Beck 2000). Beck describes the history of CBT and his ideas in Beck (1979).

35. On the brain, see Sapolsky (2017); Kaufman (2015); plus the references below. For the quotation, see Hume ([1739] 1896).

36. For reviews of this strand of emotion research, see Loewenstein and Lerner (2003), Lerner et al. (2015), Ferrer et al. (2017), and Pearlman (2013, 2017). Note that not all emotions embolden or exaggerate like this. Others, like fear, sadness, and shame, push us the opposite way, to pessimism and risk aversion. For example, when we are sad and fearful, our misconstrual goes in the other direction: We see the idiosyncrasy in others'

actions; we view them as driven by the situation, not the person; and we become more cautious and security seeking. We don't just see this in the lab, we see it in stock markets as well. Share prices fall the day after things that bring sadness or disappointment: a World Cup loss, worse-than-usual weather, or fewer hours of sunlight (Edmans, García, and Norli 2007; Hirshleifer and Shumway 2003; and Kamstra, Kramer, and Levi 2003).

37. See, for example, Friedman et al. (2004) and Tagar, Federico, and Halperin (2011).
38. For the quotation, see Hume ([1739] 1896). For a review of stereotyping in intergroup relations, see Fiske (1998) and Mackie, Smith, and Ray (2008). The literature on dehumanization is largely descriptive and correlational, but demonizing enemies is associated with a higher risk of conflict (Kteily et al. 2015; Kteily, Hodson, and Bruneau 2016; Kteily and Bruneau 2017).
39. For reviews of group-based emotions and intergroup relations, see Mackie, Smith, and Ray (2008) and Porat, Halperin, and Tamir (2016).
40. On American college student support for invasion, see Cheung-Blunden and Blunden (2008). On Indian violence and food taboos, see Atkin, Colson-Sihra, and Shayo (2021).
41. See Jervis (2010). See also Levy and Thompson (2011) and McDermott (2004). Americans were convinced they were Saddam's enemy number one; they never imagined they were enemy number four. Saddam's true pressures and interests had proved hard for others to fathom—even other Middle Eastern powers misjudged his intentions. Then, in the buildup to invasion, as new information arrived, Saddam's opponents discounted it more than they should have. Misperception and motivated reasoning may not have caused the US invasion of Iraq on their own, but they surely made an uncertain America readier to gamble on war.
42. On this polarization, see also Ripley (2021).
43. The phrase comes from Gartzke (1999), who made similar points. My own dabbling in prediction echoes the difficulty of war prediction. With all the computing power and artificial intelligence techniques available today, we can forecast events better than ever before, as long as we have the right information to feed in. There are two countries in the world that have those two rare ingredients—namely a huge amount of violence and great data: Colombia and Indonesia. The countries, both middle income with amazing statistical bureaus, have seen decades of civil wars, terror attacks, violent clashes, and a host of other bloodshed. The deaths are chillingly well cataloged, every year, down to the municipal level. Some colleagues and I gathered all the databases we could muster—economic fluctuations, demographic movements, political changes, hundreds of variables in all—and tried training algorithms that could predict violence. The results were less than we hoped. We could see which places were at the highest risk of conflict over time. But predicting the year that deaths would spike proved difficult. Maybe with different data we could do a better job. My hunch is that war was often in the error term. See Bazzi et al. (forthcoming).

CHAPTER 7. INTERDEPENDENCE

1. See Reagan (1982).
2. See Hoffman (1999).
3. There are parallels between my quartet and a so-called "liberal" school of thought in international relations that holds that the basis of peace comes from representative democracy, international law and organizations, and commerce and trade (Russett and Oneal 2001). As we'll see, I will argue for a broader view of integration than commerce,

however. I also think checked and institutionalized power is the essential political ingredient, rather than democracy. And we will see a wider range of organizations and institutions of violence control, because we are looking at many levels (from gangs to countries) and not just the international system.

4. See Pinker (2011), as well as Elias ([1939] 2000). This seems to be especially true for violence within societies. Strong states and security forces, accountable government, competitive political systems, the rule of law, and cultures and norms of nonviolence and human rights mean that groups within a nation are much less likely to resort to prolonged violence than ever before. When it comes to civil and international wars, however, the decline is less clear. Some argue that international wars have become less frequent, albeit more destructive when they do happen (Levy and Thompson 2011). Looking at civil and international wars, Braumoeller (2019) sees some signs of a decline in war since the 1990s, but no evidence of a decline in total war deaths over the previous two centuries.

5. For background on the march and the incident, as well as details of the political movement, see Jha (2018), BBC (2017), and Ellis-Petersen (2020). One study estimates that the pilgrimage to Ayodhya was so successful that it increased BJP votes by 5 percentage points, dramatically boosting its expected margin of victory (Blakeslee 2018).

6. Medieval harbors needed coastal indentations for smooth sailing. A number of these harbors subsequently silted and became inaccessible to trade, so there's little current advantage to indentations. So Jha can compare these ancient ports to other coastal cities to see the effect on Muslim settlement and institutional formation (Jha 2013, 2014, 2018).

7. See Montesquieu ([1750] 1989), Paine (1791), and Mill ([1848] 1909).

8. The effect of civil war on incomes comes from Mueller (2012). The argument that intellectual and financial capital temper incentives for coercion and seizure comes from Gartzke (2007) and Rosecrance (1986). The argument is often attributed to the early twentieth-century British politician and Nobel Peace Prize winner Norman Angell.

9. Also, trade and commerce aren't magical solutions. For instance, a nation that trades with dozens of countries might not feel commercial penalties from warring with just one, unless those other trading partners have the motive and means to restrain the aggressor. It's also possible, as we discussed in chapter 2, for some groups of industrialists and investors to have a stake in war—the famous military-industrial complex, for example. So not every industry may seek a capitalist peace. For discussions of the theory, the evidence, and some of these nuances, see Russett and Oneal (2001); Gartzke (2007); Martin, Mayer, and Thoenig (2008a, 2008b); Rohner, Thoenig, and Zilibotti (2013); and Lee and Pyun (2016).

10. See Jha and Shayo (2019).

11. See Moretti et al. (2019).

12. See Ross (2008, 2012).

13. See Benzell and Cooke (2021).

14. See Dahl (1956) and Lipset and Rokkan (1967).

15. See Smith (1759) as well as an analysis in Forman-Barzilai (2010).

16. See Smith et al. (2009); Cikara, Bruneau, and Saxe (2011); Baron-Cohen (2012); and Cikara et al. (2014). There are few examples outside the lab, or employing real identities, and so I think it remains to be seen how empirically common schadenfreude is in practice.

17. See Varshney (2003a) and Brass (1997).

18. For a meta-analysis and a comprehensive discussion of the strengths and weaknesses of this literature, see Paluck, Green, and Green (2019). For the Nigeria, India, and Iraq

studies, see Scacco and Warren (2018), Lowe (2021), and Mousa (2020). These programs don't always work as well across hardened divides, however.

19. Bazzi et al. (2019).

20. I base my discussion of ethnic politics in Africa, and the usefulness of crosscutting identities, on Fearon and Laitin (1996); Brubaker and Laitin (1998); Posner (2004); Miguel and Gugerty (2005); and Eifert, Miguel, and Posner (2010).

21. On the Kurukan Fuga, see Niang (2006). On cousinage and ethnic politics, see Dunning and Harrison (2010).

Notably, Mali has a different cleavage that I don't get into here: the tensions between the country's southern savannah, where most Malians live and the population is mainly Black and settled; and the north, a vast peripheral territory in the Sahara, home to a largely seminomadic, pastoral Berber people called the Tuareg. For simplicity, the research I highlight focuses on the politics in the dense southern core, without getting into the many other cleavages and details of what is still a sometimes unstable country.

22. One reason for caution is that intermingling could be a consequence of harmonious relations, and not a cause. Still, the theory is intuitive and the pattern can be found across diverse cleavages and places, from Africa to South Asia to Southeast Asia (Selway 2011; Gubler and Selway 2012; Gubler, Selway, and Varshney 2016).

23. See Depetris-Chauvin, Durante, and Campante (2020).

24. The idea that social identities are constructed and malleable comes from a vast literature across the social sciences and history (Brubaker and Laitin 1998; Akerlof and Kranton 2000; Fearon and Laitin 2000; Chandra 2005; Green 2005; Tajfel 2010; Wimmer 2013).

25. On imagined communities, and nationalism in particular, see Anderson (2006). On the roots of the expanding circle in both biology and culture, see Singer (2011).

26. See Ignatieff (2008, 2011), Pinker (2011), Hunt (2007), and Forman-Barzilai (2010). See also Singer (2011) for the biological basis of the narrow circle and the reasoned basis of the expanded one.

27. See Hirschman (2013).

CHAPTER 8. CHECKS AND BALANCES

1. See Sawyer (1992, 2004, 2005). He is not the only one who focuses on too much concentration of power. These unequal orders go by many names. Daron Acemoglu and James Robinson named them extractive regimes; Douglass North, John Wallis, and Barry Weingast call it a limited access order; Bruce Bueno de Mesquita labeled it a narrow selectorate with a smaller winning coalition; James Scott thinks of this as the classic coercive state; and Mancur Olson spoke of dictatorship (Bueno de Mesquita et al. 2003; Acemoglu and Robinson 2006; North, Wallis, and Weingast 2009a; Olson 1993; Scott 2010). This is a good description for how power was structured in many of the cases considered in this book: for gangs in Chicago or Medellín, sectarian leaders in Indian cities, ethnic politics in sub-Saharan Africa, dictators (e.g., Saddam Hussein) staring down foreign enemies, or warlords in weak states from Afghanistan to Tajikistan to Liberia to early modern Europe (Roessler 2016; Mukhopadhyay 2014; Driscoll 2015; North, Wallis, and Weingast 2009a; Myerson 2015; Sawyer 1992).

2. On the design of stable, institutionalized autocratic systems, see Gandhi (2008); Gandhi and Lust-Okar (2009); Egorov, Guriev, and Sonin (2009); Svolik (2012); and Gehlbach, Sonin, and Svolik (2016).

3. Institutionalizing power is tricky for a few reasons. The first is that institutions and rules are slow to change and hard to build. All these splits are feasible in theory, but in

practice, when power has been cemented under the president for such a long time, nimble changes and fine slices can be hard. Power is divisible, but it is lumpy. The split that puts you in the bargaining range isn't always available. The second is that the ruler has to worry about giving away *too much* power and risking a coup. Suppose the all-powerful president gives the challenger a piece of the armed forces or an arm of government as a form of credible commitment. (This is one reason why many countries have many military agencies.) Who is to say that the upstart won't knock him out? See Roessler (2016) for a detailed look at this coup–civil war dilemma, especially in modern-day Africa.

Throughout history, powerful rulers have had a hard time making firm commitments, despite huge incentives to get it right. An example comes not from peace, but from public finance. Suppose the king wants the lesser lords and the merchants to give the central state a share of their earnings. In return, the ruler pledges to build roads, run courts, defend the nation, and provide other public goods. But how can the nobles and businesspeople trust an almighty king or dictator to deliver on the promise? It's a commitment problem. Monarchs and emperors have the same issue borrowing money, because lenders are worried that a too-powerful ruler won't repay. The ability to raise taxes or borrow lots of money is essential. They let rulers build their armies, threaten neighboring states, and gain concessions. Taxes and loans are the lifeblood of the state. So, if rulers can solve this public finance commitment problem, then they can fight or bargain their way to world domination.

I simplify a vast historical and political economy literature here. The Nobel-winning economic historian Douglass North is one of the clearest exponents of this view (1994, 1989). This role of democratic institutions in commitment is summarized nicely by Acemoglu and Robinson (2012). On autocratic institutions as solutions to commitment problems, see Myerson (2008), Gehlbach and Keefer (2011), and Boix and Svolik (2013).

4. For a discussion of the many things democracy means and has meant, see Ostrom (1997) and Stasavage (2020).

5. For this and other descriptions of the early US presidency, I draw heavily on Howell (2015, 2022).

6. I draw Madison's description and deeds from Brookhiser (2011); Hamilton, Madison, and Jay (2008); and Madison (1793).

7. For a discussion of polycentrism, see Ostrom (2010).

8. A vast literature illustrates how different countries followed different political paths based on their early resource allocations. Places with climates and crops suited to smallholder agriculture and industry trended on a more democratic path than places where there were economies of scale in agriculture (leading to plantations and coercive labor) or concentrated natural resources, like precious metals (see Mahoney 2001; Engerman and Sokoloff 2005; Nugent and Robinson 2010). On oil and autocracy, see Ross (2012, 2008). The exceptions tend to be places where democratic institutions were established before valuable resources were discovered.

9. For the association between regime type and war, see Weeks (2012, 2014). Similar arguments are made by Geddes, Wright, and Frantz (2018). For the measure of legislative constraints, see Choi (2010).

10. See Kant ([1795] 2011) for this early articulation of the democratic peace. This can be found in the philosophical writings of Jean-Jacques Rousseau and Jeremy Bentham, as well as in the thought of scholar-politicians like Woodrow Wilson. See Gartzke (2007) and Hegre (2014) for a broader discussion of the idea and the many connections between political institutions and armed conflict. Note that advocates of the democratic

peace weren't just thinking of checks and balances as the reason democracy reduced violence. Among other things, they were also thinking that democracy fostered a cultural disposition that cooled passions and made dealmaking and deliberation a norm.

For a more modern treatment, one that focuses on solving the agency problem, see Jackson and Morelli (2007). Wars between democracies are avoided not because of similar norms or cultural affinities, they argue, but because of a lack of political bias in the bargaining process. This is similar to the logic of Bueno de Mesquita et al. (2003). The literature on the democratic peace and the mechanisms proposed are vast (Maoz and Russett 1993; Russett et al. 1995; Bueno de Mesquita et al. 1999).

None of this is to say there is some simple linear relationship between democracy and peace, however. To the extent that the voting public operates with limited information, or bounded rationality, leaders can lose office for conceding too much, for starting a war and then settling, or for losing a war. How this affects their decision is more complicated than "more democracy is good for peace" (Baliga, Sjöström, and Lucca 2011; Ashworth and Ramsay 2020).

11. See Hegre (2014) for a summary of the evidence. See Walter (2015) for repeated civil wars and the commitment problems that drive their recurrence. Finally, several scholars have noticed that places transitioning to democracy can be more belligerent. Some argue that these in-between moments are prone to aggression, whereby a small elite still has disproportionate influence and can manipulate masses into supporting their foreign adventures (Snyder 2000; Mansfield and Snyder 2002). This, too, implies that the lack of checks on elites is the key issue.

    On more consensus-based governments being a stable form for diverse and cleaved societies, see, for instance, the case analysis of Lijphart (2012). There is also a large cross-national literature consistent with this claim (Wimmer, Cederman, and Min 2009; Cederman, Wimmer, and Min 2010; Francois, Rainer, and Trebbi 2015). A study of Northern Ireland also found that areas where both Protestants and Catholics had seats on the local council were less violent, a fact the authors argue is evidence of the importance of power-sharing arrangements (Mueller and Rohner 2018).

12. The literature on the origins of democracy is vast (Stasavage 2020; Acemoglu and Robinson 2006, 2012; North, Wallis, and Weingast 2009b, 2009a). The quotation comes from Ake (2000).

13. On Brazil, see Fujiwara (2015). On Benin and Sierra Leone, see Casey et al. (2018); Bidwell, Casey, and Glennerster (2020); Wantchekon (2003); and Wantchekon and Vermeersch (2011). On China, see Martinez-Bravo et al. (2017). Finally, in Uganda, some colleagues and I worked with a huge alliance of civil society organizations to run a campaign against vote buying in thousands of villages. The campaign encouraged residents to meet and decide collectively to refuse to accept money and gifts from politicians. When the villagers met, they seemed to prefer the idea of taking the money and voting with their conscience. "Eat widely and vote wisely" was their motto. Either way, the result was a big reduction in votes for the well-funded incumbents, enough to swing many local races (Blattman et al. 2018).

14. Naidu (2012).

15. On the US Voting Rights Act, see Lacroix (2020). On England, see Rohner and Saia (2020). Consider Nigeria, too, where sudden increases in resource wealth are less likely to be conflictual when local governments are elected rather than appointed, as various arms and groups try to carve up rents (Fetzer and Kyburz 2018).

16. On the problematic incentives from aid, see Moss, Pettersson, and Van de Walle (2006). Another example comes from Somaliland, which isn't recognized as a country and doesn't receive much foreign aid. Eubank (2012) makes the case that because elites in

the country didn't have access to overseas finance, they had to depend more on more local taxation. This gave taxpaying non-elites more voice and influence with elites. They also didn't go to war.

CHAPTER 9. RULES AND ENFORCEMENT

1. Social science has a grim history of exploiting prisoners for research. Today protections exist for prisoners, and it is possible to do prison research like ours. We worked closely with human subjects review committees in both Colombia and the United States. In particular, we took great care to get informed consent from our interviewees, our notes conceal their identities, and we obtained certain guarantees not to seek our data from the police, minister of justice, and the national prosecutor's office. The men we interviewed were intelligent and powerful, fully understood our objectives, and decided whether or not to speak with us and what to say. For more on the challenges, ethics, human subject protections, and results of our interviews, see Blattman, Duncan, et al. (2021a, 2021b).

2. See Tilly (1985), Olson (1993), and Sánchez de la Sierra (2020).

3. See Restrepo (2015). One worry is that the people who settle within one hundred kilometers of a Mountie fort are different from those who do not. Outlaws might choose to be far from the law. This possibility may have played a role. But this seems an unlikely explanation of the size of the effect. Also, today all these areas have police. The persistence of a more violent culture far from the state is not in doubt.

4. See Hobbes ([1651] 2017). For the account of Hobbes's life and views, here and later in the chapter, I draw on several historians and political philosophers (Sommerville 1992; Hamilton 2009; Curran 2002).

5. See Pinker (2011) for a collection of evidence on violence within nations. Levitt and Miles (2006) and Chalfin and McCrary (2017) review the evidence on increased policing and discuss how, across dozens of studies, more police are usually associated with falling crime citywide, especially a reduction in violent crimes. In addition to these correlations, there are also many natural experiments and actual randomized experiments that intensify police, mostly in the United States and the United Kingdom. The vast majority of these show reductions in crime and violence (Braga, Weisburd, and Turchan 2018). There are indications, some of it from my own policing research in Colombia, that this crime might just get pushed to the less policed places (Blattman, Green, et al. 2021). Still, that's largely consistent with police reducing crime. My reading of the evidence is that a citywide expansion of police reduces aggregate crime. For tackling social disorder, evaluations of other municipal services are rarer. Braga, Welsh, and Schnell (2015) review interventions designed to tackle social and physical disorder, but the majority of these interventions tend to be a policing strategy rather than attempts at urban renewal. There is some evidence that street lighting reduces crime (Welsh and Farrington 2008). Cassidy et al. (2014) review five studies suggesting there is weak evidence that urban renewal reduces youth violence.

6. Indeed, professional, paid police forces like the Mounties, or city police forces, didn't exist in most developed countries until the nineteenth century, not even in the biggest and richest cities in the world (Chang 2002). For a long time, moreover, these forces were massively partisan and corrupt. One only need consider the police riot of 1857 in New York City to see what order looked like in those early days. The mayor of New York and his Municipal Police force were massively partisan and corrupt. So the governor disbanded the force and created a new Metropolitan Police for the five boroughs. When the mayor refused to disband his "Municipals" and had them swear fealty to

him, the state issued a warrant for his arrest. A Metropolitan officer tried to make the arrest, but a few hundred Municipals were stationed in city hall to stop that from happening. They tossed the captain into the street. That's when a detachment of Metropolitans arrived. For a half hour they battled one another on the steps and in the corridors of city hall. This New York story is from Herbert Asbury's somewhat sensational account, *The Gangs of New York* (1928), an inspiration for the Martin Scorsese film by the same name.

7. See Nisbett and Cohen (1996), Gould (1999), Thrasher and Handfield (2018), and Bastaki (2020).

8. See Pinker (2011).

9. For the clearest articulation of the culture of honor hypothesis, and some social psychology experiments illustrating it in the American South, see Nisbett and Cohen (1996). For quantitative evidence supporting the tie to homicide levels today, see Grosjean (2014).

10. See Leovy (2015).

11. See Lake (2007, 2011). There's some evidence in support of this view. Butt (2013) looks at South America during the 1930s and 1940s, when the United States was distracted by a depression and world war, and argues this inattention led to more political disorder on the continent. Cunningham (2016) codes up every nation's proximity to the United States in terms of hegemonic relations, and finds that this is correlated with fewer civil wars and more nonviolent political movements. We have to be careful here, because the United States might not have tried to exercise hegemony over violence-prone states.

12. See Mearsheimer (1994). For a broader discussion of the debate between realists like Mearsheimer and the liberal institutionalists in this period, see Martin and Simmons (1998).

13. See, for example, Ignatieff (2008, 2011); Power (2013); and a review in Frieden, Lake, and Schultz (2013). On norm entrepreneurship and norm diffusion, see Finnemore and Sikkink (1998).

14. You can see Frieden, Lake, and Schultz (2013) for a more detailed introduction to international institutions.

15. I have one more point to make about rules and enforcers. It marries the themes of the last chapter with this one, to explain why checked states and constrained international institutions are the most likely to produce peace. After all, we can't all be happy and idealistic little Canadians, with peace, order, and good government. And even those nineteenth-century Mounties were not all that impartial, professional, or fair. They were the agents of a colonizing, taxing government three thousand kilometers away, trying to crowd native peoples off their lands as Canadians gradually extended their empire!

    The state is a force for peace in some places but an agent of oppression in others. A lot of organizations that control violence are centralized, unaccountable, and prone to capture. Hegemons, empires, and police states might be extremely good at keeping the peace in their domains, with repression if need be. But as we've seen, unconstrained governments will be more likely to attack other states. And a lack of checks can mean a higher risk of violent revolution at home.

    This wasn't something Hobbes worried about in *Leviathan*. He had little interest in restraining his ruler. Hobbes was a committed royalist, a tutor to the Prince of Wales. He wanted to vest supreme power in an unchecked king. England didn't need a parliament, for Hobbes believed the king truly speaks for the people. He also thought the monarch deserved almost unlimited power and should not be bound by promises or the law. In one passage of his book, Hobbes compares ruling with a parliament to playing tennis in a wheelbarrow, with a bunch of people pushing you around, some of whom are hoping you will lose. Better to have these advisers on the sidelines or (better yet) in the stands, the philosopher thought.

Everything we've learned about peace says that is wrong. What we really want is the constrained state. The economists Daron Acemoglu and James Robinson call it the Shackled Leviathan. This, as it happens, was also the famous reply to Hobbes by the English philosopher John Locke. All these thinkers wanted to see a Leviathan strong enough to exercise authority, enforce rules and deals, and ensure that its subgroups don't fight. But control of this beast needed to be spread out among the subgroups to prevent the state from going to war with other nations. For more on this theme, see Locke ([1690] 1988), Migdal (1988, 2001), and Acemoglu and Robinson (2020). Checking state power has other benefits. Locke believed in the Shackled Leviathan because he treasured individual liberty. His target was repression, whose violence is more one-sided than war. It's how the powerful keep the peace (and a large share of the pie at the same time). Woe to the peasant, the heretic, or the conquered minority in Hobbes's country.

Indeed, for most of history, from Africa to the Americas, from the fields of Europe to those of South and East Asia, most people have been subjects, not citizens, of the state. They lived in conditions of servitude. They were conscripted, plundered, and forced to work. To tax, extract, and control them, states mapped, counted, enclosed, administered, and reordered the societies beneath them. When given the opportunity, most people ran away from the unshackled Leviathan, not toward it. For one of the most detailed and eloquent descriptions of life under most states, see Scott (2010). An example from Europe is North, Wallis, and Weingast (2009a), and an example from Africa is Herbst (2000). Another poignant illustration comes from the fact that, until relatively recently, rulers counted their dominion in terms of people, not territory. So, it was the king of the Franks, not the king of France; the king of the English, not the king of England (Spruyt 2017). For a discussion of the repression literature, see Davenport (2007).

Constraining the state at lower levels probably leads to checks and balances at higher levels. In recent decades, the freest and most shackled states have pushed hardest for the international institutions we have, and they are largely responsible for their expansion. Also, the fact that these liberal international institutions have been so successful at promoting economic growth, have been semisuccessful at creating more peace, and enjoy such broad legitimacy all augurs well for their continuation, especially because there are many vested interests in this order. For a discussion of the liberal international order, see Lake, Martin, and Risse (2021).

CHAPTER 10. INTERVENTIONS

1. If you want a more nuanced and detailed take, see Flint and de Waal (2008). You can also read a critique of Prendergast's advocacy by the scholar Mamdani (2010).
2. One summary is Rittel and Webber (1973). For a recent expansion and application to development in general, and to me one of the most important books I've read on solving social problems, see Andrews, Pritchett, and Woolcock (2017).
3. For the best account of the transactional, personalized politics in the Horn of Africa, see de Waal (2015).
4. For an extended discussion of the strengths and weaknesses of sanctions, see Hufbauer, Schott, and Elliott (1990); Pape (1997, 1998); Elliott and Hufbauer (1999); Hufbauer et al. (2008); Drezner (2011); and Biersteker (2019).

5. On focused deterrence and murder in US cities, see Kennedy (2011). On conditional repression and making peace with drug lords, see Lessing (2017). On targeting incentives and other interventions among the most likely criminal offenders in general, see Abt (2019).

6. See Elliott and Hufbauer (1999), Hufbauer et al. (2008), and Biersteker (2019).

7. See Draca et al. (2019).

8. See Braga, Wesiburd, and Turchan (2018).

9. The Failed State Package comes from Ellis (2006). The peacekeeping-humanitarian complex comes from conversations with James Fearon.

10. Peacekeepers must interact with some civilians, because they have a lot of sex. Some colleagues of mine interviewed a random sample of women aged eighteen to thirty in the capital, Monrovia (where countries other than Pakistan patrolled). An astonishing three-quarters of the women said they'd had sex for money or gifts with someone from the UN. Three-quarters! Even if that is way off the average in other places, it is still a depressing number, just one sign of the many unintended consequences of the presence of troops who are otherwise there to do good (Beber et al. 2017).

11. I keep the ambassador anonymous to preserve her ability to speak freely.

12. The details draw on field research by my research staff, Johnny Ndebe, Ayouba Karzu, and Prince Williams, and compiled by my collaborator Alexandra Hartman. They were collected in the course of a study of violence and dispute resolution in the region (Blattman, Hartman, and Blair 2014; Hartman, Blair, and Blattman 2021). For a news report, see Ackerman (2010). On the land issues that often underpin these seeming religious conflicts, see Hartman (2015).

13. For a wider look at the ways in which much conflict originates and aggregates from local conflicts, rivalries, and score settling, see Autesserre (2010) on central Africa, and Kalyvas (2006) on a range of cases, including in southern Europe.

14. The question of armed humanitarian intervention, with or without UN support, is a huge topic. For what I think is one of the best and more measured discussions, see Stewart and Knaus (2011). Of course the distinction is not always easy. Acts of genocide and state repression typically happen during civil wars (as in Sudan, Rwanda, or Kosovo). In these cases, I would group any humanitarian military interventions under the umbrella of peacekeeping, and I'd comfortably apply the theory and evidence in this book. Other interventions clearly do not belong in this category, such as Western interventions in Afghanistan in 2001 or in Iraq in 2003. These are, in essence, conflicts in which the United States and its allies were one of the sides.

15. See Fortna (2008). On what peacekeepers do, see also Howard (2008, 2019) and Nomikos (2021). On increasing the duration of peace, see Doyle and Sambanis (2006), Fortna (2004, 2008), Gilligan and Sergenti (2008), Stedman (1997), and Goldstein (2012). On where peacekeepers go, see these sources and Gilligan and Stedman (2003) as well as Blair (2021). For case studies, see also Caplan and Hoeffler (2017). The results suggest that larger, more robust missions mandated to use armed force if necessary are the most effective, especially in the first decade or two after the Cold War. On peacekeepers reducing the lethality of conflict, see Hultman, Kathman, and Shannon (2014, 2019). On contagion, see Beardsley (2011a). On how peacekeeping interacts with mediation, see Beardsley, Cunningham, and White (2019).

    As far as I can tell, however, there no is pooled analysis of all these time periods and outcomes. Most papers look at a snapshot of a few decades (the Cold War, the 1990s, post-2001, and so on). The closest is Hegre, Hultman, and Nygård (2019), who try to simulate how much more peace would have happened if the world had more and bigger peace missions.

16. See Walter (1997) on how guaranteeing an existing truce is easier. See Fearon (2020) on some of the possible limits to peacekeeping in the twenty-first century.

17. Syria in the past decade is an example of a place where peacekeepers would go with peril. See, for instance, Lake (2016), Fearon (2017, 2020), or Kalyvas (2020). This runs against the idea that peacekeepers go to the hard cases. But it's not clear that we have many cases in the "treatment" and "control" groups of conflicts of this nature—more ideological, strategically important, and involving rival superpowers. If not, then we can't easily generalize from peacekeeping missions of the past to the peacekeeping missions of the future.

18. On negotiations between the United Kingdom and the IRA, see Powell (2008). On his own role mediating other peaces, see Powell (2015). The quotations draw on his 2018 lecture at the University of Chicago and my conversations with him at the time (Powell 2018).

19. For these theoretical links between the reasons for conflict and mediation, see, for instance, Beber (2012), Smith and Stam (2003), Kydd (2006), and Beardsley (2011b). The Kissinger story comes from the latter article. On the interaction of peacekeepers and mediators, see Beardsley, Cunningham, and White (2019). For the most part, mediators don't solve commitment problems through enforcement, or offer concrete carrots and sticks to self-interested leaders. Those are different tools, complementary to mediation, and we'll come to those soon. For a broad look at the formal theory and evidence on a variety of interventions, see Rohner (2018).

20. See Beber (2012).

21. I've sat with several mediators in Chicago—usually former gang leaders turned social workers who step in to try to build a tunnel between the warring sides. I've not seen any formal study of these brave people. Some other better documented examples include El Salvador, Honduras, Haiti, South Africa, Trinidad and Tobago, Japan, and Jamaica (Kan 2014; Cockayne, de Boer, and Bosetti 2017; Brown et al. 2020). The officials who helped negotiate the 2012 gang truce in El Salvador were later convicted.

22. Ballah, a Liberian, worked for the UN refugee agency, UNHCR. He and a local nonprofit named the Justice and Peace Commission ran the program. The techniques are drawn from alternative dispute resolution, a set of practices used worldwide, especially in the United States and Europe. Robert Blair, Alexandra Hartman, and I helped them set it up as a randomized control trial (Blattman, Hartman, and Blair 2014; Hartman, Blair, and Blattman 2021). For the broader evidence on how UN legal and dispute resolution programs affect peace and security, see Blair (2020, 2021).

23. There had been innumerable small-scale studies, mostly nonexperimental evaluations, in American juvenile institutions. The practice of CBT for delinquents was well established. But whether it really worked as well as its practitioners hoped was anyone's guess. For this literature and the details of our evaluation, see Blattman, Jamison, and Sheridan (2017).

24. On Tony D, whose full name is Anthony Ramirez-Di Vittorio, see the interview by Waters (2016). For the BAM program evaluation, see Heller, Shah, Guryan, Ludwig, Mullainathan, and Pollack (2017). I'm lucky to have one of these as a coauthor now, and four others as friends and colleagues at the University of Chicago and the Crime Lab.

25. See Bertrand, Bhatt, Blattman, Heller, and Kapustin (2022).

26. On negotiation professionals, see, for example, the celebrated negotiator Mnookin (2010). These distortions, he says, are wrapped up in emotion, and they lead us to overestimate the benefits of fighting.

27. There have been several rigorous studies of peace propaganda in countries such as post-genocide Rwanda (Paluck 2009a, 2009b; Blouin and Mukand 2018). The perspective-

taking literature tends to be more lab-based but comes to similar conclusions (Epley et al. 2004; Eyal, Steffel, and Epley 2018).

28. On the post-Soviet republics, see Driscoll (2015). On Afghanistan, see Mukhopadhyay (2014) and Cheng, Goodhand, and Meehan (2018). On sub-Saharan Africa, see Roessler (2016). On how rebel groups participating in politics is pacifying, see Matanock (2017).

29. See, for instance, Bates (2008); North, Wallis, and Weingast (2009a); Myerson (2015, 2020c); Lake (2016); and Rohner (2018).

30. DeLong and Eichengreen (1991) show that the Marshall Plan was not actually that large—the transfer was only a small fraction of the war-ravaged European economy. Nonetheless, it offered foreign exchange and trade at a crucial moment, helping to tip Western Europe away from the unfree economic and political model promoted by the Soviets (and by Western Europeans who, after fifteen years of economic and political turmoil, were disillusioned with the liberal democratic and capitalist order).

31. On comparisons between peacebuilding and imperialism, see Paris (2010) and Cunliffe (2012). On the ritual of democracy, the quotation comes from Marina Ottaway, reproduced and discussed in Schaffer (2000). The co-option of election by the powerful is a common feature of autocratic elections (Gandhi and Lust-Okar 2009; Gehlbach, Sonin, and Svolik 2016).

32. On overburdened, low-capacity states, see Thomas (2015). On premature load bearing, see Andrews, Woolcock, and Pritchett (2017). On hasty transitions and the need for supporting institutions to come first, see Paris (2004).

33. There are big literatures on playing the long game with elites (Fearon 2020); on fostering good enough governance (Grindle 2004, 2007; Börzel and Grimm 2018; Krasner 2020); on tilting a public administration away from kleptocratic rule (Blum and Rogger 2020); and on encouraging checks and balances through polycentric governance, especially the devolution of power locally (Myerson 2020c; Sawyer 2005).

CHAPTER 11. WAYWARD PATHS TO WAR AND PEACE

1. "What drives people to kill and maim each other so savagely?" Einstein asked Freud, in the letters I described in chapter 6. "I think it is the sexual character of the male that leads to such wild explosions," the physicist concluded. More recently, psychologist Steven Pinker has written about how "over the long sweep of history, women have been and will be a pacifying force" (Pinker 2011).

2. For an evolutionary biology view on male aggression in humans and other apes, see Wrangham and Peterson (1996); Glowacki, Wilson, and Wrangham (2017); and Van Vugt (2011). For women's roles in war, see Goldstein (2001).

3. For reviews of this evidence, see Barnhart et al. (2020) and Eichenberg and Stoll (2017).

4. For a discussion of some of this evidence, see Bigio and Vogelstein (2016). My own view is that most of the evidence is consistent with general inclusion increasing prospects for peace; whether or not that's gender-specific is hard to say. But that's because only one gender is usually excluded from processes of decision-making!

5. For a discussion see Hafner-Burton et al. (2017). Another way of putting this: individual pathologies don't automatically add up to group pathologies. As one anthropologist wrote, "Maleness is one part of biology. Biology is one part of aggression. Aggression is one part of combat. Combat is one part of war" (Ferguson 2011). The point is that hostile biological instincts can get diluted amid the many other drives and decisions, so the sum effect can be quite weak.

6. See Horowitz, Stam, and Ellis (2015).

7. We don't know whether selection effects and discrimination make successful female leaders more aggressive on average. But the evidence does suggest it makes them better performers, since the ones who succeed have leapt over a higher bar than men. Most of our evidence about women's performance comes from modern US politics. For example, although conditional on winning, women perform better in US Congress than do men (Anzia and Berry 2011). On discrimination and self-selection into politics, see discussions in that paper and in Fox and Lawless (2011); and Ashworth, Berry, and Bueno de Mesquita (2021).

8. For details of the Tudor line, I draw on Ackroyd (2013).

9. We call this technique instrumental variables (IV) estimation. You take something like the correlation between women leaders and years of war, where it's hard to figure out what causes what. You look for something that seems to randomly shift the likelihood of women leaders, like birth order under rules of primogeniture, and then use IV statistical methods to isolate the effects of that idiosyncratic variation on years of warfare. The variables that have this randomness (in this case, these birth order indicators) we call "instruments." So long as these birth order measures have a large enough effect on queenly reigns, and so long as they only affect years of war through their influence on the chances of queenly reigns, we can be mostly confident that the researchers have nailed down the causal effect of queenliness on warfare. I say "mostly," because historical researchers often have to work with small samples and are never certain in their assumptions. In this case, they can't know for sure that the randomness is uncontaminated, or that birth order acts on warfare through queenly reigns alone. But most of the obvious worries are not borne out by history or the data, in this case. Credible instruments like this one are as valuable as they are rare. For all the statistical blood and gore, see Dube and Harish (2020).

10. See Dube and Harish (2020).

11. Under uncertainty, queens might also use skirmishes and small wars to signal their toughness. If signaling, then you might think that queens fight earlier in their reigns, as Dube and Harish suggest. But they don't see evidence of that. So maybe signaling isn't so common. With a small sample and few unmarried queens, however, we can't dismiss signaling outright. In general, the number of queenly reigns is small enough that we should be cautious about overinterpreting any one mechanism.

12. See Blattman, Hwang, and Williamson (2007). The idea of countries winning or losing a commodity lottery is part of a long tradition of comparative history in the Americas (Innis 1933; Diaz-Alejandro 1983).

13. The quotation comes from Nieto (1942) and is reproduced in Safford and Palacios (2002). As for the idea that plunging incomes can cause conflict, economists sometimes call this the opportunity cost theory of banditry and conflict, and it is rooted in the economic approach to crime (Becker 1968; Grossman 1991; Hirshleifer 1995a; Collier and Hoeffler 1998, 2004). As we will see, however, these are models of predation and banditry, but not necessarily of war. There's no strategizing in these models.

14. See Miguel, Satyanath, and Sergenti (2004); Miguel and Satyanath (2011); and Dube and Vargas (2013). Dube and Vargas also found that rising oil prices raised conflict levels in oil-producing regions. This probably happened for a different reason than poverty; more valuable oil raised incentives to arm and invest in fighting on both sides, as the local pie grew.

15. This isn't to say a devastating economic shock could never derail a peaceful deal. A large and sudden depression could exacerbate problems of uncertainty, greedy leaders, or commitment. In societies that are navigating a narrow gorge, a big collapse in income or

in government revenues might be enough to destabilize the whole system. If so, we might see a slight effect of these bad shocks on warfare, but not a big or systematic one. For an example, see Chassang and Padró-i-Miquel (2009), who illustrate how, in the presence of a commitment problem, a shock can produce conflict. Note that it is not the level of income that matters in this context, but a sudden shift—the power shift that is so essential to commitment problem stories.

I want to make three more nuanced and technical points. First, when you mix conflict onset and conflict continuation, you mechanically end up estimating the effect of something on continuation. That's because wars are long. The average civil war, for example, runs for about ten years. Suppose I code any year of war with 1 and years of peace with 0, and I correlate that outcome with a price plunge or drought. For every year when war breaks out, there are nine years where war continued. Mostly, then, the correlation you estimate is going to tell you how volatility affects whether wars continue or get more intense.

Second, it's not so easy to pinpoint wars breaking out, or to separate this onset from war intensity. Scholars find it surprisingly hard to agree on what years countries have wars. But it makes sense when you look at the details. Does it start when one side declares war, even if the fighting starts next year? What about interludes of calm, where war is officially declared, but no one is battling? You can disagree on whether those years should be ones or zeros, and people do. A lot of scholars use a threshold for recorded battle deaths to code a war—usually twenty-five or one thousand per year. That's a useful approach, but on reflection, you can see how it conflates outbreaks with intensity. In principle, we might see falling incomes causing new wars not because it caused the bargain to break down, but because it pushed a country from a few hundred to a few thousand battle deaths a year. So a lot of the variation driving a "war onset" regression is still coming from war intensity and continuation.

Third, when scholars have driven the analysis down to a more micro level, such as fifty-by-fifty kilometer grid cells, diverse shocks in those cells are associated with conflict onset in those cells. For an example with commodity prices, see Berman and Couttenier (2015). But this is still a kind of "continuation" or "intensity," because it's assessing whether an ongoing war in the area spread to that area. Again, hungry men are more willing to rebel when there's an existing fight.

16. See Bazzi and Blattman (2014) for the commodity price analysis. To be fair, not all the evidence agrees with my conclusion. A recent paper analyzes all the commodity shock and conflict papers out there and comes to a slightly different conclusion (Blair, Christensen, and Rudkin 2020). They treat all papers as equally good and look at what they say on average—a meta-analysis. They do see some evidence that as agricultural prices fall, wars are more likely to break out. It's an impressive study, but I stick with my view for a few reasons. First, every researcher overweights their own papers, and I am probably guilty of that a little. Second, a meta-analysis is only as good as the underlying studies, and I worry about mistakes in some of them. Third, a subnational study that looks at war onset in grid cells or subregions is still measuring war intensity, not war onset, as I explained above. Finally, if some scholars didn't publish null results, then there's an inherent bias in what studies we average in a meta-analysis. We don't see all the null results.

I don't think it matters for the argument I'm trying to make, however. I wouldn't be surprised if massive volatility in trade helped push a country to war sometimes. It's one of the forces that can send a pilot careening into the cliff face, even when a bargain makes sense. The resiliency of most countries to huge shocks is, for me, the big takeaway.

As for the fact that shocks only explain war when the country is fragile, this makes sense alongside another result all these papers share: the rainfall or price shock usually explains a puny share of conflict. Ninety-nine percent or more of the variation in peace and war comes from other factors—other shocks maybe, but probably most of these are explained by the five logics I describe in this book. I'm referring here to the very small change in explained variance from adding income shocks like these to a conflict regression, as measured by the R^2 statistic, for example. Often this is at most 1 or 2 percent.

17. See Blattman and Miguel (2010).

18. There are dozens of papers in this literature. See Blattman and Miguel (2010) for a detailed review of the role of ethnicity in civil wars.

19. See Miguel and Satyanath (2011); Harrington (2014); Burke, Hsiang, and Miguel (2015).

20. For climate analyses, see Burke at al. (2009); Hsiang, Burke, and Miguel (2013); and Burke, Hsiang, and Miguel (2015). The main theoretical model underlying the analysis in these papers is one where a commitment problem is the fundamental issue, and the price shock is the power shift that is too large to be accommodated given the assumed inflexibility (Chassang and Padró-i-Miquel 2009). It's not clear why a climate shock should aggravate a commitment problem, however. Another possibility is that climate shocks are simply driving the intensity of wars alone, but that phenomenon shows up as a new conflict onset because of the way political scientists code conflict with battle death thresholds. Once again, however, as with price shocks, temperature changes explain only a tiny amount of conflict. We should always be careful to distinguish a statistically significant cause from one that explains substantial variation in the phenomenon. I believe climate shocks are an example of the former.

21. See Licklider (1995) for the point that peace interventions freeze in place an unstable equilibrium. See Luttwak (1999) for a famous and influential *Foreign Affairs* article. A large empirical literature finds negotiated settlements are more likely to see subsequent conflict than wars ending in a decisive victory by one side (e.g., Quinn, Mason, and Gurses 2007; Toft 2010). For examples of arguments that weak states might be more stable long term if they fight now, see Herbst (1990) and Weinstein (2005). See Rohner (2018) for a review and careful discussion of the strengths and limits of this view, especially the difficulties of a causal claim. Below I focus mainly on why, even if it's true that decisive victories lead to more peace, we should not forget the very human cost. But it's not even clear that decisive victories are indeed more peaceful. It could be a spurious correlation for a few reasons. Selection effects are one—the places where two sides are in stalemate are inherently more conflictual. Or it could be driven by omitted factors that make peace settlements less likely.

22. See Scheidel (2018).

23. For Tilly's view, see Tilly (1985, 1992). Some also argue that not only did war make the state, but democracy too—some societies developed constrained governments and mass participation as a result of fighting wars. That's because recruiting all those troops, collecting all those taxes, and amassing the necessary loans required not only a bureaucracy. It also required money and recruits, and autocrats had to make concessions to the people with labor and capital. Tilly and others have made a version of this democratization argument. For a broader review of the long-run determinants of democracy, see Stasavage (2020). A recent popular summary of the argument is Morris (2014). On the role of war in the development of cities, see Dincecco and Onorato (2017). Finally, for formal theory and some informative correlations, see Gennaioli and Voth (2015) and Besley and Persson (2009). Weinstein (2005) has also argued that

some civil wars forge political movements that are capable of governing and shaping society—a kind of state-building capacity. This is most likely, he points out, when there aren't external great powers or natural resources supporting the movement, forcing them to develop a local tax base and govern civilians.

24. Who decides on behalf of future generations is a difficult question. If war has long-run positive externalities, then leaders will choose less war than is optimal. But if we're going to ask leaders to be so farsighted over gains so ambiguous, then we also ought to ask two philosophical questions. The first is how to account for the interests of unborn generations. They probably don't enter most group decisions either. It's hard to know how much weight to give them, but the answer probably isn't "zero." The second question is "Who gets to decide?" In practice, a small elite group decides for their group. Even if their society is democratic, the unborn don't get a vote. Again, it's not clear how to bring this into our decisions. Every policy affects future generations. But some decisions affect who will one day live more than others, and again this is an externality that should probably push us all to be more cautious.

25. For example, once cannons were invented, medieval walls were no match for them. Cities now required massive earthworks, covered in bricks, to withstand artillery fire. But these defenses raised the cost of attacking still higher. Now invaders had to prepare for lengthy sieges. They needed engineers, equipment, and large armies, all in the field year-round. Decade after decade, century after century, Europe's many polities needed ever-greater monies and ever-larger and more efficient administrations to simply endure. In addition to Tilly, see Hoffman (2017) and Spruyt (2017) for discussions of this period.

26. See Hoffman (2017) and Spruyt (2017) for this argument. For a comparison of Europe to China, see Ko, Koyama, and Sng (2018). For Latin America see Centeno (2003), as well as Bates, Coatsworth, and Williamson (2007). The latter shows how Latin America's century of conflict meant that most countries lost out on the first great era of globalization and growth from the 1870s to World War I, falling further behind the rest of the West. They never caught back up. Finally, the absence of warfare is also held responsible for the lack of bureaucratic development in Africa (Herbst 1990). In principle, this is used to support Tilly's argument, as a negative case. It does not automatically follow, however, that war making would have produced strong states in Africa.

What is important, however, is that it's not clear how well the story holds in Europe outside of the gunpowder era. Fighting was already frequent on the continent before 1500, but strong states mostly failed to develop. Even in the supposedly prime period from 1500 to 1800, war's effects on development were erratic (Gennaioli and Voth 2015). Charles Tilly himself admitted that "most of the European efforts to build states failed" (Spruyt 2017). Instead, what we should take away from this survey of wars is just how peculiar the circumstances needed to be for conflict to promote development.

On what made Europe and the Gunpowder Revolution special, there are many theories: a politically fragmented continent of many small players, where no one hegemon ever emerged; political systems that insulated rulers from the costs of warfare while their cultures rewarded fighting with prestige and glory; an absence of easily exploited natural resource wealth; and a particular phase of military technology, focused on gunpowder and large professionalized armies, which demanded and rewarded mass mobilization of labor, capital, and innovation. None of this denies the part warfare played in Europe's rise. But from the end of the Middle Ages to the Industrial Revolution, the circumstances in the West were so weird, they are almost unique.

27. In international relations, inefficient arming is one aspect of what is called the security dilemma. Anarchy means that the things groups do to increase their security has the opposite effect, because arming induces the same investments in their rivals. The name echoes the famous prisoner's dilemma, a simple game theoretic model where two prisoners would benefit from both refusing to confess, but neither one can trust the other to comply alone, and so they each implicate the other. See Herz (1950), Jervis (1978), and Glaser (1997).

In economics, most early theoretical models were also models of inefficient arming in anarchy. They showed how competition gave groups incentives to invest in military might. Interestingly, there was seldom any explicit fighting violence in these models, unless it was an assumed by-product of arming. For examples, see Tullock (1974), Garfinkel (1990), Grossman (1991), Hirshleifer (1991), Skaperdas (1992), Hirshleifer (1995b), and Garfinkel and Skaperdas (2007). For newer and more general discussions of formal models of arming versus fighting, and the inefficiency of arming, see Skaperdas (2006), Fearon (2018), and Baliga and Sjöström (2013).

28. For some impressive theory, data collection, and the correlation between conflict and development, see Dincecco and Onorato (2017) on cities, and Besley and Persson (2009) on nations. In addition to the omitted variable problem, there is also a risk of reverse causality—maybe things that drove development also led to war, not the other way around.

29. I overlook civil wars, which were more common than ever in the late twentieth century. Still, even if there were a lot of civil conflicts, they were mostly low intensity, killing relatively few people a year. Despite a few counterexamples, like Uganda and Rwanda, the average civil war was hugely destructive to economies and state development. For a discussion of these counterexamples, each one fascinating, see Weinstein (2005).

30. Histories that emphasize internal competition among the elites or between the elites and the masses include Acemoglu and Robinson (2012, 2020); North, Wallis, and Weingast (2009a); Bueno de Mesquita et al. (2003); and Stasavage (2020).

CONCLUSION: THE PEACEMEAL ENGINEER

1. From Popper ([1945] 2013). See also Popper ([1957] 2013). For details of his life, I draw on Popper (2005).

2. See Florio and Shapiro (2020).

3. Places as different as Djibouti, Botswana, and St. Lucia (among others) have constitutions that are three-quarters identical to a generic one (Law and Versteeg 2012). One reason, surely, is that there are some ideals these countries share. But another reason, undoubtedly, is the allure of the best practice. The existence of a generic constitution indicates an almost complete lack of national deliberation and input into what are supposed to be the foundational rules for that society.

On the mimicking of form over function, and the perils of bureaucracy, see Meyer and Rowan (1977); Weber (2014); Barnett and Finnemore (1999, 2012); and Andrews, Pritchett, and Woolcock (2017). The contradiction is seldom discussed: how a fragile state is corrupt and has no capacity, and the government should do everything (Mkandawire 2001).

On institutional monocropping, see Evans (2004). On isomorphic mimicry, see DiMaggio and Powell (1983) and Andrews, Pritchett, and Woolcock (2017). They argue that isomorphism is not just a bureaucratic impulse in the imitating countries, it's actively encouraged by the rich donor countries to reward form over function. In the arena of growth and development policy in general, see Rodrik (2007) for illustrations of how there are many recipes for institutional and economic organization that spring from some broad shared economic principles (as he argues against the more mainstream view of a generic recipe for all).

4. See Jacobs ([1961] 2016). "The pseudoscience of planning seems almost neurotic in its determination to imitate empiric failure and ignore empiric success," she also wrote.

5. See Scott (1998). For a discussion of the kinds of policy problems where seeing like a state, ordering society, and best practices might work, see Seabright (1999).

6. On how bureaucracies get their legitimacy, and the mistakes they're prone to make, see Barnett and Finnemore (1999, 2012).

7. See Ferguson (1990).

8. See Easterly (2006, 2014).

9. See Autesserre (2014).

10. On the failure of big solutions and the importance of marginal improvements in international development, see Easterly (2001) and Banerjee and Duflo (2011).

11. Fortunately, other American cities had social workers and criminologists thinking like peacemeal engineers. They were trying new things, on the lookout for impacts on violence. Eventually, they came to the same conclusion: a handful of neighborhoods, a few dozen groups, and a few thousand people are responsible for most of the homicides. Once they understood this, they began to ask why these particular people were violent, and what set them apart from the vast number that weren't. They had different answers (they attacked different margins) in different places, depending on the circumstances. Gang outreach and CBT made sense for disorganized gangs with long-running feuds. More organized mobs, on the other hand, might respond to conditional repression. The answers were different but the mode of thinking was not. Marginal thinking lies behind some of the most promising violence-reduction approaches in the country, from violence interruption (Slutkin, Ransford, and Decker 2015; Brantingham et al. 2018), to focused deterrence, a variety of conditional repression (Kennedy 2011; Braga, Weisburd, and Turchan 2018). Mediation, to my knowledge, is the least studied and documented, and is either secretive or rare. Marginal thinking also lies behind place-based criminological strategies (Weisburd et al. 1993; Weisburd, Groff, and Yang 2012; Braga, Papachristos, and Hurreau 2012; Blattman, Green, et al. 2021). For a review of this literature, see Abt (2019).

12. This could be a case of something economists call increasing returns—each additional increment has a more-than-proportional impact on the outcome. That would be the case if the second tranche of five thousand peacekeepers had a larger impact on peace than the first five thousand. It's possible. Another kind of increasing return happens when a multipronged intervention is more effective than the individual components— where the whole is greater than the sum of the parts. This calls for coordination, and what some policymakers call a "big push." Bold claims require bold evidence, however, and I've not seen persuasive evidence of increasing returns. I'm sure there are some situations. Commitment problems in civil wars might offer one of them. But, overwhelmingly, we seem to live in a world of decreasing returns—each additional increment has a less-than-proportional impact on the outcome.

Also, peacekeeping missions might not be as nonincremental as you think. Countries count police density by officers per one hundred thousand people (not counting their military, national guards, and other security forces). The United States is about two hundred, France is over four hundred, and other countries range from one hundred to five hundred. A ten-thousand-strong peacekeeping force in a country of twenty million people raises that nation's ratio by about fifty. This is not a trivial amount, but it's also not that huge an increase, especially for a country at war.

13. This trial and error lies behind some of the great policy successes of the past century, not just of peace but development too (Hirschman 1970). Take one of the greatest explosions of wealth in human history—East Asia's rapid industrialization in the late twentieth century. Economists trace this success to a rejection of blueprints and an embrace of trial and error in policy (Bardhan 2002; Xu 2011; Ang 2016; Bai, Hsieh, and Song 2020). For a discussion of trial and error and industrial policy as self-discovery, see Hausmann and Rodrik (2003) and Rodrik (2007). See Roland (2000, 2004) for a discussion of the importance of experimentation in Communist regimes, and especially the transition from Communist to more open regimes. For a formal analysis and a review of the literature on experimentation in successful policy, see Majumdar and Mukand (2004) and Mukand and Rodrik (2005).

14. For the "Torah" on iteration and adaptation, see Harford (2011).

15. See, for example, the Design Kit from ideo.org: www.designkit.org/resources/1. Or see the April 2011 *Harvard Business Review* for a special issue on failing: https://hbr.org/archive-toc/BR1104.

16. Do I have to formally reference evening conversations after the kids have gone to bed? I'll say no. For more on the Airbel lab, see https://airbel.rescue.org.

17. I don't like to start with Afghanistan, because it's an example of a victor trying to impose a settlement, rather than a societal effort to find peace (though there are elements of that too). But there's no mistaking that it's a major social experiment and an attempt to engineer a different society. See Thomas (2015) and Mukhopadhyay (2014) for terrific accounts.

18. See Thomas (2015).

19. This is a broad problem across many areas of international development. Take the United Nations Millennium Development Goals (MDGs). Clemens, Kenny, and Moss (2007) show how the United Nations set targets that are implausible for a large number of countries. Many recipients of aid missed the goals, and "failed," even though their progress was rapid by any standard.

20. For a brief introduction to these ideas, and support for many of the points I make in this section, see Ostrom (2001, 2010). A version applied to foreign aid is Ostrom et al. (2002).

21. On the importance of decentralization in fragile settings, see Honig (2018, 2019). On the problem with experts, see Easterly (2014). In aid agency ratings, the United States and the United Nations routinely perform poorly (Easterly and Pfutze 2008; Knack, Rogers, and Eubank 2011).

    Piecemeal engineers also benefit from accountability above, often in the form of a powerful central government. It's easy to romanticize the small and local. But that can get just as mired down. Polycentrism needs a strong center and also a strong local component—they complement one another (e.g., Tandler 1997; Xu 2011). Centralized authorities have at least two big roles to play. One is dissemination. If the small and local idea is successful, something needs to help it spread to other decentralized piecemeal engineers. Polycentric systems have ways for the center to fund experimentation, harvest ideas, and propagate successes. The second thing the center can do is to counterbalance local elites who will skew any experimentation in their own favor. In a lot of developing countries, minorities and the poor often look to central actors for protection and relief from local oppression.

22. This is a vast literature. For an example, see Tendler's (1997) famous case study of a Brazilian state for an illustration of how to foster civil society and downward accountability in a poor, corrupt, and weak state. Roger Myerson, who won the Nobel Prize for his contributions to game theory, has spent most of the last few decades developing

some of the formal theory and historical evidence for similar claims (Myerson 2015, 2020a, 2020b).

23. See Autesserre (2021).

24. This balance between strong states and society is one of the most fundamental lessons of history. We saw this in earlier chapters, and it is a theme echoed by most economic and political historians (Migdal 1988, 2001; North, Wallis, and Weingast 2009a; Fukuyama 2011; Acemoglu and Robinson 2020).

BIBLIOGRAPHY

Abrams, Douglas E. 2017. "The Cuban Missile Crisis, Historian Barbara W. Tuchman, and the 'Art of Writing.'" Columbia: University of Missouri School of Law Scholarship Repository.

Abt, Thomas. 2019. *Bleeding Out: The Devastating Consequences of Urban Violence—and a Bold New Plan for Peace in the Streets.* New York: Basic Books.

Acemoglu, Daron. 2003. "Why Not a Political Coase Theorem? Social Conflict, Commitment, and Politics." *Journal of Comparative Economics* 31 (4): 620–52.

Acemoglu, Daron, and James A. Robinson. 2006. *Economic Origins of Democracy and Dictatorship.* Cambridge: Cambridge University Press.

———. 2012. *Why Nations Fail: The Origins of Power, Prosperity, and Poverty.* New York: Crown.

———. 2020. *The Narrow Corridor: States, Societies, and the Fate of Liberty.* New York: Penguin Press.

Ackerman, Ruthie. 2010. "A Girl's Murder Sparks Riots." *Daily Beast*, March 26, 2010. https://www.thedailybeast.com/a-girls-murder-sparks-riots.

Ackroyd, Peter. 2013. *Tudors: The History of England from Henry VIII to Elizabeth I.* New York: Thomas Dunne Books.

Acland, Dan, and Matthew R. Levy. 2015. "Naiveté, Projection Bias, and Habit Formation in Gym Attendance." *Management Science* 61 (1): 146–60.

Adena, Maja, Ruben Enikolopov, Maria Petrova, Veronica Santarosa, and Ekaterina Zhuravskaya. 2015. "Radio and the Rise of the Nazis in Prewar Germany." *Quarterly Journal of Economics* 130 (4): 1885–939.

Ager, Philipp, Leonardo Bursztyn, Lukas Leucht, and Hans-Joachim Voth. Forthcoming. "Killer Incentives: Relative Position, Performance and Risk-Taking Among German Fighter Pilots, 1939–45." *Review of Economic Studies.*

Ake, Claude. 2000. *The Feasibility of Democracy in Africa.* Dakar: Council for the Development of Social Science Research in Africa.

Akerlof, George A., and Rachel E. Kranton. 2000. "Economics and Identity." *Quarterly Journal of Economics* 115 (3): 715–53.

Anderson, Benedict. 2006. *Imagined Communities: Reflections on the Origin and Spread of Nationalism.* London: Verso Books.

Anderson, Jon Lee. 2004. *The Fall of Baghdad.* New York: Penguin Books.

Anderton, Charles H., and Jurgen Brauer. Forthcoming. "Mass Atrocities and Their Prevention." *Journal of Economic Literature.*

Andrew, Christopher. 2004. "Intelligence Analysis Needs to Look Backwards before Looking Forward." History & Policy, Policy paper. https://www.historyandpolicy.org/policy-papers/papers/intelligence-analysis-needs-to-look-backwards-before-looking-forward.

———. 2009. *Defend the Realm: The Authorized History of MI5*. New York: Vintage Books.

Andrews, Matt, Lant Pritchett, and Michael Woolcock. 2017. *Building State Capability: Evidence, Analysis, Action*. Oxford: Oxford University Press.

Ang, Yuen Yuen. 2016. *How China Escaped the Poverty Trap*. Ithaca: Cornell University Press.

Anzia, Sarah F., and Christopher R. Berry. 2011. "The Jackie (and Jill) Robinson Effect: Why Do Congresswomen Outperform Congressmen?" *American Journal of Political Science* 55 (3): 478–93.

Asbury, Herbert. 1928. *The Gangs of New York: An Informal History of the Underworld*. New York: Knopf.

Asher-Schapiro, Avi. 2016. "The Young Men Who Started Syria's Revolution Speak about Daraa, Where It All Began." *Vice*, March 15, 2016. https://www.vice.com/en/article/qv5eqb/the-young -men-who-started-syrias-revolution-speak-about-daraa-where-it-all-began.

Ashworth, Scott, Christopher R. Berry, and Ethan Bueno de Mesquita. 2021. *Theory and Credibility: Integrating Theoretical and Empirical Social Science*. Princeton: Princeton University Press.

Ashworth, Scott, and Kristopher W. Ramsay. 2020. "Optimal Domestic Constraints in International Crises." Working paper.

Ashworth, Scott, and Greg Sasso. 2019. "Delegation to an Overconfident Expert." *Journal of Politics* 81 (2): 692–96.

Atkin, David, Eve Colson-Sihra, and Moses Shayo. 2021. "How Do We Choose Our Identity? A Revealed Preference Approach Using Food Consumption." *Journal of Political Economy* 129 (4): 1193–251.

Aumann, Robert J. 1976. "Agreeing to Disagree." *Annals of Statistics* 4 (6): 1236–39.

Autesserre, Séverine. 2010. *The Trouble with the Congo: Local Violence and the Failure of International Peacebuilding*. Cambridge: Cambridge University Press.

———. 2014. *Peaceland: Conflict Resolution and the Everyday Politics of International Intervention*. Cambridge: Cambridge University Press.

———. 2021. *The Frontlines of Peace: An Insider's Guide to Changing the World*. Oxford: Oxford University Press.

Ayittey, George B. N. 1998. *Africa in Chaos*. New York: St. Martin's Press.

Aytaç, S. Erdem, Luis Schiumerini, and Susan Stokes. 2018. "Why Do People Join Backlash Protests? Lessons from Turkey." *Journal of Conflict Resolution* 62 (6): 1205–28.

Azam, Jean-Paul. 1995. "How to Pay for the Peace? A Theoretical Framework with References to African Countries." *Public Choice* 83 (1–2): 173–84.

Backus, Matthew, and Andrew Little. 2020. "I Don't Know." *American Political Science Review* 114 (3): 724–43.

Bai, Chong-En, Chang-Tai Hsieh, and Zheng Song. 2020. "Special Deals with Chinese Characteristics." *NBER Macroeconomics Annual 2019* 34 (1): 341–79.

Bailyn, Bernard. 2017. *The Ideological Origins of the American Revolution*. Cambridge: Harvard University Press.

Baliga, Sandeep, Ethan Bueno de Mesquita, and Alexander Wolitzky. 2020. "Deterrence with Imperfect Attribution." *American Political Science Review* 114 (4): 1155–78.

Baliga, Sandeep, and Tomas Sjöström. 2008. "Strategic Ambiguity and Arms Proliferation." *Journal of Political Economy* 116 (6): 1023–57.

———. 2013. "Bargaining and War: A Review of Some Formal Models." *Korean Economic Review* 29 (2): 235–66.

———. 2020. "The Strategy and Technology of Conflict." *Journal of Political Economy* 128 (8): 3186–219.

Baliga, Sandeep, David O. Lucca, and Tomas Sjöström. 2011. "Domestic Political Survival and International Conflict: Is Democracy Good for Peace?" *Review of Economic Studies* 78 (2): 458–86.

Banerjee, Abhijit V., and Esther Duflo. 2011. *Poor Economics: A Radical Rethinking of the Way to Fight Global Poverty*. PublicAffairs.

Barberis, Nicholas C. 2018. "Psychology-Based Models of Asset Prices and Trading Volume." In *Handbook of Behavioral Economics: Foundations and Applications 1*, edited by B. Douglas Bernheim, Stefano DellaVigna, and David Laibson, 79–175. Amsterdam: Elsevier.

Bardhan, Pranab. 2002. "Decentralization of Governance and Development." *Journal of Economic Perspectives* 16 (4): 185–205.

Barnett, Michael N., and Martha Finnemore. 1999. "The Politics, Power, and Pathologies of International Organizations." *International Organization* 53 (4): 699–732.

———. 2020 *Rules for the World: International Organizations in Global Politics.* Ithaca: Cornell University Press.

Barnhart, Joslyn N., Allan Dafoe, Elizabeth N. Saunders, and Robert F. Trager. 2020. "The Suffragist Peace." *International Organization* 74 (4): 633–670.

Baron-Cohen, Simon. 2012. *The Science of Evil: On Empathy and the Origins of Cruelty.* New York: Basic Books.

Bastaki, Basil. 2020. "The Retaliatory Imperative: How Blood Feuding Deters Societal Predation in Contexts of Honor." Master's thesis, University of Chicago.

Bates, Robert H. 2008. *When Things Fell Apart: State Failure in Late-Century Africa.* Cambridge: Cambridge University Press.

Bates, Robert H., John H. Coatsworth, and Jeffrey G. Williamson. 2007. "Lost Decades: Postindependence Performance in Latin America and Africa." *Journal of Economic History* 67 (4): 917–43.

Bauer, Michal, Christopher Blattman, Julie Chytilová, Joseph Henrich, Edward Miguel, and Tamar Mitts. 2016. "Can War Foster Cooperation?" *Journal of Economic Perspectives* 30 (3): 249–74.

Bazerman, Max H., and Don A. Moore. 2012. *Judgment in Managerial Decision Making.* New York: John Wiley & Sons.

Bazzi, Samuel, Robert A. Blair, Christopher Blattman, Oeindrila Dube, Matthew Gudgeon, and Richard M. Peck. Forthcoming. "The Promise and Pitfalls of Conflict Prediction: Evidence from Colombia and Indonesia." *Review of Economics and Statistics.*

Bazzi, Samuel, and Christopher Blattman. 2014. "Economic Shocks and Conflict: Evidence from Commodity Prices." *American Economic Journal: Macroeconomics* 6 (4): 1–38.

Bazzi, Samuel, Arya Gaduh, Alexander D. Rothenberg, and Maisy Wong. 2019. "Unity in Diversity? How Intergroup Contact Can Foster Nation Building." *American Economic Review* 109 (11): 3978–4025.

BBC. 2017. "How the Babri Mosque Destruction Shaped India," December 6, 2017. https://www.bbc.com/news/world-asia-india-42219773.

Bean, Kevin. 2010. *Ed Moloney: Voices from the Grave: Two Men's War in Ireland.* London: Faber and Faber.

Beardsley, Kyle. 2011a. "Peacekeeping and the Contagion of Armed Conflict." *Journal of Politics* 73 (4): 1051–64.

———. 2011b. *The Mediation Dilemma.* Cornell University Press.

Beardsley, Kyle, David E. Cunningham, and Peter B. White. 2019. "Mediation, Peacekeeping, and the Severity of Civil War." *Journal of Conflict Resolution* 63 (7): 1682–709.

Beber, Bernd. 2012. "International Mediation, Selection Effects, and the Question of Bias." *Conflict Management and Peace Science* 29 (4): 397–424.

Beber, Bernd, Michael J. Gilligan, Jenny Guardado, and Sabrina Karim. 2017. "Peacekeeping, Compliance with International Norms, and Transactional Sex in Monrovia, Liberia." *International Organization* 71 (1): 1–30.

Beck, Aaron T. 1979. *Cognitive Therapy and the Emotional Disorders.* New York: Plume Books.

———. 2000. *Prisoners of Hate: The Cognitive Basis of Anger, Hostility and Violence.* New York: Harper Perennial.

Becker, Gary S. 1968. "Crime and Punishment: An Economic Approach." *Journal of Political Economy* 76 (2): 169–217.

Bellows, John, and Edward Miguel. 2009. "War and Local Collective Action in Sierra Leone." *Journal of Public Economics* 93 (11–12): 1144–57.

Bénabou, Roland. 2013. "Groupthink: Collective Delusions in Organizations and Markets." *Review of Economic Studies* 80 (2): 429–62.

Benjamin, Milton R. 1980. "France Plans to Sell Iraq Weapons-Grade Uranium." *Washington Post,* February 28, 1980. https://www.washingtonpost.com/archive/politics/1980/02/28/france-plans-to-sell-iraq-weapons-grade-uranium/da7187fb-6e77-4e09-9c1f-f2d4f7634561/.

Benner, Erica. 2017. *Be Like the Fox: Machiavelli in His World.* New York: W. W. Norton.

Benzell, Seth G., and Kevin Cooke. 2021. "A Network of Thrones: Kinship and Conflict in Europe, 1495–1918." *American Economic Journal: Applied Economics* 13 (3): 102–33.

Berge, Lars Ivar Oppedal, Kjetil Bjorvatn, Simon Galle, Edward Miguel, Daniel N. Posner, Bertil Tungodden, and Kelly Zhang. 2020. "Ethnically Biased? Experimental Evidence from Kenya." *Journal of the European Economic Association* 18 (1): 134–64.

Berkowitz, Leonard. 1993. *Aggression: Its Causes, Consequences, and Control.* New York: McGraw-Hill.

Berman, Eli, and David A. Lake, eds. 2019. *Proxy Wars: Suppressing Violence through Local Agents.* Ithaca: Cornell University Press.

Berman, Nicolas, and Mathieu Couttenier. 2015. "External Shocks, Internal Shots: The Geography of Civil Conflicts." *Review of Economics and Statistics* 97 (4): 758–76.

Bertrand, Marianne. 2009. "CEOs." *Annual Review of Economics* 1 (1): 121–50.

Bertrand, Marianne, Monica Bhatt, Christopher Blattman, Sara B. Heller, and Max Kapustin. 2022. "Predicting and Preventing Gun Violence: Experimental Results from READI Chicago." Working paper.

Besley, Timothy, and Torsten Persson. 2009. "The Origins of State Capacity: Property Rights, Taxation, and Politics." *American Economic Review* 99 (4): 1218–44.

Betts, Richard K. 1978. "Analysis, War, and Decision: Why Intelligence Failures Are Inevitable." *World Politics: A Quarterly Journal of International Relations* 31 (1): 61–89.

Bidwell, Kelly, Katherine Casey, and Rachel Glennerster. 2020. "Debates: Voting and Expenditure Responses to Political Communication." *Journal of Political Economy* 128 (8): 2880–924.

Biersteker, Thomas. 2019. "Understanding Effectiveness of International Sanctions." *MGIMO Review of International Relations* 3 (66): 7–16.

Bigio, Jamille, and Rachel Vogelstein. 2016. *How Women's Participation in Conflict Prevention and Resolution Advances U.S. Interests.* Council on Foreign Relations.

Blainey, Geoffrey. 1973. *The Causes of War.* London: Macmillan.

Blair, Graeme, Darin Christensen, and Aaron Rudkin. 2021. "Do Commodity Price Shocks Cause Armed Conflict? A Meta-analysis of Natural Experiments." *American Political Science Review*, 115 (2): 709–16.

Blair, Robert A. 2020. *Peacekeeping, Policing, and the Rule of Law after Civil War.* Cambridge: Cambridge University Press.

———. 2021. "UN Peacekeeping and the Rule of Law." *American Political Science Review* 115 (1): 51–68.

Blakeslee, David S. 2018. "The Rath Yatra Effect: Hindu Nationalist Propaganda and the Rise of the BJP." Working paper.

Blattman, Christopher. 2009. "From Violence to Voting: War and Political Participation in Uganda." *American Political Science Review* 103 (2): 231–47.

———. 2011. "Post-Conflict Recovery in Africa: The Micro Level." In *The Oxford Companion to the Economics of Africa,* edited by Ernest Aryeetey, Shantayanan Devarajan, Ravi Kanbur, and Louis Kasekende, 124–30. Oxford: Oxford University Press.

Blattman, Christopher, and Jeannie Annan. 2016. "Can Employment Reduce Lawlessness and Rebellion? A Field Experiment with High-Risk Men in a Fragile State." *American Political Science Review* 110 (1): 1–17.

Blattman, Christopher, Gustavo Duncan, Benjamin Lessing, and Santiago Tobón. 2021a. "Gang Rule: Understanding and Countering Criminal Governance." Working paper.

———. 2021b. "Gangs of Medellín: How Organized Crime Is Organized." Working paper.

Blattman, Christopher, Donald Green, Daniel Ortega, and Santiago Tobón. 2021. "Place-Based Interventions at Scale: The Direct and Spillover Effects of Policing and City Services on Crime." National Bureau of Economic Research, Working Paper 23941.

Blattman, Christopher, Alexandra C. Hartman, and Robert A. Blair. 2014. "How to Promote Order and Property Rights under Weak Rule of Law? An Experiment in Changing Dispute Resolution Behavior through Community Education." *American Political Science Review* 108 (1): 100–120.

Blattman, Christopher, Jason Hwang, and Jeffrey G. Williamson. 2007. "Winners and Losers in the Commodity Lottery: The Impact of Terms of Trade Growth and Volatility in the Periphery 1870–1939." *Journal of Development Economics* 82: 156–79.

Blattman, Christopher, Julian C. Jamison, and Margaret Sheridan. 2017. "Reducing Crime and Violence: Experimental Evidence from Cognitive Behavioral Therapy in Liberia." *American Economic Review* 107 (4): 1165–206.

Blattman, Christopher, Horacio Larreguy, Benjamin Marx, and Otis Reid. 2018. "A Market Equilibrium Approach to Reduce the Incidence of Vote-Buying: Evidence from Uganda." Working paper.

Blattman, Christopher, and Edward Miguel. 2010. "Civil War." *Journal of Economic Literature* 48 (1): 3–57.

Blouin, Arthur, and Sharun W. Mukand. 2018. "Erasing Ethnicity? Propaganda, Nation Building and Identity in Rwanda." *Journal of Political Economy* 127 (3): 1008–62.

Blount, Sally. 1995. "When Social Outcomes Aren't Fair: The Effect of Causal Attributions on Preferences." *Organizational Behavior and Human Decision Processes* 63 (2): 131–44.

Blum, Jurgen Rene, and Daniel Rogger. 2020. "Public Service Reform in Post-Conflict Societies." *World Bank Research Observer* 36 (2): 260–87.

Boix, Carles, and Milan W. Svolik. 2013. "The Foundations of Limited Authoritarian Government: Institutions, Commitment, and Power-Sharing in Dictatorships." *Journal of Politics* 75 (2): 300–316.

Börzel, Tanja A., and Sonja Grimm. 2018. "Building Good (Enough) Governance in Postconflict Societies & Areas of Limited Statehood: The European Union & the Western Balkans." *Daedalus* 147 (1): 116–27.

Bowles, Samuel, and Herbert Gintis. 2004. "The Evolution of Strong Reciprocity: Cooperation in Heterogeneous Populations." *Theoretical Population Biology* 65 (1): 17–28.

———. 2013. *A Cooperative Species: Human Reciprocity and Its Evolution*. Princeton: Princeton University Press.

Boyd, Robert, Herbert Gintis, Samuel Bowles, and Peter J. Richerson. 2003. "The Evolution of Altruistic Punishment." *Proceedings of the National Academy of Sciences of the United States of America* 100 (6): 3531–35.

Braga, Anthony A., David Weisburd, and Brandon Turchan. 2018. "Focused Deterrence Strategies and Crime Control: An Updated Systematic Review and Meta-analysis of the Empirical Evidence." *Criminology & Public Policy* 17 (1): 205–50.

Braga, Anthony A., Brandon C. Welsh, and Cory Schnell. 2015. "Can Policing Disorder Reduce Crime? A Systematic Review and Meta-analysis." *Journal of Research in Crime and Delinquency* 52 (4): 567–88.

Braga, Anthony, Andrew V. Papachristos, and David M. Hurreau. 2012. "An Ex Post Facto Evaluation Framework for Place-Based Police Interventions." *Evaluation Review* 35 (6): 592–626.

Brantingham, P. Jeffrey, Baichuan Yuan, Nick Sundback, Frederick P. Schoenberg, Andrea L. Bertozzi, Joshua Gordon, Jorja Leap, Kristine Chan, Molly Kraus, Sean Malinowski, and Denise Herz. 2018. "Does Violence Interruption Work?" Working paper.

Brass, Paul R. 1997. *Theft of an Idol: Text and Context in the Representation of Collective Violence*. Princeton: Princeton University Press.

Braumoeller, Bear F. 2019. *Only the Dead: The Persistence of War in the Modern Age*. Oxford: Oxford University Press.

Braut-Hegghammer, Målfrid. 2020. "Cheater's Dilemma: Iraq, Weapons of Mass Destruction, and the Path to War." *International Security* 45 (1): 51–89.

Brito, Dagobert L., and Michael D. Intriligator. 1985. "Conflict, War, and Redistribution." *American Political Science Review* 79 (4): 943–57.

Brookhiser, Richard. 2011. *James Madison*. New York: Basic Books.

Brosnan, Sarah F., and Frans B. M. de Waal. 2003. "Monkeys Reject Unequal Pay." *Nature* 425 (6955): 297–99.

Brown, Zach Y., Eduardo Montero, Carlos Schmidt-Padilla, and Maria Micaela Sviatschi. 2020. "Market Structure and Extortion: Evidence from 50,000 Extortion Payments." National Bureau of Economic Research, Working Paper 28299.

Brubaker, Rogers, and David D. Laitin. 1998. "Ethnic and Nationalist Violence." *Annual Review of Sociology* 24 (1): 423–52.

Bueno de Mesquita, Bruce, James D. Morrow, Randolph M. Siverson, and Alastair Smith. 1999. "An Institutional Explanation of the Democratic Peace." *American Political Science Review* 93 (4): 791–807.

Bueno de Mesquita, Bruce Bueno, Alastair Smith, Randolph M. Siverson, and James D. Morrow. 2003. *The Logic of Political Survival*. Cambridge: MIT Press.

Bueno de Mesquita, Bruce, and Alastair Smith. 2016. *The Spoils of War: Greed, Power, and the Conflicts That Made Our Greatest Presidents*. New York: PublicAffairs.

Bueno de Mesquita, Ethan. 2008. "Terrorist Factions." *Quarterly Journal of Political Science* 3 (4): 399–418.

Buford, Bill. 2001. *Among the Thugs*. New York: Random House.

Burke, Marshall, Solomon M. Hsiang, and Edward Miguel. 2015. "Climate and Conflict." *Annual Review of Economics* 7 (1): 577–617.

Burke, Marshall B., Edward Miguel, Shanker Satyanath, John A. Dykema, and David B. Lobell. 2009. "Warming Increases the Risk of Civil War in Africa." *Proceedings of the National Academy of Sciences* 106 (49): 20670–74.

Bush, George W. 2010. *Decision Points*. New York: Crown Books.

Busse, Meghan R., Devin G. Pope, Jaren C. Pope, and Jorge Silva-Risso. 2012. "Projection Bias in the Car and Housing Markets." National Bureau of Economic Research, Working Paper 18212.

Butt, Ahsan I. 2013. "Anarchy and Hierarchy in International Relations: Examining South America's War-Prone Decade, 1932–41." *International Organization* 67 (3): 575–607.

———. 2019. "Why Did the United States Invade Iraq in 2003?" *Security Studies* 28 (2): 250–85.

Cacault, Maria Paula, and Manuel Grieder. 2019. "How Group Identification Distorts Beliefs." *Journal of Economic Behavior & Organization* 164: 63–76.

Camerer, Colin F. 2011. *Behavioral Game Theory: Experiments in Strategic Interaction*. Princeton: Princeton University Press.

Camerer, Colin, and Dan Lovallo. 1999. "Overconfidence and Excess Entry: An Experimental Approach." *American Economic Review* 89 (1): 306–18.

Caplan, Richard, and Anke Hoeffler. 2017. "Why Peace Endures: An Analysis of Post-Conflict Stabilization." *European Journal of International Security* 2 (2): 133–52.

Casey, Katherine, Rachel Glennerster, Edward Miguel, and Maarten Voors. 2018. "Skill versus Voice in Local Development." National Bureau of Economic Research, Working Paper 25022.

Cassidy, Tali, Gabrielle Inglis, Charles Wiysonge, and Richard Matzopoulos. 2014. "A Systematic Review of the Effects of Poverty Deconcentration and Urban Upgrading on Youth Violence." *Health & Place* 26: 78–87.

Cederman, Lars-Erik, Andreas Wimmer, and Brian Min. 2010. "Why Do Ethnic Groups Rebel? New Data and Analysis." *World Politics: A Quarterly Journal of International Relations* 62 (1): 87–119.

Centeno, Miguel Ángel. 2003. *Blood and Debt: War and the Nation-State in Latin America*. University Park: Penn State University Press.

Chalfin, Aaron, and Justin McCrary. 2017. "Criminal Deterrence: A Review of the Literature." *Journal of Economic Literature* 55 (1): 5–48.

Chandra, Kanchan. 2005. "Ethnic Parties and Democratic Stability." *Perspectives on Politics* 3 (2): 235–52.

Chang, Ha-Joon. 2002. *Kicking Away the Ladder: Development Strategy in Historical Perspective*. London: Anthem Press.

Charness, Gary, and Matthew Rabin. 2002. "Understanding Social Preferences with Simple Tests." *Quarterly Journal of Economics* 117 (3): 817–69.

Charness, Gary, and Matthias Sutter. 2012. "Groups Make Better Self-Interested Decisions." *Journal of Economic Perspectives* 26 (3): 157–76.

Chassang, Sylvain, and Gerard Padró-i-Miquel. 2009. "Economic Shocks and Civil War." *Quarterly Journal of Political Science* 4 (3): 211–28.

Chen, Yan, and Sherry Xin Li. 2009. "Group Identity and Social Preferences." *American Economic Review* 99 (1): 431–57.

Cheng, Christine. 2018. *Extralegal Groups in Post-Conflict Liberia: How Trade Makes the State*. Oxford: Oxford University Press.

Cheng, Christine, Jonathan Goodhand, and Patrick Meehan. 2018. "Synthesis Paper: Securing and Sustaining Elite Bargains That Reduce Violent Conflict." Elite Bargains and Political Deals Project, United Kingdom Stabilization Unit. https://assets.publishing.service.gov.uk/government/uploads/system/uploads/attachment_data/file/765882/Elite_Bargains_and_Political_Deals_Project_-_Synthesis_Paper.pdf.

Chenoweth, Erica, Evan Perkoski, and Sooyeon Kang. 2017. "State Repression and Nonviolent Resistance." *Journal of Conflict Resolution* 61 (9): 1950–69.

Chernow, Ron. 2010. *Washington: A Life.* New York: Penguin Books.

Cheung-Blunden, Violet, and Bill Blunden. 2008. "The Emotional Construal of War: Anger, Fear, and Other Negative Emotions." *Peace and Conflict: Journal of Peace Psychology* 14 (2): 123–50.

Chilcot, Sir John. 2016. "Iraq Inquiry." http://www.iraqinquiry.org.uk/the-report/.

Choi, Seung-Whan. 2010. "Legislative Constraints: A Path to Peace?" *Journal of Conflict Resolution* 54 (3): 438–70.

Christia, Fotini. 2012. *Alliance Formation in Civil Wars.* Cambridge: Cambridge University Press.

Cikara, Mina, Emile G. Bruneau, and Rebecca R. Saxe. 2011. "Us and Them: Intergroup Failures of Empathy." *Current Directions in Psychological Science* 20 (3): 149–53.

Cikara, Mina, Emile G. Bruneau, Jay J. Van Bavel, and Rebecca R. Saxe. 2014. "Their Pain Gives Us Pleasure: How Intergroup Dynamics Shape Empathic Failures and Counter-Empathic Responses." *Journal of Experimental Social Psychology* 55: 110–25.

Cikara, Mina, and Jay J. Van Bavel. 2014. "The Neuroscience of Intergroup Relations: An Integrative Review." *Perspectives on Psychological Science* 9 (3): 245–74.

Clark, Christopher M. 2006. *Iron Kingdom: The Rise and Downfall of Prussia, 1600–1947.* Cambridge: Harvard University Press.

———. 2013. *The Sleepwalkers: How Europe Went to War in 1914.* New York: Harper Perennial.

Clemens, Michael A., Charles J. Kenny, and Todd J. Moss. 2007. "The Trouble with the MDGs: Confronting Expectations of Aid and Development Success." *World Development* 35 (5): 735–51.

CNN. 2003. "Bush, Blair: Time Running out for Saddam." January 31, 2003. https://www.cnn.com/2003/US/01/31/sprj.irq.bush.blair.topics/.

Coase, Ronald H. 1960. "The Problem of Social Cost." In *Classic Papers in Natural Resource Economics,* 87–137. Cham: Springer.

Cockayne, James, John de Boer, and Louise Bosetti. 2017. "Going Straight: Criminal Spoilers, Gang Truces and Negotiated Transitions to Lawful Order," Crime-Conflict Nexus Series, no. 5. United Nations University Centre for Policy Research.

Coe, Andrew J. 2018. "Containing Rogues: A Theory of Asymmetric Arming." *Journal of Politics* 80 (4): 1197–1210.

Coe, Andrew J., and Jane Vaynman. 2020. "Why Arms Control Is So Rare." *American Political Science Review* 114 (2): 342–55.

Collier, Paul, and Anke Hoeffler. 1998. "On Economic Causes of Civil War." *Oxford Economic Papers* 50 (4): 563–73.

———. 2004. "Greed and Grievance in Civil War." *Oxford Economic Papers* 56 (4): 563–95.

———. 2007. "Civil War." In *Handbook of Defense Economics, vol. 2, Defense in a Globalized World,* edited by Keith Hartley and Todd Sandler, 711–39. Princeton: North-Holland.

Collins, Randall. 2008. *Violence: A Micro-Sociological Theory.* Princeton: Princeton University Press.

Conlin, Michael, Ted O'Donoghue, and Timothy J. Vogelsang. 2007. "Projection Bias in Catalog Orders." *American Economic Review* 97 (4): 1217–49.

Cook, Philip J., and Jens Ludwig. 2000. *Gun Violence: The Real Costs.* Oxford: Oxford University Press.

Cooter, Robert D., and Daniel L. Rubinfeld. 1989. "Economic Analysis of Legal Disputes and Their Resolution." *Journal of Economic Literature* 27 (3): 1067–97.

Copeland, Dale C. 2001. *The Origins of Major War.* Ithaca: Cornell University Press.

———. 2014. "International Relations Theory and the Three Great Puzzles of the First World War." In *The Outbreak of the First World War: Structure, Politics and Decision-Making,* edited by Jack S. Levy and John A. Vasquez, 167–98. Cambridge: Cambridge University Press.

Coughlin, Con. 2005. *Saddam: His Rise & Fall.* New York: HarperCollins.

Cowen, Tyler. 2018. "Daniel Kahneman on Cutting through the Noise (Episode 56 - Live at Mason)." In *Conversations with Tyler.* Podcast. December 19, 2018.

Cunliffe, Philip. 2012. "Still the Spectre at the Feast: Comparisons between Peacekeeping and Imperialism in Peacekeeping Studies Today." *International Peacekeeping* 19 (4): 426–42.

Cunningham, David E. 2006. "Veto Players and Civil War Duration." *American Journal of Political Science* 50 (4): 875–92.

———. 2016. "Preventing Civil War: How the Potential for International Intervention Can Deter Conflict Onset." *World Politics: A Quarterly Journal of International Relations* 68 (2): 307–40.

Curran, Eleanor. 2002. "A Very Peculiar Royalist. Hobbes in the Context of His Political Contemporaries." *British Journal for the History of Philosophy* 10 (2): 167–208.

Dafoe, Allan, Jonathan Renshon, and Paul Huth. 2014. "Reputation and Status as Motives for War." *Annual Review of Political Science* 17 (1): 371–93.

Dahl, Robert A. 1956. *A Preface to Democratic Theory*. Chicago: University of Chicago Press.

Davenport, Christian. 2007. "State Repression and Political Order." *Annual Review of Political Science* 10 (1): 1–23.

de Quervain, Dominique, Urs Fischbacher, Valerie Treyer, Melanie Schellhammer, Ulrich Schnyder, Alfred Buck, and Ernst Fehr. 2004. "The Neural Basis of Altruistic Punishment." *Science* 305 (5688): 1254–58.

de Waal, Alex. 2015. *The Real Politics of the Horn of Africa: Money, War and the Business of Power*. New York: John Wiley & Sons.

de Waal, Alex, and Julie Flint. 2008. *Darfur: A New History of a Long War*. London: Zed Books.

Debs, Alexandre, and Nuno P. Monteiro. 2014. "Known Unknowns: Power Shifts, Uncertainty, and War." *International Organization* 68 (1): 1–31.

Dell, Melissa, and Pablo Querubin. 2018. "Nation Building through Foreign Intervention: Evidence from Discontinuities in Military Strategies." *Quarterly Journal of Economics* 133 (2): 701–64.

DeLong, J. Bradford, and Barry Eichengreen. 1991. "The Marshall Plan: History's Most Successful Structural Adjustment Program." National Bureau of Economic Research, Working Paper 3899.

Depetris-Chauvin, Emilio, Ruben Durante, and Filipe Campante. 2020. "Building Nations through Shared Experiences: Evidence from African Football." *American Economic Review* 110 (5): 1572–1602.

Des Forges, Alison. 1999. *Leave None to Tell the Story: Genocide in Rwanda*. Human Rights Watch.

Diaz-Alejandro, Carlos F. 1983. "Stories of the 1930s for the 1980s." In *Financial Policies and the World Capital Market: The Problem of Latin American Countries*, 5–40. Chicago: University of Chicago Press.

DiMaggio, Paul J., and Walter W. Powell. 1983. "The Iron Cage Revisited: Institutional Isomorphism and Collective Rationality in Organizational Fields." *American Sociological Review* 48 (2): 147–60.

Dincecco, Mark, and Massimiliano G. Onorato. 2017. *From Warfare to Wealth: The Military Origins of Urban Prosperity in Europe*. Cambridge: Cambridge University Press.

Dorison, Charles A., Julia A. Minson, and Todd Rogers. 2019. "Selective Exposure Partly Relies on Faulty Affective Forecasts." *Cognition* 188: 98–107.

Dostoyevsky, Fyodor. (1873) 2013. *The Possessed*. Translated by Constance Garnett. e-artnow.

Dowden, Richard. 1994. "'The Graves of the Tutsi Are Only Half Full—We Must Complete the Task': Richard Dowden, Africa Editor, Reports on the Rising Tide of Blood in Rwanda." *Independent*, May 24, 1994. https://www.independent.co.uk/news/the-graves-of-the-tutsi-are -only-half-full-we-must-complete-the-task-richard-dowden-africa-editor-1438050.html.

Dowell, William. 1980. "Iraqi-French Nuclear Deal Worries Israel." *Christian Science Monitor*, July 31, 1980. https://www.csmonitor.com/1980/0731/073155.html.

Doyle, Michael W. 1997. *Ways of War and Peace: Realism, Liberalism, and Socialism*. New York: W. W. Norton.

Doyle, Michael W., and Nicholas Sambanis. 2006. *Making War and Building Peace: United Nations Peace Operations*. Princeton: Princeton University Press.

Draca, Mirko, Leanne Stickland, Nele Warrinnie, and Jason Garred. 2019. "On Target? The Incidence of Sanctions across Listed Firms in Iran." LICOS Discussion Paper, no. 413.

Drezner, Daniel W. 2011. "Sanctions Sometimes Smart: Targeted Sanctions in Theory and Practice." *International Studies Review* 13 (1): 96–108.

———. 2015. *Theories of International Politics and Zombies: Revived Edition*. Princeton: Princeton University Press.

Driscoll, Jesse. 2015. *Warlords and Coalition Politics in Post-Soviet States*. Cambridge: Cambridge University Press.

Dube, Oeindrila, and S. P. Harish. 2020. "Queens." *Journal of Political Economy* 128 (7): 2579–652.

Dube, Oeindrila, and Juan F. Vargas. 2013. "Commodity Price Shocks and Civil Conflict: Evidence from Colombia." *Review of Economic Studies* 80 (4): 1384–421.

Duelfer, Charles. 2005. *Comprehensive Report of the Special Advisor to the DCI on Iraq's WMD, with Addendums*. McLean: Central Intelligence Agency.

Dunning, Thad, and Lauren Harrison. 2010. "Cross-Cutting Cleavages and Ethnic Voting: An Experimental Study of Cousinage in Mali." *American Political Science Review* 104 (1): 21–39.

Easterly, William. 2001. *The Elusive Quest for Economic Growth: Economists' Adventures and Misadventures in the Tropics*. Cambridge: MIT Press.

———. 2006. *The White Man's Burden: Why the West's Efforts to Aid the Rest Have Done So Much Ill and So Little Good*. New York: Penguin Books.

———. 2014. *The Tyranny of Experts: Economists, Dictators, and the Forgotten Rights of the Poor*. New York: Basic Books.

Easterly, William, and Tobias Pfutze. 2008. "Where Does the Money Go? Best and Worst Practices in Foreign Aid." *Journal of Economic Perspectives* 22 (2): 29–52.

Edmans, Alex, Diego García, and Øyvind Norli. 2007. "Sports Sentiment and Stock Returns." *Journal of Finance* 62 (4): 1967–98.

Egorov, Georgy, Sergei Guriev, and Konstantin Sonin. 2009. "Why Resource-Poor Dictators Allow Freer Media: A Theory and Evidence from Panel Data." *American Political Science Review* 103 (4): 645–68.

Ehrenreich, Barbara. 2011. *Blood Rites: Origins and History of the Passions of War*. London: Granta Books.

Eichenberg, Richard C., and Richard J. Stoll. 2017. "The Acceptability of War and Support for Defense Spending: Evidence from Fourteen Democracies, 2004–2013." *Journal of Conflict Resolution* 61 (4): 788–813.

Eifert, Benn, Edward Miguel, and Daniel N. Posner. 2010. "Political Competition and Ethnic Identification in Africa." *American Journal of Political Science* 54(2): 494–510.

Einstein, Albert. 1932. Albert Einstein to Sigmund Freud, July 30, 1932. *UNESCO Courier*, May 15, 1985, https://en.unesco.org/courier/may-1985/why-war-letter-albert-einstein-sigmund -freud.

———. (1933) 2011. *The Fight Against War*, edited by Alfred Lief. Whitefish: Literary Licensing.

———. 2017. *Einstein on Peace*, edited by Otto Nathan and Heinz Nordan. London: Arcole.

Elbadawi, Ibrahim, and Nicholas Sambanis. 2002. "How Much War Will We See? Explaining the Prevalence of Civil War." *Journal of Conflict Resolution* 46 (3): 307–34.

Elias, Norbert. (1939) 2000. *The Civilizing Process*. Translated by Edmund Jephcott. Blackwell.

Elliott, Kimberly Ann, and Gary Clyde Hufbauer. 1999. "Same Song, Same Refrain? Economic Sanctions in the 1990's." *American Economic Review* 89 (2): 403–8.

Ellis, Stephen. 2006. *The Mask of Anarchy: The Destruction of Liberia and the Religious Dimension of an African Civil War*. 2nd ed. New York: New York University Press.

Ellis-Petersen, Hannah. 2020. "India's BJP Leaders Acquitted over Babri Mosque Demolition." *The Guardian*, September 30, 2020. https://www.theguardian.com/world/2020/sep/30/india -bjp-leaders-acquitted-babri-mosque-demolition-case.

Engerman, Stanley L., and Kenneth L. Sokoloff. 2005. "Institutional and Non-institutional Explanations of Economic Differences." In *Handbook of New Institutional Economics*, edited by Claude Menard and Mary M. Shirley, 639–65. Cham: Springer.

English, Richard. 2008. *Armed Struggle: The History of the IRA*. London: Pan Macmillan.

Epley, Nicholas. 2015. *Mindwise: Why We Misunderstand What Others Think, Believe, Feel, and Want*. New York: Vintage Books.

Epley, Nicholas, and Thomas Gilovich. 2016. "The Mechanics of Motivated Reasoning." *Journal of Economic Perspectives* 30 (3): 133–40.

Epley, Nicholas, Boaz Keysar, Leaf Van Boven, and Thomas Gilovich. 2004. "Perspective Taking as Egocentric Anchoring and Adjustment." *Journal of Personality and Social Psychology* 87 (3): 327–39.

Esteban, Joan, Massimo Morelli, and Dominic Rohner. 2015. "Strategic Mass Killings." *Journal of Political Economy* 123 (5): 1087–132.

Esteban, Joan, and Debraj Ray. 2008. "On the Salience of Ethnic Conflict." *American Economic Review* 98 (5): 2185–202.

Eubank, Nicholas. 2012. "Taxation, Political Accountability and Foreign Aid: Lessons from Somaliland." *Journal of Development Studies* 48 (4): 465–80.

Evans, Peter. 2004. "Development as Institutional Change: The Pitfalls of Monocropping and the Potentials of Deliberation." *Studies in Comparative International Development* 38 (4): 30–52.

Eyal, Tal, Mary Steffel, and Nicholas Epley. 2018. "Perspective Mistaking: Accurately Understanding the Mind of Another Requires Getting Perspective, Not Taking Perspective." *Journal of Personality and Social Psychology* 114 (4): 547–71.

Eyster, Erik. 2019. "Errors in Strategic Reasoning." In *Handbook of Behavioral Economics: Foundations and Applications 2*, edited by B. Douglas Bernheim, Stefano DellaVigna, and David Laibson, 187–259. Amsterdam: Elsevier.

Falk, Armin, and Urs Fischbacher. 2006. "A Theory of Reciprocity." *Games and Economic Behavior* 54 (2): 293–315.

Fanon, Frantz. (1952) 2008. *Black Skin, White Masks.* Translated by Constance Farrington. New York: Grove Press.

———. (1963) 2004. *The Wretched of the Earth.* Translated by Richard Philcox. New York: Grove Press.

Fearon, James D. 1995. "Rationalist Explanations for War." *International Organization* 49 (3): 379–414.

———. 1997. "Signaling Foreign Policy Interests: Tying Hands versus Sinking Costs." *Journal of Conflict Resolution* 41 (1): 68–90.

———. 1998. "Commitment Problems and the Spread of Ethnic Conflict." In *The International Spread of Ethnic Conflict*, edited by David A. Lake and Donald Rothchild, 107–126. Princeton: Princeton University Press.

———. 2004. "Why Do Some Civil Wars Last So Much Longer Than Others?" *Journal of Peace Research* 41 (3): 275–301.

———. 2013. "Fighting Rather Than Bargaining." Working paper.

———. 2017. "Civil War & the Current International System." *Daedalus* 146 (4): 18–32.

———. 2018. "Cooperation, Conflict, and the Costs of Anarchy." *International Organization* 72 (3): 523–59.

———. 2020. "State Building in the Post-post-Cold War World." Presented at the Conference on Foreign Assistance and Political Development in Fragile States, University of Chicago, May 15–16.

Fearon, James D., and David D. Laitin. 1996. "Explaining Interethnic Cooperation." *American Political Science Review* 90 (4): 715–35.

———. 2000. "Violence and the Social Construction of Ethnic Identity." *International Organization* 54 (4): 845–77.

Fehr, Ernst, and Simon Gächter. 2000. "Fairness and Retaliation: The Economics of Reciprocity." *Journal of Economic Perspectives* 14 (3): 159–81.

———. 2002. "Altruistic Punishment in Humans." *Nature* 415: 137–40.

Fehr, Ernst, Lorenz Goette, and Christian Zehnder. 2009. "A Behavioral Account of the Labor Market: The Role of Fairness Concerns." *Annual Review of Economics* 1 (1): 355–84.

Fehr, Ernst, and Ian Krajbich. 2014. "Social Preferences and the Brain." In *Neuroeconomics*, edited by Paul W. Glimcher and Ernst Fehr, 193–218. 2nd ed. Cambridge: Academic Press.

Fehrler, Sebastian, Baiba Renerte, and Irenaeus Wolff. 2020. "Beliefs about Others: A Striking Example of Information Neglect." Working paper.

Ferguson, James. 1990. *The Anti-politics Machine: "Development," Depoliticization, and Bureaucratic Power in Lesotho.* Cambridge: Cambridge University Press.

Ferguson, R. Brian. 2011. "Born to Live: Challenging Killer Myths." In *Origins of Altruism and Cooperation*, edited by Robert W. Sussman and C. Robert Cloninger, 249–70. Cham: Springer.

Ferrer, Rebecca A., Alexander Maclay, Paul M. Litvak, and Jennifer S. Lerner. 2017. "Revisiting the Effects of Anger on Risk-Taking: Empirical and Meta-analytic Evidence for Differences between Males and Females." *Journal of Behavioral Decision Making* 30 (2): 516–26.

Fetzer, Thiemo, and Stephan Kyburz. 2018. "Cohesive Institutions and Political Violence." Working paper.

Fey, Mark, and Kristopher W. Ramsay. 2007. "Mutual Optimism and War." *American Journal of Political Science* 51 (4): 738–54.

———. 2019. "Reasoning about War with Uncertainty about Victory." Working paper.

Finnemore, Martha, and Kathryn Sikkink. 1998. "International Norm Dynamics and Political Change." *International Organization* 52 (4): 887–917.

Fiske, Alan Page, and Tage Shakti Rai. 2014. *Virtuous Violence: Hurting and Killing to Create, Sustain, End, and Honor Social Relationships.* Cambridge: Cambridge University Press.

Fiske, Susan T. 1998. "Stereotyping, Prejudice, and Discrimination." In *The Handbook of Social Psychology, vol. 2*, edited by Daniel T. Gilbert, Susan T. Fiske, and Gardner Lindzey, 357–411. 4th ed. Oxford: Oxford University Press.

Florio, John, and Ouisie Shapiro. 2020. "How New York City Vaccinated 6 Million People in Less Than a Month." *New York Times*, December 18, 2020. New York. https://www.nytimes.com /2020/12/18/nyregion/nyc-smallpox-vaccine.html.

Forman-Barzilai, Fonna. 2010. *Adam Smith and the Circles of Sympathy: Cosmopolitanism and Moral Theory*. Ideas in Context 96. Cambridge: Cambridge University Press.

Fortna, Virginia Page. 2004. "Does Peacekeeping Keep Peace? International Intervention and the Duration of Peace after Civil War." *International Studies Quarterly* 48 (2): 269–92.

———. 2008. *Does Peacekeeping Work? Shaping Belligerents' Choices after Civil War*. Princeton: Princeton University Press.

Fox, Richard, and Jennifer L. Lawless. 2011. "Gendered Perceptions and Political Candidacies: A Central Barrier to Women's Equality in Electoral Politics." *American Journal of Political Science* 55 (1): 59–73.

Francois, Patrick, Ilia Rainer, and Francesco Trebbi. 2015. "How Is Power Shared in Africa?" *Econometrica* 83 (2): 465–503.

Freud, Sigmund. (1930) 2021. *Civilization and Its Discontents*. Translated by James Strachey. New York: W. W. Norton.

———. 1932. Sigmund Freud to Albert Einstein, September 1932. *UNESCO Courier*, May 15, 1985. https://en.unesco.org/courier/marzo-1993/why-war-letter-freud-einstein.

Frieden, Jeffry A., David A. Lake, and Kenneth A. Schultz. 2013. *World Politics: Interests, Interactions, Institutions*. New York: W. W. Norton.

Friedman, Jeffrey A. 2019. *War and Chance: Assessing Uncertainty in International Politics*. Oxford: Oxford University Press.

Friedman, Jeffrey A., Jennifer S. Lerner, and Richard Zeckhauser. 2017. "Behavioral Consequences of Probabilistic Precision: Experimental Evidence from National Security Professionals." *International Organization* 71 (4): 803–26.

Friedman, Ray, Cameron Anderson, Jeanne Brett, Mara Olekalns, Nathan Goates, and Cara Cherry Lisco. 2004. "The Positive and Negative Effects of Anger on Dispute Resolution: Evidence from Electronically Mediated Disputes." *Journal of Applied Psychology* 89 (2): 369–76.

Fujiwara, Thomas. 2015. "Voting Technology, Political Responsiveness, and Infant Health: Evidence from Brazil." *Econometrica* 83 (2): 423–64.

Fukuyama, Francis. 2011. *The Origins of Political Order: From Prehuman Times to the French Revolution*. New York: Farrar, Straus and Giroux.

Galiani, Sebastian, and Gustavo Torrens. 2016. "Why Not Taxation and Representation? A Note on the American Revolution." National Bureau of Economic Research, Working Paper 22724.

———. 2019. "Why Not Taxation and Representation? British Politics and the American Revolution." *Journal of Economic Behavior & Organization* 166: 28–52.

Galland, Adolf. 2014. *The First and the Last*. Seattle: Stellar.

Gallop, Max. 2017. "More Dangerous Than Dyads: How a Third Party Enables Rationalist Explanations for War." *Journal of Theoretical Politics* 29 (3): 353–81.

Gandhi, Jennifer. 2008. *Political Institutions under Dictatorship*. Cambridge: Cambridge University Press.

Gandhi, Jennifer, and Ellen Lust-Okar. 2009. "Elections under Authoritarianism." *Annual Review of Political Science* 12 (1): 403–22.

Garfinkel, Michelle R. 1990. "Arming as a Strategic Investment in a Cooperative Equilibrium." *American Economic Review* 80 (1): 50–68.

Garfinkel, Michelle R., and Stergios Skaperdas. 2007. "Economics of Conflict: An Overview." In *Handbook of Defense Economics, vol. 2, Defense in a Globalized World*, edited by Keith Hartley and Todd Sandler, 649–709. Amsterdam: Elsevier.

Gartzke, Erik. 1999. "War Is in the Error Term." *International Organization* 53 (3): 567–87.

———. 2007. "The Capitalist Peace." *American Journal of Political Science* 51 (1): 166–91.

Gat, Azar. 2008. *War in Human Civilization*. Oxford: Oxford University Press.

Gay, Peter. 1998. *Freud: A Life for Our Time*. New York: W. W. Norton.

Geddes, Barbara, Joseph Wright, and Erica Frantz. 2018. *How Dictatorships Work: Power, Personalization, and Collapse*. Cambridge: Cambridge University Press.

Gehlbach, Scott, and Philip Keefer. 2011. "Investment without Democracy: Ruling-Party Institutionalization and Credible Commitment in Autocracies." *Journal of Comparative Economics* 39 (2): 123–39.

Gehlbach, Scott, Konstantin Sonin, and Milan W. Svolik. 2016. "Formal Models of Nondemocratic Politics." *Annual Review of Political Science* 19 (1): 565–84.

Gennaioli, Nicola, and Hans-Joachim Voth. 2015. "State Capacity and Military Conflict." *Review of Economic Studies* 82 (4): 1409–48.

Gilligan, Michael J., and Ernest J. Sergenti. 2008. "Do UN Interventions Cause Peace? Using Matching to Improve Causal Inference." *Quarterly Journal of Political Science* 3 (2): 89–122.

Gilligan, Michael, and Stephen John Stedman. 2003. "Where Do the Peacekeepers Go?" *International Studies Review* 5 (4): 37–54.

Gilpin, Robert. 1981. *War and Change in World Politics*. Cambridge: Cambridge University Press.

Girard, René. 1977. *Violence and the Sacred*. Translated by Patrick Gregory. Baltimore: Johns Hopkins University Press.

Glaser, Charles L. 1997. "The Security Dilemma Revisited." *World Politics: A Quarterly Journal of International Relations* 50 (1): 171–201.

Glowacki, Luke, Michael L. Wilson, and Richard W. Wrangham. 2020. "The Evolutionary Anthropology of War." *Journal of Economic Behavior & Organization* 178: 963–82.

Goldstein, Joshua S. 2001. *War and Gender: How Gender Shapes the War System and Vice Versa*. Cambridge: Cambridge University Press.

———. 2012. *Winning the War on War: The Decline of Armed Conflict Worldwide*. New York: Plume Books.

Gordon, Michael R., and Bernard E. Trainor. 2006. *Cobra II: The Inside Story of the Invasion and Occupation of Iraq*. New York: Vintage.

Gould, John P. 1973. "The Economics of Legal Conflicts." *Journal of Legal Studies* 2 (2): 279–300.

Gould, Roger V. 1999. "Collective Violence and Group Solidarity: Evidence from a Feuding Society." *American Sociological Review* 64 (3): 356–80.

Green, Elliott D. 2005. "What Is an Ethnic Group? Political Economy, Constructivism and the Common Language Approach to Ethnicity." Working paper.

Grindle, Merilee S. 2004. "Good Enough Governance: Poverty Reduction and Reform in Developing Countries." *Governance* 17 (4): 525–48.

———. 2007. "Good Enough Governance Revisited." *Development Policy Review* 25 (5): 533–74.

Grosjean, Pauline. 2014. "A History of Violence: The Culture of Honor and Homicide in the US South." *Journal of the European Economic Association* 12 (5): 1285–316.

Grossman, Herschel I. 1991. "A General Equilibrium Model of Insurrections." *American Economic Review* 81 (4): 912–21.

Gubler, Joshua R., and Joel Sawat Selway. 2012. "Horizontal Inequality, Crosscutting Cleavages, and Civil War." *Journal of Conflict Resolution* 56 (2): 206–32.

Gubler, Joshua R., Joel Sawat Selway, and Ashutosh Varshney. 2016. "Crosscutting Cleavages and Ethno-Communal Violence: Evidence from Indonesia in the Post-Suharto Era." Working paper.

Gurr, Ted Robert. 2015. *Why Men Rebel*. London: Routledge.

Habyarimana, James, Macartan Humphreys, Daniel N. Posner, and Jeremy M. Weinstein. 2007. "Why Does Ethnic Diversity Undermine Public Goods Provision?" *American Political Science Review* 101 (4): 709–25.

Hafner-Burton, Emilie M., Stephan Haggard, David A. Lake, and David G. Victor. 2017. "The Behavioral Revolution and International Relations." *International Organization* 71 (S1): S1–31.

Hafner-Burton, Emilie M., D. Alex Hughes, and David G. Victor. 2013. "The Cognitive Revolution and the Political Psychology of Elite Decision Making." *Perspectives on Politics* 11 (2): 368–86.

Hamilton, Alexander, James Madison, and John Jay. 2008. *The Federalist Papers*. Oxford: Oxford University Press.

Hamilton, James J. 2009. "Hobbes the Royalist, Hobbes the Republican." *History of Political Thought* 30 (3): 411–54.

Hanson, Victor D. 1998. Introduction to *The Landmark Thucydides: A Comprehensive Guide to the Peloponnesian War*, edited by Robert B. Strassler and translated by Richard Crawley, ix–xxiv. New York: Touchstone.

Harford, Tim. 2011. *Adapt: Why Success Always Starts with Failure.* New York: Farrar, Straus and Giroux.

Harrington, Cameron. 2014. "Water Wars? Think Again: Conflict over Freshwater Structural Rather Than Strategic." *New Security Beat* (blog). Woodrow Wilson International Center for Scholars. April 15, 2014. https://www.newsecuritybeat.org/2014/04/water-wars/.

Hartman, Alexandra C. 2015. "This Land Is My Land: Access to Justice and the Sacred Stakes of Land Disputes in Liberia." PhD diss., Yale University. ProQuest (AAT 10006741).

Hartman, Alexandra C., Robert A. Blair, and Christopher Blattman. 2021. "Engineering Informal Institutions: Long-Run Impacts of Alternative Dispute Resolution on Violence and Property Rights in Liberia." *Journal of Politics* 83 (1): 381–89.

Hassner, Ron E. 2003. "'To Halve and to Hold': Conflicts over Sacred Space and the Problem of Indivisibility." *Security Studies* 12 (4): 1–33.

Hastorf, Albert H., and Hadley Cantril. 1954. "They Saw a Game; a Case Study." *Journal of Abnormal and Social Psychology* 49 (1): 129–34.

Haushofer, Johannes, Anat Biletzki, and Nancy Kanwisher. 2010. "Both Sides Retaliate in the Israeli–Palestinian Conflict." *Proceedings of the National Academy of Sciences* 107 (42): 17927–32.

Hausmann, Ricardo, and Dani Rodrik. 2003. "Economic Development as Self-Discovery." *Journal of Development Economics* 72 (2): 603–33.

Heath, Chip, and Dan Heath. 2006. "The Curse of Knowledge." *Harvard Business Review*, December 2006, 20–23.

Heaton, Colin D., and Anne-Marie Lewis. 2011. *The German Aces Speak: World War II through the Eyes of Four of the Luftwaffe's Most Important Commanders.* Duluth: Zenith Press.

Hedges, Chris. 2003. *War Is a Force That Gives Us Meaning.* New York: Anchor Books.

Hegre, Håvard. 2014. "Democracy and Armed Conflict." *Journal of Peace Research* 51 (2): 159–72.

Hegre, Håvard, Lisa Hultman, and Håvard Mokleiv Nygård. 2019. "Evaluating the Conflict-Reducing Effect of UN Peacekeeping Operations." *Journal of Politics* 81 (1): 215–32.

Heller, Sara B., Anuj K. Shah, Jonathan Guryan, Jens Ludwig, Sendhil Mullainathan, and Harold A. Pollack. 2017. "Thinking, Fast and Slow? Some Field Experiments to Reduce Crime and Dropout in Chicago." *Quarterly Journal of Economics* 132 (1): 1–54.

Henrich, Joseph, Robert Boyd, Samuel Bowles, Colin Camerer, Ernst Fehr, and Herbert Gintis. 2004. *Foundations of Human Sociality: Economic Experiments and Ethnographic Evidence from Fifteen Small-Scale Societies.* Oxford: Oxford University Press.

Herbst, Jeffrey. 1990. "War and the State in Africa." *International Security* 14 (4): 117–39.

———. 1996. "Responding to State Failure in Africa." *International Security* 21 (3): 120–44.

———. 2000. *States and Power in Africa: Comparative Lessons in Authority and Control.* Princeton: Princeton University Press.

Herz, John H. 1950. "Idealist Internationalism and the Security Dilemma." *World Politics: A Quarterly Journal of International Relations* 2 (2): 157–80.

Hirschman, Albert O. 1970. "The Search for Paradigms as a Hindrance to Understanding." *World Politics: A Quarterly Journal of International Relations* 22 (3): 329–43.

———. 2013. *The Passions and the Interests: Political Arguments for Capitalism before Its Triumph.* Princeton: Princeton University Press.

Hirshleifer, David, and Tyler Shumway. 2003. "Good Day Sunshine: Stock Returns and the Weather." *Journal of Finance* 58 (3): 1009–32.

Hirshleifer, Jack. 1991. "The Technology of Conflict as an Economic Activity." *American Economic Review* 81 (2): 130–34.

———. 1995a. "Anarchy and Its Breakdown." *Journal of Political Economy* 103 (1): 26–52.

———. 1995b. "Theorizing about Conflict." In *Handbook of Defense Economics, vol. 1,* edited by Keith Hartley and Todd Sandler, 165–89. Amsterdam: Elsevier.

Hobbes, Thomas. (1651) 2017. *Leviathan.* London: Penguin Classics.

Hoffman, David. 1999. "'I Had a Funny Feeling in My Gut.'" *Washington Post*, February 10, 1999, sec. A.

Hoffman, Philip T. 2017. *Why Did Europe Conquer the World?* Princeton Economic History of the Western World 54. Princeton: Princeton University Press.

Honig, Dan. 2018. *Navigation by Judgment: Why and When Top-Down Management of Foreign Aid Doesn't Work.* Oxford: Oxford University Press.

———. 2019. "The Power of Letting Go." *Stanford Social Innovation Review*, Winter 2019.

Horowitz, Donald L. 2000. *Ethnic Groups in Conflict*, 2nd ed. Berkeley: University of California Press.
———. 2001. *The Deadly Ethnic Riot*. Berkeley: University of California Press.
Horowitz, Michael C., Allan C. Stam, and Cali M. Ellis. 2015. *Why Leaders Fight*. Cambridge: Cambridge University Press.
Howard, Lise Morjé. 2008. *UN Peacekeeping in Civil Wars*. Cambridge: Cambridge University Press.
———. 2019. *Power in Peacekeeping*. Cambridge: Cambridge University Press.
Howell, William G. 2015. *Thinking about the Presidency: The Primacy of Power*. Princeton: Princeton University Press.
———. 2022. *An American Presidency: Institutional Foundations of Executive Politics*. Princeton: Princeton University Press.
Hsiang, Solomon M., Marshall Burke, and Edward Miguel. 2013. "Quantifying the Influence of Climate on Human Conflict." *Science* 341 (6151): 1212–28.
Hufbauer, Gary C., Jeffrey J. Schott, and Kimberly A. Elliott. 1990. *Economic Sanctions Reconsidered: History and Current Policy*. Washington: Institute for International Economics.
Hufbauer, Gary Clyde, Jeffrey J. Schott, Kimberly Ann Elliott, and Barbara Oegg. 2008. "Economic Sanctions: New Directions for the 21st Century." Presentation, Peterson Institute for International Economics. https://www.piie.com/commentary/speeches-papers/economic-sanctions-new-directions-21st-century.
Hultman, Lisa, Jacob D. Kathman, and Megan Shannon. 2019. *Peacekeeping in the Midst of War*. Oxford: Oxford University Press.
Hultman, Lisa, Jacob Kathman, and Megan Shannon. 2014. "Beyond Keeping Peace: United Nations Effectiveness in the Midst of Fighting." *American Political Science Review* 108 (4): 737–53.
Hume, David. (1739) 1896. *A Treatise of Human Nature*, edited by Sir Lewis A. Selby-Bigge. Oxford: Claredon Press. Reprinted by the Online Library of Liberty. https://oll.libertyfund.org/title/bigge-a-treatise-of-human-nature.
Humphreys, Macartan. 2003. "Economics and Violent Conflict." Working paper.
Hunt, Lynn. 2007. *Inventing Human Rights: A History*. New York: W. W. Norton.
Ignatieff, Michael. 2008. *The Rights Revolution*. Toronto: House of Anansi Press.
———. 2011. *Human Rights as Politics and Idolatry*. Princeton: Princeton University Press.
Innis, Harold A. 1933. *Problems of Staple Production in Canada*. Toronto: Ryerson Press.
Isaacson, Walter. 2008. *Einstein: His Life and Universe*. New York: Simon & Schuster.
Jackson, Matthew O., and Massimo Morelli. 2007. "Political Bias and War." *American Economic Review* 97 (4): 1353–73.
———. 2012. "The Reasons for Wars: An Updated Survey." In *The Handbook on the Political Economy of War*, edited by Christopher J. Coyne and Rachel L. Mathers, 34–53. Cheltenham: Edward Elgar.
Jackson, Robert H., and Carl G. Rosberg. 1982. *Personal Rule in Black Africa: Prince, Autocrat, Prophet, Tyrant*. Berkeley: University of California Press.
Jacobs, Jane. (1961) 2016. *The Death and Life of Great American Cities*. New York: Vintage Books.
Janis, Irving L. 1972. *Victims of Groupthink: A Psychological Study of Foreign-Policy Decisions and Fiascoes*. Boston: Houghton Mifflin.
Jervis, Robert. 1976. *Perception and Misperception in International Politics*. Princeton: Princeton University Press.
———. 1978. "Cooperation under the Security Dilemma." *World Politics: A Quarterly Journal of International Relations* 30 (2): 167–214.
———. 2010. *Why Intelligence Fails: Lessons from the Iranian Revolution and the Iraq War*. Ithaca: Cornell University Press.
———. 2017a. *How Statesmen Think: The Psychology of International Politics*. Princeton: Princeton University Press.
———. 2017b. *Perception and Misperception in International Politics: New Edition*. Princeton: Princeton University Press.
Jha, Saumitra. 2013. "Trade, Institutions, and Ethnic Tolerance: Evidence from South Asia." *American Political Science Review* 107 (4): 806–32.
———. 2014. "'Unfinished Business': Historic Complementarities, Political Competition and Ethnic Violence in Gujarat." *Journal of Economic Behavior & Organization* 104: 18–36.
———. 2018. "Trading for Peace." *Economic Policy* 33 (95): 485–526.

Jha, Saumitra, and Moses Shayo. 2019. "Valuing Peace: The Effects of Financial Market Exposure on Votes and Political Attitudes." *Econometrica* 87 (5): 1561–88.

Johnson, Dominic D. P., Rose McDermott, Emily S. Barrett, Jonathan Cowden, Richard Wrangham, Matthew H. McIntyre, and Stephen Peter Rosen. 2006. "Overconfidence in Wargames: Experimental Evidence on Expectations, Aggression, Gender and Testosterone." *Proceedings of the Royal Society B: Biological Sciences* 273 (1600): 2513–20.

Kagan, Donald. 1996. *On the Origins of War and the Preservation of Peace*. New York: Anchor Books.

———. 2004. *The Peloponnesian War*. New York: Penguin Books.

Kahneman, Daniel. 2011. *Thinking, Fast and Slow*. New York: Farrar, Straus and Giroux.

Kahneman, Daniel, and Jonathan Renshon. 2007. "Why Hawks Win." *Foreign Policy*, January–February 2007: 34–38.

Kahneman, Daniel, Andrew M. Rosenfield, Linnea Gandhi, and Tom Blaser. 2016. "Noise: How to Overcome the High, Hidden Cost of Inconsistent Decision Making." *Harvard Business Review*, October 2016, 36–43, https://hbr.org/2016/10/noise.

Kahneman, Daniel, and Amos Tversky. 2013. "Choices, Values, and Frames." In *Handbook of the Fundamentals of Financial Decision Making: Part I*, edited by Leonard C. MacLean and William T. Ziemba, 269–78. Singapore: World Scientific.

Kalyvas, Stathis N. 1999. "Wanton and Senseless? The Logic of Massacres in Algeria." *Rationality and Society* 11 (3): 243–85.

———. 2000. "Commitment Problems in Emerging Democracies: The Case of Religious Parties." *Comparative Politics* 32 (4): 379–98.

———. 2006. *The Logic of Violence in Civil War*. Cambridge: Cambridge University Press.

———. 2007. "Civil Wars." In *The Oxford Handbook of Comparative Politics*, edited by Carles Boix and Susan Stokes, 416–34. Oxford: Oxford University Press.

———. 2020. "Armed Conflict and State-Building after WWII." In *Conference on Foreign Assistance and Political Development in Fragile States*. Chicago: University of Chicago Press.

Kalyvas, Stathis N., and Laia Balcells. 2010. "International System and Technologies of Rebellion: How the End of the Cold War Shaped Internal Conflict." *American Political Science Review* 104 (3): 415–29.

Kamstra, Mark J., Lisa A. Kramer, and Maurice D. Levi. 2003. "Winter Blues: A SAD Stock Market Cycle." *American Economic Review* 93 (1): 324–43.

Kan, Paul Rexton. 2014. "Malicious Peace: Violent Criminal Organizations, National Governments and Truces." *International Journal of Criminology and Sociology* 3: 125–32.

Kant, Immanuel. (1795) 2011. *Perpetual Peace: A Philosophical Essay*. Translated by William Hastie.

Kaplan, Edward. 2015. *To Kill Nations: American Strategy in the Air-Atomic Age and the Rise of Mutually Assured Destruction*. Ithaca: Cornell University Press.

Kaufman, Bruce E. 2015. "Integrating Emotions into Economic Theory." In *Handbook of Contemporary Behavioral Economics: Foundations and Developments*, edited by Morris Altman, 100–120. London: Routledge.

Keen, David. 2005. *Conflict and Collusion in Sierra Leone*. Basingstoke: Palgrave Macmillan.

Kennan, John, and Robert Wilson. 1993. "Bargaining with Private Information." *Journal of Economic Literature* 31 (1): 45–104.

Kennedy, David M. 2011. *Don't Shoot: One Man, a Street Fellowship, and the End of Violence in Inner-City America*. New York: Bloomsbury.

Kennedy, Gavin. 2005. "A 'Night Watchman' State?" In *Adam Smith's Lost Legacy*. Basingstoke: Palgrave Macmillan.

Kerr, Norbert L., and R. Scott Tindale. 2004. "Group Performance and Decision Making." *Annual Review of Psychology* 55 (1): 623–55.

Kleinfeld, Rachel. 2019. *A Savage Order: How the World's Deadliest Countries Can Forge a Path to Security*. New York: Vintage Books.

Klepper, Michael, and Robert Gunther. 1996. *The Wealthy 100: From Benjamin Franklin to Bill Gates—A Ranking of the Richest Americans, Past and Present*. Secaucus: Citadel Press.

Knack, Stephen, F. Halsey Rogers, and Nicholas Eubank. 2011. "Aid Quality and Donor Rankings." *World Development* 39 (11): 1907–17.

Knoch, Daria, Alvaro Pascual-Leone, Kaspar Meyer, Valerie Treyer, and Ernst Fehr. 2006. "Diminishing Reciprocal Fairness by Disrupting the Right Prefrontal Cortex." *Science* 314 (5800): 829–32.

Ko, Chiu Yu, Mark Koyama, and Tuan-Hwee Sng. 2018. "Unified China and Divided Europe." *International Economic Review* 59 (1): 285–327.

Krasner, Stephen D. 2020. "Learning to Live with Despots: The Limits of Democracy Promotion." *Foreign Affairs* 99 (2): 49.

Krawczyk, Michał, and Maciej Wilamowski. 2017. "Are We All Overconfident in the Long Run? Evidence from One Million Marathon Participants." *Journal of Behavioral Decision Making* 30 (3): 719–30.

Kreps, David M., and Robert Wilson. 1982. "Reputation and Imperfect Information." *Journal of Economic Theory* 27 (2): 253–79.

Kteily, Nour, and Émile Bruneau. 2017. "Backlash: The Politics and Real-World Consequences of Minority Group Dehumanization." *Personality and Social Psychology Bulletin* 43 (1): 87–104.

Kteily, Nour, Emile Bruneau, Adam Waytz, and Sarah Cotterill. 2015. "The Ascent of Man: Theoretical and Empirical Evidence for Blatant Dehumanization." *Journal of Personality and Social Psychology* 109 (5): 901–31.

Kteily, Nour, Gordon Hodson, and Emile Bruneau. 2016. "They See Us as Less Than Human: Metadehumanization Predicts Intergroup Conflict via Reciprocal Dehumanization." *Journal of Personality and Social Psychology* 110 (3): 343–70.

Kube, Sebastian, Michel André Maréchal, and Clemens Puppe. 2012. "The Currency of Reciprocity: Gift Exchange in the Workplace." *American Economic Review* 102 (4): 1644–62.

Kunda, Ziva. 1990. "The Case for Motivated Reasoning." *Psychological Bulletin* 108 (3): 480–98.

Kydd, Andrew H. 2006. "When Can Mediators Build Trust?" *American Political Science Review* 100 (3): 449–62.

Lacroix, Jean. 2020. "Ballots Instead of Bullets? The Effect of the Voting Rights Act on Political Violence." Working paper.

Lake, David A. 2007. "Escape from the State of Nature: Authority and Hierarchy in World Politics." *International Security* 32 (1): 47–79.

———. 2010. "Two Cheers for Bargaining Theory: Assessing Rationalist Explanations of the Iraq War." *International Security* 35 (3): 7–52.

———. 2011. *Hierarchy in International Relations*. Ithaca: Cornell University Press.

———. 2016. *The Statebuilder's Dilemma: On the Limits of Foreign Intervention*. Ithaca: Cornell University Press.

Lake, David A., Lisa L. Martin, and Thomas Risse. 2021. "Challenges to the Liberal Order: Reflections on *International Organization*." Special issue, *Challenges to the Liberal International Order: International Organization at 75: International Organization* 75 (2): 225–57.

Landes, William M. 1971. "An Economic Analysis of the Courts." *Journal of Law and Economics* 14 (1): 61–107.

Larwood, Laurie, and William Whittaker. 1977. "Managerial Myopia: Self-Serving Biases in Organizational Planning." *Journal of Applied Psychology* 62 (2): 194–98.

Law, David S., and Mila Versteeg. 2012. "The Declining Influence of the United States Constitution." *New York University Law Review* 87 (3): 762–858.

Lebow, Richard Ned. 2014. "What Can International Relations Theory Learn from the Origins of World War I?" *International Relations* 28 (4): 387–410.

———. 2020. *Between Peace and War: 40th Anniversary Revised Edition*. London: Palgrave Macmillan.

Lee, Jong-Wha, and Ju Hyun Pyun. 2016. "Does Trade Integration Contribute to Peace?" *Review of Development Economics* 20 (1): 327–44.

Leovy, Jill. 2015. *Ghettoside: A True Story of Murder in America*. New York: Spiegel & Grau.

Lerner, Jennifer S., Ye Li, Piercarlo Valdesolo, and Karim S. Kassam. 2015. "Emotion and Decision Making." *Annual Review of Psychology* 66 (1): 799–823.

Lessing, Benjamin. 2017. *Making Peace in Drug Wars: Crackdowns and Cartels in Latin America*. Cambridge: Cambridge University Press.

Levitt, Steven D., and Thomas J. Miles. 2006. "Economic Contributions to the Understanding of Crime." *Annual Review of Law and Social Science* 2 (1): 147–64.

Levy, Jack S. 1990. "Preferences, Constraints, and Choices in July 1914." *International Security* 15 (3): 151–86.

———. 1991. "The Role of Crisis Management in the Outbreak of World War I." In *Avoiding War: Problems of Crisis Management*, edited by Alexander L. George, 62–102. London: Routledge.

———. 2014. "The Sources of Preventive Logic in German Decision-Making in 1914." In *The Outbreak of the First World War: Structure, Politics, and Decision-Making*, 139–66. Cambridge: Cambridge University Press.

Levy, Jack S., and William R. Thompson. 2011. *Causes of War*. New York: John Wiley & Sons.

Levy, Jack S., and John A. Vasquez, eds. 2014. *The Outbreak of the First World War: Structure, Politics, and Decision-Making*. Cambridge: Cambridge University Press.

Licklider, Roy. 1995. "The Consequences of Negotiated Settlements in Civil Wars, 1945–1993." *American Political Science Review* 89 (3): 681–90.

Liebenow, J. Gus. 1987. *Liberia: The Quest for Democracy*. Bloomington: Indiana University Press.

Lijphart, Arend. 2012. *Patterns of Democracy: Government Forms and Performance in Thirty-Six Countries*. New Haven: Yale University Press.

Lipset, Seymour Martin, and Stein Rokkan. 1967. *Cleavage Structures, Party Systems, and Voter Alignments: An Introduction*. New York: Free Press.

Locke, John. (1690) 1988. *Locke: Two Treatises of Government*. Edited by Peter Laslett. Cambridge: Cambridge University Press.

Loewenstein, George, and Jennifer S. Lerner. 2003. "The Role of Affect in Decision Making." In *Handbook of Affective Sciences*, edited by Richard J. Davidson, Klaus S. Scherer, and H. Hill Goldsmith, 619–42. Oxford: Oxford University Press.

Loewenstein, George, Ted O'Donoghue, and Matthew Rabin. 2003. "Projection Bias in Predicting Future Utility." *Quarterly Journal of Economics* 118 (4): 1209–48.

Lowe, Matt. 2021. "Types of Contact: A Field Experiment on Collaborative and Adversarial Caste Integration." *American Economic Review* 111 (6): 1807–44.

Luttwak, Edward N. 1999. "Give War a Chance." *Foreign Affairs* 78 (4): 36–44.

Machiavelli, Niccolò. (1532) 2006. *The Prince*. Translated by William K. Marriott. El Paso: El Paso Norte Press.

Mackie, Diane M., Eliot R. Smith, and Devin G. Ray. 2008. "Intergroup Emotions and Intergroup Relations." *Social and Personality Psychology Compass* 2 (5): 1866–80.

MacMillan, Margaret. 2013. *The War That Ended Peace: The Road to 1914*. New York: Random House.

———. 2020. *War: How Conflict Shaped Us*. New York: Random House.

Madarász, Kristóf. 2015. "Projection Equilibrium: Definition and Applications to Social Investment and Persuasion." Working paper.

Madison, James. 1793. "'Helvidius' Number 4," September 14, 1793, National Archives Founders Online. https://founders.archives.gov/documents/Madison/01-15-02-0070.

Mahoney, James. 2001. "Path-Dependent Explanations of Regime Change: Central America in Comparative Perspective." *Studies in Comparative International Development* 36 (1): 111–41.

Maier, Pauline. 1991. *From Resistance to Revolution: Colonial Radicals and the Development of American Opposition to Britain, 1765–1776*. New York: W. W. Norton.

Majumdar, Sumon, and Sharun W. Mukand. 2004. "Policy Gambles." *American Economic Review* 94 (4): 1207–22.

Malmendier, Ulrike. 2018. "Behavioral Corporate Finance." In *Handbook of Behavioral Economics: Foundations and Applications 1*, edited by B. Douglas Bernheim, Stefano DellaVigna, and David Laibson, 277–379. Amsterdam: Elsevier.

Mamdani, Mahmood. 2010. *Saviors and Survivors: Darfur, Politics, and the War on Terror*. New York: Random House Digital.

———. 2018. *Citizen and Subject: Contemporary Africa and the Legacy of Late Colonialism*. Princeton: Princeton University Press.

Mansfield, Edward D., and Jack Snyder. 2002. "Democratic Transitions, Institutional Strength, and War." *International Organization* 56 (2): 297–337.

Maoz, Zeev, and Bruce Russett. 1993. "Normative and Structural Causes of Democratic Peace, 1946–1986." *American Political Science Review* 87 (3): 624–38.

Markey, Daniel. 1999. "Prestige and the Origins of War: Returning to Realism's Roots." *Security Studies* 8 (4): 126–72.

Martin, Lisa L., and Beth A. Simmons. 1998. "Theories and Empirical Studies of International Institutions." *International Organization* 52 (4): 729–57.

Martin, Mike. 2018. *Why We Fight*. London: Hurst.

Martin, Philippe, Thierry Mayer, and Mathias Thoenig. 2008a. "Civil Wars and International Trade." *Journal of the European Economic Association* 6 (2–3): 541–50.

———. 2008b. "Make Trade Not War?" *Review of Economic Studies* 75 (3): 865–900.

Martin, Thomas R. 2013. *Ancient Greece: From Prehistoric to Hellenistic Times*. New Haven: Yale University Press.

Martinez-Bravo, Monica, Gerard Padró i Miquel, Nancy Qian, and Yang Yao. 2017. "The Rise and Fall of Local Elections in China: Theory and Empirical Evidence on the Autocrat's Trade-Off." National Bureau of Economic Research, Working Paper 24032.

Mas, Alexandre. 2006. "Pay, Reference Points, and Police Performance." *Quarterly Journal of Economics* 121 (3): 783–821.

———. 2008. "Labour Unrest and the Quality of Production: Evidence from the Construction Equipment Resale Market." *Review of Economic Studies* 75 (1): 229–58.

Massey, Cade, and Richard H. Thaler. 2013. "The Loser's Curse: Decision Making and Market Efficiency in the National Football League Draft." *Management Science* 59 (7): 1479–95.

Matanock, Aila M. 2017. *Electing Peace: From Civil Conflict to Political Participation*. Cambridge: Cambridge University Press.

McCullough, David. 2005. *1776*. New York: Simon & Schuster.

McDermott, Rose. 2004. *Political Psychology in International Relations*. Ann Arbor: University of Michigan Press.

McGuirk, Eoin, Nathaniel Hilger, and Nicholas Miller. 2021. "No Kin in the Game: Moral Hazard and War in the U.S. Congress." Working paper.

Mearsheimer, John J. 1994. "The False Promise of International Institutions." *International Security* 19 (3): 5–49.

Meyer, John W., and Brian Rowan. 1977. "Institutionalized Organizations: Formal Structure as Myth and Ceremony." *American Journal of Sociology* 83 (2): 340–63.

Middlekauff, Robert. 2016. *Washington's Revolution: The Making of America's First Leader*. New York: Vintage Books.

Migdal, Joel S. 1988. *Strong Societies and Weak States: State-Society Relations and State Capabilities in the Third World*. Princeton: Princeton University Press.

———. 2001. *State in Society: Studying How States and Societies Transform and Constitute One Another*. Cambridge: Cambridge University Press.

Miguel, Edward, and Mary Kay Gugerty. 2005. "Ethnic Diversity, Social Sanctions, and Public Goods in Kenya." *Journal of Public Economics* 89 (11–12): 2325–68.

Miguel, Edward, and Shanker Satyanath. 2011. "Re-examining Economic Shocks and Civil Conflict." *American Economic Journal: Applied Economics* 3 (4): 228–32.

Miguel, Edward, Shanker Satyanath, and Ernest Sergenti. 2004. "Economic Shocks and Civil Conflict: An Instrumental Variables Approach." *Journal of Political Economy* 112 (4): 725–53.

Mill, John Stuart. (1848) 1909. *Principles of Political Economy with Some of Their Applications to Social Philosophy*, edited by W. J. Ashley, reprinted by the Library of Economics and Liberty. https://www.econlib.org/library/Mill/mlP.html.

Mitra, Anirban, and Debraj Ray. 2014. "Implications of an Economic Theory of Conflict: Hindu-Muslim Violence in India." *Journal of Political Economy* 122 (4): 719–65.

Mkandawire, Thandika. 2001. "Thinking about Developmental States in Africa." *Cambridge Journal of Economics* 25 (3): 289–314.

Mnookin, Robert. 2010. *Bargaining with the Devil: When to Negotiate, When to Fight*. New York: Simon & Schuster.

Montesquieu, Charles de. (1750) 1989. *Montesquieu: The Spirit of the Laws*, edited and translated by Anne M. Cohler, Basia C. Miller, and Harold S. Stone. Cambridge: Cambridge University Press.

Moore, Don A., Elizabeth R. Tenney, and Uriel Haran. 2015. "Overprecision in Judgment." In *The Wiley Blackwell Handbook of Judgment and Decision Making*, edited by Gideon Keren and George Wu, 2:182–209. Chichester: Wiley Blackwell.

Moore, Don A., and Paul J. Healy. 2008. "The Trouble with Overconfidence." *Psychological Review* 115 (2): 502–17.

Moore, Barrington, Jr. 2016. *Injustice: The Social Bases of Obedience and Revolt*. London: Routledge.

Moretti, Enrico, Claudia Steinwender, and John Van Reenen. 2019. "The Intellectual Spoils of War? Defense R&D, Productivity and International Spillovers." National Bureau of Economic Research, Working Paper 26483.

Morris, Ian. 2014. *War! What Is It Good For?: Conflict and the Progress of Civilization from Primates to Robots*. New York: Farrar, Straus and Giroux.

Moss, Todd J., Gunilla Pettersson, and Nicolas van de Walle. 2006. "An Aid-Institutions Paradox? A Review Essay on Aid Dependency and State Building in Sub-Saharan Africa." Working paper.

Mousa, Salma. 2020. "Building Social Cohesion between Christians and Muslims through Soccer in Post-ISIS Iraq." *Science* 369 (6505): 866–70.

Mueller, Hannes. 2012. "Growth Dynamics: The Myth of Economic Recovery: Comment." *American Economic Review* 102 (7): 3774–77.

Mueller, Hannes, Lavinia Piemontese, and Augustin Tapsoba. 2017. "Recovery from Conflict : Lessons of Success." World Bank, Policy Research Working Paper 7970. https://openknowledge.worldbank.org/handle/10986/26137.

Mueller, Hannes, and Dominic Rohner. 2018. "Can Power-Sharing Foster Peace? Evidence from Northern Ireland." *Economic Policy* 33 (95): 447–84.

Mukand, Sharun W., and Dani Rodrik. 2005. "In Search of the Holy Grail: Policy Convergence, Experimentation, and Economic Performance." *American Economic Review* 95 (1): 374–83.

Mukhopadhyay, Dipali. 2014. *Warlords, Strongman Governors, and the State in Afghanistan.* Cambridge: Cambridge University Press.

Muthoo, Abhinay. 1999. *Bargaining Theory with Applications.* Cambridge: Cambridge University Press.

Myerson, Roger B. 2008. "The Autocrat's Credibility Problem and Foundations of the Constitutional State." *American Political Science Review* 102 (1): 125–39.

———. 2015. "Moral Hazard in High Office and the Dynamics of Aristocracy." *Econometrica* 83 (6): 2083–126.

———. 2020a. "Local Agency Costs of Political Centralization." Working paper.

———. 2020b. "State-Building Lessons from the British Empire." Working paper.

———. 2020c. "Introductory Remarks." Presented at the Conference on Foreign Assistance and Political Development in Fragile States, University of Chicago, May 15–16.

Myerson, Roger B., and Mark A. Satterthwaite. 1983. "Efficient Mechanisms for Bilateral Trading." *Journal of Economic Theory* 29 (2): 265–81.

Naidu, Suresh. 2012. "Suffrage, Schooling, and Sorting in the Post-Bellum U.S. South." National Bureau of Economic Research, Working Paper 18129.

Niang, N. 2006. "The Kurukan Fuga Charter: An Example of an Endogenous Governance Mechanism for Conflict Prevention." In *Intergenerational Forum on Endogenous Governance in West Africa,* vol. 2. Organized by Sahel and West Africa Club & OECD, Ouagadougou, Burkina Faso, June 26–28, 2006. https://www.oecd.org/swac/events/38516561.pdf.

Nieto, Luis E. 1942. *Economía y Cultura en la Historia de Colombia.* Bogotá: Ediciones Librería Siglo XX.

Nisbett, Richard E., and Dov Cohen. 1996. *Culture of Honor: The Psychology of Violence in the South.* Boulder: Westview Press.

Nomikos, William G. 2021. "Peacekeeping and the Enforcement of Intergroup Cooperation: Evidence from Mali." Working paper.

North, Douglass C. 1994. "Institutions and Credible Commitment." Working Paper in Economic History 9412002. Washington University in St. Louis.

North, Douglass C., John Joseph Wallis, and Barry R. Weingast. 2009a. *Violence and Social Orders: A Conceptual Framework for Interpreting Recorded Human History.* Cambridge: Cambridge University Press.

———. 2009b. "Violence and the Rise of Open-Access Orders." *Journal of Democracy* 20 (1): 55–68.

North, Douglass C., and Barry R. Weingast. 1989. "Constitutions and Commitment: The Evolution of Institutions Governing Public Choice in Seventeenth-Century England." *Journal of Economic History* 49 (4): 803–32.

Nugent, Jeffrey B., and James A. Robinson. 2010. "Are Factor Endowments Fate?" *Revista de Historia Económica* 28 (1): 45–82.

Ober, Josiah. 2015. *The Rise and Fall of Classical Greece.* Princeton: Princeton University Press.

Odean, Terrance. 1999. "Do Investors Trade Too Much?" *American Economic Review* 89 (5): 1279–98.

Olson, Mancur. 1993. "Dictatorship, Democracy, and Development." *American Political Science Review* 87 (3): 567–76.

O'Neill, Barry. 2001. *Honor, Symbols, and War.* Ann Arbor: University of Michigan Press.

Organski, A. F. K., and Jacek Kugler. 1980. *The War Ledger.* Chicago: University of Chicago Press.

Ortoleva, Pietro, and Erik Snowberg. 2015. "Overconfidence in Political Behavior." *American Economic Review* 105 (2): 504–35.

Ostrom, Elinor. 2001. "Decentralization and Development: The New Panacea." In *Challenges to Democracy: Ideas, Involvement and Institutions,* edited by Keith Dowding, James Hughes, and Helen Margetts, 237–56. Cham: Springer.

———. 2010. "Beyond Markets and States: Polycentric Governance of Complex Economic Systems." *American Economic Review* 100 (3): 641–72.

Ostrom, Elinor, Clark Gibson, Sujai Shivakumar, and Krister Andersson. 2002. *Aid, Incentives, and Sustainability: An Institutional Analysis of Development Cooperation* (Main Report). Sida Studies in Evaluation 02/01. https://www.oecd.org/derec/sweden/37356956.pdf.

Ostrom, Vincent. 1997. *The Meaning of Democracy and the Vulnerability of Democracies: A Response to Tocqueville's Challenge.* Ann Arbor: University of Michigan Press.

Pace, Eric. 1989. "Barbara Tuchman Dead at 77; A Pulitzer-Winning Historian." *New York Times,* February 7, 1989, sec. A.

Paine, Thomas. 1791. *Rights of Man: Being an Answer to Mr. Burke's Attack on the French Revolution.* 2nd ed. J. S. Jordan. Reprinted by the Online Library of Liberty. https://oll.libertyfund.org/title/paine-the-rights-of-man-part-i-1791-ed.

Paluck, Elizabeth L. 2009a. "Reducing Intergroup Prejudice and Conflict Using the Media: A Field Experiment in Rwanda." *Journal of Personality and Social Psychology* 96 (3): 574–87.

———. 2009b. "What's in a Norm? Sources and Processes of Norm Change." *Journal of Personality and Social Psychology* 96 (3): 594–600.

Paluck, Elizabeth Levy, and Donald P. Green. 2009. "Deference, Dissent, and Dispute Resolution: An Experimental Intervention Using Mass Media to Change Norms and Behavior in Rwanda." *American Political Science Review* 103 (4): 622–44.

Paluck, Elizabeth Levy, Seth A. Green, and Donald P. Green. 2019. "The Contact Hypothesis Re-evaluated." *Behavioural Public Policy* 3 (2): 129–58.

Pape, Robert A. 1997. "Why Economic Sanctions Do Not Work." *International Security* 22 (2): 90–136.

———. 1998. "Why Economic Sanctions *Still* Do Not Work." *International Security* 23 (1): 66–77.

Paris, Roland. 2004. *At War's End: Building Peace after Civil Conflict.* Cambridge: Cambridge University Press.

———. 2010. "Saving Liberal Peacebuilding." *Review of International Studies* 36 (2): 337–65.

Patton, Desmond Upton, Robert D. Eschmann, and Dirk A. Butler. 2013. "Internet Banging: New Trends in Social Media, Gang Violence, Masculinity and Hip Hop." *Computers in Human Behavior* 29 (5): A54–A59.

Pearlman, Wendy. 2011. *Violence, Nonviolence, and the Palestinian National Movement.* Cambridge: Cambridge University Press.

———. 2013. "Emotions and the Microfoundations of the Arab Uprisings." *Perspectives on Politics* 11 (2): 387–409.

———. 2017. *We Crossed a Bridge and It Trembled: Voices from Syria.* New York: HarperCollins.

Petersen, Roger D. 2001. *Resistance and Rebellion: Lessons from Eastern Europe.* Cambridge: Cambridge University Press.

———. 2002. *Understanding Ethnic Violence: Fear, Hatred, and Resentment in Twentieth-Century Eastern Europe.* Cambridge: Cambridge University Press.

———. 2011. *Western Intervention in the Balkans: The Strategic Use of Emotion in Conflict.* Cambridge: Cambridge University Press.

Pierce, Marlyn R. 2014. Review of *The German Aces Speak II: World War II through the Eyes of Four More of the Luftwaffe's Most Important Commanders,* by Colin D. Heaton and Anne-Marie Lewis. *Military Review* 94 (6): 134.

Pinker, Steven. 2011. *The Better Angels of Our Nature: Why Violence Has Declined.* New York: Viking.

———. 2015. *The Sense of Style: The Thinking Person's Guide to Writing in the 21st Century.* New York: Penguin Books.

Plutarch. 2009. *Greek Lives,* edited by Philip A. Stadter and translated by Robin Waterfield. Oxford: Oxford University Press.

Popper, Karl. (1945) 2013. *The Poverty of Historicism.* 2nd ed. London: Routledge.

———. (1957) 2013. *The Open Society and Its Enemies: New One-Volume Edition.* Princeton: Princeton University Press.

———. 2005. *Unended Quest*. 2nd ed. London: Routledge.

Porat, Roni, Eran Halperin, and Maya Tamir. 2016. "What We Want Is What We Get: Group-Based Emotional Preferences and Conflict Resolution." *Journal of Personality and Social Psychology* 110 (2): 167–90.

Posner, Daniel N. 2004. "The Political Salience of Cultural Difference: Why Chewas and Tumbukas Are Allies in Zambia and Adversaries in Malawi." *American Political Science Review* 98(4): 529–45.

Posner, Richard A. 1973. "An Economic Approach to Legal Procedure and Judicial Administration." *Journal of Legal Studies* 2 (2): 399–458.

Powell, Jonathan. 2008. *Great Hatred, Little Room: Making Peace in Northern Ireland*. New York: Random House.

———. 2015. *Terrorists at the Table: Why Negotiating Is the Only Way to Peace*. New York: St. Martin's Press.

———. 2018. "The Reverend Dr. Richard L. Pearson Annual Lecture." Lecture presented at the University of Chicago, April 16, 2018.

Powell, Robert. 1996. "Uncertainty, Shifting Power, and Appeasement." *American Political Science Review* 90 (4): 749–64.

———. 2002. "Bargaining Theory and International Conflict." *Annual Review of Political Science* 5 (1): 1–30.

———. 2004. "The Inefficient Use of Power: Costly Conflict with Complete Information." *American Political Science Review* 98 (2): 231–41.

———. 2006. "War as a Commitment Problem." *International Organization* 60 (1): 169–203.

———. 2013. "Monopolizing Violence and Consolidating Power." *Quarterly Journal of Economics* 128 (2): 807–59.

Power, Samantha. 2013. *"A Problem from Hell": America and the Age of Genocide*. New York: Basic Books.

Pronin, Emily. 2007. "Perception and Misperception of Bias in Human Judgment." *Trends in Cognitive Sciences* 11 (1): 37–43.

Pronin, Emily, Daniel Y. Lin, and Lee Ross. 2002. "The Bias Blind Spot: Perceptions of Bias in Self versus Others." *Personality and Social Psychology Bulletin* 28 (3): 369–81.

Quinn, J. Michael, T. David Mason, and Mehmet Gurses. 2007. "Sustaining the Peace: Determinants of Civil War Recurrence." *International Interactions* 33 (2): 167–93.

Rabin, Matthew. 1993. "Incorporating Fairness into Game Theory and Economics." *American Economic Review* 83 (5): 1281–302.

———. 2002. "A Perspective on Psychology and Economics." *European Economic Review* 46 (4–5): 657–85.

———. 2004. "Behavioral Economics." In *New Frontiers in Economics*, edited by Michael Szenberg and Lall Ramrattan, 68–102. Cambridge: Cambridge University Press.

Ramsay, Kristopher W. 2017. "Information, Uncertainty, and War." *Annual Review of Political Science* 20 (1): 505–27.

Ray, Debraj. 2009. "Costly Conflict under Complete Information." Working paper.

Reagan, Ronald. 1982. "Address at Commencement Exercises at Eureka College in Illinois, May 9, 1982." Public Papers of the Presidents of the United States 1: 585.

Reno, William. 1999. *Warlord Politics and African States*. Boulder: Lynne Rienner.

Restrepo, Pascual. 2015. "The Mounties and the Origins of Peace in the Canadian Prairies." Working paper.

Ricks, Thomas E. 2006. *Fiasco: The American Military Adventure in Iraq*. New York: Penguin Books.

Ripley, Amanda. 2021. *High Conflict: Why We Get Trapped and How We Get Out*. New York: Simon & Schuster.

Rittel, Horst W., and Melvin M. Webber. 1973. "Dilemmas in a General Theory of Planning." *Policy Sciences* 4 (2): 155–69.

Rodrik, Dani. 2007. *One Economics, Many Recipes: Globalization, Institutions, and Economic Growth*. Princeton: Princeton University Press.

Roessler, Philip. 2016. *Ethnic Politics and State Power in Africa: The Logic of the Coup–Civil War Trap*. Cambridge: Cambridge University Press.

Rohner, Dominic. 2018. "Success Factors for Peace Treaties: A Review of Theory and Evidence." Working paper.

Rohner, Dominic, and Alessandro Saia. 2020. "Ballot or Bullet: The Impact of UK's Representation of the People Act on Peace and Prosperity." Working paper.

Rohner, Dominic, and Mathias Thoenig. 2021. "The Elusive Peace Dividend of Development Policy: From War Traps to Macro-Complementarities." *Annual Review of Economics* (13)1: 111–31.

Rohner, Dominic, Mathias Thoenig, and Fabrizio Zilibotti. 2013. "War Signals: A Theory of Trade, Trust, and Conflict." *Review of Economic Studies* 80 (3): 1114–47.

Roland, Gérard. 2000. *Transition and Economics: Politics, Markets, and Firms.* Cambridge: MIT Press.

———. 2004. "Understanding Institutional Change: Fast-Moving and Slow-Moving Institutions." *Studies in Comparative International Development* 38 (4): 109–31.

Rosecrance, Richard N. 1986. *Rise of the Trading State: Commerce and Conquest in the Modern World.* New York: Basic Books.

Rosecrance, Richard N., and Steven Miller, eds. 2014. *The Next Great War?: The Roots of World War I and the Risk of U.S.-China Conflict.* Cambridge: MIT Press.

Ross, Lee. 1990. "Recognizing the Role of Construal Processes." In *The Legacy of Solomon Asch: Essays in Cognition and Social Psychology,* edited by Irvin Rock, 77–96. Marwah: Lawrence Erlbaum Associates.

———. 2013. "Perspectives on Disagreement and Dispute Resolution: Lessons from the Lab and the Real World." In *The Behavioral Foundations of Public Policy,* edited by Eldar Shafir, 108–25. Princeton: Princeton University Press.

Ross, Lee, and Richard E. Nisbett. 2011. *The Person and the Situation: Perspectives of Social Psychology.* London: Pinter & Martin.

Ross, Michael L. 2001. *Timber Booms and Institutional Breakdown in Southeast Asia.* Cambridge: Cambridge University Press.

———. 2008. "Blood Barrels: Why Oil Wealth Fuels Conflict." *Foreign Affairs* 87 (3): 2–8.

———. 2012. *The Oil Curse: How Petroleum Wealth Shapes the Development of Nations.* Princeton: Princeton University Press.

Russett, Bruce, Christopher Layne, David E. Spiro, and Michael W. Doyle. 1995. "The Democratic Peace." *International Security* 19 (4): 164–84.

Russett, Bruce, and John Oneal. 2001. *Triangulating Peace: Democracy, Interdependence, and International Organizations.* New York: W. W. Norton.

Sadka, Joyce, Enrique Seira, and Christopher Woodruff. 2020. "Information and Bargaining through Agents: Experimental Evidence from Mexico's Labor Courts." National Bureau of Economic Research, Working Paper 25137.

Safford, Frank, and Marco Palacios. 2002. *Colombia: Fragmented Land, Divided Society.* Oxford: Oxford University Press.

Sambanis, Nicholas. 2004. "What Is Civil War? Conceptual and Empirical Complexities of an Operational Definition." *Journal of Conflict Resolution* 48 (6): 814–58.

Sánchez de la Sierra, Raúl. 2020. "On the Origins of the State: Stationary Bandits and Taxation in Eastern Congo." *Journal of Political Economy* 128 (1): 32–74.

Sanfey, Alan G., James K. Rilling, Jessica A. Aronson, Leigh E. Nystrom, and Jonathan D. Cohen. 2003. "The Neural Basis of Economic Decision-Making in the Ultimatum Game." *Science* 300 (5626): 1755–58.

Sapolsky, Robert M. 2017. *Behave: The Biology of Humans at Our Best and Worst.* New York: Penguin Press.

Saunders, Elizabeth N. 2017. "No Substitute for Experience: Presidents, Advisers, and Information in Group Decision Making." *International Organization* 71 (S1): S219–S247.

Sawyer, Amos. 1992. *The Emergence of Autocracy in Liberia: Tragedy and Challenge.* San Francisco: ICS Press.

———. 2004. "Violent Conflicts and Governance Challenges in West Africa: The Case of the Mano River Basin Area." *Journal of Modern African Studies* 42 (3): 437–63.

———. 2005. *Beyond Plunder: Toward Democratic Governance in Liberia.* Boulder: Lynne Rienner.

Scacco, Alexandra, and Shana S. Warren. 2018. "Can Social Contact Reduce Prejudice and Discrimination? Evidence from a Field Experiment in Nigeria." *American Political Science Review* 112 (3): 654–77.

Schaffer, Frederic Charles. 2000. *Democracy in Translation: Understanding Politics in an Unfamiliar Culture*. Ithaca: Cornell University Press.

Scheidel, Walter. 2018. *The Great Leveler: Violence and the History of Inequality from the Stone Age to the Twenty-First Century*. Princeton: Princeton University Press.

Schelling, Thomas C. 1960. *The Strategy of Conflict*. Cambridge: Harvard University Press.

———. 2020. *Arms and Influence*. New Haven: Yale University Press.

Schemo, Diana Jean. 1997. "Colombia's Death-Strewn Democracy." *New York Times*, July 24, 1997, sec. A.

Schub, Robert. 2015. "Are You Certain? Leaders, Overprecision, and War." Working paper.

Scott, James C. 1998. *Seeing Like a State: How Certain Schemes to Improve the Human Condition Have Failed*. New Haven: Yale University Press.

———. 2010. *The Art of Not Being Governed: An Anarchist History of Upland Southeast Asia*. New Haven: Yale University Press.

Seabright, Paul. 1999. "The Aestheticising Vice." *London Review of Books*, May 27, 1999.

Selway, Joel Sawat. 2011. "Cross-Cuttingness, Cleavage Structures and Civil War Onset." *British Journal of Political Science* 41 (1): 111–38.

Sen, Amartya. 1999. *Development as Freedom*. Oxford: Oxford University Press.

Simon, Herbert A. 1956. "Rational Choice and the Structure of the Environment." *Psychological Review* 63 (2): 129–38.

Singer, Peter. 2011. *The Expanding Circle: Ethics, Evolution, and Moral Progress*. Princeton: Princeton University Press.

Skaperdas, Stergios. 1992. "Cooperation, Conflict, and Power in the Absence of Property Rights." *American Economic Review* 82 (4): 720–39.

———. 2006. "Bargaining versus Fighting." *Defence and Peace Economics* 17 (6): 657–76.

Slantchev, Branislav L. 2012. "Borrowed Power: Debt Finance and the Resort to Arms." *American Political Science Review* 106 (4): 787–809.

Slantchev, Branislav L., and Ahmer Tarar. 2011. "Mutual Optimism as a Rationalist Explanation of War." *American Journal of Political Science* 55 (1): 135–48.

Slomp, Gabriella. 2000. *Thomas Hobbes and the Political Philosophy of Glory*. Basingstoke: Palgrave Macmillan.

Slutkin, Gary, Charles Ransford, and R. Brent Decker. 2015. "Cure Violence: Treating Violence as a Contagious Disease." In *Envisioning Criminology*, edited by Michael D. Maltz and Stephen K. Rice, 43–56. Cham: Springer.

Smith, Adam. 1759. *The Theory of Moral Sentiments*. Reprinted by the Library of Economics and Liberty, https://www.econlib.org/library/Smith/smMS.html?chapter_num=2#book-reader.

———. (1776) 1904. *An Inquiry into the Nature and Causes of the Wealth of Nations*. London: Methuen and Co. Reprinted by the Library of Economics and Liberty, https://www.econlib.org/library/Smith/smWN.html.

Smith, Alastair. 1998. "Fighting Battles, Winning Wars." *Journal of Conflict Resolution* 42 (3): 301–20.

Smith, Alastair, and Allan Stam. 2003. "Mediation and Peacekeeping in a Random Walk Model of Civil and Interstate War." *International Studies Review* 5 (4): 115–35.

———. 2004. "Bargaining and the Nature of War." *Journal of Conflict Resolution* 48 (6): 783–813.

Smith, Richard H., Caitlin A. J. Powell, David J. Y. Combs, and David Ryan Schurtz. 2009. "Exploring the When and Why of *Schadenfreude*." *Social and Personality Psychology Compass* 3 (4): 530–46.

Snyder, Jack. 1989. *The Ideology of the Offensive: Military Decision Making and the Disasters of 1914*. Cornell Studies in Security Affairs 2. Ithaca: Cornell University Press.

Snyder, Jack L. 2000. *From Voting to Violence: Democratization and Nationalist Conflict*. New York: W. W. Norton.

Snyder, Richard. 2006. "Does Lootable Wealth Breed Disorder? A Political Economy of Extraction Framework." *Comparative Political Studies* 39 (8): 943–68.

Sommerville, Johann P. 1992. *Thomas Hobbes: Political Ideas in Historical Context*. Basingstoke: Palgrave Macmillan.

Spruyt, Hendrik. 2017. "War and State Formation: Amending the Bellicist Theory of State Making." In *Does War Make States?: Investigations of Charles Tilly's Historical Sociology*, edited by Lars Bo Kaspersen and Jeppe Strandsbjerg, 73–97. Cambridge: Cambridge University Press.

Stasavage, David. 2020. *The Decline and Rise of Democracy: A Global History from Antiquity to Today*. Princeton Economic History of the Western World 96. Princeton: Princeton University Press.

Staub, Ervin. 1989. *The Roots of Evil: The Origins of Genocide and Other Group Violence*. Cambridge: Cambridge University Press.

Stedman, Stephen John. 1997. "Spoiler Problems in Peace Processes." *International Security* 22 (2): 5–53.

Stewart, Rory, and Gerald Knaus. 2011. *Can Intervention Work?* New York: W. W. Norton.

Straus, Scott. 2006. *The Order of Genocide: Race, Power, and War in Rwanda*. Ithaca: Cornell University Press.

———. 2015. *Making and Unmaking Nations: War, Leadership, and Genocide in Modern Africa*. Ithaca: Cornell University Press.

Sunstein, Cass R., and Reid Hastie. 2008. "Four Failures of Deliberating Groups." Working paper.

———. 2015. *Wiser: Getting beyond Groupthink to Make Groups Smarter*. Cambridge: Harvard Business Review Press.

Svenson, Ola. 1981. "Are We All Less Risky and More Skillful Than Our Fellow Drivers?" *Acta Psychologica* 47 (2): 143–48.

Svolik, Milan W. 2012. *The Politics of Authoritarian Rule*. Cambridge: Cambridge University Press.

Tagar, Michal Reifen, Christopher M. Federico, and Eran Halperin. 2011. "The Positive Effect of Negative Emotions in Protracted Conflict: The Case of Anger." *Journal of Experimental Social Psychology* 47 (1): 157–64.

Tajfel, Henri. 2010. *Social Identity and Intergroup Relations*. European Studies in Social Psychology 7. Cambridge: Cambridge University Press.

Tarabay, Jamie. 2018. "For Many Syrians, the Story of the War Began with Graffiti in Dara'a." CNN. March 15, 2018. https://www.cnn.com/2018/03/15/middleeast/daraa-syria-seven-years-on-intl/index.html.

Taylor, Alan. 2016. *American Revolutions: A Continental History, 1750–1804*. New York: W. W. Norton.

Taylor, A. J. P. 2011. *Bismarck*. New York: Vintage Books.

Tendler, Judith. 1997. *Good Government in the Tropics*. Baltimore: Johns Hopkins University Press.

Tetlock, Philip E. 2017. *Expert Political Judgment: How Good Is It? How Can We Know?* Princeton: Princeton University Press.

Thaler, Richard H. 2016. "Behavioral Economics: Past, Present, and Future." *American Economic Review* 106 (7): 1577–1600.

Thaler, Richard H., and Cass R. Sunstein. 2008. *Nudge: Improving Decisions about Health, Wealth, and Happiness*. New Haven: Yale University Press.

Thomas, M. A. 2015. *Govern Like Us: U.S. Expectations of Poor Countries*. New York: Columbia University Press.

Thompson, C. Bradley. 2019. *America's Revolutionary Mind: A Moral History of the American Revolution and the Declaration That Defined It*. New York: Encounter Books.

Thrasher, John, and Toby Handfield. 2018. "Honor and Violence: An Account of Feuds, Duels, and Honor Killings." *Human Nature* 29 (4): 371–89.

Thucydides. 1998. *The Landmark Thucydides: A Comprehensive Guide to the Peloponnesian War*, edited by Robert B. Strassler and translated by Richard Crawley. New York: Touchstone.

Tilly, Charles. 1985. "War Making and State Making as Organized Crime." In *Bringing the State Back In*, edited by Peter B. Evans, Dietrich Rueschemeyer, and Theda Skocpol, 169–91. Cambridge: Cambridge University Press.

———. 1992. *Coercion, Capital, and European States, AD 990–1992*. Oxford: Blackwell.

Tindale, R. Scott, and Jeremy R. Winget. 2019. "Group Decision-Making." In *Oxford Research Encyclopedia of Psychology*. Oxford: Oxford University Press. https://doi.org/10.1093/acrefore/9780190236557.013.262.

Toft, Monica Duffy. 2010. "Ending Civil Wars: A Case for Rebel Victory?" *International Security* 34 (4): 7–36.

Tuchman, Barbara W. 1994. *The Guns of August*. New York: Random House Trade Paperbacks.

Tullock, Gordon. 1974. *The Social Dilemma: The Economics of War and Revolution*. Blacksburg: University Publications.

Tversky, Amos, and Daniel Kahneman. 1974. "Judgment under Uncertainty: Heuristics and Biases." *Science* 185 (4157): 1124–31.

Tzu, Sun. 2016. *The Art of War*. Translated by Lionel Giles. Sweden: Wisehouse Classics.

Valentino, Benjamin A. 2004. *Final Solutions: Mass Killing and Genocide in the 20th Century*. Cornell Studies in Security Affairs. Ithaca: Cornell University Press.

Vallone, Robert P., Lee Ross, and Mark R. Lepper. 1985. "The Hostile Media Phenomenon: Biased Perception and Perceptions of Media Bias in Coverage of the Beirut Massacre." *Journal of Personality and Social Psychology* 49 (3): 577–85.

Van Evera, Stephen. 1999. *Causes of War: Power and the Roots of Conflict*. Ithaca: Cornell University Press.

———. 2013. *Causes of War: Power and the Roots of Conflict*. Ithaca: Cornell University Press.

Van Vugt, Mark. 2011. "The Male Warrior Hypothesis." In *The Psychology of Social Conflict and Aggression*, edited by Joseph P. Forgas, Arie W. Kruglanski, and Kipling D. Williams, 233–48. Sydney: Sydney Symposium of Social Psychology. Psychology Press.

Varshney, Ashutosh. 2003a. *Ethnic Conflict and Civic Life: Hindus and Muslims in India*. New Haven: Yale University Press.

———. 2003b. "Nationalism, Ethnic Conflict, and Rationality." *Perspectives on Politics* 1 (1): 85–99.

Verwimp, Philip. 2003. "Testing the Double-Genocide Thesis for Central and Southern Rwanda." *Journal of Conflict Resolution* 47 (4): 423–42.

Volkov, Vadim. 2016. *Violent Entrepreneurs: The Use of Force in the Making of Russian Capitalism*. Ithaca: Cornell University Press.

Walt, Stephen M. 1985. "Alliance Formation and the Balance of World Power." *International Security* 9 (4): 3–43.

Walter, Barbara F. 1997. "The Critical Barrier to Civil War Settlement." *International Organization* 51 (3): 335–64.

———. 2002. *Committing to Peace: The Successful Settlement of Civil Wars*. Princeton: Princeton University Press.

———. 2009a. "Bargaining Failures and Civil War." *Annual Review of Political Science* 12 (1): 243–61.

———. 2009b. *Reputation and Civil War: Why Separatist Conflicts Are So Violent*. Cambridge: Cambridge University Press.

———. 2015. "Why Bad Governance Leads to Repeat Civil War." *Journal of Conflict Resolution* 59 (7): 1242–72.

Waltz, Kenneth N. 2010. *Theory of International Politics*. Long Grove: Waveland Press.

Wantchekon, Leonard. 2003. "Clientelism and Voting Behavior: Evidence from a Field Experiment in Benin." *World Politics: A Quarterly Journal of International Relations* 55 (3): 399–422.

Wantchekon, Leonard, and Christel Vermeersch. 2011. "Information, Social Networks, and the Demand for Public Goods: Experimental Evidence from Benin." In *Accountability through Public Opinion: From Inertia to Public Action*, edited by Sina Odugbemi and Taeku Lee, 123–35. Washington: World Bank.

Waters, Rob. 2016. "A Conversation with Tony D: How 'Becoming A Man' Got to the White House." *Forbes*, March 9, 2016. https://www.forbes.com/sites/robwaters/2016/03/09/a-conversation-with-tony-d-how-becoming-a-man-got-to-the-white-house/?sh=19cc0b0f666b.

Weber, Max. 2014. *From Max Weber: Essays in Sociology*, edited by Hans H. Gerth and C. Wright Mills. London: Routledge.

Weeks, Jessica L. 2012. "Strongmen and Straw Men: Authoritarian Regimes and the Initiation of International Conflict." *American Political Science Review* 106 (2): 326–47.

———. 2014. *Dictators at War and Peace*. Ithaca: Cornell University Press.

Weinstein, Jeremy M. 2005. "Autonomous Recovery and International Intervention in Comparative Perspective." Center for Global Development, Working Paper 57.

Weisburd, David, Elizabeth R. Groff, and Sue-Ming Yang. 2012. *The Criminology of Place: Street Segments and Our Understanding of the Crime Problem*. Oxford: Oxford University Press.

Weisburd, David, Lisa Maher, and Lawrence Sherman. 1993. "Contrasting Crime General and Crime Specific Theory: The Case of Hot Spots of Crime." In *Advances in Criminological Theory*, vol. 4, edited by Freda Adler and William S. Laufer, 45–70. Abingdon: Transaction.

Weisiger, Alex. 2013. *Logics of War: Explanations for Limited and Unlimited Conflicts*. Ithaca: Cornell University Press.

Welsh, Brandon C. and David P. Farrington. 2008. "Effects of Improved Street Lighting on Crime: A Systematic Review." *Campbell Systematic Reviews* 4 (1): 1–51.

Westad, Odd Arne. 2005. *The Global Cold War: Third World Interventions and the Making of Our Times*. Cambridge: Cambridge University Press.

Wilkinson, Steven I. 2004. *Votes and Violence: Electoral Competition and Ethnic Riots in India*. Cambridge: Cambridge University Press.

———. 2009. "Riots." *Annual Review of Political Science* 12 (1): 329–43.

Wimmer, Andreas. 2013. *Ethnic Boundary Making: Institutions, Power, Networks*. Oxford: Oxford University Press.

Wimmer, Andreas, Lars-Erik Cederman, and Brian Min. 2009. "Ethnic Politics and Armed Conflict: A Configurational Analysis of a New Global Dataset." *American Sociological Review* 74 (2): 316–37.

Wittman, Donald. 1979. "How a War Ends: A Rational Model Approach." *Journal of Conflict Resolution* 23 (4): 743–63.

Wolford, Scott. 2019. *The Politics of the First World War: A Course in Game Theory and International Security*. Cambridge: Cambridge University Press.

Wolton, Stephane. 2019. "Signaling in the Shadow of Conflict." Working paper.

Wood, Elisabeth Jean. 2003. *Insurgent Collective Action and Civil War in El Salvador*. Cambridge: Cambridge University Press.

Wood, Gordon S. 2002. *The American Revolution: A History*. Modern Library.

Woods, Kevin M., with Michael R. Pease, Mark E. Stout, Williamson Murray, and James G. Lacey. 2006. *Iraqi Perspectives Project: A View of Operation Iraqi Freedom from Saddam's Senior Leadership*. Norfolk: United States Joint Forces Command Joint Center for Operational Analysis, https://www.hsdl.org/?view&did=461392.

Wrangham, Richard. 2019. *The Goodness Paradox: The Strange Relationship between Virtue and Violence in Human Evolution*. New York: Vintage Books.

Wrangham, Richard W., and Dale Peterson. 1996. *Demonic Males: Apes and the Origins of Human Violence*. Boston: Houghton Mifflin Harcourt.

Xu, Chenggang. 2011. "The Fundamental Institutions of China's Reforms and Development." *Journal of Economic Literature* 49 (4): 1076–1151.

Yanagizawa-Drott, David. 2014. "Propaganda and Conflict: Evidence from the Rwandan Genocide." *Quarterly Journal of Economics* 129 (4): 1947–94.

Young, Christopher. 2019. "Agonistic Behavior." In *Encyclopedia of Animal Cognition and Behavior*, edited by Jennifer Vonk and Todd Shackelford. Cham: Springer International. https://doi.org/10.1007/978-3-319-47829-6.

Zimmermann, Florian. 2020. "The Dynamics of Motivated Beliefs." *American Economic Review* 110 (2): 337–61.

INDEX

Note: Italicized page numbers indicate material in photographs or illustrations.